ADMINISTRATION OF THE PUBLIC LIBRARY

by
ALICE GERTZOG
and
EDWIN BECKERMAN

The Scarecrow Press, Inc.
Metuchen, N.J., & London
1994

British Library Cataloguing-in-Publication data available

Library of Congress Cataloging-in-Publication Data

Gertzog, Alice.
    Administration of the public library / by Alice Gertzog and
Edwin Beckerman.
                p. cm.
    Includes bibliographical references and index.
    ISBN 0-8108-2857-X (acid-free paper)
    1. Public libraries--United States--Administration.
I. Beckerman, Edwin, 1927-   II. Title.
Z678.G442 1994
025.1 '97473--dc20   94-9880

For
Max, Ben and Sam
The Next Generation

TABLE OF CONTENTS

Table of Contents

LIST OF FIGURES

FOREWORD

The challenges of management in the public library are as varied and complex as is this remarkable institution itself. While rooted firmly in nineteenth-century idealism, it is yet forced to compete for support and status in the political and technological arenas of the late twentieth century. Revered as fundamental to society's values, it nonetheless lacks legal mandate or a secure fiscal niche at most levels of government. Small wonder that the direct application of business-based management principles fall short of the mark in public library administration.

Fortunately, the major premise of this long-needed book about administering public libraries is that management of any enterprise flows from the nature of the institution to be managed. Making sound management decisions for public libraries depends on a thorough understanding of the nature of the public library business, its total context, its past, the texture of the current public library world, including its ethical precepts and its prospects for the future. The authors explore current management thinking (greater staff participation in management, the "planning process," output measures, legal aspects of staff treatment, and so on), against a backdrop of all of the major elements of public library service. The synthesis of the rich heritage, complex problems and major controversies together form the rich and unique mosaic that is today's public library.

The authors articulate and reaffirm the profession's traditional and too often overlooked articles of faith -- that the public library is a civil libertarian institution, predicated on and dedicated to free access to information for all citizens and is a pillar of a democratic society; that intellectual freedom and freedom from censorship are essential; that the library plays an important role in preserving and disseminating society's humanistic documents is; that a basic tenet of the library faith is that citizens have a right to self-education; and that the library must assume a pluralistic stance to feminism, to the rights of the handicapped, to racial and ethnic minorities, and to other multicultural concerns.

The book looks at controversial and continuing library issues such as "demand versus quality," "fee versus free," library cooperation at all levels, and appropriate services to children and youth, presenting differing opinions of library practitioners and theorists as a means of encouraging the reader toward more informed individual judgements. By following the flow of these critical matters, librarians gain a sense of where the profession currently is and where it is headed. Thus, the implications for the future of public libraries of where technology is going or of what part staff will play in making organizational decisions are profound. The authors have taken care to weigh societal and public library countervailing forces, examining not only factors that currently facilitate change, but also those that serve to limit it.

Finally, the text is virtually jargon-free, logical, comprehensive, clear, and simple. It will serve students, librarians, and those in managerial positions. Between them, the authors have utilized their over sixty years of library experience to produce a wise, readable, sensible and helpful book.

In *Arsenals of a Democratic Culture* (American Library Association, 1947), Sidney Ditzion could aver that "the tax-supported public library not only answered the criteria inherent in the democratic premise, but also offered an instrument as responsive to varying social requirements as democracy itself." As these requirements continue to evolve, a delicate balance of administrative, political, and missionary skills will be needed. The blueprint is in this excellent and most welcome volume.

Arthur Curley
Boston Public Library

INTRODUCTION

The science of management, largely a twentieth-century creation, developed as a response to the need to organize the large-scale enterprises spawned by the industrial revolution. While initially managers were thoroughly versed in the products and processes for which they were responsible, subtle changes over time shifted the emphasis to a knowledge of management skills, with the nature of the enterprise to be managed being of lesser importance.

This volume departs from some current management thinking by maintaining that successful administration can only occur when managers are familiar with all aspects of the institutions which they supervise as well as with management principles and practices. They must be aware of its aims, goals, problems, procedures and controversial issues. To this end, *The Administration of the Public Library* presents chapters on the major functions of public libraries -- circulation, reference, technical processes, youth services, outreach, readers' advisory -- as well as sections on human resources, the director, finances, the building and marketing, always within a library context that includes a historical perspective and a contemporary definition.

The structure of the volume owes a debt to *Lyle's Administration of the College Library*, 6th ed. (Scarecrow Press, 1992) which served as its model. It is designed, as was that one, to follow a middle-ground approach, to be both experiential and philosophical; and to take a broad view, but also to include a practical component.

We would like to acknowledge a few of the many people who assisted us in the development of the text. Elaine McConnell of the Ocean County (NJ) Library was generous with her time and expertise during the embryonic stages of the work. Liz Scott, also from Ocean County, not only shared her ideas, but supplied crucial materials as they were requested. The chapter on Youth Services would have been difficult without the advice of Cynthia Woodruff. Professor Barbara Kwasnik counselled us about cataloging. The Allegheny College Library staff, in particular Jane Westenfeld and Nancy Brenot, actively sought the materials we required through interlibrary loan. The staffs of the Woodbridge (NJ) Public Library, the Meadville (PA) Public Library and the New Jersey State Library lent invaluable assistance in supplying materials and advising us. Particular thanks are due Barbara Sullivan, Judith Yurenda, Glenda Moore, Sharon Counselman, Linda Cooper, Louise Kassoff, Ellen Bonacarti, Sandra Horrocks, Florence (Jackie) Rapacki, Jean Chabot, Kathryn Lancier-Drogram, Leslie Keiser, John Walz, Karen Spak and Mary Lee Minnis. Without Aggie Sakanich the production of the final manuscript would have been impossible. Brent Nordstrom lent invaluable technical assistance.

Finally, the patience, tolerance and goodwill of Jean Beckerman and Irwin Gertzog deserve recognition and praise that far exceeds mere mention on this page. It is, however, a start. We thank you both.

Alice Gertzog
Edwin Beckerman

CHAPTER 1

THE PUBLIC LIBRARY IN CONTEXT

To paraphrase Charles Dickens, today may be the best of times and the worst of times to be working in a public library. Profound forces are shaking the institution. Change is not a stage through which it will pass, but an omnipresent, ongoing state. Technological pressures are driving *environmental* change. Librarians now have the capability to control, organize, structure and disseminate information in ways that their predecessors could scarcely imagine. New comprehension of how institutions and people behave is propelling *organizational* change. Theories regarding staff management and roles are appearing at a dizzying pace. The future is fluid, exciting, uncertain and perilous. We continue to inhabit a zero-sum system of finite resources. Diminished willingness to fund public services, coupled with severe economic constraints, has spawned major consequences for the coffers of American public institutions, public libraries among them. Stasis or retrenchment is a way of life for many libraries, particularly those in metropolitan areas where tax bases have endured critical declines. Some Cassandras have even prophesied the death of libraries and of the profession in view of the competition from other segments of the work force, particularly from computer engineers. Secretly, some librarians worry that lack of vision and failure of courage and imagination may prevent their leaders from seizing the opportunities and that apathy and stagnation will prevail, resulting in irrelevant, non-responsive institutions.

Ironically, librarians face a world of rising expectations about their abilities and behavior. They are commanded to be aggressive, to provide not only for society's haves, but also for its less fortunate citizens. They are expected to be accountable, to manage with fewer dollars while providing new services; to further traditional humanistic values; to bear responsibility for preserving the human record and other cultural artifacts; to create an information-literate public and champion books and encourage the reading habit. In addition, they are expected to be better prepared when they enter the profession and to have mastered far more skills than were required from their predecessors. Fears of a crisis of leadership may be unfounded in light of claims by library schools of mounting numbers of applicants with impressive credentials. On the other hand, library schools may be hard-pressed to provide what future librarians need.

Libraries are busier now than they have ever been. The new services as well as unemployment and recession problems have swelled the ranks of users. Current abilities to gain rapid access to materials provide what is tantamount to a national electronic highway, "an extraordinary roadway of the intellect, carrying vast stores of ideas and information across the nation, almost at the speed of light."[1]

On the horizon, difficult questions confront the profession. Balancing between conflicting perceptions of the library's role is not easy. The following three scenarios help to illuminate some of the difficult decisions that lie ahead for public libraries. Consider this scenario:

Picture, if you will, a book -- one whose size and weight are not more or less than any other ordinary volume. Fingers rubbed across the cover produce the same feeling as they would from any fabric and cardboard book.

But this book is different from other books. No title or author appears on its cover or spine. It opens only to a single blank paper page. What resembles a book is, in reality, a computer. A touch to the left-hand corner of the page turns the "book" on. A finger placed on the right- hand corner causes page 88 of Faulkner's *As I Lay Dying* to appear. The page "turns" at a touch to the middle of the screen. Another book replaces the Faulkner one after a series of finger presses signal responses to a group of user-friendly questions.

Who says you can't curl up with a computer?

Think about another scenario:

> It is past midnight. Unable to sleep, you decide to begin work on a new research project. After fixing yourself a cup of tea, you pad into your home office and fire up your personal computer. Using a modem, you log-on to your public library's computer system.
>
> First, you check the library's catalog of holdings and place electronic reserves on those monographs you would like to examine. Those items may be picked up at the nearest branch library or delivered to your office the following day. Next, you search the electronic index of periodical literature. You read the abstracts and determine which articles you would like to read in full. The full text of those items may then be downloaded to your computer where you will read them at a later date, either in electronic format or from printed copy.
>
> Before signing off you remember that you are planning to buy your son a bicycle for his birthday, and you consult the electronic version of *Consumer Reports*. Finally, able to sleep and secure in the knowledge that you have a jump on your research, you return to bed.[2]

Neither of these scenes is far-fetched, nor far off. But "book computers" and "libraries without walls" tell only part of the story. After all, only a small percentage of Americans have personal computers at home, and the number is not growing as rapidly as once predicted. Consider yet one more scenario:

I can't read. My daughter doesn't know that. I bring her to the library where they read to her and give her a look into a world far different than the one in which we live. I can't afford a computer.

Wouldn't know what to do with one if I could. The librarians teach my older son how to find information and then how to decide whether the information is useful. Sometimes when I come to the library, I see other people from my neighborhood. One day I saw the blind man who lives downstairs using a special computer that read information aloud to him. The old lady who lives in the next apartment tells me she comes to the library for book discussions. When she was laid up last year, people from the library delivered books to her. She's been trying to get me to join the library's literacy program. But then I'd have to admit I can't read.

I heard talk that they are going to cut the library's budget. What will I do then?

A public library is an organized collection of materials, operated by trained staff, regularly made available for public use and supported by public funds. It differs from special, academic and school libraries in its lack of a specified constituency and in its universal availability, two factors with strong implications for service and collection management. The resources of public libraries range from minimal to extensive and deep. Their staffs may be sparse or ample. Yet no matter the nature of the public library, its fundamental activities and concerns remain similar. Methods may vary in particular libraries, but major functions must be fulfilled and successful techniques to achieve them do not differ greatly from one library to another.

ENVIRONMENTS

The purpose of this book is to describe the work involved in administering a public library. All public libraries are products of and are influenced by
 •factors existing in the greater society
 •the nature of the community or municipality in which the library is located
 •the internal organization of the library

•the nature of the relationships between these elements and how they interact.

Successful administration of a contemporary public library requires an understanding of how to manage a library and knowledge of the context in which it functions. Public library service, its provision and use, occurs in, is affected by, and affects what happens in its immediate and greater environment.

Public librarians could, at one time, assume that their libraries occupied a relatively stable place in a slowly changing library world. The time has long passed when public libraries can be thought of as isolated institutions. Like all of American society, their horizons have expanded. The 1980s produced a sea change in attitudes towards knowledge and information, and in the delivery of library services. These shifts, coupled with the accelerated pace of social ferment, technological strides, the applications of both systems theories to social organizations and management theories to non-profit organizations ended forever any notion that libraries were independent of their environments.

Six environments can be considered to surround a public library. Figure 1 represents the way in which a public library is embedded within them.

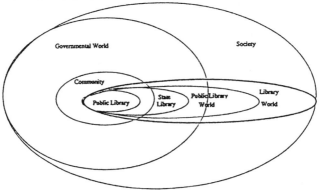

Figure 1
Environments of the Public Library

Each of these environments is described below, and is accompanied by an example that illustrates how one event or occurrence may produce a ripple effect and the way in which influence may be exerted or experienced.

They are:

The *Society*, which encompasses social, economic, political and cultural trends. Among these may be public attitudes towards learning and society's assessments of the importance of information.

The rapid growth of the aging population, with its particular needs and demands, will affect the demand for and nature of library services.

The *Library* World which is comprised of the sectors of practice, scholarship, and those that service the profession, as, for instance, the library associations and the organs of communication, the library periodicals.

The degree to which the profession is currently successful in promoting librarianship as a challenging and rewarding career will influence a public library's ability to recruit a capable staff in the immediate future.

The *Governmental* World which includes, among other elements, current understanding of the role of knowledge, supply of resources and demand for services, fiscal trends, requirements for accountability and adherence to rules for treatment of particular populations.

The Americans with Disabilities Act means that all public libraries will have to be universally accessible.

The *Public Library* World which includes methods and practices, both new and traditional, for the provision of efficient and effective public library service.

The development of new methods to train reference librarians which pay particular attention to satisfying specific patron information needs, will alter the manner in which Library X responds to requests for reference assistance.

The *State Library* World, which includes the establishment of standards for public libraries promulgated in order to dispense state aid, establishment of access points such as interlibrary loan networks and continuing education opportunities. *State libraries' insistence that local libraries join statewide interlibrary loan programs insures that the distinction between access and acquisition will become increasingly blurred.*

The *Community*, the most direct context in which the library operates, includes the members of the library's service area -- its users, nonusers and municipal authority. It has a social structure produced by, among other factors, its history, traditions, geography, cultural climate, resources, size and economic condition. *Lack of a community's success in retaining a sufficient industrial base may result in diminished resources available to the library.*

SYSTEMS THEORY

Public librarians often have to confront the question about the extent to which the library is meeting its purpose or potential. Mere facts do not supply answers. Knowing, for instance, that more than 50% of a community's residents hold library cards says little about whether that library is serving its community adequately. Measuring the extent to which this fulfills objectives is one avenue to learning about success. Another is studying the question in context. In recent years, system theory has been widely applied to help describe and explain the workings of a library. This approach assumes that the elements and structures of an institution should be thought of as parts of a whole and affecting one another, rather than as distinct entities to be examined separately.

The following are some generalizations regarding system theory:

1. Systems are composed of interrelated parts;
2. They are not merely the sum of parts, but a totality and should be viewed holistically;
3. Systems are relatively *open* or *closed* depending on the extent to which information, energy or material is exchanged with their environments;
4. They are more or less bounded and separated from their environments;
5. Systems have *inputs* and *throughputs* as well as *outputs* which in turn provide feedback and appear as future *inputs*;
7. Systems generally achieve something. In other words they are organized for a particular purpose.[3]

Public libraries are relatively *open* systems that depend on their environment for inputs and for feedback. They both draw on and contribute to their environments in order to meet social expectations. A system model (Figure 2) based on one devised by Joanne Euster,[4] utilizes a two environment approach to describe the dynamics of a public library.

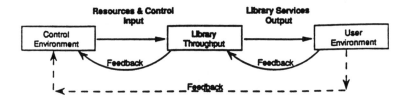

Figure 2
Community Environments

The *Control* Environment provides the input -- the resources and controls on which the library depends for survival -- and evaluates the goals, methods and outputs. Inputs are generally regarded as money, services, personnel and information. Among the controls are the degree of autonomy granted the library. This includes its ability to define or reshape its mission, goals, and scope of activities, and its freedom to devise methods to meet its goals and conduct its program.

The *User* Environment refers to all segments of the community that receive the services of the library -- the outputs. Outputs may be thought of in terms of measurable activities and operations, including circulation, in-house library use, assistance in locating information, and programs offered. Alternately, outputs may refer to transformations in library patrons as a result of library use.[5]

Feedback in this model is delivered directly to the Library from its User Environment and from the Library to its Control Environment. Feedback from the User Environment flows weakly to the Control Environment. User and Control Environments in a public library community sometimes share personnel who play different roles in each setting. Municipal officials, for instance, are members of the Control Environment but function, at times, as library service consumers.

The *Library* is the place where the elements and activities are converted from energy and information (inputs) into exportable products (outputs). Elements used in the process are the collection and its surrogate, the catalog. The activities usually involved in the conversion are:

Technical Processes - acquisitions, cataloging, classification and collection maintenance;

Public Services - circulation, reference services, readers advisory services, programming;

Administration - planning, organizing, motivating and controlling.

Figure 3 illustrates the internal process of converting energy and information (inputs) into usable library products (outputs).Of these activities, some are more boundary-spanning -- located closer to the system's borders -- than others. Cataloging, for instance, has traditionally been relatively remote from the library's clientele, although it has open boundaries with book dealers, jobbers and bibliographic networks, among others in the library world. Public services, on the other hand, deal directly with library users, and library administrators continually confer and negotiate with the control environment, the municipality or others.

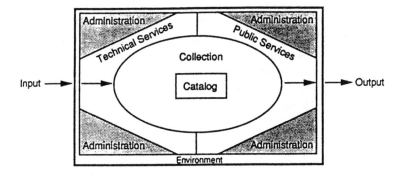

Figure 3
A Systems Model

Libraries, like other organizations, react to the environment in two ways. First, they adapt the library to it. Second, they modify the environment to lessen the need for internal adaptation. A library wishing to enhance its output, for instance, must alter the value of its output either through improved internal processes or through manipulation of the environment's perception of its value -- or both.

MANAGEMENT FOR PUBLIC LIBRARIANS

Most budding librarians intend to practice librarianship when they enroll in library school. Few, however, start out with any clear thought of becoming library managers. For many, the management responsibilities associated with most professional library positions come as something of a shock. Professional library managers must master not only the philosophy and techniques of management, but must also have firmly in place an understanding of all other phases of librarianship -- the context in which management skills take place and are utilized.

No formula can help library managers determine an optimum mode of action; each management situation has its own set of dynamics and each manager differs in temperament and skills. Management wisdom begins with the recognition that formulas are simply guidelines and generalizations subject to the exigencies of a particular set of circumstances. The needs of an organization do not always fit the skills of a manager. Some managers may be dynamic entrepreneurs, functioning most effectively when faced with the challenge to improve substantially the coffers of a library currently receiving low levels of financial support. Others may be better suited to situations that require more efficient organization and use of resources, but that have already achieved financial stability. Some managers may be able to handle both jobs, improving funding and managing the organization equally well, but experience suggests it is unlikely.

Some skills and some issues, however, are universally important and managers must pay particular attention to them:

1. Organizations require focus. Without it, performance is likely to be erratic, at best. Planning is a process designed to

produce focus for organizations. For libraries, the American Library Association's planning and role setting process can achieve this purpose.

2. A key element in public library organizational life is the kind of relationship encouraged by the organization between and among managers, other staff, and trustees. Are all factions essentially members of the same organization who share in corporate decision-making, or is staff divided into groups of managers who make decisions, and other employees who simply carry them out? Organizations take action primarily through their staffs. Relations between staff and management may not always be characterized by perfect harmony, but they must always be based on mutual respect, equity of treatment, concern for staff welfare and creation of opportunities for the staff to state their opinions and concerns about the welfare of the institution in a meaningful fashion.

3. Most public libraries are supported by funds controlled by local politicians. Local library managers are, de facto, part of the local political processes and therefore require strategies for dealing with the world of formal and informal community politics. It is this world in which they must survive.

4. Most institutions require some degree of modification in order to meet their goals. Change agents may be internal (the staff and governing body), or external (the funding body, the state and federal governments or the public at large). In either case, adequate communication is essential to bring it about. A public relations program based on an intense planning effort with clear goals to give it shape may be the surest method of generating support for institutional improvement, both inside and outside the library.

5. An important corollary to systems theory is that all management actions taken within an organization are interrelated. No single act can be made without generating an impact on every other

facet of management. Exercising foresight helps to eliminate the remediation necessitated by blindness or hindsight.

CHAPTER HIGHLIGHTS

The chapters that follow are organized according to the conceptual framework described above. The initial section, *Chapters One* through *Four*, places the public library in context. *Chapter Two* explores the public library movement as it has existed in the past and as it has evolved over the years. *Chapter Three* presents a snapshot of the public library today, describes the library profession and contemplates the future of both in light of societal and technological demands. The public library from the late 1880s to the early 1990s can be seen as a paradigm for the growth of American society operating out of rural and small town America, with its local institutions and perspectives, largely independent of the organizations and establishments of other small communities, and gradually evolving into a network of increasingly interconnected elements.

Chapters Four, Five and *Six* deal with the community environment. *Chapter Four* places the library within the framework of its service area, suggests methods to acquire and analyze community information and illustrates how community demographics, history, traditions and other factors can be used to help predict the nature and extent of public library use.

Chapter Five deals with the legal basis of a public library and with its governance, areas in which stability rather than rapid shifts seem to prevail. Most public libraries are still governed by lay boards of library trustees who, although occasionally criticized as unrepresentative and lacking in energy, have endured because they have managed the library as independent bodies and in the public interest.

Chapter Six describes how the library structures itself internally in order to operate and meet its goals, demonstrating how organizations have begun to shift from command driven pyramidal entities to more cooperative, consensus driven organizations.

Beginning with *Chapter Seven*, attention is turned to more substantive issues. *Chapter Seven* traces the growth of technological advances within all segments of public libraries and compares them with transformations occurring in American society. Automation has already significantly improved library service and promoted cooperation. Now, questions about fundamental differences in the way libraries do business are being raised.

Chapter Eight is devoted to the construction and management of the knowledge base, the library's materials collections. Vexing problems including intellectual freedom, demand versus quality arguments, the nature of the collection and its relationship to the community it serves, as well as descriptions of selection and acquisition procedures are discussed.

Chapter Nine, Technical Services, describes how materials, once acquired, are organized and processed for use, the mechanisms designed to give access to them and how the process has altered since automation. Included are such traditional technical functions as cataloging, processing, binding and preservation.

Chapter Ten deals with how a library, after it has properly marked and placed its materials, disseminates them. Current circulation practices are investigated as are questions about who may borrow which materials for what length of time and the consequences of their nonreturn.

Specific users are the focus of *Chapters Eleven* through *Fourteen*. Assisting patrons in their pursuit of knowledge, answering questions, is clearly one of the fundamental public library services. *Chapter Eleven* looks at how Reference activities are delivered and examines the Fee versus Free controversy, delivery of service to particular interest groups, the extent to which Information and Referral can be sustained, and the integration of technology into existing reference departments.

Chapter Twelve, Reader Services, discusses programming efforts, stresses the humanistic responsibilities of librarians to further reading, and rehearses some of the hazards of providing public library service including security and other problems caused by difficult patrons.

Chapter Thirteen is devoted to services libraries provide for young people, both children and young adults. Children are habitually short-changed by the society. Children's services in libraries, despite considerable success, have sometimes suffered a similar fate. Such difficult matters as service to latchkey and sheltered children, and to parents of those "at risk" are addressed.

Chapter Fourteen deals with constituents who are deemed "special" and who require so-called outreach services. Among these are aging populations, racial minority groups, immigrants, non-literate people, institutionalized and homebound populations, and rural residents.

Chapter Fifteen describes how to market the output of library efforts. The undertaking we call public relations, an essential tool for helping to secure public knowledge and approval of the library's services, is explained as are reasons why it has sometimes failed to function effectively. Such efforts as attracting media attention, organizing Friends of the Library Groups, holding book sales and other methods are presented.

Chapters Sixteen through *Nineteen* concern the administrative tasks of staffing, financing and housing the library. *Chapter Sixteen* looks at how leadership in the person of the Library Director is manifested and exercised, and the impact this may have on the organization. Recruitment, retention and evaluation of the chief executive are also discussed, as is the relationship between the chief executive, the library's board and staff, and the municipality's administration.

Questions relating to other library staff, especially those about the conditions of employment that make it possible to organize and sustain effective activity, are explored in *Chapter Seventeen*, Human Resources. Particular difficulties of working under restrictions engendered by union and civil service regulations are discussed as are other troublesome problems such as burnout and utilizing volunteers.

Difficulty in finding sufficient funds to operate the library, a matter that has plagued public librarians since the inception of the institution, continues with increasing intensity today. Scarce resources, the need to be accountable and productive have made understanding the budget process as a financial plan of action essential.   *Chapter Eighteen* presents several budget options, explores sources of revenue both private and public and ponders the importance of political relationships in securing appropriate library funding.

Chapter Nineteen examines the utility of American public libraries as they attempt to accommodate to the changing needs of the public for a building that houses and disseminates information resources. Having an acceptable structure for the public and staff means intimate knowledge of the uses to which it will be put. The tasks associated with preparing for a new building, including writing a building program, hiring a consultant and assuring that it meets handicapped access regulations are reviewed.

The final chapter, *Twenty,* is devoted to evaluation. The key question of how to assess library goodness or value is addressed and mechanisms that permit librarians to learn how well the library is meeting its goals and objectives and servicing its community are explained.

SUMMARY

Public libraries are deeply embedded in a variety of environments, all of which influence the services they provide. Understanding public libraries as open systems with environmental inputs, boundary-spanning activities, outputs and feedback mechanisms furnishes librarians with a framework in which to examine what they do and with whom they do it. Understanding them as institutions requiring honed management skills as well as library technical proficiency improves performance and assures a smooth-running organization.   Ultimately these theoretical approaches permit libraries to exercise greater flexibility and more control over their environments. Systems and management theory must always be combined with intimate knowledge of a particular institution's framework and resources, both human and material.

The best library managers are said to combine the attributes of psychiatrist, confessor, snake-oil seller and mathematician, a formidable array of talents.

NOTES AND SUGGESTED READINGS

Notes

1. Richard Dougherty, ALA Inaugural Address, as delivered, July 1990.

2. Marilyn Gell Mason, "Library Automation: The Next Wave," *Library Administration and Management* 5 (Winter 1991): 34.

3. Freemont E. Kast and James Rosenzweig, "General Systems Theory" in *Management Strategies for Libraries,* ed. Beverly Lynch (New York: Neal-Schuman, 1985) 132.

4. Joanne Euster, *Activities and Effectiveness of the Academic Library Director* (Westport, CT: Greenwood Press, 1987), 36.

5. Maurice Marchant, "The Library as Open System," in *Management Strategies for Libraries,* ed. Beverly Lynch (New York: Neal-Schuman, 1985) 154-6.

Suggested Readings

Childers, Thomas and Nancy Van House. "The Grail of Goodness: The Effective Public Library." *Library Journal* 114 (October 1, 1989): 44-49.

OCLC (Online Computer Library Center) Inc. *The Future of the Public Library. Conference Proceedings.* Dublin, OH: OCLC, 1988.

"Proceedings of the H.W. Wilson Symposium on the Future of Public Libraries." *Wilson Library Bulletin* 65 (May 1991): 25-54.

Pungitore, Verna. *Public Librarianship; An Issues-Oriented Approach*

New York: Greenwood Press, 1989.

Sager, Don, ed. "Professional Views. Critical Issues Facing Public Libraries." *Public Libraries* (Jan/Feb 1991): 13-20.

Shuman, B.A. *The Library of the Future: Alternative Scenarios for the Information Profession.* Littleton, CO: Libraries Unlimited, 1989.

Williams, Patrick. *The American Public Library and the Problem of Purpose.* New York: Greenwood Press, 1988.

Woodrum, Pat. *Managing Public Libraries in the 21st Century.* New York: Haworth, 1989.

CHAPTER 2

HISTORY OF THE PUBLIC LIBRARY IN THE UNITED STATES

The public library in the United States today, as in the past, is a reflection of the changing priorities of the society in which it is embedded. Beginning with the colonial period, its growth has been intimately bound to the country's political and economic fortunes, to the prevailing social ethic and to national needs. Changes in the rural and urban landscape, industrialization and immigration, for instance, found strong echoes in the course of public library development. Changes in social conditions, wars and depressions, to name two, produced substantial shifts in the quantity and nature of required services. The public library has been seen, in turn, as a place where persons in poverty have an equal chance, as a positive alternative to the tavern and brothel, and as an antidote to radicalism.

Social movements or agencies must, by necessity, derive sustenance from their environments, but they also require the support of strong, innovative, forceful leaders in order to flourish. The path which the public library has followed was charted, among others, by Justin Winsor, George Ticknor, William Poole and, of course, the two most influential actors, Melvil Dewey and Andrew Carnegie. Their early visions are responsible for an institution, remarkable, flawed and uniquely American.

THE COLONIAL AND POST-REVOLUTIONARY PERIODS

Pinpointing when private libraries became public ones and

which forms of early libraries represent significant predecessors to public libraries, is difficult. Historians generally agree they did not begin on a specific date or in a specific place, but rather, as Jesse Shera asserted, "a multiplicity of forces, accumulating over a long period of time, converged to shape this new library form."[1]

The first attempt to create a public library in the new world might have been made by Captain Robert Keayne when, in 1656, he willed his book collection to Boston with the proviso that the City provide a place for it. Books represented real wealth in the early colonies. Colleges, for instance, often measured their worth by the value of the gifts and donations which formed their library collections. Boston willingly complied with Keayne's stipulation, supplying a room in its Town House for the books. Unfortunately, little subsequent attention was paid to the collection and it was ultimately devoured by fire in 1747 -- a fate that befell many public and private collections in the eighteenth and nineteenth centuries.

The most prevalent form of collections of publicly shared books in the early 18th century were those in Church and parish libraries. Reverend Thomas Bray, an Anglican priest, established during a nine year period (1695-1704) seventy libraries, five of which were termed "provincial" and were large. Unfortunately, like Keayne's bequest, no provisions were made for acquiring new materials once the collections were established and the vast majority of them withered and disappeared.

It is possible to doubt the importance of Keayne's and Bray's contributions, but few would deny that *social libraries* were significant predecessors of the public library. Though there is a tendency to group them under a single rubric, they adopted many differing forms. Some were elite social institutions, others were housed in mills and factories. What they had in common was shared book collections for specific users.

One of the earliest social libraries grew out of Benjamin Franklin's reputedly insatiable thirst for knowledge and desire for self-improvement. He and twelve young Philadelphians from modest backgrounds organized Junto, a group whose purpose was to "nurture honest and decorous debate and thought, and to contribute in any way possible to the betterment of mankind." [2] In order to further these ends, members were to create a common library in the clubroom. While Junto's library never grew beyond modest size, the notion of sharing materials to provide for wider access caused Franklin, in 1731, to "set on foot my first Project of a Public Nature, that of a Subscription Library." [3] It reached fruition when, in 1742, the Library Company of Philadelphia was chartered and became a model for many other communities. The Library Company was a joint stock company where each member owned one or more shares in the corporation. Some social libraries collected annual fees in addition to an initial stock purchase; others permitted non-shareholders to join on a year-to-year basis or even, occasionally, for briefer periods of time.

Another form of social library, the Athenaeum, emphasized collections of scholarly newspapers and magazines. Considered the aristocrat of social library forms, it could cost as much as $300 to join one. In addition to their collections of materials, Athanaeums frequently provided cultural and recreational activities. The Boston Athenaeum, founded in 1807, was the first of its kind. Members were drawn from the ranks of the city's most affluent and influential citizens and included, among others, a number of men who would later become the strongest advocates of a public library for that city. Women, however, were rarely welcomed in social libraries.

"Mechanics" or "mercantile" libraries, institutions sponsored by community elites to keep aspiring middle class young men off the streets and "to promote orderly and virtuous habits, diffuse knowledge and the desire for knowledge, improve the scientific skill" and create good citizens,[4] were yet another example of social library. William Wood, a Boston merchant and philanthropist, established the first apprentice or mechanics library in the 1820's and collected money from other philanthropists for libraries for young mercantile clerks, as well. The success and popularity of these occupational libraries can be traced, in part, to that important article of nineteenth century American faith -- that with proper knowledge, people could succeed. The Horatio Alger myth enjoyed widespread belief by both workingmen and employers.

While social libraries were beginning to meet the needs of some of the citizenry, a lack of guaranteed funding rendered them problematic. In times of prosperity they would grow, increase their hours of operation, and additional staff would be hired. When recessions and depressions occurred, they often failed *completely*. Finding a more stable method of financial support for libraries became crucial. Many social libraries were integrated into the public libraries that began to form in the latter part of the eighteenth century. Others, particularly those in major cities, still exist. The importance of social libraries cannot be underestimated. They symbolized a determination to emphasize knowledge and literacy as valuable to individual growth and the advancement of society.

A second strand of library development which would ultimately be incorporated into the definition of public library were "circulating" libraries. Those who had formed social libraries saw them as serious sources of knowledge about important subjects. On the other hand, circulating or rental libraries, housed in book stores or in print shops, offered popular materials -- the newest and most exciting fiction, particularly novels, an 18th century literary innovation. Circulating libraries first appeared prior to the Revolutionary War, had their heyday in the period around 1830 and then ran their course, particularly as public libraries began to form.

A third and important thread in the fabric of public library history was the *school district library*. Reading was seen as an important adjunct to formal education, and therefore supporting libraries -- collections of books -- was considered legitimate for school districts. Some indication of the prominent role that reading and books held in the mind of early educators can be seen in the following excerpt from Horace Mann's *Third Annual Report* which he delivered as Secretary of the Massachusetts Board of Education in 1839.

> After the rising generation have acquired habits of Intelligent reading...*what shall they read?* for, with no books to read, the power of reading will be useless; and with bad books to read, the

consequences will be as much worse than ignorance as wisdom is better. What books, then, are there accessible to the great mass of the children in the State, adapted to their moral and intellectual wants, and fitted to nourish their minds with the elements of uprightness and wisdom?[5]

School district libraries originated in New York, then spread throughout New England and subsequently to the Midwest. Unfortunately, they generally lacked interesting materials and adequate quarters. Their collections were composed primarily of textbooks and inspirational tracts, and collections were often stored in teachers' homes.

These three early forms of libraries scarcely resembled what we have come to think of as the public library, although each played a role in setting a principle that would later be integrated into the institution. *Social libraries* contributed quality as a goal, as well as the notion of sharing; *circulating libraries* introduced popular materials as legitimate items to collect and disseminate; *school district libraries* established the principle of public funding.

If the definition of a public library includes the concept of public financial support, the town library in Peterborough, New Hampshire, founded in 1833 probably deserves to be considered the progenitor of all public libraries in America. The State of New Hampshire had collected taxes on capital stock of banks operating there for the purpose of starting a state college. When the attempt was abandoned in 1828, the accumulated funds were apportioned among New Hampshire towns to be used in support of free schools or other kinds of educational endeavors. Peterborough decided to allocate some of the money to purchase books for a town library, an institution that would be both publicly owned and supported and free to all residents of the community.

Later, in 1849, New Hampshire became the first state to pass a law permitting the levying of local taxes to support public libraries. Massachusetts followed in 1851 and Maine in 1854. After the Civil War many states adopted similar measures, thereby establishing the legitimacy of libraries as recipients of local taxes.

THE BOSTON PUBLIC LIBRARY

Peterborough may have had the first tax-supported public library, but without the Boston Public Library, the idea of a popular library might not have become viable.[6] On the eve of the Civil War, the United States was becoming an industrialized, urban nation, attracting millions of poorly educated immigrants who were increasingly seen as unable to participate in democratic society. At the same time, workingmen were beginning to view publicly supported educational institutions as a means to gain political and economic power and prosperity.

Mid-nineteenth century Boston seemed ready to establish a public library. Not only was it experiencing the typical growing pains of an Ante-Bellum community, but it was exhibiting positive signs indicating that it was prepared to welcome this new institution. First, it commanded sufficient resources to support it financially; Second, its population had grown large enough; Third, the community was sympathetic to public support of education; and, finally, there was a favorable cultural milieu which included a spirit of intellectual and cultural competition fanned by interurban rivalries.

In 1852, the Trustees of the Boston Public Library issued their *Report*, written jointly by Edward Everett and George Ticknor, which delineated what is still considered the ideal concept of public library service. It read, in part:

> Reading ought to be furnished to all, as a matter of public policy and duty, on the same principle that we furnish free education, and in fact, as a part and a most important part of the education of all. For it has been rightly judged that--under political, social and religious institutions like ours--it is of paramount importance that the means of general information should be so diffused that the largest possible number of persons should be induced to read and understand questions going down to the very foundations of social order, which are constantly presenting themselves, and which we, as a people, are constantly required to decide, and do decide, either ignorantly or wisely.[7]

In this statement can be read the basic tenets of the early public library movement. That is, there is close linkage between knowledge and right thinking; the future of the democracy is contingent on an educated citizenry; there is a strong correlation between the public library movement and public education; and, every citizen has the right of free access to community-owned resources.

In 1854, with the permission of the Massachusetts legislature, the Boston Public Library opened its doors. Charles Coffin Jewett, lately of the Smithsonian Institution, agreed to serve as its first Superintendent. Known for his organizational abilities, he is remembered for his early attention to collecting and cataloging materials. After twelve years he stepped down, relinquishing his place to Justin Winsor, an eminent, albeit reclusive, historical scholar.

Winsor brought to Boston, and by virtue of Boston's place in the intellectual life of the nation, to the entire country a broadened vision of what public libraries should be doing. The series of innovations he instituted were designed to make the library more attractive and accessible to those he hoped to reach. He circulated fiction, insisting that mass tastes would improve over time and that people would progress from inferior to good literature. He prepared annotated book lists. Branch libraries and delivery stations were opened. A public card catalog was installed. Hours were extended so that the library was closed only five days a year. That Winsor was successful can be seen in book circulation records which indicated that loans increased from 175,727 in 1868 to 1,140,572 in 1877.

After a squabble with the Boston Common Council which left him with a sharply reduced salary, Winsor resigned his Boston Public Library position to become Head Librarian at Harvard University. There he was able to continue his liberalizing innovations and is credited with transforming the library from a mere repository of knowledge to a workshop for scholars.

There were additional legacies to libraries resulting from the establishment of the Boston Public Library. In petitioning the State of Massachusetts for permission to appropriate a maximum of

$5,000 annually, the legitimacy of using local tax money to fund the library was affirmed. A citizen board of trustees with specified powers and tasks was given responsibility for the library although the municipality retained funding and oversight duties. They could spend money, decide on policies and set conditions of employment, including remuneration, for all but the Librarian.

Few library historians deny the seminal role played by Boston Public Library, but a lively and interesting debate centers around the motivations ascribed to those who were instrumental in its establishment. What did those who formed the Boston Public Library and other like institutions hope to achieve? Were they genteel missionaries, as some have claimed, seeking to uplift the masses and be their moral guardians?[8] Were they followers of the humanitarian ideal, liberal middle-class leaders who attempted to bring educational opportunity to the common people? Did they rise out of that group of Americans who would later foster abolition, women's rights, the peace movement, prison reform and other enlightened policies?[9] Or were they authoritarian, conservative elitists who saw the public library as a means of stabilizing the society, of restraining the behavior of those who would follow the leadership of unscrupulous politicians, and those who were woefully ignorant and incapable of handling universal suffrage -- especially the new immigrants? Was the library to serve as an intellectual resource for the elite minority -- the country's best men -- who would become the leaders of the political, social and literary affairs of the nation? Were the founders motivated by *fear* of the dangerous masses, by a commitment to preserve their elite status, to continuing conservative mores and social refinements?[10]

Motivations are difficult to ascribe. Hindsight seems to differ with each age and conclusions are drawn based on currently prevailing interpretations of history. That the library profession attracted to its early ranks middle-class, native born, Protestant, well-educated, apolitical North-Easterners who shared a definition of reality and believed that the "best reading" would have a salutary effect on the moral health of the public seems clear. Whether they were fundamentally conservative or liberal is debatable. That the nation required educational opportunities for its citizens is undeniable.

THE AMERICAN LIBRARY ASSOCIATION AND THE AGE OF MELVIL DEWEY

Five first events crucial to American public library history occurred in 1876: the initial meeting of the American Library Association, the premier edition of the *American Library Journal,* the release of the first volumes of Dewey's Decimal Classification, publication of Cutter's *Rules for a Printed Dictionary Catalogue* and the issuance of the Department of Education's *Report on Public Libraries in the United States,* the first true survey of the number and extent of United States public libraries and their collections. According to the Education Department's report there had been, in 1776, 29 so-called public libraries with holdings of 45,623 volumes. By 1876 there were 3,682 public libraries with 12 million volumes which were "open to the public without charge or for a nominal fee only." Librarianship was beginning to exhibit the hallmarks of a profession: an organization that set standards and a literature that treated its concerns. The missing element, an educational component, would not be long in making its appearance.

On the sixth of October, in 1876, the centennial year of the United States, in the Centennial City, Philadelphia, 103 librarians convened

> for the purpose of promoting the library interests of the country, and of increasing reciprocity of intelligence and goodwill among librarians and all interested in library economy and bibliographic studies[11]

and called themselves the American Library Association.

Attempts to organize the profession dated as far back as 1852, occurring earlier than the cohesive efforts of most other occupations in the United States. Still, convening the initial meeting was no mean feat. The idea had originated with John Eaton, U.S.

Commissioner of Education, who suggested it to Frederick Leypoldt, coeditor with Richard Bowker of *Publishers Weekly*. Leypoldt, in turn, mentioned it to Melvil Dewey, formerly Amherst College Librarian and currently a businessman trying to establish a library supply manufacturing company, during negotiations about a new periodical devoted to library affairs they hoped to publish. When Dewey agreed to accept the editorship of the magazine, Leypoldt suggested they launch it simultaneously with a librarians' conference.

To all intents and purposes, Dewey now accepted responsibility for the campaign to start a library organization, one which would give support to previously isolated library leaders, but one which would also further his own ends; that is, provide an arena where he could sell his products, gain support for his new magazine, and in which he could begin to disseminate the ideas for library standardization that he was beginning to envision.

The call for a library meeting was greeted with mixed response. Winsor asserted that he was "willing to do anything helpful for the cause of public library interests"[12] but could not attend. William Poole of the Chicago Public Library said he was unfamiliar with those who had issued the invitation. Finally, Dewey was able to convince not only Winsor and Poole, but Boston Athenaeum Librarian Charles Ammi Cutter, Harvard College Library Director John Langdon Sibley and a number of other prominent librarians to attend.

Of the 103 participants, 13 were women, none of whom, it should be noted, ventured to speak except through male peers. (This despite the fact that by 1878 two-thirds of the library workers at the Boston Public Library were women.) Public librarians predominated and while many of the subjects discussed were of interest to academic librarians, the main focus was public libraries. Winsor became the fledgling organization's first president, and was joined in leadership positions by Poole, Smith (Philadelphia Library Company) and Spofford (Librarian of Congress). Dewey was one of three secretaries.

Next to Justin Winsor, William Frederic Poole was the nation's most prominent librarian. A Yale graduate and former head of the Boston Athenaeum, he had organized the Cincinnati Public Library prior to performing the same role in Chicago. An index to periodicals he had produced while a student at Yale became the preeminent model of a periodical finding guide. Poole was a strong personality, somewhat less patrician and more outspoken than Winsor, who often found himself at odds with Dewey. Initially, Dewey's petty practices, producing minutes in his own unreadable simplified spelling, for instance, were mere irritants. Gradually, however, Poole found himself increasingly unhappy with Dewey's attempts to standardize the profession. More a bookman than an administrator, he was intent, as was Winsor and the vast majority of other early ALA officials, on expanding public exposure to good literature, even if this meant initially supplying lesser works.

Dewey was different from the others. The baby of the group, he was from far less privileged circumstances than his fellow library leaders. Complex in character, never quite accepted by the Brahmins who populated ALA from its inception almost to the turn of the century, he exhibited a greater interest in standardizing library procedures and making services available more efficiently than he was in the contents of books. His decimal classification system, developed while he was still a student at Amherst, had its trial run there. Like his other innovations, the classification system was designed to make the library accessible and efficient, enabling librarians to supply "The best reading, for the largest number, at the least cost," a Dewey motto that ALA accepted as its own. By 1899, he said "run the library smoothly, and let people get their own meat or poison."[13]

Preoccupied with library mechanics, Dewey concentrated on minute details, decreeing, for instance, that

> the standard library card has lines 6 mm apart, or four spaces to the inch. Of these the small letters should be 2 1/2 mm high; and b, f, h, k and 15 mm high, thus leaving a 1 mm margin below the top of the tallest letter and the line above.[14]

about which Dee Garrison comments, "the length of 1 mm, in case

anyone wanted to compute it, was about the width of six hairs."
And, she adds, "Perhaps it really is not possible to truly compre-
hend the intricacies of Melvil Dewey's mind."[15]

Through force of his personality, and despite the opposition of
Columbia trustees, Dewey was able to convince the President of the
University to establish a library school in 1886. Twenty-four hours
before the school was to open, Dewey was informed that because
seventeen of the class's twenty students were women he was not to
be given a room on campus. Undaunted, he garnered old furniture,
cleaned out an unused storeroom above the chapel, and greeted the
first library school class -- on time! Dewey had openly courted
women to the profession, particularly cultured and educated ones.
From the beginning librarians of both genders were of uncommon
intellect. Yet, without much thought he misused his primarily
female recruits. At Albany, where the library school moved when
Dewey was appointed director of the New York State Library
students paid fees, bought their own books and supplies, and spent
a substantial amount of time working in the library. Though he
demanded that his students have earned an undergraduate degree
before enrolling in his school, much of the curriculum was devoted
to menial or mechanical concerns.[16]

The contradictions surrounding Dewey's contributions to the
library field are almost endless. His election to the presidency of
ALA in 1890 has been seen as a triumph of standardization in
library work. But his emphasis on mechanical and technical
concerns created a profession that is, sometimes, according to
Howard Mumford Jones, devoted more to books as objects in
space, than to what is inside them. [17] Wearing too many hats led
to Dewey's eventual downfall within ALA. The organization
requested his resignation from office when they learned that he had
comingled the accounts of ALA, his magazine, and his library
company. The establishment of his Lake Placid Club with its
restrictive covenants against Jews, African-Americans and other
"undesirables," and accusations of womanizing, continued his
downslide.

By the turn of the century, ALA had coalesced, spawned

countless organizations devoted to particular library interests, and could be characterized as "merely a humdrum professional organization, wrapped round with tradition, settled in its habits of thought and chiefly occupied with matters of technical detail."[18]

THE CARNEGIE DECADES

The years 1890 through the onset of World War I marked a period of major expansion and change for public libraries. Not only did they grow in number, collection and staff, but they changed in orientation and purpose. The transfer in 1902 from Boston to Chicago of American Library Association headquarters was both an actual and symbolic relocation. From its inception, the organization had gradually, but steadily, turned towards Midwesternization and feminization, and seen its executive board membership shift from public librarians to those from academic institutions, state libraries and the Library of Congress.[19]

The decade of the 1890's witnessed the rise of big city free public libraries, New York in 1895, New Orleans in 1896, Brooklyn in 1897 and Los Angeles in 1889 as well as the burgeoning of smaller ones, due, in large measure, to big and little philanthropy. Men of means contributed to the good fortune of their communities, primarily to the educational and cultural institutions. Whether their munificence was generated by a new imperative to share their fortunes rather than follow the "old-world practice of devoting wealth to insure permanent comfort and luxury to a few people"[20] or because they wished to insure a world that maintained the "status quo" is a matter of some contention. Probably both are true.

Industrialist Andrew Carnegie and some others aimed libraries at workingmen. Socialites Astor, Lenox and Tilden whose private collections formed the New York Public Library were, initially at least, more intent on serving scholars and people of a certain class. John Jacob Astor had bequeathed $400,000 in 1838 to form a new library, with his secretary Joseph Cogswell as librarian. Unfortunately, the funds became available only after Astor died. When Cogswell finally ascended to the position, he closed the stacks, installed no gas lighting (meaning the library was only available during the day) and put the minimum age of use at 17. His attitudes toward the public are reflected in his statement that "It would have crazed me to have seen a crowd ranging lawlessly among the books and throwing everything into confusion."[21]

Andrew Carnegie, on the other hand, was dedicated to an institution which he considered conservatively progressive and civilizing. An immigrant from Scotland, Carnegie had amassed an enormous fortune from the steel industry. A devotee of Social Darwinism, he saw the library as the university of workingmen where those who wished to improve themselves could do so. He also thought the library capable of calming the inflamed sensibilities of would-be radicals.

> the result of knowledge [gleaned from libraries] is to make men not violent revolutionists, but cautious evolutionists;   not destroyers, but careful improvers.[22]

Carnegie limited his philanthropy to library buildings which he agreed to supply to those communities willing to guarantee funding once they were erected. Ironically, his actions were attacked by the right and left. His demand for community support was labelled Communist by those citizens who said, "Don't tax me, I'll give willingly." Conversely, labor leaders greeted the library with skepticism, asserting that the wages of workingmen were taken away in great amount and only a little was returned in the form of the public library. Union leader Eugene Debs cried "shame" upon the workers who had "uncritically accepted gifts from the hands of Andrew Carnegie, red with the blood of their slain comrades."[23]

By 1920 Carnegie had provided $50,000,000 for the erection of at least 2,500 buildings, of which 1,679 were in the United States. Some communities refused Carnegie's money because it was "tainted," because they resented his stipulations about further support, or because they had local benefactors willing to contribute. Enoch Pratt Library in Baltimore and Cossit Library in Memphis are two such examples.

Along with the growth in facilities, libraries were beginning to offer new services. Reference departments and reference librarians, creations of the 1890s, had become standard components of service by the turn of the century. Open shelves, despite the hesitations of librarians worried about misplacement of materials and extra wear and tear on books, became the norm. A system of interlibrary loan of special books for students and scholars was instituted. In large public libraries, book collections were arranged into subject and departmental libraries, leading, in turn, to a division of labor and specialization. Shortly after John Cotton Dana assumed the librarianship of Denver Public in 1894, he established a business and medical collection, as well as one of the first children's libraries.

The last decade of the nineteenth century marked the appearance of children's services. Early public libraries had been envisioned as adult institutions, extensions of the public education system. As late as 1894, seventy percent of the libraries still had age restrictions. In most, those under twelve or thirteen were ineligible to enter the building. Now, in a reversal of mission, children became important components of the library program. Response was swift and widespread. By 1908, circulation of materials to children accounted for thirty to forty percent of total lending. Storytelling, touted as a way to socialize immigrants, soften voices, teach courtesy and good manners, quickly became a dominant feature of children's services. Discipline was stressed for both children and adults. Policemen and janitors were omnipresent and it was not unusual for children to be arrested for misbehavior.

Adult immigrants continued to be a focus of activities, as local libraries of the progressive era came more to resemble community centers. Librarians felt they were waging a war against evil and ignorance and for "Americanization." The library at Mt. Vernon, NY, for instance, targeted special ethnic groups, by offering lectures on American life in Italian, publishing an "immigrant's guide" in Italian, Polish and Yiddish, and providing ethnic musical events in its building.[24] By 1914, most large public libraries had a well-developed branch library system, with the bulk of their units located in poor neighborhoods.

WORLD WARS AND THE DEPRESSION

A dispiriting air descended on public librarians as their missionary period entered its final days. Immigration was down, reading habits, despite the good efforts of dedicated librarians, were not improving. As a matter of fact, book circulation was in decline. Libraries were used by few people and fewer men. There were, indeed, periods of ups and downs. Bad times -- recessions and depressions -- brought people back into the library. But when economic fortunes improved, the public disappeared. The "library spirit," belief in the uplifting power of the institution, was losing its cachet.

World War I, for all its devastation, had a salutary effect on public librarianship. The Library War Service Program, under the auspices of the American Library Association, assumed responsibility for providing books for the armed forces both at home and abroad. Librarians performed superbly. On the civilian front, however, they were not as stalwart in guarding their materials from the hysteria that kept German books off the shelf in many American public libraries.[25]

The term "adult education" entered the library lexicon in the mid 1920's. While adults had often been the focus of library service, their formal education had been almost overlooked. What was proposed now was a massive campaign to service and help those who wanted to learn something. Libraries were urged to install readers advisory desks in main circulation areas, to interview patrons, assess their levels of reading, give them individualized lists and follow their progress. An impractical plan in light of the scarcity of funds to hire sufficient personnel, it was abandoned by the mid 1930's, only to be succeeded by the concept of the public library as a "people's university," a place for self-education.

The depression years, particularly 1933 and 1934, were as difficult for public libraries as they were for the rest of the nation. Financial support was curtailed, but demand for services burgeoned. With no place else to go, people found solace and warmth in the reading rooms of libraries. Among the new priorities, was a mandate to "provide for 'greatly increased leisure,' a popular euphemism for permanent unemployment."[26] In addition, librarians were now to supply information on social problems and carry materials on leisure and self-help activities.

A new strain of public librarianship emerged in the 1930's. Born of social necessity, fueled by the specter of the rise of dictatorships in Europe, librarians began to look at themselves as guardians of the people's right to know. This was a difficult stance for many librarians who had previously regarded themselves as, if not apolitical, then certainly religiously, socially and politically neutral. In their assiduous attempts to avoid arbitrary appointments to and dismissals from their ranks, they had cloaked themselves in a mantle of professionalism and adopted neutrality as a norm of behavior. In the past, censorship had been excused on the grounds of moral uplift. Librarians had followed a code that prevented them from taking stands on controversial material and subjects. Even ALA employed this rationale when it declined to join with other groups in matters of anti-censorship and civil liberties issues.[27] Now, librarians were asked to become watchdogs of free speech and guarantors of access to all ideas as moral imperatives.

Adding to the thrust for a different kind of public librarianship was a new spirit of inquiry in the library profession as a whole, a partial consequence of the efforts of the recently formed doctoral program at the University of Chicago. In his landmark report, *Training for Library Service* issued in 1923, Charles Williamson, had called for far-reaching improvements to library education including the abolition of emphasis on routines and technique and more attention to theory, philosophy and research. Responding to the documented need, the Chicago Library School was formed in 1926 and the doctoral program instituted in 1928. An eclectic blend of diversely qualified faculty were hired, a research-oriented curriculum adopted and a wide-ranging publishing program inaugurated. By the mid-1930's, Chicago was producing a new literature of librarianship that paid close attention to such philosophical considerations as the purpose of libraries and the nature of reading, a literature that utilized the empirical methodologies developed for other social sciences.

Still another harbinger of change was Stanley Kunitz, a poet who edited the *Wilson Library Bulletin* and continually criticized the profession's lack of social conscience and commitment. In one editorial, "Specter at Richmond," published in May 1936, he descried as outrageous the fact that the American Library Association had scheduled its upcoming meeting in racially segregated facilities at Richmond, VA.[28] Unfortunately the problem he identified did not receive attention until the 1960's. By 1939, librarians had coalesced around the theme of intellectual freedom and had adopted the first Library Bill of Rights. Chapter 8 treats contemporary questions about intellectual freedom and censorship and copies of relevant documents (Library Bill of Rights, Freedom to Read, Complaint Form) appear in Appendix 1. Reports of book burning and other abominations of Hitler and Mussolini helped to solidify for librarians the vital role they could play in promoting and preserving democracy. President Roosevelt lent further support when he issued a Presidential Proclamation late in 1941 declaring that

> Libraries are directly and immediately involved in the conflict which divides our world, and for two reasons: first because they are essential to the functioning of a democratic society; second, because the contemporary conflict touches the integrity of scholarship, the freedom of the mind, and even the survival of culture and libraries are the great tools of scholarship, the great repositories of culture and the great symbols of the freedom of the mind.[29]

One final development during the 1930's seems worthy of note. The American Library Association issued, in 1935, its *A National Plan for Libraries* which reflected the then current thinking of social and economic planners. What the plan represented was the first step on the long road toward bringing to the federal government an understanding that public libraries are both a natural resource and a nationwide service, and that financial support for them should be a matter of national concern. Many librarians shared with other citizens a widespread distrust of the federal government and feared granting it a role in education, maintaining that to be a state and local responsibility. Since libraries were considered part of the educational system, the principle of state and local control became embedded in all legislation relating to them. States retained responsibility for establishing standards of performance, equalizing expenditures and certifying personnel.

Unfortunately, the fight for national recognition was slow and it was not until 1956 that federal funding for libraries in the form of the Library Services Act became a reality. On the way, however, national planning had generated useful by-products, among which were clear distinctions between functions and services of various types of libraries, assessments of the current status of libraries, attention to particular types of library problems such as service to rural communities, and, above all, interest in defining what it is that libraries do, that is, in what we have come to call the library mission.

THE ERA OF THE PUBLIC LIBRARY INQUIRY

World War II may have marked a watershed for all types of libraries not only in the United States, but in the entire world. The realization that libraries with unique holdings could be and had been destroyed, their contents forever lost, led to cooperative collection schemes, extensive microfilming and new commitments to fund libraries. An introspective mood spawned perhaps by the planning movement caused librarians to worry about what it is they were doing, and perhaps what it is they should be doing. A steady stream of studies began to document the lack of good library service available to all but a few Americans. The most important of these, *The Public Library Inquiry,* had a profound and lasting effect on the public library community. It cut librarians lose from their traditional moorings and faith, and left a demoralized populace in its wake.

The Public Library Inquiry was undertaken by the Social Science Research Council at the behest of the American Library Association under the leadership of Carl Milam and was funded by the Carnegie Corporation of New York. Robert Leigh, a political scientist directed the project, assisted by a number of library educators and other social scientists. Begun in 1948, the summary volume was published in 1950. While all seven books of the study were important, the one which had the greatest influence was authored by Bernard Berelson, Dean of the University of Chicago Library School, and was called *The Library's Public*.[30]

Berelson reported that

--25 to 30% of adult Americans read at least one book a month, and then contrasted that figure with the 50% of the population who saw one motion picture every two weeks and the 90% who read newspapers and listened to the radio.

--the public library supplied only one-fourth of the books read. 18% of the population used the public library once a year; 10% used it once a month. Of these latter, those who used it once a month, 10% of adults and 33% of children could be considered "real users."

--a small group of heavy users borrowed a majority of books. 5% of users borrowed 40% of the books circulated annually and 20% borrowed 70%.

--half of the books circulated were juvenile and two-thirds were fiction. Nonfiction was concentrated among a small group of students and well-educated adults.

--the young used the public library more than the old, women far more than men, well educated rather than less educated. In other words they found the public library a middle-class institution whether defined by occupation or economic status.[31]

He contended on the basis of the study's findings that the library had two sets of objectives, one stated and the other unwritten. One described educational goals, the other sought to supply books that a certain population wanted. He concluded that it well might be wise for public libraries to serve the needs of the "serious" and "culturally alert" rather than attempt to reach all the people; that today's library clientele is small and no prestige would be lost by serving an even smaller group with a higher quality of service.

It seemed almost as if librarians heard Berelson's findings, but turned a deaf ear toward his recommendations, becoming more intent on seeking ways to broaden their spheres of influence rather than limit them. They did not wish to be thought of as a middle-class institution. There were, of course, societal reasons developing that promoted their choice.

First, however, librarians had to contend with the very real threat of McCarthyism. Senator Joseph McCarthy of Wisconsin, a Cold War warrior, had targeted libraries as major enemies in his fight against Communism. He was joined by like-minded citizens throughout the United States who were successful in such endeavors as causing the firing of Elizabeth Haas of Enoch Pratt Library in Baltimore for refusing to take a loyalty oath and having Librarian Ruth Brown of Bartlesville, Oklahoma, relieved of her duties for buying subversive periodicals including *The Nation* and *The New Republic*. In 1952, the Boston Public Library was accused of promoting communist materials.

McCarthy, himself, attacked the overseas libraries maintained by the United States Department of State. He identified 418 "suspect" authors whose books were included in State Department library collections, among them Edna Ferber, Dashiell Hammett and Stephen Vincent Benet. Under pressure, the State Department removed many of the so-called questionable books, even *burning* some, a step denounced by both President Eisenhower and the press. The library profession stood fast this time adopting, first, a strong statement against labelling materials, and, second, a *Freedom to Read* document which gave librarians, in effect, the responsibility to guard the public's freedom to read and to contest encroachments on that freedom, steps which provoked one state American Legion publication to identify the American Library Association as a Red Front.[32]

THE GOLDEN AGE OF AMERICAN PUBLIC LIBRARIES

For librarians, the highpoint of the decade of the 1950's occurred in 1956 when the Library Services Act, the first national legislation to grant aid to the country's libraries, was passed. It provided federal subsidies based on each state's percentage of rural inhabitants, required state matching funds, limited expenditures to those communities of less than 10,000 persons and demanded that a state supply a plan for dissemination of funds before it could be accepted into the program. Between its initial introduction and final passage, the rural population of America had substantially diminished and one of the bill's first alterations was to delete the restrictions based on population. As a result of LSA countless bookmobiles appeared, there was substantial improvement in state libraries and various library experiments, some inventive and exciting, were attempted.

Two other 50's developments had major impacts on libraries. One was the launching, in 1957, of the Russian space satellite Sputnik, an event that marked the onset of a three decade space race. School children began building rockets, studying the planets, learning what it meant to be an astronaut, and packing the libraries. The second occurrence was the arrival of the so-called "knowledge explosion." Books were rolling off the presses in record numbers and demand for them was high. Fortunately, there were now public sector funds available, sometimes even for public libraries.

The Library Services Act was expanded in 1962 into the Library Services and Construction Act. Now, funds could be used for buildings as well as programs.

Words such as *community*, *integration* and *poverty* entered the national and library vocabularies during the 1960's. The Great Society, the War on Poverty, Meeting the Needs of the Community, slogans of the Kennedy and Johnson administrations, served as clarion calls to librarians as well. Urged to be proactive, not reactive, to institute measures that would stimulate use, librarians were told they could not wait for patrons to cross their thresholds, but must reach out and serve all of the people in whatever ways were necessary.

In reality, necessity as well as good intentions, propelled the outreach movement. The flight of the middle-class from central cities had left a poverty-stricken, poorly educated underclass in its stead, a group traditionally alienated from the library and its contents. Librarians could either flee themselves or remain and change. A new breed of librarian, committed to the library as an agency of social activism, took up the task. "Change agents," they saw themselves as instrumental in helping to achieve a just, humane and democratic society. Public libraries participated in Model Cities, Upward Bound, Head Start and Community Center programs. Librarians joined with social workers in Neighborhood Information Centers where information and referral services as well as wide-ranging activities for children and adults were offered.

The spirit of outreach is reflected in this statement which appeared in *Library Service to the Disadvantaged,* one of the period's texts:

Can this be the American Public Library -- that smug, impressive edifice that housed a multitude of books for the scholar, the researcher, the middle-class, average reader, lo these many years? It can be and it is. The new American public library has retraced its steps from a slow death march and has found a more proper role in society.[33]

The new library professionals also played an increasingly activist role in the American Library Association. There they fought against segregation and sexism. When Kunitz had pointed accusingly at ALA for meeting in segregated facilities in the late 1930's, he had identified only one manifestation of a deep-seated problem. For many years, according to E.J. Josey, who is credited with pricking the conscience of the profession, ALA did everything possible to avoid dealing with the issue of discrimination.[34] Most library associations in the South did not permit African-Americans to join. After ALA was finally prevailed upon to condemn this practice, the majority of those units dissociated themselves from the national organization rather than integrate.

Some librarians, though perhaps fewer than might have been anticipated, joined the fight to desegregate libraries in the South, sitting in and participating in court fights. The battle was not an easy one. An insidious example of how far one community was willing to go to try to discourage integration was its decision to remove all public chairs from the public library, effecting what has come to be called "vertical integration." Eric Moon, then Editor of *Library Journal (LJ)* spearheaded the drive for Civil Rights, both in the public sector and in the profession. While historically *LJ*, like the rest of librarianship, had tried to remain neutral, Moon believed that objectivity in editorial columns was not good journalism or good for the profession.[35] Reporting facts objectively, but opening the pages to controversy was the approach he followed, one which the magazine continues today.

Community another of the words entering the national idiom during the 1960s also helped to focus library activities. Providing services not according to some national scheme, but targeted to a particular audience became the goal. Knowing the community meant understanding its demographics, its socio-economic conditions, its traditions, and its culture.

Gradually the community library concept expanded to include information for the people, and then to mean: *"All information* must be available to *all people* in *all formats* purveyed through *all communication channels* and delivered at *all levels of comprehension,*[36] which meant, not only understanding what it is that people want and need, but establishing mechanisms for making it available.

Unfortunately, that catchy phrase, "information for the people," did not include a definition of the word "information," which now received a variety of interpretations. Charles Robinson of the Baltimore County Library, advocate of the "give them what they want," approach marketed his books, bought best sellers in great numbers, and sometimes sold little read poetry books to pay for them.[37] Conversely, noted author and library consultant Lowell Martin contended that the "libraries have a responsibility to ideas, to sustaining, preserving and making readily available the intellectual capital of our society to anyone who may want or need it, now or in the future"[38] and eschewed collecting frivolous material, including fiction.

At the end of the 1970's, facing economic hardship and uncertainty, public librarians were once again at a crossroads, wondering about their role in the lately arrived Information Age. A different set of problems had emerged, as well. Many public libraries, beset by financial problems, and experiencing increased demands for unique information, were contemplating or had instituted fees for such activities as data-base searching or inter-library loan. A changed demographic landscape produced calls for new types of services, to the senior citizen community, for instance, or to new immigrant groups.

Ironically, both the development of Sputnik and the knowledge explosion, may have presaged the later eclipse of the public library in the library constellation. The new importance attached to scientific research and to technology able to control information and allow access to it demanded heavy investment in institutions of higher learning where scientific experiments were being conducted or where collections able to sustain research were located. Resources were poured into honing the interlibrary loan delivery system and to other methods of resource sharing. Information science joined library science in the titles of most university library schools and often dynamic tension best characterized the relationships between the students and prac-titioners of each. Public libraries were scrambling to keep pace.

The following chapter, "The Public Library Today" describes current and prevailing thinking about the role that libraries now play and how they may function in the future.

SUMMARY

Despite changes over time, today's public library is a recognizable successor of the one created in Boston so many years ago, even utilizing as its foundation many of the premises articulated in the statements of the founders of that institution. There remains, for instance, a shared commitment to the value of an enlightened citizenry, to an acceptance of the importance and utility of information in books and other media, to the idea that the library's primary financial support should come from local taxes, to the concept that the material collected, organized and disseminated is owned by the whole community and to the overriding article of faith -- that the library is free to all, as is still written above the portal of the Boston Public Library.

While the public library may be a familiar descendent of its earlier ancestor, the roles it has played have varied over time. Whether Michael Harris is correct when he asserts that the public library was "conceived as a deterrent to irresponsibility, intemperance, and rampant democracy, and administered in an elitist and authoritarian fashion by librarians and trustees from the middle and upper classes,"[39] there is no doubt that it came to be the guardian of the people's right to know and of their intellectual freedom.

It may also be true, as Jesse Shera contends, that the public library is an agency which follows, not creates, social change; that its true frame of reference is its coeval culture.[40] On the other hand, librarians have often so closely followed the cultural and social leadership as to be perceived to be in the vanguard.

NOTES AND SUGGESTED READINGS

Notes

1. Jesse Shera, *Foundations of the Public Library* (Chicago: The University of Chicago Press, 1949), 200.

2. Michael Harris, *History of Libraries in the Western World* (Metuchen, NJ: Scarecrow Press, 1984), 171.

4. Ibid., 173.

5. Ibid., 176.

6. Ditzion, Sidney, *Arsenals of a Democratic Culture* (Chicago: American Library Association, 1947), 3.

7. Harris, 226.

8. Dee Garrison, *Apostles of Culture* (New York: Macmillan, 1979); and Evelyn Geller, *Forbidden Books in American Public Libraries* (Westport, CT: Greenwood Press, 1984).

9. Ditzion, 68.

10. Michael Harris, "The Purposes of the Public Library: A Revisionist Interpretation of History," *Library Journal* 98 (Sept. 15, 1973): 2509-2514.

11. Wayne Wiegand, *The Politics of an Emerging Profession* (New York: Greenwood Press, 1986), 1.

12. Ibid., 5.

13. Garrison, 96.

14. Ibid., 131.

15. Ibid.

16. Ibid.

17. Ibid., 194.

18. Patrick Williams, *The American Public Library and the Problem of Purpose* (New York: Greenwood Press, 1988), 235.

19. Wiegand, 129.

20. Ditzion, 131.

21. Ibid., 144.

22. Harris (1973), 2514.

23. Ditzion, 162.

24. Garrison, 217.

25. Ibid., 94.

26. Geller, 149.

27. Ibid., 155.

28. Stanley J. Kunitz, "Specter at Richmond," *Wilson Library Bulletin* 10 (May 1936): 592-3.

29. Quoted in Williams.

30. The following titles comprise The Public Library Inquiry: Robert Leigh, *The Public Library in the United States: The general report of the Inquiry, by its director*; Bernard Berelson, *The Library's Public*; Alice Bryan, *The Public Librarian*; Oliver Garceau, *The Public Library in the Political Process*; James McCamy, *Government Publications for the Citizen*; William Miller, *The Book Industry;* Gloria Waldron, *The Information Film.* All were published by Columbia University Press.

31. Summarized from Leigh.

32. Williams, 86.

33. Ibid., 104.

34. E.J. Josey, "The Civil Rights Movement and American Librarianship: The Opening Round," in Mary Lee Bundy and Frederick J. Stielow, *Activism in American Librarianship, 1962-1973* (New York: Greenwood Press, 1987), 15.

35. Moon, Eric, with Frederick J. Stielow, "The Library Press and Eric Moon: An Interview," in Bundy and Stielow, 107.

36. Williams, 117.

37. Ibid., 118-119.

38. Ibid., 130.

39. Harris (1973), 2514.

40. Shera, 248.

Suggested Readings

Bundy, Mary Lee and Frederick J. Stielow. *Activism in American Librarianship 1962-1973.* New York: Greenwood Press, 1987.

Ditzion, Sidney. *Arsenals of a Democratic Culture.* Chicago: American Library Association, 1947.

DuMont, Rosemary. *Reform and Reaction: The Big City Public Library in American Life.* Westport, CT: Greenwood Press, 1977.

Garrison, Dee. *Apostles of Culture: The Public Library and American Society 1876-1920.* New York: Macmillan, 1979.

Geller, Evelyn. *Forbidden Books in American Public Libraries, 1876-1939.* Westport, CT: Greenwood Press, 1984.

Harris, Michael. *History of Libraries in the Western World.* Metuchen, NJ: Scarecrow Press, 1984.

Harris, Michael. "The Purpose of the American Public Library: A Revisionist Interpretation of History." *Library Journal* 98 (Sept. 15, 1973): 2509-2514.

Leigh, Robert D. *The Public Library in the United States.* New York:

Columbia University Press, 1950.

Molz, Redmond Kathleen. *National Planning for Library Service, 1935-1975*. Chicago: American Library Association, 1984.

Shera, Jesse H. *Foundations of the Public Library: The Origins of the Public Library Movement in New England, 1629-1855*. Chicago: University of Chicago Press, 1949.

Whitehill, Walter Muir. *Boston Public Library*. Cambridge, MA: Harvard University Press, 1956.

Wiegand, Wayne A. *The Politics of an Emerging Profession: The American Library Association, 1876-1917*. New York: Greenwood Press, 1986.

Williams, Patrick. *The American Public Library and the Problem of Purpose*. New York: Greenwood Press, 1988.

Winger, Howard, issue ed. "American Library History." *Library Trends* 25 (July, 1976).

CHAPTER 3

THE PUBLIC LIBRARY TODAY

The contemporary public library stands once again at a crossroads faced by difficult choices and decisions that will redefine its mission and activities. Technology has transformed the processes and procedures of its operation, but technology is only a tool, one of many that managers can use to meet the needs of their service populations. The main task now is to determine what kind of institution members of the community wish the public library to be in the future; what services they want it to deliver; in what form; and the extent to which they are willing to provide the funds required to accomplish the job.

SOCIAL FORCES

In addition to the geopolitical events of the past few years, other trends are influencing the course of public libraries. Among the most salient are:

An aging population. By 1983, more Americans were over the age of 65 than were teenagers. The oldest baby boomers, those born between 1946 and 1964, are now in their fifties. There has been a commensurately precipitous drop in birthrates. In 1960 there were 23.7 births per thousand population; by 1975 this had fallen to 14.6 per thousand. Though we are in the middle of a baby boomlet, there will be a dramatic decrease in the number of young adults between the ages of 18 and 26 in the next decade.

An increase in racial and ethnic diversity. Birth rates among African-Americans and Latinos remain at high levels as does immigration from Asia and Latin America. Demographers predict that by 2010, one of three persons in the United States will be African-American, Latino or Asian-American. A heightened awareness of the need to address multicultural concerns is anticipated.

Population shifts. Rural populations will continue to shrink while metropolitan areas, primarily suburban, will continue to expand. Older central cities will continue to deteriorate in the face of growing crime, increased poverty and homelessness, shrinking tax base and decaying infrastructures. Internal population migrations are predicted to result in population growth in the South and Southwest.

Transformation to a service oriented global economy. The economy of the United States is affected by the economy of other countries. The percentage of people involved in farming and manufacturing is decreasing, while the proportion of the population involved in managerial and professional enterprises is increasing. There will be intense need for workers with skills in identifying, obtaining, organizing, selecting, evaluating, managing and using information. The ranks of the unemployed will be swelled by those unable to acquire new skills.

New work force patterns. The work force itself is shrinking. Today there are three workers for every retiree. The ratio is anticipated to undergo even further reduction. The "learning society," in which rapid change requires a lifetime of learning in order to survive, will be reflected in the increasing number of adults who return to school for job retraining. More women will be in the work force. The number of part-time and temporary jobs will increase; more flexible work hours will be permitted; more work will be accomplished in homes using interactive computer programs. New educational skills are required for those whose jobs have been superannuated by technology and who face the prospect of accepting non-skilled entry-level service industry jobs.

A proliferation of information. What was once an industrial society is now an information society. People have easier access to more information than ever before. The amount of information is said to double every seven years. But availability of information does not guarantee that knowledge will be produced.

A continuing high illiteracy rate. Twenty-five million Americans cannot read road signs; 35 million more cannot read well enough to function in the society. The problem is expected to continue unabated. A learning society presupposes literacy. Without the tools to learn, the information society described above becomes inaccessible.

Changing assumptions about the course of human development. Most society members have been led to believe that life in society is a competitive struggle for existence and that material progress can be realized through technological and economic growth. Students of society, however, have identified a gradual paradigm shift away from these positions and a spreading pessimism. The futurist Alvin Toffler, for instance, contends that there is an assumption that moral, aesthetic, political and environmental degradation will overwhelm society no matter the material or technological progress it enjoys.

All of the societal forces described above have serious consequences for public libraries. They are being asked to become lifelong learning institutions, to serve the particular needs and demands of older users, to serve multicultural populations, to help combat literacy and to harness for a hungry public the information promise of the new technology.

Against this background of difficult societal trends what does today's public library look like and how is it faring?

A CONTEMPORARY PROFILE

In 1993, there were 9,097 public library jurisdictions in the United States and 15,312 separate library buildings, including library branches.[1]

The majority of these libraries serve populations of less than 10,000[2] and typically employ staffs of five full-time employees or less.[3] More than half of these smaller libraries serve populations of under 5,000 and average only two (in full-time equivalents) employees.

Patterns of statewide library organization vary greatly. Published statistics about libraries generally refer to jurisdictions, not buildings. One public library, administered by the state, serves all of Hawaii. In New York State, there are 760 public libraries. California, the most populous state in the country, has only 168 libraries, while Iowa has 500.[4]

Most public libraries in the United States tend to be small though in the aggregate they employ 108,246 paid staff members[5] and expend about 4.1 billion dollars. About 45 percent of public libraries reported operating expenditures of less than $50,000; about 36% expended between $50,000 and $399,000 and nearly 19% exceeded $400,000. Of the total funds, 63% is devoted to personnel and another 16% is used for collection development.[6] Public libraries are visited annually by 507 million users who borrow nearly 1.4 billion items.[7]

Libraries serving populations under 10,000 constitute a numerical majority of public libraries, but they account for only 6.6% of total budgets, employ only 9.1% of all employed library workers and circulate only 9.6% of all materials.[8] The bulk of public library activity actually occurs in institutions that are larger in size; 51.3% of all public library materials are circulated by libraries serving 100,000 or more and 20 libraries provided service for 34,000,000 people.[9]

Public libraries can also be classed according to the jurisdictional units they service.

--4,982 (59%) serve local communities.
--956 (11%) serve counties.
--1,049 (12%) are non-profit corporations, usually association libraries contracting with one or more local governments.
--372 (4%) serve more than one local jurisdiction.
--758 (9%) serve independent taxing districts.
--339 (4%) serve school district jurisdictions.[10]

LOCAL LIBRARIES

Local libraries exist in a variety of shapes, offer a variety of services and face discrete problems.

Small Public Libraries. As noted above, most public libraries in the United States fall under this rubric. The demands made on them depend on the nature of the population they serve. In communities with high educational levels, patrons are likely to request a broad range of sophisticated services. Where the public is less educated, fewer demands for service may be articulated, but librarians know that there are as many needs waiting to be met.

The staff of a small library is certain to be limited in size -- typically less than five full-time equivalents -- and responsible for a broader range of services than their larger library counterpart. Specialization rarely exists. Professionals serve all age groups, an endeavor affording them well-rounded views of patrons needs, but limiting the opportunities to cultivate specialized skills. Children's librarians, for instance, are apt to spend considerable time doing adult and young adult reference. Conversely, adult or reference personnel are likely to have substantial contact with younger patrons. Library directors deal with everyone, charge-out books, and shovel snow off walks.

The geographic isolation of many small libraries promotes the importance of networking so that their patrons may have access to larger materials collections and greater staff specialization. It is ironic that though smallness fosters this need, smallness itself sometimes breeds an attitude of fierce independence that checks local efforts to cooperate with others.

Medium Size Urban Libraries. Medium size urban libraries serve populations ranging between 25,000 and 100,000 people. They number about 1,350 and represent 15% of the libraries in the U. S.[11] Their per capita expenditures vary from a median of $21.06 for libraries serving from 25,000 to 49,999, to $23.75 for libraries serving from 50,000 to 99,999.[12] Staffing for this population ranges from a median of 20.5 for libraries serving from 25,000 to 49,999 to 43 for libraries serving 50,000 to 99,999.[13] Typically, urban libraries of this size create branch operations when populations of their service areas exceed 50,000 and/or the geographical configuration of the community requires multiple units.

Many medium size American urban centers, particularly those in the North East, Middle Atlantic and Far West States have experienced declining economic bases, deteriorating school systems, and degenerating infrastructures. There have also been profound changes in the character of their populations. Urban libraries in this group, mirroring their parent communities, have encountered mounting funding problems, declining patron use and decaying building facilities, as well as a commensurate shift from populations that made intensive use of their facilities to populations that do not. Such changes require wholesale redefinitions of the focus of the public library.

The decline in the tax base has produced serious deficits in materials collections, caused staff layoffs and left buildings in desperate need of repair. In yet another ironic turn, medium size urban libraries, long considered the bastions of regional and statewide networks, have found it increasingly difficult to contribute to their upkeep while drawing upon them more frequently for basic support.

Non-Urban Medium Size Libraries. In contrast with medium size urban libraries that have fallen on hard times, non-urban rural and suburban medium size libraries tend to be newer and to be experiencing substantial success, demonstrating once more how closely the fortunes of a public library are tied to that of its parent community.

Suburban, and to some extent rural libraries came into their own during the second half of the 20th century, as did their communities, both benefitting from America's economic boom. The result was experimentation with consolidation and strengthened city-county and county libraries.

The question of who is to pay for services to support these libraries has plagued librarians as the rapid blossoming of suburban and rural life has effaced community boundaries. Increasingly, mobile residents live, work and conduct their business with only limited consciousness of crossing municipal lines. Often they are uncertain in which community they actually reside. Private enterprise can respond swiftly to new consumer patterns. All consumers pay for a product at the time of purchase; where they live is irrelevant. Public institutions have more difficulty with geography.

User-fees to cover the cost of non-resident use have generally been imposed by public libraries. But fees are rarely set at a level that adequately compensates a community. If the use by non-residents is heavy, the problem is compounded. In addition, many non-residents avail themselves of reference and information services for which no card, and therefore no fee, is required. Local libraries that make serious attempts to analyze and recover actual costs directly from non-resident users, or from the communities in which they live, are likely to incur substantial resentment, particularly since these groups rarely have a voice in the way the library operates and sometimes number as high as 40% of the service area. Planning future service for a library that has no firm base of support is a problem. Securing capital financing for building expansion or other allied purposes is almost impossible. In the long run, non-resident fees hold no answer. A more formal mechanism involving the communities in which non-residents live is required.

Large Urban Libraries. About 2% of all public libraries -- 236 -

- serve populations of 100,000 or above. The median staff size for them ranges from 63 to 476, depending on population size. Among the 20 libraries serving more than 1,000,000 people, staff sizes range from a low of 88 to a high of 1213. Though a substantial number of people work in these libraries when compared with their rural and suburban cousins, by private enterprise standards they are small indeed. Included in this grouping are the "crown jewels" of the American public library movement, the large metropolitan libraries of America's great cities with their tentacled branch systems, significant subject collections and staffs with sufficient training to serve the most specialized and sophisticated of needs. In these libraries were the first services geared to different age groups -- to children, young adults, and adults -- and the first for specialized audiences -- labor and business, for instance.

Large urban libraries remain the core of the public library movement in the United States despite the significant changes in American cities -- the flight of white, middle class populations to the suburbs and rural areas and the severe erosion of the tax base. Urban libraries have been hard pressed to maintain their high standards. The economic strains of the past four decades have sapped their strength. State agencies and others have attempted to pick up the slack by advocating an infusion of state and federal funding for those parts of urban library service that support regional, statewide and even national needs. Despite occasional successes, they are confronting increasing resistance from librarians in suburban and rural areas who prefer to see available aid expended in ways more amenable to their interests.

The changed public -- more minorities, poorer residents, more illiterates, increasing breakdown of public order and erosion of the local tax base -- of the urban library challenges the institution to find new ways of linking public services to the needs of this more difficult to serve constituency.

Large Suburban Library Systems. As the economic life of the large urban centers declined, some of the strength and vitality of the city migrated to its outskirts. In suburban settings service has been consolidated, often along county lines and large, unified libraries have emerged, most frequently in areas where patterns of consolidated local governmental services already existed. Maryland, for example, with a tradition of governmental service based on the county as a unit, has witnessed the growth of some of the strongest libraries in the country.

Today, large suburban library systems enjoy high usage, substantial levels of public support, many branches covering wide geographical areas, buildings located in shopping areas and proximate to major roadways and strong general, nonspecialized collections designed to meet popular rather than scholarly needs. The libraries of large suburban areas are among the best in the county. They are centers for experimentation and innovation, and they provide leadership to the profession both regionally and nationally.

Non-Headquarters Library Systems. In recent years, a new form of library, one without a strong central facility, has appeared on the horizon. This distributed model responds to a number of current developments. One is the diminished residential populations in "downtown" urban areas. Another is adherence to the "give em what they want" philosophy which implies supplying the most popular literature to the greatest numbers of people where they are and relying on interlibrary loan to meet the requests of those whose needs remained unsatisfied by their local neighborhood collections. Finally, technology in the form of online-public access catalogs, on-line remote data base searching, electronic means of transmission and rapid intra-system delivery mean that materials and information from far-flung locations can be made available without undue delay.

Libraries adopting this arrangement may choose to have a separate administrative complex for the system's non-public services, or to house administrators in a larger branch. Metaphorically, this system no longer has a central trunk with branches, but now can be pictured as nodes (branches) in a network.

Regional Service Centers. Regional service centers do not usually offer direct patron library service. Nonetheless they have a dramatic effect on the quality of service available to users of local libraries. Initially, regional libraries attempted to provide patrons of smaller libraries with access to materials previously available only to users of larger ones. Now, typically, regional service centers assist with technical processing, with public relations, in facilitating "open borrowing" arrangements between local libraries, in supplying specialized service consultants, in enhancing inter-library loan and reference services, and in generating improved specialized materials collections.

The spark that ignited the regional service center movement was an infusion of state and federal aid funds for the purpose of experimenting with ways to augment local library service without threatening local sovereignty. The insistence by local libraries on autonomy generated this model as an alternative to consolidation among contiguous districts. The desire to maintain local autonomy is often cast in villainous terms, as a regressive impulse impeding progress. Indeed, its wellsprings may be an instinct to protect turf, no matter how small, from encroachments by larger jurisdictions. But the desire to make grass roots decisions about desirable levels of local service based on local values, rather than composite values of a larger area, may result in more responsible institutions.

Another cross-jurisdictional institution -- the *multitype library service center* -- spanning both geographic boundaries and library types has been gaining favor. Designed to include academic, school, public and special libraries, it exists in a variety of forms throughout the United States. In New Jersey, six regional multi-type library centers with membership open to all libraries have been established by the state. Through multitype libraries, cooperation is stimulated by the increased availability of material and expertise. In the process, however, new and perhaps unnecessary levels of bureaucracy have been created, a fact that many librarians find troubling.

SIZE LIMITATIONS OF LOCAL LIBRARIES

The majority of public libraries are small, relatively isolated and limited in service. How to overcome these obstacles, extend improved services to local constituencies and maximize the nation's resources poses one of the great challenges. Technology offers some answers; organization still others. Consolidating, federating or entering cooperative systems are among the options available to small libraries.

Consolidation. The simplest method of establishing larger units of service has also proven to be the most difficult to implement. Consolidated library systems achieve cohesion by placing all facets of service under a single jurisdiction, with a single administration and one policy-making body. A large-scale operation produces economies of scale, allows the introduction of sophisticated services such as automation, staff specialization, broad and deep collection resources, good delivery systems, and other improvements difficult to achieve in smaller units.

Some consolidation has occurred -- notably the merger of units within a county, creating city-county libraries -- and some libraries have increased their scopes of operation through municipal annexation of unincorporated areas surrounding existing incorporated municipalities. In localities where traditions of local government remain strong, consolidation of library districts has proven impossible. New Jersey, for example, has had a Regional Library Law authorizing the creation of a consolidated library system serving two or more counties for many years. It has never been used. New York legislation providing for consolidated districts was abandoned in favor of cooperative library systems when it became clear that consolidation attracted few takers. Consolidation appears to be a factor of the general structure of a state's local government. Maryland has strong countywide libraries. The other Middle Atlantic and the New England States, with strong traditions of independent local municipal government, have tended toward experimentation in cooperation, rather than consolidation. Different patterns have emerged in other parts of the country. County libraries are most common in the South and Far West, particularly in California which pioneered the development of these types of libraries.

Federations. Library federations are organizations composed of two or more separate library jurisdictions for the purposed of conducting combined operations in one or more areas to meet specific objectives. In federated systems, individual identity of member libraries is preserved. Essentially cooperative endeavors, they are called federations because they are so identified by state enabling legislation and bearing that mantle may entitle them to increased state aid.

Cooperative Library Systems. In recent years, the most popular approach to dealing with networking has been through the creation of cooperative library systems, groups of public libraries within given geographical areas joined together in common effort to achieve stated purposes. State library agencies, using state aid and federal funding, have supported these efforts. Without these new moneys, and despite their innate benefits, cooperative systems would not have succeeded. Cooperation, or networking, links together the resources of many libraries, creating effective service and optimizing use of available resources. Among their attractions is that they are cooperative rather than coercive and are predicated on voluntary surrender of limited amounts of local sovereignty rather than on total relinquishment as demanded by consolidation. Retention of local identity helps to explain the rapid spread of networking in recent years. The degree of cooperation and the available funding varies from state to state, as does the level of participation required of local libraries. A variant of the public library cooperative system is the multi-type library system described above.

One political drawback of cooperative systems is the inherent necessity to create a separate administration to manage system activities, a unit that duplicates ones in local libraries and introduces an unnecessary level of bureaucracy. Cooperative system supporters argue that the duplication is more apparent than real. System directors, they contend, concentrate on activities of the cooperative, activities beyond the responsibilities of local library directors.

SERVING EMERGENT POPULATIONS

America is greying, becoming multi-hued, multi-lingual, poorer, homeless or institutionalized, less able to read and navigate the institutions of society; in other words, what used to be considered non-traditional clientele are the emerging majority and will require services unneeded by the traditional white, middle-class, middle-aged female library usership. The extent to which this group can be assisted will depend first on the willingness of librarians to consider service to them a current priority, and, second, the willingness of the society to fund the library at a level adequate to give these groups the type of help they need. There is growing conflict among those who see the library's role as collector and purveyor of the cumulative records of civilization -- the guarantor that all people may enter the world of learning, literature, and the arts that was formerly the private preserve of the aristocracy, clergy and privileged middle class[14]; those who consider the library's role to be responding to popular demand and collecting and distributing only what is requested; and those who see a more activist role, one of reaching out to those unwilling or unable to utilize those information services that would make their lives safer, easier and more comfortable.

ORGANIZATION AND PLANNING

The public library today plans its future far differently than it did a decade or two ago, perhaps as a response to the pressures to be accountable to funding bodies, as well as escalating ones to be productive. As the importance of goal, role and objective setting, and of evaluation have been realized, the profession has produced workshops and manuals to assist practitioners in devising them. Beginning with Ernest DeProspo's construction of "Performance Measures" in 1973 through the ALA's *Planning Process, Output Measures* and most recently *Planning and Role Setting* in the 1980's, attention to the importance of knowing what we are all about has never been greater. The public library world has also been alert to adapting organizational trends extent in the wider community to its uses, particularly the new attention to employee participation that has engaged a growing segment of American industry.

Technology has implications for organizational change within public libraries. Personnel are added and decreased. Changes in the ratio of professional to support staff have already been noted. As day-to-day operations become more routine, as tasks of sorting, filing, counting are taken over by computers the need for support staff grows, but support staff with greater skills, experience and training. Automation deprofessionalizes some formerly professional tasks. On the other hand, technology may have the opposite impact on public service departments. Online reference service, for instance, may necessitate additional professional staff. There may also be changes in the decision-making structure of the library. Systems theory and the interrelatedness of automated modules elevates the level at which decisions must be reached. As a result, the planning process is yet more important, with each decision requiring thorough preparation and deliberation.

TECHNOLOGICAL CHANGE

Not all libraries will experience full-scale technological transformations during the next few years. All, however, will become objects of greatly increased expectations and all are faced by a dizzying and continually expanding array of new technologies applicable to library operations. The new technology offers not only ever widening access to information, but avenues to eliminating routine, repetitive functions that every library must perform.

Technology has been responsible for facilitating cooperation among libraries where little or none existed. A typical pre-technological attempt to secure economies of scale through the creation of larger service units can be seen in early and recent advancements in technical processing. Joint cataloging, it was felt, could produce a standard product and result in significant savings for all who participated. In practice, many local libraries resisted, preferring the "standardized" version they already used. Regional cooperatives organized in the 1950s to provide this and other services were forced either to customize their technical processing operations by largely manual means or compel local libraries to accept their standardized product, an alienating action. Similar problems arose when centers attempted to standardize their acquisitions procedures. Resistance at the local level was intense.

Passage of time and the acceptance of computer technology has diminished these difficulties. Local libraries are able to introduce some level of customization to what is essentially a standard product. Expanded power of computers has made coordination even more feasible. The Online Computer Library Center (OCLC), a nationwide non-profit service utility, offers cataloging, both online and in hard copy, with customized options to libraries throughout the country. Further, OCLC operates a nationwide interlibrary loan network.

Technology renders local libraries, particularly those in rural areas, less isolated, permits transcending of regional jurisdictional lines and allows broadened citizen access to information.

For all its benefits, technology must be harnessed to suit libraries' needs lest it become the end rather than the means. Herb White asserts that "Technology becomes our servant rather than our master when we remember to tell it what we want, rather than have it tell us what we can provide."[15]

Among the technological innovations expected in the near future are more software with enhanced user-friendly access features; increased use of on-line communication; formation and implementation of expert systems for access to information; increased demand and expectation for faster access to computer-generated information; emerging technologies for handicapped populations, including voice enhancement devices and speaker-independent speech recognition systems; forged links between related bodies of information in formats such as hypertext and hypermedia permitting readers to jump to books and articles mentioned in citation footnotes, seek further information in related topics presented to match users' levels of knowledge and learning styles; storage technologies, optical warehouses for instance, to meet space needs; integrated information work stations that provide problem solving formulation support as well full texts; and laser technology, robotics, interactive-TV and home document delivery from combined computer-television.

All of these developments may result in "infoglut" and "meaning lag" becoming widespread. Difficult problems in copyright will emerge over the confusion about intellectual ownership. And, importantly, the size of the knowledge gap between classes, between the "haves" and "have-nots" will be stretched, perhaps beyond the limits of retraction.

FINANCIAL SUPPORT

Worries about public library finances are not new; reading public library history of any period reveals similar anxieties. However, events of the past two decades suggest that library fortunes may be curtailed for some time to come.

For about 25 years following World War II, the United States enjoyed unparalleled prosperity. In the last two decades, however, spendthrift government, the arms race, and unrealistically low taxes have combined to drive the U.S. economy to the verge of bankruptcy. Virtually every component of the social infrastructure has suffered, as the means or the willingness to fund agencies or institutions has diminished.[16]

Practitioners involved with day-to-day operations of public

libraries have voiced similar concerns. A recent survey revealed that 42% of library personnel managers had to reduce staffing levels -- by freezing hiring, through terminating some positions, or by furloughing or reducing the hours of some employees.[17] And they anticipate further cutbacks during the next few years. Hours of operation, materials budgets, special services and programs have suffered similar fates.

In California, for instance, public libraries are closing in record numbers. Fifty of its 700 library buildings closed in 1992. In Los Angeles County, alone, ten library buildings closed in November, 1992.[18] Many other states, especially Massachusetts and Illinois, have found it necessary to tighten their belts.

Difficulties created by budget decreases are compounded by the increased activity that economic downturns generate. Libraries across the country report heavier use than ever before. In 1989, the average increase in circulation was 4.3%, in 1990, 7.8%[19] and in 1991, 4.7%.[20]

Even with an upturn in public revenues, continued curtailment of public services seems likely. There will be little margin for error. Careful spending must be based on thorough community understanding, good planning and thoughtful establishment of priorities. Expert marketing and public relations will maximize those services that remain available.

Some publicly-funded organizations, libraries among them, may turn to the private sector for greater proportions of their income. These may be in the form of donations on the one hand or fees for service, on the other.

If the average public library is experiencing considerable difficulty, many urban libraries exist in near depression environments. Public services are funded primarily by local taxes that are based on the value of local property. Many urban communities suffer from low property values and low levels of tax collection. Yet the needs for public services are heightened by disadvantaged populations who require large amounts of sophisticated assistance. Other levels of government are unwilling to supply the resources that these local communities lack. Hard times in America means even harder times in the cities. In one hopeful sign, David Dinkins, Mayor of New York City, proposed, as the major plank in his 1993 budget to open the city's 205 branch libraries six days a week for the first time since 1948 in an effort to strengthen neighborhood communities. It passed with little opposition.

Other financial problems are likely to plague libraries. Computing power will command increasing percentages of budgets. The cost of information resources will be substantially higher than the anticipated low-to-moderate rate of inflation. In this environment, priority-setting and role-definition assume heightened importance.

A related, difficult question is whether and to what extent the library can afford to supply information and materials free to its patrons. Many libraries have begun charging fees for on-line data base searching, for video rentals and for other services. Will this result, eventually, in providing information to those who can afford to pay and effectively deny service to those without funds, rendering the "free" public library an anachronism? Both sides of the "free or fee" debate are presented in Chapter 11.

ADDITIONAL LIBRARY CONCERNS

The shortage of able librarians, particularly in public libraries will continue unabated unless there are immediate efforts to recruit talented people to the field. Becoming a librarian is not easy. The multitude of new technologies requires that students be trained in subject disciplines, computers and in interactive people skills. The numbers of public librarians subject to burnout will enlarge by virtue of the stress placed on them as public clamors for reference assistance to manipulate the new electronic information formats and as machinery fails and requires attention. Librarians will be challenged to enlarge their roles from providers of information to information consultants; to help users make sense of the information; to help them determine which of the answers is the best solution to their needs.

Space will become a critical issue and decisions will have to be made about the appropriate use of library buildings. New information transmissions may change the infrastructures of libraries.

THE LIMITATIONS OF CHANGE

Despite the heady excitement induced by new technology and the rush to automate, in some important respects only limited change has occurred in public libraries. It is true that experimentation with networking and the introduction of various forms of library cooperation has been widespread in post World War II America. Yet the small public library remains the predominant public library institution. The one-library building still comprises a majority of all library districts, enduring as the interpreter of local library needs and dispenser of local library service.

A second feature of public library service that has persisted is its use by the public as a source of reading material for personal enrichment. Professional library rhetoric in recent years has concentrated on public libraries as information providers, purveyors of fact to eager patrons who need to be kept up to date on the fast changing world of knowledge. Since the advent of "Sputnik" the Soviet space satellite on October 4, 1957, librarians have also stressed the tie to educational institutions. Yet surveys of public library continue to reveal that the heaviest use of public libraries is made by those who borrow materials to read at home. In the rush to make common cause with other institutions, librarians sometimes forget that libraries assist patrons to refine their sensibilities, help them reflect on human and societal values, enhance their cultural and leisure pursuits and, in general, improve the quality of their lives.

A final unchanging fact of library life is that, however much the techniques and tools of the profession may change, service is a product of the skill and ingenuity of individual librarians. Technology and organizational change may assist or hinder the way that librarians fulfill their assignments, but nonetheless it is they who must design and bear responsibility for providing the service that the public requires.

THE WHITE HOUSE CONFERENCE ON LIBRARY AND INFORMATION SERVICES, 1991

From July 9-13, 1991, 700 delegates from the 50 states and six U.S. territories, the District of Columbia, and the Native American Community met in Washington, D.C. at the second national White House Conference on Library and Information Services to consider the future role of library and information services in a rapidly changing society. It represented the culmination of many years of grass roots activity and interest, but stemmed directly from a Joint Congressional Resolution (PL 100 382) calling on the president to authorize and request a second White House Conference.[21] The first had been held in 1979.

The single most important aspect of the White House Conference -- symbolically, at least -- was that it was held, that recognition of their importance was accorded the nation's libraries. Its second benefit was that it served as a forum in which to identify major questions in the field. Third, it provided a mechanism to establish priorities for action.

Following five days of deliberations, delegates reported out 95 wide-ranging policy proposals, conferring priority status on eleven of them. Several of the priority items addressed the problems of literacy, others the need for widening information access and opportunities. Following is a summary of major recommendations.

Literacy. Two of the priorities directly involved literacy. One called for an omnibus children and youth literacy initiative and another urged literacy initiatives including the implementation of a national training model for library literacy programs.

A third recommendation asked that libraries be designated educational institutions for lifelong learning and be included in all legislation, regulations, and policies designed to support and improve American education. Recognizing this role furthers the concept of libraries as "people's universities," and underscores the importance of insuring access to other literacies besides reading -- cultural, numeric, and computer, to name a few. (The public library's role in furthering literacy is discussed in Chapter 14.)

Access to Information. Six of the eleven priorities were related, in one form or another, to insuring access of all people to all information.

Among the most favored recommendations was one calling for creation and funding of the National Research and Education Network (NREN) that would grant speedy acquisition of the products of educational research. Following the conference, Congress passed the High Performance Computer Act creating the National Research and Educational Network, often referred to as the Electronic Superhighway. A primitive form of this channel was created by the Department of Defense in the 1960s to link universities, research laboratories, and military bases. Operating today over existing telephone lines, "Internet," as it is called, links information centers in 102 countries. The High Performance Computing Act authorized the expenditure of 2.9 billion dollars, to enhance the capacity of Internet to transmit information. Currently researchers at five centers are creating the technologies required for an "electronic superhighway." Yet unclear is the access that the non-research public will have to the network. Also unknown is who will own the network. Will it be the public, or will it be privatized and operated commercially? Advocates of this path contend that the quickest way to produce a data superhighway is to permit the deployment by phone companies of a digital system called Integrated Services Digital Network (I.S.D.N.).[22] The answer to this question could well determine whether the costs incurred in gaining access to this network will be so prohibitive that public libraries will be unable to afford their patrons "free" access.

A second access proposal advocated the formation of networks containing rural, small, urban and tribal libraries. The inclusion of this proposal gives continuing recognition of the isolation of these libraries and the distance yet to be traveled to ameliorate the problem.

Several of the proposals referred to specific access problems. The importance of halting the deterioration of the nation's library resources was recognized in the recommendation that a national information preservation policy be adopted. The problem of copyright was addressed in a request to Congress for amendments to copyright legislation respective to new and emerging technologies. The Conference also advocated expanding the Freedom of Information Act to insure access to all nonexempt information whether received by the federal government or created at public expense regardless of physical form or characteristics. Finally delegates supported the creation of library programs and materials for multicultural, multilingual populations. (Preservation problems, copyright and access to government information are discussed in Collection Development and Management, Chapter 8 and problems of multicultural, multilingual populations in Outreach, Chapter 14.)

Funding. Not unexpectedly, the Conference recommended that sufficient funding for libraries to provide the information resources needed for increased U.S. productivity and competitiveness be made available.

Marketing. A priority calling for the creation of a model library marketing system reflects the concern felt by many librarians that they are better are creating library services than they are at marketing them to the public. (Marketing is covered in Chapter 15, Marketing, Publicizing and Interpreting the Library.)

STAYING CURRENT AND PROFESSIONAL

Professions, as distinct from occupations or trades, are characterized by formal training in a field whose core is a cognitive body of knowledge, the generation of skills relating to this knowledge, and an institutional framework controlling the application of these skills.

Every profession demands that individual practitioners maintain and enhance their skills and knowledge. Many states mandate that beginning library professionals possess a minimum level of education -- generally a Master's Degree from an ALA accredited library science program. However, no regulations exist to insure that competence is maintained and enhanced. It redounds to individual staff members and employing libraries to insure that skills are constantly upgraded. Most librarians, like workers in other professions, have little time to spend in diagnosis, planning, innovation, deliberate change and growth. Day-to-day demands mean that most efforts are spent in routine, goal-directed activities. In these circumstances, how can professionals maintain currency in professional matters as well as obtain technical proficiency in their primary areas of responsibility?

Continuing Education

Participating in conferences, visiting other libraries to study procedures and attending courses, workshops and institutes help to maintain continued excellence in library service. While professional development money for tuition and travel is likely to be limited at most institutions, funding at least a few experiences annually should be viewed as part of the cost of operating a library.

Unfortunately, as a rule, public librarians pursue continuing education at their own expense, and often on their own time. School systems are likely to reimburse teachers for efforts to enhance their knowledge and skills and to reward them for their pursuits. Public librarians rarely receive additional compensation for their continuing education endeavors. A more supportive attitude on the part of administrations could well lead to the enhancement of their staffs' service skills.

Opportunities for library professionals to continue their training have been created in a variety of settings:

State Library Agencies. Since their inception, state library agencies have engaged in training librarians. Prior to the emergence of professional library schools and professional certification, their role was seminal. Now, though still active, they concentrate their continuing education efforts on emerging areas of library interest such as planning, networking and automation.

Library Schools. Universities represent the main training grounds for librarians. In recent years, many university library schools have recognized the importance of offering continuing education to their graduates, sometimes in extension centers located in less accessible geographic areas.

Library Associations. A major source of continuing education opportunities can be found in workshops sponsored by national, state and local library associations. The American Library Association (ALA) and its public library division, the Public Library Association (PLA), other ALA divisions, and regional organizations sponsor a wide range of programs at their annual meetings and at other times.

Libraries and Private Contractors. These may take the form of courses and workshops conducted by outside consultants on library premises, attendance at commercially-run institutes, or in-house staff-led discussion and training sessions.

Professional Reading

Among the best ways of tracking changes in librarianship is by constantly reviewing the literature, particularly periodicals. Together with continuing education and on-the-job training, professional periodical reading affords the most expeditious method of updating skills and knowledge. Frequently consulted sources of professional reading for public librarians are:

American Libraries. Official publication of the American Library Assocation includes news and features of interest to the profession.

Bowker Annual. Reviews significant happenings in the library world during the previous year. Particularly valuable for statistics.

Library Journal. Covers most completely the general news of the profession as well as including a wide range of provocative features.

Library Technology Reports. Provides information about and evaluations of new technology for libraries.

Public Libraries. Presents news and features specifically for public librarians.

Public Library Quarterly. Contains articles of particular concern to administrators and managers of public libraries.

Wilson Library Bulletin. Includes articles of interest to all librarians.

Librarians, especially those in larger libraries, involved in a particular phase or specialization of public librarianship normally ally themselves with others who perform similar functions, joining such divisions of ALA as Reference and Adult Services, Library Administration and Management Association, Library and Information Technology Association and the Association for Library Collections and Technical Services, all of which have their own publications.

Professional Association Activities

The larger purposes of public libraries as institutions in American culture and the responsibilities of library professionals are the substance of professional organization consideration. Professional associations furnish bonds through which the community coalesces and mediate relationships between practitioners and the outside world. In practical terms, professional associations try to safeguard the welfare of their members, improve working conditions, press for advancement opportunities and work toward legally enforced standards of professional competence.[23] For public librarians the national American Library Association (ALA) and its two divisions, the Public Library Association and the American Library Trustee Association, as well as the various state, regional and local library associations that operate throughout the United States fulfill that role. Librarians, like other professionals, need to confer, to compare notes, consult, share experiences and explore common purposes and mutual interests. Professionals who do not participate in such activities forego a rich and broadening aspect of their occupational lives and they deprive their librarian colleagues of the benefit of their insights and counsel. Library Directors who do not encourage their staffs to be professionally active deny their own libraries the advantages of the learning that occurs when professionals share experiences.

Most public libraries cannot afford to defray completely the costs of employee participation in professional meetings. Even-handed treatment of staff is best assured by guidelines that describe how existing funds are to be apportioned. Among the criteria for making decisions about allocating travel monies are whether staff are members of the organization whose conference they wish to attend, whether they hold an office, have committee responsibilities, are presenting a paper or participating in a panel. While libraries, by necessity, may offer scant financial support to those travelling to meetings, they can recognize the value of participation by permitting attendance on library time.

ETHICS

A code of ethics defining the relationship 1) between the individual or group and the society, and 2) with each other is an integral part of a profession's social ethos. In 1981, the American Library Association issued its "Code of Ethics for Professional Librarians," a revision of an earlier version adopted in 1939.

Following is the text of the 1981 statement:

I. Librarians must provide the highest level of service through appropriate and usefully organized collections, fair and equitable circulation and service policies, and skillful, accurate, unbiased and courteous responses to all requests for assistance.

II. Librarians must resist all efforts by groups or individuals to censor library materials.

III. Librarians must protect each user's right to privacy with respect to information sought or received, and materials consulted, borrowed or acquired.

IV. Librarians must adhere to the principles of due process and equality of opportunity in peer relationships and personnel actions.

V. Librarians must distinguish clearly in their actions and statements between their personal philosophies and attitudes and those of an institution or professional body.

VI. Librarians must avoid situations in which personal interests might be served or financial benefits gained at the expense of library users, colleagues, or the employing institution.[24]

The statement makes explicit that librarians have a responsibility to be honest stewards of the resources entrusted to their care, to be fair in their dealings with all individuals, to speak out in support of the rights of patrons to gain access to information and to insure the confidentiality of library circulation records. Care must be taken not to adopt an "ends justifies the means" stance when setting policies and determining goals. The need to retrench, for instance, requires honest and realistic appraisal of priorities rather than retreat to traditional library practices. Attaching undue importance to numbers of library holdings leads to dubious methods of counting, to abandonment of materials selections principles, or to inadequate weeding. Over infatuation with library statistics of all kinds brings with it the danger of emphasizing quantity rather than quality of performance. Ethical conduct in personnel affairs is discussed in Chapter 17, Human Resources. Responses to the ethics statements have been varied, reflecting both the complexity of the ethical issues involved as well as fundamental disagreement on ethical principles.[25]

Promulgating an ethics statement is one action; interpreting and enforcing it yet another. The public's trust can only be claimed if a means of ensuring compliance with a code of ethics exists.

SUMMARY

Today's public library is a multi-faceted institution offering services to a wide variety of users. It takes many shapes and sizes, almost all reflecting the current status and historical traditions of their parent municipalities. In the past few decades change has come to public libraries in the form of new technologies, recent advances in the field of organizational management, new constituencies and new fiscal realities. The pressures to cooperate generated by scarce resources and relative isolation have resulted in networks of libraries banding together to achieve specific library objectives creatively.

Worrisome problems beset the public library field, but the possibilities for continued and expanded participation in the nation's future are exhilarating. Innovation and change are the lifeblood of any institution or profession. Without them, stasis -- a slower form of death -- prevails.

NOTES AND SUGGESTED READINGS

Notes

1. *American Library Directory 1993-94.* (New Providence, NJ: RR Bowker, 1993), vii, x.

2. National Center for Educational Statistics. *Public Libraries in the U.S.: 1990.* (Washington, DC: Government Printing Office, 1992), 11.

3. Ibid., iii, 28.

4. Ibid., 11-13.

5. Ibid., iii.

6. Ibid.

7. Ibid., iv.

8. Ibid., 27, 37, 88.

9. Ibid., 88.

10. Public Library Association. *Statistical Report, 1992.* (Chicago: American Library Association, 1992).

11. Ibid., 5.

12. Ibid., 45.

13. Ibid., 70.

14. Leonard Freiser, *Library Journal* 113 (May 1, 1988): 51.

15. Herbert White.

16. Christinger Tomer, in *Bowker Annual*, 37th ed., (New York: Bowker, 1992), 79.

17. Ibid., 3.

18. *Meadville (PA) Tribune* (January 18, 1993): 2.

19. Ibid.

20. Preliminary 1991 figures issued by the National Center for Education Statistics, U.S. Department of Education.

21. White House Conference on Library and Information Services, *Information 2000.* Washington, DC: U.S. Govt. Printing Office 1991.

22. *New York Times,* Sec 3, 6. (Jan. 24, 1993).

23. Anthony Abbott, *System of Professions.* (Chicago: University of Chicago Press, 1988), 35.

24. American Library Association. *ALA Handbook of Organizations 1992-93.* (Chicago: American Library Association, 1992), 148.

25. See, for instance, a provocative series of articles by Lillian Gerhardt entitled "Ethical Book Talk," in *School Library Journal* 36(2)4; 36(6)4; 36(8)4; 36(6)4; 36(8)4; 36(10)3; 36(12)4. (1990).

Suggested Readings

Cargill, Jennifer and Gisela Webb. *Managing Libraries in Transition.* Phoenix, AZ: Oryx Press, 1987.

Crismond, Linda. "The Future of Public Library Services." *Library Journal* 111 (Nov. 1986): 42-9.

Fox, Beth Wheeler. *The Dynamic Community Library.* Chicago: American Library Association. 1988.

Gaines, Ervin J. "Public Responsibility for a Public Library." *Public Library Quarterly* 6 (Spring 1985): 51-61.

Hennen, Thomas J., Jr. "Attacking the Myths of Small Libraries." *American Libraries* 17 (Dec. 1986): 830-4.

Lange, Janet M. "Public Library Users, Nonusers, and Type of Library Use." *Public Library Quarterly* 8 (1987/88): 49-67.

Martin, Susan K. *Library Networks 1986-1987: Libraries in Partnership.* White Plains, New York: Knowledge Industry Publications, 1986.

Owen, A. "Current Issues and Patterns in State Standards for Public Library Service." *Public Libraries* 31 (July/August 1992): 213-20.

Riggs, Donald and Gordon Sabine, eds. *Libraries in the 90s: What the Leaders Expect.* Phoenix, AZ: Oryx Press, 1989.

Shavit, David. *The Politics of Public Librarianship.* Westport, CT: Greenwood, 1986.

Weingand, Darlene. *Administration of the Small Public Library.* Chicago: American Library Association, 1992.

CHAPTER 4

THE COMMUNITY CONTEXT

All communities are products of the same general components. The generic community has a history, traditions, multi-faceted populations, political, social, economic, cultural and educational systems, and most have a library. The particular mixture of these elements is what determines the community's character and renders it unique. The factors themselves, examined separately reveal information essential to all those who seek to understand the community's ethos and the library's place within it, including, of course, the library director and staff. The library professional, contemplating employment with a public library who makes a decision based solely on the library, without considering its environment as well, is indeed short-sighted.

A fundamental tenet of the contemporary practice of library planning is that it must be based on intimate and thorough knowledge of the community in which it is embedded. Traditional library planning tended to treat all communities of a given size as identical or at least alike, making wide use of input measures, the numbers of books and staff per capita, for instance. Current planning efforts focus, instead, on the unique qualities of a community that reveal its information needs and act as a basis for the construction of library goals and objectives.

The questions raised here represent a broad range of community life. What the answers may infer is subject to varying interpretation. For example, lack of population mobility may signal inertia or contentment, a stagnant environment or one that provides a satisfying milieu for residents. Other data would be required before any assumption could be ventured about the relationship between mobility and community morale.

The variables described below have direct importance for the library. The materials collection and programming, for example, should reflect the educational backgrounds and interests of community members.

Constructing a community profile is complex and time-consuming, and should not be undertaken lightly. Two difficulties become apparent while developing items for analysis. The first is determining what are the really important questions to ask and the second is deciding when to stop asking questions. An important rule to follow is that data collection should be limited to information that will be used in a profile statement. The basic questions, then, to be asked of a community analysis are: What are the characteristics of a community and its members, and what are their information needs? And, where do I find the data that will supply the answers?

Statistical and non-statistical data are fed into the crucible of community analysis. While documenting assertions is important, intuition is useful and not to be denied. Both impressions and fact play a role. The building blocks of a community profile are its history and topography, its economy, its cultural and social organizations and opportunities, its educational institutions, its communication and transportation networks, its political profile, its religious life, and, finally, its demographic factors, those that describe in statistical terms, the socio-economic characteristics of its population.

Much of the data produced here is measurable and can be compared with numbers produced by like communities. Care must be taken, however, to use comparisons only in the most general way. Intervening variables play an important part in determining the personality of a community. Two municipalities with equal populations and socio-economic levels may have substantial variance in their library use due to geographical considerations.

Like a zoom lens that focuses first broadly, and then narrows its scope, a community survey may begin impressionistically with a walk or ride around the downtown and the neighborhoods noting conditions -- ages of buildings, deterioration, new construction, empty stores, for sale signs, evidence of children, and so on. Conversations with area influentials -- planning office personnel, political figures, educational administrators, members of the Chamber of Commerce and other civic organizations -- will corroborate or correct inferences drawn from the walkabout.

THE COMMUNITY

Systematic data gathering starts with a description of the community's *history*: Perhaps the most important single question to pose is whether or not a municipality is a viable community. The move to suburbanization in twentieth century America described in Chapter 3 has created numerous contiguous areas that cannot lay claim to the traditional definition of community. They have no municipal complex, commercial or other center of gravity. Has the community produced famous people?   What is the community's age? What are its unique traditions? How old is the library? Does the community heritage include establishing and supporting a library?

Geography, Topography, Climate and Transportation. Geographically-isolated communities without diverse sources of information may have the greatest need to turn to the library. The reverse may be true for urban areas where other outlets and resources exist. Questions about the location of the community might include. Is the community classified as urban, rural, or suburban? Are there topographical features such as hills or rivers that may influence library use?   Is there a state or local environmental plan that identifies areas as protected, flood plains, gamelands or wetlands, for instance?   Does the community experience periods of excessive heat or cold that may have an impact on library use?

Compactness of a community, citizens' abilities to traverse it, traffic patterns, public transportation systems all help to determine how accessible the library is to its residents. How isolated is the library? Where is the library located in the community? Is it within walking distance of many residential neighborhoods? Does an expressway bisect the community preventing walkers from reaching it. Must citizens drive to the library? Library research indicates that most users live within five miles of the library; that use declines as the distance increases from the nearest branch or bookmobile stop; and that few regular users live ten or more miles from library facilities.[1]

Economic Life. The growth and development of a community is predicated on a sound economy. The degree to which it will be *able* to support the library despite its intentions and traditions depends on it. A shrinking tax base, for instance, severely limits the ability to impose new or larger local taxes. What is the community's budget? Has it grown or shrunk in recent years? Identifying economic trends, becoming familiar with economic forecasts and looking at employment and dominant occupational patterns helps librarians to understand a community's present and anticipated fortunes. Other questions might relate to factory openings and closings; seasonal factors, tourism and migrant labor, for instance; to location of commercial centers, for example malls and downtown businesses or to the extent of agricultural endeavors.

Educational Institutions. The availability to citizens of educational opportunities may be consequential to library use. Whether there are professional schools, universities, colleges (four year or community) or trade schools located in close proximity to the community, their nature and quality, whether they are residential or commuter, the extent to which they have been able to develop their own information resources, may predict the demand for public library services.

Similarly, the quality of public and parochial secondary and grade schools and their media centers, their proximity to the public library and their dependence on it, has important ramifications for collection development and allocation of library resources, as do opportunities for informal education and for remediation.

Cultural, Civic, Recreational and Social Opportunities and Organizations. How a community organizes itself into voluntary civic, social and cultural organizations describes its social structure and its networks of interactions. This includes service clubs, special interest and hobby groups, arts councils, educational and cultural support groups, and literary and current affairs groups as well as those of a purely social nature, private or country clubs, for instance. The availability of recreational outlets such as swimming pools or skating rinks and cultural outlets, symphonies, museums and movie theaters, may show how a community entertains itself. Library programming is often predicated on the extent to which cultural opportunities are available within the community; the subject matter of programming dependent on the interests of residents as indicated by the nature of the groups. In addition, service-oriented groups can be prevailed upon to help the library. Lions groups, for instance, have adopted, as a service goal, the improvement of sight and may see large print materials as furthering their mission. Creating a file of these groups not only assists in learning the community, but provides a resource for the Library's Information and Referral services (See Chapter 11). The following page lists typical organizations and groups found within a community.

Governance and Politics. How a government is structured -- Mayor/Council, City Manager, for example -- how long its members have served and the size of the bureaucracy may reveal the extent to which the political structure is relatively fixed and unchanging. Whether the library is independent or a municipal dependent, and its physical and psychological proximity to local seats of government may prophesy the library's relationships to the municipal authority as a supplier of services and a recipient of resources. Knowledge of how frequently citizens vote, the relative strength of political parties, the locus of decision-making powers within the community may determine, for instance, the success or

Figure 4
Groups Found in Communities

1. Business/Professional
   service clubs
   Chamber of Commerce
   Vocational Groups
   Cooperatives
   Industrial Development Orgs.

2. Political
   good government
   taxpayers associations
   political party organizations
   veterans associations
   neighborhood planning assocs.
   community councils symphony

3. Environmental/Conservation
   nature societies
   Big Brother

4. Education
   better school groups
   Parent-teacher organizations
   adult education groups

5. Fraternal
   lodges, fraternities/sororities
   ethnic group fraternal assocs.

6. Recreation
   athletic clubs and teams
   hobby clubs
   outdoor clubs
   golden age clubs
   Y's
   skating rinks
   swimming facilities
   spectator sports
   singles clubs

7. Religious
   churches & synagogues
   bible study/worship groups
   ministerial associations
   Council of Churches

8. Cultural
   choral groups
   study groups
   art societies
   drama groups
   literary societies
   museum groups
   symphony

9. For Children and Youth
   child welfare
   Big Brother
   Police athletic league
   youth organizations

10. Health
    support groups
    handicapped
    Planned Parenthood
    Right-to-Life
    La Leche League
    hospital auxiliaries

11. County-wide organizations
    chests
    councils
    coordinating committees
    intergroup agencies
    federation of clubs

(adapted from Ocean County, NJ, Library)

failure of a library referendum. Local interest in the political process may bear on collections and programming. The political culture of a community often determines its willingness to support schools and libraries.

Studies reveal little difference in level of library between adherents of the two major parties. However, voters are more likely to be library users than are non-voters.

Community Institutions and Services. How a community provides for its health and welfare -- its elderly, sick, indigent, delinquent and abused populations -- indicates not only its needs for these special services, but the willingness of citizens to furnish them. Determining the size of these services and their locations helps rationalize the provision of library services to them. Does the hospital supply reading matter to its patients? If not, can the library assume this responsibility? Similarly, are there libraries in the jail, in the women's shelter, in nursing homes and senior citizens' centers? To what extent can the library participate in the life of its institutionalized citizens?

Communication. What are the formal and informal networks by which people gather information? How many and what types of media cover the local area? What is their relative strength in terms of frequency of publication or airing and how many readers, viewers or listeners do they have? Are there informal gathering places in communities where information is exchanged? Media not only contribute to an understanding of the community, but also provide outlets for dissemination of information about the library.

DEMOGRAPHICS

The demographic profile of a community, its population's characteristics, may be the most crucial determinant of its needs for library service. Recent studies have shed considerable light on how demographic factors affect library use.[2] Of particular interest are those completed by the Eagleton Institute and by Louis Harris and Associates. Following are some of the appropriate demographic questions to be posed in a community study and what their answers may reveal.

Population Size and Density. Is the community growing or shrinking? What are its long-range population trends? The percentage of the population using the public library appears to be increasing rather than decreasing, in spite of the intense competition being waged for attention by other media. Current surveys demonstrate that between 52% and 66% of the population are library users, among whom 42% can be considered heavy, 24% moderate and 33% light?[3]

Indications of population density can be used in conjunction with other factors in decisions about the number and placement of branch libraries.

Age. What is the age group range of the community? How many children, young adults and older people are there and what percentage of the total population does each group represent? Different age groups require different materials collections, formats, services and facilities. For pre-school children, for instance, story hours and other programs represent vital early educational experiences. Large numbers of senior citizens may suggest the need for home delivery of materials.

Research reveals that the use of libraries varies with age. There is evidence, for instance, that older people utilize the public library less than younger ones. Currently over sixty percent of adults 29 years old or younger are reported to use the library compared with 40% or lower for those 50 or over.

Education. What is the educational profile of the community? How many of its citizens have college or graduate degrees? How many are without high school diplomas, without six years of schooling?

Educational achievement has broad implications for library

service. Library use data consistently demonstrate the close
relationship between library use and levels of education. The
Eagleton and Harris studies reveal the following use of libraries by
educational background:

Figure 5
Educational Background of Library Users

Educational Group	Eagleton 1989	Harris* 1990
College	73%	81-90%
High School	48	61
Grade School	16.2	48

*Harris data includes both telephone and in-person library use.
Eagleton does not.

A college educated adult is almost twice as likely to be a library
user as is someone with a high school education. Education has
implications for types, levels, formats and programs the library
needs to provide. The nature and extent of literacy programs, for
example, depends on the community's educational achievement.

Income and Occupation Factors. Are community members of
relatively high or low economic status? At what kinds of jobs do
they work? What proportion is professional, skilled, unskilled?
Household and individual income are, like education, closely tied
to library use. White collar and professional workers are far more
likely to use public libraries than are blue collar workers or
laborers. High concentrations of poverty may indicate the need for
introduction of outreach services.

Inferences may be drawn from the types of positions held by
a community's employed persons about the materials they will
require to improve their skills.

Together with educational data, the level of income and nature
of occupation within a community may determine when to offer
home-computer access to the library and how many ports may be

essential.

Race, religion, ethnicity and recent immigration. What groups are represented in the community? Do they have special material needs?

African-Americans and Latinos are slightly less likely to use public librarians than are Anglos. However, intervening variables such as income and education may cause the discrepancy more than does race or ethnicity. In fact, based on fragmentary data,

> somewhat more than half of all blacks and Spanish speaking respondents in the sample report that at least one member of their household has a public library card...This compares with 49% of all those with annual family incomes of $10,000-14,999, and 32% of all those with annual family incomes of under $10,000.[4]

Recent immigrants, with little or no English, may use libraries as socializing agencies, for English as a Second Language (ESL) training and for materials in native languages.

Based on demographics, a highly educated community of 25,000 people may require as much as twice as many material resources than a more average one. Not only would a better educated community visit their library more frequently, but they would require enhanced reference and information services. On the other hand, the combination of factors that produces low socio-economic status also produces the need for more individualized services that are often expensive and difficult to provide.

THE USES OF THE LIBRARY

The final questions relate to the reasons community members use libraries. Unfortunately, the Eagleton and Harris studies do not utilize the same classification scheme to analyze their data on library use. As a result, the findings are presented separately, below.

Figure 6
Library Uses

Eagleton	*Percent*	*Harris*	*Percent*
Borrow books	51	Took out a book	91
Getting information	44	Used reference mats.	77
Used reference section	30	Read periodicals	49
Children's activities	15	Borrowed AV mats.	30
Relaxation	10	Used computer terminal	25
Borrow AV mats.	8	Attended program	24
Social activities	10	Took a class	12
Read periodicals	5		
To study	5		
View exhibits	3		
Other	7		

While the results vary, there seems little doubt that both studies demonstrate that borrowing books remains the most frequent activity of public library users today. The levels of information seeking manifested in both studies is significant and suggests that even the smallest communities have need for well-trained reference/information specialists.

LIMITATIONS OF COMMUNITY ANALYSIS

Community analysis is a valuable tool to assist public libraries in responding to community needs but there are limitations to its usefulness. Once community data have been produced, there is an assumption that it can serve as a basis for action. In practice, however, "the environment of the library is changing even as the community analysis is being conducted."[5] Community analysis can only be effective if it tracks the community over time, and within a changing context. A static analysis of a community at one point

in time will provide a distorted view.
In addition, we have not yet directly linked community analysis with information needs.

Study of general population information needs has involved all the dedication of microbe hunting. We have asked people to tell about their information needs only to be greeted by a nonplussed reaction from the respondents...Attractive as this concept is, however, we have not isolated needs or been able to design library programs on the basis of what we've found.[6]

Community analysis as a method of needs assessment is useful in aiding librarians to focus on community needs, but it is not yet scientifically precise. Collected data have no intrinsic meaning. Their significance is provided by collectors and interpreters who are often so overwhelmed by the mass of information that they are unable to make sense of it.

SOURCES OF INFORMATION

The most important sources of demographic information are U.S. census reports, both decennial and supplementary. Census data is available for entire communities, for entire states and for the nation. Individual census district reports within the community also exist. Of only limited significance for smaller communities, they are crucial to understanding diverse areas within larger municipalities. Other sources are local census materials, reports of planning and zoning authorities, state and local, surveys of business and industry and labor organizations, state municipal books and school records. Building data on new and projected housing and commercial development can be invaluable in forecasting the amount and kind of growth likely to occur in a community and the location of this growth.

New technology is making available even more sophisticated analytical tools for community analysis. Data now available through the U. S. Bureau of the Census on CDROM can provide information on "block groups," a level of detail that penetrates below the traditional census tract to reveal block-by-block neighborhood statistics. Also available from commercial vendors in varied information packages, such data permit analysts to map library service areas with great precision, enabling branch communities to be identified and described.

There are additional places to seek community information. Local telephone books are particularly useful in providing clues to community institutions and agencies, as are local histories and Chamber of Commerce brochures. Interviews and focus groups are helpful in non-statistical data collection.

STUDYING THE LIBRARY

One could gather all the information involved in a community analysis and still not have a grasp on a particular community. Obviously it is more than the sum of all of these parts.

Similarly, a generic library is a product of its political, economic and social structure. How it is governed, funded, staffed, the services it provides, who it serves and does not serve and what it is used for all contribute to a library's profile. Yet its sum, too, is more than its individual parts.

In studying the library, one would ask many of the same questions as would be posed about the community. What is its history? Is it well supported? well stocked? well used? Who serves on its Board? Who uses it and for what purpose? What does it look like? Is it down at the heels, or in good repair? Is it well located? In close proximity to public transportation? Is parking provided? What are the qualifications of its director and staff?

The remainder of this book focuses on the internal public library, on its structure, its organization, resources, services, users, staff, finances, buildings and describes how to evaluate the institution and its output; in other words to ask the significant questions about the library and utilize the answers to assess the library's "goodness."

SUMMARY

Learning a community is a complex process, one that can engage the energies of an intelligent seeker for a long period of time. Data gathered from this kind of "community-scanning" should be compared with information about similar communities. While all communities have similar components, their individuality lies in how they have traditionally provided for these elements and how they are meshed. Libraries, too, have unique personalities, are products of their history, tradition and context. Studying communities and libraries in this way, leads to a understanding of both expressed and unarticulated needs that can be used to fuel the library's plan of development.

Community and library profiles represent motion pictures of development rather than snapshots. Still photographs reveal the present, movies capture the past, present and future.

NOTES AND SUGGESTED READINGS

Notes

1. Sharon Baker and F. Wilfred Lancaster, *The Measurement and Evaluation of Library Services*, 2nd ed. (Arlington, VA: Information Resources Press, 1991), 29.

2. See, for instance, Alan Westin and Anne Finger. *Using the Public Library in the Computer Age* (Chicago: American Library Association, 1991), based on data from a 1990 national survey by Louis Harris and Associates, *Consumers in the Information Age*, sponsored by Equifax; and Eagleton Institute of Politics, *Library Utilization in New Jersey* (New Brunswick, NJ: Rutgers University, 1989).

3. Eagleton and Harris respectively.

4. Harris, 16-7.

5. Douglas Zweizig, "Community Analysis," in Ellen Altman, ed. *Local Public Library Administration.* 2nd ed. (Chicago: American Library Assocation, 1980), 40.

6. Ibid., 41.

Suggested Readings

Barron, Daniel and Charles Curran. "A Look at Community Analysis." *Public Libraries* 20 (Spring, 1981): 29-30.

Cassell, K.A. *Knowing the Community and Its Needs.* Chicago: American Library Association, 1988.

Coghlin, Robert. *Urban Analysis for Branch Library System Planning.* Westport, CT: Greenwood Press, 1972.

Goldhor, Herbert. "Community Analysis for the Public Library." *Illinois Libraries* 62 (April 1980): 296-302.

Guerena, S. "Community Analysis and Needs Assessment." *Latino Librarianship.* Jefferson, NC: McFarland, 1990.

Hutton, B. and S. Walters. "Focus Groups: Linkages to the Community." *Public Libraries* 27 (Fall, 1988): 149-50+.

Kirkup, M.H., et al. "The Marketing of Public Library Services." *Public Library Journal* 4 (September/October 1989): 93-100.

McClure, Charles. *Planning and Role Setting for Public Libraries.* Chicago: American Library Association, 1987.

Monroe, Margaret. "Community Development as Model of Community Analysis," *Library Trends* 24 (January 1976): 497-514.

Whittle, S. "How to Assess Your Community," in *Fundraising for Nonprofit Insitutions.* Greenwich, CT: JAI Press, 1987.

Zweizig, Douglas. "Community Analysis," in Altman, Ellen ed. *Local Public Library Administration.* 2nd ed. Chicago: ALA, 1980.

CHAPTER 5

LEGAL STATUS, GOVERNANCE AND POLITICS

The *legal status* of a library refers to those characteristics specified by charter and to its statutory placement within the world of other organized groups. *Governance* is the codified arrangement whereby a given state or municipality assigns to its constituents responsibilities and rights. *Politics* is the process by which individuals and constituencies seek to influence decisions about the distribution of resources. The administrative structure within which a system manages its operations is discussed Chapter 6.

LEGAL STATUS

The legal status of a library derives primarily from state law, often in statutes relating to education, but also in general municipal law.

Cities and other municipal corporations as well as townships and counties, are creatures of the state. The state creates them and can dissolve them, subject of course to constitutional limitations.[1]

Three key provisions appear in every general library law. The first grants power from the legislature to a municipality (city, village, township or county). The second authorizes the corporate authority of the local government unit (not the public library board) to levy taxes for library purposes. The third describes the governance of the public library, generally a board of directors of a specified number to be appointed by the corporate authorities or elected by the people for a specified term of years. The law also enumerates the powers and duties of the board.[2] For those jurisdictions that operate without boards, the law similarly describes the governance of the public library. In such cases, the library operates as a department of local government, responsible to the executive of the municipality.

Many of the library's general powers, however, can be traced to "case-law," court decisions which clarify or modify written statutes. For the most part, state legislation enables, rather than mandates, public libraries.

Further, general state and federal acts or legal decisions concerning broad societal concerns also apply to public libraries. State anti-discrimination laws, for instance, or federal statutes about handicapped access are illustrative of ordinances that must be universally observed.

In addition, regulations promulgated by state agencies have the force of law by virtue of the powers vested in them by state legislatures. State libraries are responsible for planning, developing and implementing public library services throughout the state. They promulgate statewide plans for library growth, coordinate library systems, offer consulting services, establish systems of interlibrary loan, gather and analyze statistics, review library legislation, develop interstate library compacts, and provide opportunities for continuing education, among other activities. Their authority over local libraries derives primarily from their ability to dispense federal and state aid based on compliance with state-generated standards of library behavior.[3] The ambiguity of the authority relationship between state and local libraries is an irritant to many public libraries and a source of tension.

Finally, the authority of the local library may be defined in local statutes and regulations to the extent that they do not conflict with ones enacted by the state or nation.

> The library board of a municipal library... does not have the power to levy taxes, for the library is not a separate government entity but a part of the municipal government that it serves. At most it is a department of the municipal administration.[4]

Public libraries do have certain rights and powers which exist independent of local government conferred on them by state statute. But courts have held that in those cases where specific powers have not been delegated to local libraries by state law, the library is essentially bound by the authority of local government. Becoming and remaining familiar with the laws pertaining to local libraries means understanding state and federal statutes, relevant court decisions, applicable regulations of state agencies and local legislation, tradition and practice.

GOVERNANCE

Public libraries are quintessentially American institutions relying on lay, citizen boards of trustees and emphasizing local citizen input and involvement. Tracing the threads of American public libraries back to their sources in social, school district and municipal libraries reveals how patterns of trusteeship developed.

The social library developed into the subscription or association library with the governing trustees elected by the members of the association. The school-district library responsible through its trustees to the board of education, and the municipal public library with its trustees selected by mayor and city council, account for the major variations in modern public library government and organization.[5]

All three forms continue to exist, although the powers trustees exercise vary. Some boards are advisory rather than supervisory; a minority are constituted as departments of local government and function directly under the supervision of local appointed or elected officials. A few boards are elected. Most are appointed by municipal officials -- mayors, county commissioners, supervisors, selectmen or a city council. While a distinction is usually drawn between the policy-making role of the board and the administrative role of the executive, (the board charged with creating the policy that governs the library, and the library director implementing it), in practice the distinction is not always clear cut. Determining whether an action makes policy or executes it is difficult. The effects of an executive action may be so profound for an organization that though the action is administrative in nature, it may be wise to treat it as a matter of policy with full board review. The implications of a board policy may not be recognized when the action is first taken, and a review at the time a policy has its first major impact may serve to prepare the board for further ramifications of its actions.

The board of trustee form of governance emerged in public libraries as it did in schools and other municipal endeavors for a variety of reasons:

1. *Faith in Popular Government.* Using lay, citizen groups to govern local services appeals to the American tendency to keep government close to the people.

2. *The Need to Neutralize Political Influence.* Americans have assumed that the use of non-partisan boards of trustees in education and local government and a non-partisan civil service will curb the corrosive effects of unrestrained political partisanship. Not always successful in municipalities, on the whole the board of trustees system of governance has kept public libraries relatively free of outside, partisan political influences.

3. *The Expectation of Citizen Control: Lay Boards and Expert Administrators.* The expectation that professional "experts" will direct the institution, but lay boards will act as checks on them has kept many executives accountable for their actions and away from unrestrained behavior and excessive zeal.

4. *The Importance of Continuity.* Lay board members typically serving a three or five year term, renewable by reappointment can provide continuity of governance. In practice, board members sometimes serve indefinite, virtually permanent terms, aging in office and creating boards that change too slowly to respond to societal shifts. All library boards need new blood. A plan that

provides for rotating membership with one or two board members replacing long-serving ones each year, encourages continuity without sterility.

5. *Stimulation of Library Leadership.* The development of interested, informed laypersons, dedicated to improving local libraries has been a salutary by-product of the trustee form of governance.

> The value of the board as a body which collectively or individually represents the library to the people and officials of the city is or should be a very concrete and positive thing. It would be easy to illustrate this point by an almost unlimited series of specific examples of the weight carried by an official statement by the board or of a mere word of an influential trustee offered at the right time or in the right place.[6]

CRITICISM OF THE LIBRARY BOARD FORM OF ORGANIZATION

Some who advocate streamlining the mechanisms of local government argue that separate library corporations with governing boards create additional layers of local governments, with an agenda that varies from that of the central municipal authority. Others argue that the distinction between policy and administrative issues are too often blurred and library boards gradually become administrators of policies, rather than generators of them. Unfortunately, the difference between policy and administrative decisions is frequently so nebulous that distinction becomes impossible.

Perhaps the strongest criticism leveled against the board of trustee form of governance is that it perpetuates current practice and militates against innovation. As early as 1936, Anna Gertrude Hall identified this persistent problems when she wrote that

> they too often opposed and defeated the well-considered plans of able librarians. This obstructionist policy may have arisen from

any one of several causes: sometimes simply from a conservative temperament that hesitates before changing; sometimes from niggardliness in spending tax money or in asking for increased budgets, and sometimes from a petty and often unconscious desire to exercise authority. Restraint of the overenthusiastic librarian is a function of the board, but opposition to progress out of personal caprice or mental indolence is something entirely different.[7]

The composition of library boards may account for the difficulties in distinguishing librarian and trustee roles, and for the inaction that characterizes many boards. In 1935, Joeckel observed that the typical trustee was an over 50 year old male, well-educated lawyer.[8] Over a decade later, Garceau commented that board members were too old, overly representative of business and the professions and socially exclusive.[9] Later studies confirm the earlier findings. Almost three decades later, Ann Prentice reported that

Men still hold a considerable edge over women in the number of trustee positions and although the difference has lessened, two out of every three trustees continue to be men. In age, the medium is 53...for all the social concerns about the rights of minorities, their representation on library boards has not increased in medium-sized cities.[10]

Boards are too frequently reflections of themselves; that is, in order to join its ranks, one must embody those characteristics which already exist on the board. In one community this might be economic position; in another, affiliation with a particular church; in still another membership in an organization whose project it is to run the library. In one community, board membership may be a symbol of status; in another, the library may have to scramble to find members for its board; in still a third, board membership may bring with it the demand that members commit themselves to working in the library for a number of hours each week or month.

Among the current prescriptions for a library board is that its members ought to typify the various backgrounds and interests which make up the community.[11] The importance of representing the concerns of minority groups, or students is clear. However to mirror, for instance, the educational level of a community may not be constructive. The same holds true if a community tends to be culturally insulated and geographically isolated and its board members reflect these orientations. Finding the right formula for board membership is not an easy task.

ALTERNATE FORMS OF ORGANIZATION

A small minority of public libraries in the United States operate as agencies of local government. Their effectiveness is closely tied to the effectiveness of their municipality. An inherent advantage of this type of governance is that it provides direct access to top municipal or county policy makers. If, however, librarians report to intermediates at the departmental level rather than to top management, some of the advantage is dissipated. A real danger is that local decision-makers may not value the library and may assign it low priority. Further, a public library with its own board of trustees can galvanize public opinion in its support to influence local government. As a direct agency of local government, however, the library is blocked from this course of action since any attempt to garner general public support in opposition to decisions amounts to insubordination. Lack of flexibility becomes a significant problem.

Librarians, as department heads, have the opportunity to become influential in official capacities. They attend department head meetings, have access to municipalities' personnel, purchasing, finance and accounting systems, and communicate officially with other department heads.

THE JOB OF THE LIBRARY TRUSTEE

Library boards that are purely advisory attempt to influence local government through indirect means -- reason and moral suasion. They must win with argument what cannot be enforced through the exercise of direct power.

Those whose role bears more authority and responsibility for setting library policies and overseeing operations are charged with a number of major tasks, some fixed by law, others suggested by custom. Typically a board is responsible for:

1. *Hiring and Evaluating the Library Director and Approving other Personnel Appointments.* Among the most important functions the library board performs is to hire the library director. The board, part-time, normally lacking in professional library expertise, cannot administer an organization, but it must hire a professional library who can. The board must

> understand the functions of the library director, find and appoint a competent one, give that employee a free hand in administrative matters and evaluate the leadership, lend support and help overcome weaknesses, if any become evident.[12]

At times, boards of trustees forget that administering a library is a full-time job requiring technical competence, managerial skills and the time to exercise both and try to manage library organizations themselves. Occasionally this results from frustration with the incumbent library director. The situation is improved only when the present director's performance changes or when he or she is replaced, not from board assumption of management duties.

The performance of all public library staff requires regular and careful evaluation. For the library director, it is the board that fulfills this obligation. How it is best accomplished is discussed in Chapter 16, The Library Director.

The power of selecting additional staff, while legally a Board responsibility, is commonly delegated to library directors. If they are to be held accountable for the staff's performance, they must be able to choose those with whom they can best work.

Figure 7
2. Director/Board Responsibilities.

Board

--determining the purpose of the library;

--adopting policies which govern its operation;

--securing funds to support adequately the program;

--being cognizant of library standards and trends;

--helping to plan and support a public relations program;

--acting as a link between the community and the library;

--learning about state/local statutes, and supporting library legislation on the state and national level;

--developing policies regarding materials selection and intellectual freedom;

--adopting a library budget and presenting it to municipal authorities;

--attending all board meetings, assuring their legitimacy and maintaining adequate records;

--attending regional, state and national trustee meetings and workshops;

--understanding the functions and services of the library agency;

--reporting regularly to the local governing officials and to the public.

Director

--acting as the board's chief technical advisor;

--suggesting library policies to the board;

--recommending personnel actions and assuming responsibility for staff;

--carrying out board policies;

--preparing library progress reports about library use and current expenditure reports for the board;

--maintaining an active public relations program;

--preparing an annual budget proposal;

--knowing local and state laws and regulation, library trends and standards;

--assuming responsibility for selecting and ordering all library materials;

--attending all board meetings, except for those dealing with the director's tenure or salary;

--joining local, state, and national organizations and attending professional meetings and workshops;

--reporting regularly to the library board, to local officials and to the public.[13]

Although major distinctions exist between the functions of board and director, there are points where duties intersect and overlap. Continuing, frank dialogue between the parties helps to avoid misunderstandings about respective responsibilities.

3. *Participating in the Political Process.* To whom are trustees responsible and for what? Virginia Young answers the question in this way:

> Trusteeship by definition is an agency or a person (or persons) designated to act as governor or protector over property belonging to another. Since the public library belongs to its entire community, library boards have been created by law to act as citizen control or governing body of the library. Library trustees accordingly are public officials and servants of the public and the power delegated to library boards are a public trust.[14]

Many trustees consider their role to be standing in for the local official who was responsible for their appointment. To the extent this exists, the library remains hostage to local, sometimes narrow and sometimes parochial, interests.

The true mission of trustees is to represent the library based on a careful assessment of library needs, on intelligence, on knowledge of the community, and on the views of the library director and staff. They owe the public the use of their skills to further the library plan they have adopted. Their first loyalty is to the public. Occasionally this may mean confronting public officials, doing battle in service of the library, sometimes in opposition to those who have appointed them.

4. *Preparing and Supporting the Library Budget.* Library directors and staff prepare an initial budget. Trustees review it from the perspective of a series of questions about library objectives and planned implementation. As they consider the budget, they must first ask:

How well has the library serviced its public in the year ending?
How well is the library meeting its stated objectives?
What are the next steps to be taken in order to implement both
short-range and long-range objectives?[15]

Once trustees have assured themselves about public need and
available community and library resources, they make any
necessary adjustments. The library director and staff participate in
the entire process, interacting with the board during all
deliberations. The final budget becomes a true joint staff/board
effort.

At this point, the burden falls on the board members. They are
responsible for the budget's presentation to municipal authorities
and for lobbying for its passage. If, during its construction, boards
members have merely viewed a series of numbers that balance,
without internalizing their programmatic implications, their appeal
for funds will be less compelling. Board members are ultimately
responsible for helping local government understand the
importance of the library as a *public good*. (This concept is
explored in Chapter 18.)

5. *Promoting Favorable Public Relations.* Management is
responsible for developing a public relations program, but trustees
play both a direct and indirect role in shaping and executing it. In
their oversight capacity, trustees must make certain than an
effective program is developed by library staff. Of equal
importance, however is the way in which they represent the library
in public forums. Library trustees occupy a singular position in the
life of their communities. They are perceived as concerned citizens
motivated by sincere desire to support and improve their local
libraries, without vested interest or personal benefit. Many are also
reputational elites whose influence is often the result of anticipated
reactions, desire to emulate behavior and power exerted simply by
being, rather than by doing.[16] Like all employee-advocates,
librarians are regarded as having a personal stake in the future of
the library. For this reason, trustee-issued statements on library

matters are more persuasive and carry more weight than those delivered by librarians, particularly when financial and other potentially controversial matters are involved.

6. *Planning the Library's Future.* Organizational planning is an area in which trustee involvement is critical. Trustees cannot discharge their fiduciary responsibilities to their libraries unless the objectives of the library have been clearly articulated and precisely drawn. Without these landmarks, trustees lack evidence that the library is travelling a coherent, rational path toward presentation of appropriate library services.

Planning is discussed elsewhere in this text. However, it seems important to stress here the crucial function of trustees in communicating core community values as they bear on library service. The board's Janus-like relations to the community and the library can help to prevent misunderstandings and avoid isolation. Often former board members become the library's strongest supporters after they have moved to other community panels.

7. *Protecting Intellectual Freedom.*

> Ranking high among the most significant decision for a library is the decision to meet staunchly and forcefully and with proper preparation and advice (legal if necessary), challenges to library materials and sometimes to services offered by the library as well. Most library boards manage to avoid confrontation with the community and, when inconsequential matters are concerned, this is a wise course to follow. However, intellectual freedom, protected by the first amendment to the United States Constitution is a matter of consequence.[17]

Intellectual freedom considerations and procedures are handled in Chapter 8. Inasmuch as the board is the final arbiter of decisions about whether to continue to provide a particular title or service, it is they who feel the full force of community fury if the conclusion is an unpopular one. At such times they face angry friends and neighbors in defense of a principle which can seem abstract and distant. Without a solid grounding in the history and current practice of intellectual freedom as it pertains to libraries, controversies become quagmires from which extrication is extremely arduous.

STRUCTURE OF THE LIBRARY BOARD

The formal organization of library boards is normally made explicit in the by-laws of the library.[18] Typically they state the official names of the organization, the names of designated offices of the board, together with their powers, duties, and how officers are chosen. They also indicate when the board normally meets, the order of business for board meetings, the nature of a quorum for official meetings, the procedure for calling special meetings of the board, the basis for governing conduct at board meetings -- usually *Robert's Rules of Order* -- the committee structure, the nature of the relationships between the board and the director, and the method of amending the by-laws. The by-laws should also specify that when trustees speak on library issues, they clearly identify their statements as personal unless they have been authorized by the board to speak on its behalf.

Board sizes are often set by law, usually five to seven members. A large board can be unwieldy and make reaching consensus difficult. A small one may make gathering a quorum problematic. Sometimes the number of consecutive terms a member may serve is also specified in state law. If not, a board is well advised to include a limitation of board tenure in the library by-laws.

A committee system of governance is frequently adopted. Among the important standing committees are: personnel, budget, endowment, by-laws and building and grounds. In cases where trustees negotiate employee contracts, the board normally appoints a negotiating committee. Some boards also appoint trustee-municipal liaison committees to provide for continuing contact between the library and governmental officials.

Orienting new board members presents an opportunity to

advise them about the library values and is as important as it is for new staff. Time spent by the library director and, if possible, the board president in informing new trustees about the current state of the library is an investment that is likely to produce healthy dividends for years to come.

THE LIBRARY BOARD MEETING

Library boards, like most other public agencies, once made their decisions in meetings closed to the public "Sunshine laws" now mandate that most public discussion and actions take place in open sessions.

Meetings of the library board proceed according to a set agenda prepared by the librarian in consultation with the board president and distributed to members prior to the meeting. Minutes record all actions including member votes and statements of substance made by them or other speakers. Routinely distributing copies of minutes to municipalities that fund the library insures that, procedurally at least, officials have been informed about recommendations, resolutions or other actions taken by the library board. Typical agenda items are roll call (to establish attendance), approval of minutes, correspondence, library's report, financial report and approval of expenditures, standing and special committee reports, and any other business.

Time should be allowed during the meeting for citizen participation. A policy of openness and a willingness to listen, particularly in times of controversy, can prove valuable.

The success of the library board is determined by the attitudes toward it of the director and of the members who serve on it. They must be genuinely interested in the development of the library, and not just the prestige of serving on the board. Conversely, if the library board is seen as a rubber stamp for the actions of the director, it is unlikely to be effective either in offering advice on library matters or interpreting them to the community. Some directors have difficulty refraining from dominating meetings, a pattern of behavior that also threatens the efficacy of the board.

TRUSTEES AND THE LAW

Library trustees are responsible for governing the library pursuant to the statutes that establish the institution and provide for its affairs. Operating the library within the limits imposed by law is not easy. In the litigious American society of the 1990's, inadvertent violations of existing statutes can mean that library trustees are personally accountable for damages. Every library must have immediate access to an attorney knowledgeable about public law and willing to become familiar with statutes that pertain to libraries. Too often general municipal attorneys are assigned by local government to represent the local public library under the mistaken impression that nothing of legal consequence happens in a library. Questions affecting libraries, intellectual freedom, for instance, or homeless people in libraries, are as complex as any others covered by municipal law. Larger libraries should certainly consider retaining their own legal counsels. Many library boards now require routine attendance of their legal counsels, municipal or private, at board meetings.

Board members, too, need to be familiar with pertinent laws governing public libraries. Reasonable familiarity with library related statutes, regulations and legal decisions provides one of the best defenses against potential litigation.

THE TRUSTEE AND THE CHANGING LIBRARY WORLD

Public library trustees once focused almost exclusively on the local library scene, on its ability to meet the many and varied needs of its patrons. Librarians, trustees and the public have been proud of the ability of the library to disgorge information and materials about the most arcane subjects. Now, however, the growth of knowledge has multiplied the difficulties of satisfying local needs. Technology is one of the important enabling mechanisms in the new world. Networks of libraries banded together to cooperate in mutually supportive systems offer solutions. But these mechanisms operate within substantially larger frameworks based on delivery of service to the library's patron, rather than on who delivers the service. Without trustee approval of such ventures as OCLC, or on-line databases, or automation of libraries, these systems would never have been incorporated into contemporary public library service.

Some trustees, even some library staff, have been prey to a particular breed of "localism" and show indifference, at best, and sometimes hostility to participating in cooperative efforts, feeling that they detract from direct service. A board so oriented to local service and to traditional delivery of it is likely to deny progress and innovation and finally, to do disservice to the institution and community it is trying to serve.

TRUSTEE ASSOCIATIONS, STATE LIBRARIES AND LOCAL TRUSTEES

Trustees require a wide range of knowledge to discharge their responsibilities properly, knowledge that cannot arise spontaneously and without effort. State library agencies and state and national library trustee associations are well positioned to assist in developing both trustee skills and knowledge about libraries. State library consultants, conversant with state and federal library statutes and programs, generally transmit their knowledge in training programs for trustees and in face-to-face meetings.

State library associations and the American Library Trustee Association (ALTA) offer the collective wisdom and experience of past and present trustees, particularly about the process of decision-making. Through participation in associations, trustees can explore the issues which affect them.

SUMMARY

Wide differences appear in laws regulating public libraries throughout the United States. State laws enable libraries to exist, but local municipalities create and endow them and boards of trustees construct frameworks within which they can come to life.

Librarians add services, materials, processes and activities, the heart and bloodstream of an institution. Citizen control in a lay library board prevents vested interests from pursuing separate agendas. Libraries function best when trustee oversight and librarian administration are clearly distinguished, with each having the authority and flexibility to act in the best interests of the community. Trustees in advisory or policy-making capacities act as lynch-pins between libraries and municipalities carrying information to and from each. Without their advocacy, libraries might be seen as self-serving institutions and suffer severely at the financial trough.

NOTES AND SUGGESTED READINGS

Notes

1. Alex Ladenson, *Library Law and Legislation in the United States* (Metuchen, NJ: Scarecrow, 1982), 13.

2. Ibid., 17.

3. David Shavit, *Federal Aid and State Library Agencies* (New York: Greenwood, 1985), 17.

4. Ibid., 30.

5. Ann Prentice, *The Public Library Trustee: Image and Performance on Funding* (Metuchen, NJ: Scarecrow, 1973) 4-5.

6. C. B. Joeckel, *The Government of the American Public Library* (Chicago: University of Chicago Press, 1935), 252.

7. Anna Gertrude Hall, *The Library Trustee* (Chicago: American Library Association, 1937), 6.

8. Joeckel, 236-42.

9. Oliver Garceau, *The Public Library in the Political Process* (New York: Columbia University Press, 1949) 51-70.

10. Prentice, 47.

11. Virginia Young, "Library Governance by Citizen Boards," *Library Trends* (Fall, 1977): 287.

12. Carlton Rochell, *Wheeler and Goldhor's Practical Administration of Public Libraries* (New York: Harper, 1981), 33.

13. Summarized from Young, Virginia, *The Library Trustee* (New York: Bowker, 1978), 9.

14. Ibid., 9.

15. Charles O'Halloran, "The Trustees and Finances," in Young, 121.

16. M. Kent Jennings, *Community Influentials* (Glencoe, IL: Free Press, 1964), 21.

17. Young, 67-8.

18. A useful sample of model public library by-laws is included in Young, 165.

Suggested Readings

Guidelines for Developing Policies and Procedures in Missouri Public Libraries. Jefferson City, MO: Missouri State Library, 1990.

Hall, Gertrude Anne. *The Library Trustee.* Chicago: American Library Association, 1937.

Ihrig, Alice. *Decision Making for Public Libraries.* Hamden, CT: Library Professional Pub., 1989.

Ladenson, Alex. *Library Law and Legislation in the United States.*

Metuchen, NJ: Scarecrow Press, 1982.

Madden, Michael. "The Governance of Public Libraries." *Journal of Library Administration* 11 (1989): 81-92.

Prentice, Ann E. *The Public Library Trustee: Image and Performance on Funding.* Metuchen, NJ: Scarecrow Press, 1973.

Rochell, Carlton. *Wheeler and Goldhor's Practical Administration of Public Libraries.* New York: Harper, 1981.

Trustee Tool Kit for Library Leadership. Sacramento, CA: California State Library, 1987.

Williams, Lorraine. *The Library Trustee and the Public Librarian.* Metuchen, NJ: Scarecrow Press, 1993.

Young, Virginia, ed. *The Library Trustee.* New York: Bowker, 1978.

Young, Virginia, ed. *The Library Trustee.* Chicago: American Library Association, 1988.

CHAPTER 6

ORGANIZATION

At the end of the twentieth century, the public library finds itself, as does the rest of the organizational world, poised with one foot in an industrial environment that is passing and the other seeking solid ground in a post-industrial, information-based universe with changed values and concerns. Organizational models that prevailed during the last nine decades -- pyramidal, hierarchical arrangements with clearly defined chains of command, compartmentalized work relationships, authoritarian and nonparticipative behavioral models -- have undergone intense scrutiny and, in some cases, significant restructure.

In the early history of American public libraries, organizational arrangements were hardly necessary. One employee performed all tasks -- opened in the morning, closed for lunch from noon to one, and from five to seven if there were evening hours, and locked the door at night. Even added staff, increased hours and fatter budgets did not negate the generalist model.

The beginning of the twentieth century witnessed a shift in private sector industry toward operational efficiencies through job definition, standardization and coordination. This meant grouping tasks in related, specialized activities and hiring and training staff to perform them. Public libraries, following the industrial model, separated duties into professional and support categories, and offered specialized instruction to those whose work was considered to require library expertise. In-house library training programs and the institutes which succeeded them gave way to degree-granting library programs in colleges and graduate schools. State recognition of professional qualifications was accorded through certification and civil service classifications that reflected advanced training. In the 1960s a para-professional rank, usually called library technical assistant, was added. Only recently has automation caused new categories of both paraprofessionals and professionals to appear in the ranks of library staffs. Typically, they are people with no formal training in librarianship, but who have been prepared as programmers and system analysts, telecommunication specialists, archivists, media technicians and specialists, and conservators and restorers.

Not long after professional/support distinctions were effected, task specialization among those with professional training also emerged. There were reference librarians, children's and young adult librarians and catalogers. In addition, managerial ranks surfaced. Now there were also Directors, Assistant and Associate Directors, coordinators and department heads.

Organizations began to accommodate these new specialties, to coordinate the library's work between and among them, to define lines of authority and responsibility and to describe linear career paths for upwardly-mobile librarians.

LIBRARY ORGANIZATIONS

Organizations have been defined as

the pattern of ways in which a large number of people of a size too great to have intimate face-to-face contact and engaged in a complexity of tasks, relate themselves to each other in the conscious, systematic establishment and accomplishment of mutually agreed purposes.[1]

Public service institutions are organs of society that exist, not for their own sakes, but to fulfill a specific purpose and to satisfy a specific community need. They are not ends in themselves, but rather means to achieve certain goals. Effective public service organizations ask What am I supposed to be doing? and What are my tasks? rather than What am I?[2]

Typically, public libraries are organized as vertical hierarchies, resembling pyramids, although their exact shapes vary according to their individual histories, traditions and other local factors. The library's structure should reflect its aims, goals and roles which, in turn, serve as vehicles by which decisions are made about how staff will be arranged, coordinated and integrated. In the continuing process of defining and redefining goals and objectives, structural elastic arrangements permit organizational readjustment and manipulation in order to accomplish new aims. Two of the most important tasks of a library director are to clarify for the staff and for the community the library's roles, and to select appropriate means to carry them out.

Each of the public library's constituencies legitimately expects different quantities and kinds of services from it. Children, for instance, clamor for books useful in fulfilling school assignments; fiction readers demand best sellers and scholars seek research materials. For this reason, public libraries must assess community needs and demands and attach degrees of importance to each in order to define the institution's role and shape its organizational structure.

PLANNING

In the past two decades, public librarians have recognized the importance of incorporating careful planning into their administrative structures. Based on the premise that each library is unique and should be assessed and developed within its own context, that is, its peculiar history, traditions, user and non-user populations and environment, the new planning thrust counsels each library to devise its own mission, decide what it wants to do and then set its own goals and objectives to guide its short-range and long-term future. Understood within the planning procedure is the need for an evaluation component to measure the success of the effort. The history of public library planning efforts grew in tandem with the development of performance measures for judging a library's effectiveness.[3] In 1980 a complicated program for public library planning which leaned heavily on community participation in the process and on an elaborate level of data collection and analysis was published.[4] The process was revised in 1987[5] and is now followed by many of the nation's public libraries.

Planning enables an institution to determine what it is doing and what it wishes to achieve, to devise alternative courses of action that may produce the desired result and provides a method of evaluating the extent to which goals have been reached. At times difficult and time-consuming if properly administered, its value should not be underestimated. It is the most basic of functions, the one on which all others rest, permitting rational commitment of resources -- personnel and material -- based on the best possible knowledge of the future.

The purpose of planning is not to create a permanent document. Rather, planning embodies a continuous, never-ending process whose output is virtually obsolete upon completion. The production of a plan is a signal to begin a new cycle of planning, leading eventually to yet another plan. Two types of plans are generally produced: long-range and short-term. The former represents a master plan whose duration is typically between three and five years. Short-term goals and objectives, set for one year periods, comprise the building blocks of the longer document. These are evaluated each year and revised as circumstances dictate.

Creating a public library plan is best accomplished as a group activity, involving not only library staff and the governing authority, but the public as well. The library director may frame a working draft and present it to various constituencies or it may be generated at the departmental level and move upwards and out. Who actually composes the final statement depends on the nature of the institution and the size of the staff.

The process of producing a master plan has a number of salutary effects:

1. The act of articulating missions, goals, and objectives and of reviewing the library's current condition is, in itself, a

consciousness-raising experience. If, after completion of the project, the plan is banished to a closet shelf to gather dust, the exercise will still have been worth the effort, given the heightened understanding of the library and its role in the community that have been provided.

2. Goals and objectives help to free staffing patterns from whimsical, senseless arrangements. Individual roles and departmental groups can be compared with objectives to insure that harmony and smooth operation exists among them.

3. A public master plan acts as a contract with a community. If it has been negotiated with a variety of constituencies, it can serve to reconcile the vested interests of opposing groups.

4. A well-produced document has public relations value. Libraries face heavy competition from other community agencies for scarce dollars. Formulating a plan helps them make their best possible case by presenting a rational plan based, not on intuition, but on careful analysis.

THE PLANNING PROCESS

Utilizing the Public Library Association's 1987 *Planning and Role Setting* or other planning manuals[6] results in following a procedure not unlike the one described below:

Planning to Plan. This preliminary phase clarifies the purposes of the planning effort, allocates resources for its implementation, establishes a schedule, impanels a planning committee charged with carrying the effort to its conclusion and sees that all participants are knowledgeable about the process, the library and the community.

Looking Around. This step includes determining the kinds of information required for decision-making, gathering pertinent community and library data, analyzing them and reporting the results. Often called the community analysis segment of the planning process, it entails an environmental scan and demographic examination of the kind described in Chapter 4, The Community Context.

Developing Missions and Roles. A mission statement is generally broad, inspiring and philosophical in tone, reflecting "the fundamental reasons for the library's existence."[7] It might read, for instance:

> "The library exists to serve the educational, informational, cultural and recreational needs of its community."[8]

Selection of the library's service roles are based on the analysis it has made of the community's needs. Role statements are more concrete, stating who is to receive what services. Among the suggested roles for public libraries are to act as

1) a Community Activities Center;
2) a Community Information Center;
3) a Community Services Agency;
4) a Cultural Center;
5) an Educational Support Center;
6) an Independent Learning Center;
7) a Reference, Information and Research Center;
8) a Preschoolers Door to Learning;
9) a Recreational Center.[9]

Writing Goals and Objectives. Goals and objectives are derived from the mission statement. Goals are generally long-range statements defining broad aspirations. For instance, one might set, as a goal the establishment of a currently useful collection of materials. Objectives differ from goals in that they are narrow, entail a shorter time period, are always measurable and achievable. An objective built on the preceding goal might read, "The library will acquire and make available .5 books per capita during the calendar year 1994." At the end of 1994, the library is able to evaluate the degree to which it has met this objective.

It should be noted that "Missions," "Goals," "Aims" and "Objectives" do not always share the same meaning in library and management literature. "Goals" and "Objectives" are sometimes used interchangeably. So, too, are "Goals" and "Aims," as well as "Missions" and "Goals."

Taking Action. This stage of the planning process involves generating strategies or activities to implement objectives. Choices are made from a set of alternative paths to the achievement of objectives that have been examined for practicality, effectiveness, efficiency and potential conflicts with other services.

Writing the Planning Document. An important product of the process is the planning document. It formalizes and institutionalizes the plan, informs the public of the results of the effort and serves as a reference source for future decision making.

Implementing the Plan and Reviewing the Results. The plan is put into action and is reviewed periodically to learn how much has been accomplished and whether the roles, goals and objectives were realistic and achievable. Near the terminating date of the Master Plan, the entire effort is evaluated to learn the extent to which goals and objectives have been realized. At this point, the cycle begins once again. The mission is reaffirmed, any variations in the community noted, goals are reconsidered to learn if they still reflect accurately what the library seeks to accomplish. New or reformed objectives are constructed and implemented. A discussion of the performance measures devised to evaluate the service objectives produced during the planning process is described in Chapter 20, Evaluation.

ORGANIZING PRINCIPLES

An established mission, roles, goals and objectives statement should suggest the library's organization structure and describe the functional relationship among its job title holders, that is, its organization chart. In reality, the organizational structure is often a reflection of the patterns of behavior that have sprouted over time as adaptations to the architecture of the building, the personality of the administrator or to the skills of staff members. This is not altogether undesirable providing the work of the institution is not hampered. A talented administrator may select the right people for the library and help them grow, placing them in positions that accord with their individual skills and interests. The exact form an organization takes depends on its own circumstances. Public libraries today adopt varied organizational structures depending on their size, community and available space, among other factors. Automation, too, accounts for differing organizational structures among public libraries and also contributes to fluctuating conditions and rapid change. Among the drawbacks of current public library organization is a tendency to compartmentalize operations and to ignore the mission of the library while concentrating on the goals of an individual department. Staff sometimes forget they are part of a whole team rather than exclusively catalogers or reference librarians. The opportunity to incorporate new organizing principles, as well as discontent with the rigid structures currently exhibited by most public libraries, has given rise to numerous suggestions for reorganization. Some restructuring suggestions are considered after the following discussion of how libraries currently organize themselves.

In the small public library, there is either no elaborate organization or the library has organized its work around the unique skills of its few staff members. There is little departmentalization, and jobs are attached to those who perform them best. Adaptation to individual capabilities has potential dangers, as well as benefits. It can produce a dysfunctional, unbalanced institution, with some staff severely overburdened and others underutilized. If possible, even in the smallest libraries, duties assigned to an individual staff member should be closely related and the person should be asked to report routinely to only one supervisor.

As libraries grow larger and hire more than three or four staff members, the common pattern is to distinguish areas of responsibility and authority and distribute them among the staff. Five types of arrangements or operational units characterize most public libraries:

1. *Functional.* Public libraries, except the very smallest, are organized into functional units. A functional arrangement would include the following departments found in most public libraries:

Collection Development and Management involves evaluation and selection of materials to be added to the library, evaluation and weeding of materials no longer useful, preservation of library holdings and strategies for insuring patron satisfaction and rational collection growth.

Acquisitions includes ordering materials, monitoring deliveries and approving payments. Among the duties are searching files for ownership; collecting bibliographic information; selecting suppliers; ordering and checking deliveries; initiating claims for unreceived materials.

Cataloging and Technical Services entails recording, describing, and indexing the holdings of a library, as well as determining and establishing the number and kinds of access points for retrieving each item, and monitoring the quality control of all bibliographic records. Other technical services include physical preparation materials for circulation.

Circulation encompasses those activities revolving around the flow of library materials; that is, managing the removal and return of items to and from shelf locations and implementing policies regarding who may borrow what material for what length of time and enforcing penalties for their non-return.

Reference or Information Services involves helping users locate, retrieve and otherwise gain access to information, no matter where it is located.

Systems. Automated libraries now commonly include a systems department whose work consists of upgrading equipment, training staff to work with computerized processes, troubleshooting and adapting and integrating new technology to library uses.

It could also include *Readers Service Departments, Personnel, InterLibrary Loan* and other functional units.

2. *Location.* Branch libraries illustrate the principle of organizing libraries along territorial or geographic lines. Determination of whether or not to build a branch and where has occupied substantial library attention. Some have held that to be viable a branch must draw on a population of at least 25,000. On the other hand, geographical as well as other factors may suggest that it is reasonable to build a branch for fewer people. Many experts contend that constructing additional branches tends to dilute library support. Since World War II, there have been major efforts to create larger and larger library units in county and regional library systems across the country based on the assumption that smaller libraries are inherently inefficient and cannot provide the full range of modern library services including specialized staff, specialized information materials and periodical back files. It has also been assumed that larger units of service produce economies of scale, spreading costs of specialized service or staff members over a large number of people, reducing the cost per unit. Some feel that networks, resource sharing, rapid delivery of materials can overcome restraints of distance and size. Bill Summers maintains that:

> the impact of modern technology on library system structure has not been investigated...the availability of relatively low-cost high capacity computer systems may well have the potential to alter the most desirable configurations of library systems and should be reexamined.[10]

Online systems are "distance independent." Online public access catalogs and bibliographic data bases are accessible through any computer and are therefore not limited to a precise site. Facsimile transmission insures that periodical articles, once located can be instantly delivered. Limited collections, either reference or periodical, no longer represent stumbling blocks to quality service.

3. *Subject Orientation.* Departmentation along subject lines is more characteristic of large libraries than it is of smaller or medium-size ones. Subject specialization has distinct advantages. Disciplinary materials concentrated in one area can be serviced by staff thoroughly familiar with the subject's literature, producing levels of assistance otherwise impossible. Increased costs associated with providing specialized service militate against its being offered in communities of less than 75,000 to 100,000 people. When departmentation or divisional approaches are utilized, Local History, Fine Arts, Business and Science are the most likely subjects to be separately offered.

4. *Format.* Audio-visual materials, periodicals, manuscripts and microforms are four types of materials that public libraries often detach from their general collections. Using format as the determining factor in placing materials has merit when special care, special use or security factors are involved. On the other hand, libraries sometimes retain this status for materials when those conditions no longer prevail. Non-fiction videos, for instance, are now more routinely shelved with their print counterparts. Microforms which were once expensive and difficult to replace can now be located in areas of ready public access.

5. *Clientele.* A popular organizing principle for library public service departments is to structure them around specific clientele or consumers. Where the demand is sufficient, concentrations of resources and expertise guarantee a higher level of service. Most libraries easily justify a *Children's Department.* Somewhat fewer offer a *Young Adult Department.* Others may establish a *New Adult Readers Department* or an *Institutional Service Department*, which

includes outreach to jails, and nursing homes.

ORGANIZATION CHARTS

Libraries large enough to organize demonstrate most or all of the above principles in their formal *organization chart*, the graphic embodiment of official, standardized work relationships. The organization chart fulfills a number of important purposes. It provides a structure for job titles and describes the relations between them. It reveals, at a glance, the chain of authority and responsibility that stretches directly from the director to the most junior of library employees and back up. Most libraries today remain basically scalar, hierarchical organizations crafted along traditional functional lines.

On the following two pages are twocommon organization charts that describe contemporary public libraries.

Unfortunately, it is the rare public library director who maintains an up-to-date chart of the library's internal organization, complete with staff assignments. Most charts are assembled at the request of a new board president, when a major restructuring is contemplated, or when a new Master Plan is in the formative stage. Many librarians contend that organization charts only capture the reality of a given moment in an organization's history and while they seem to make sense on paper, they are, in truth, not observed. What they represent are the *intentions* of the framers for the way in which interactions will take place among its members. Scalar organizations are always more complex than organization charts suggest. Organization charts do not include social networks, functional contacts, decision-making or power factors, nor do they describe channels of communication. Dotted and solid lines may indicate ideal advisory, coordinating or authority and responsibility paths, but they do not reveal the quality or frequency of exchanges between individuals who hold titles. Two organization charts that seem to duplicate each other may, in fact, describe different organizations. In one, a library director may meet regularly with a dynamic board president who will then take the public library's

Figure 8
Organization Chart: District of Columbia Public Library

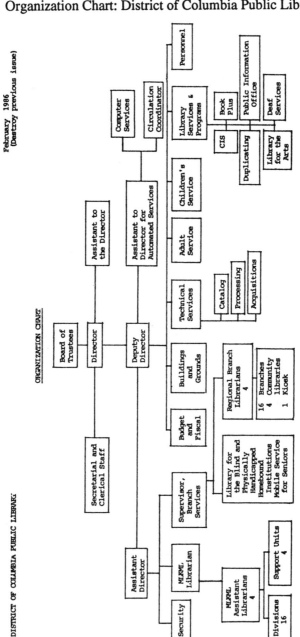

Figure 9
Hartford Public Library

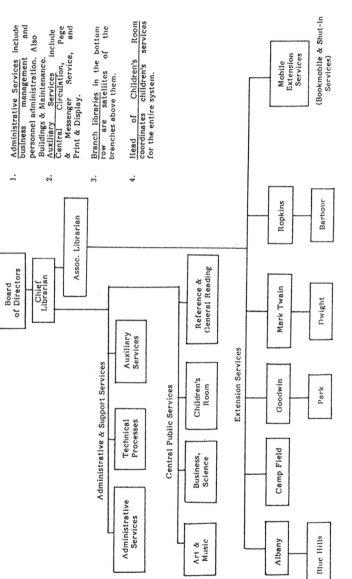

HARTFORD PUBLIC LIBRARY

1. Administrative Services include business management and personnel administration. Also Buildings & Maintenance.

2. Auxiliary Services include Central Circulation, Page & Messenger Service, and Print & Display.

3. Branch libraries in the bottom row are satellites of the branches above them.

4. Head of Children's Room coordinates children's services for the entire system.

2/85

* Associate Librarian assists Chief Librarian in various administrative duties and is his deputy. Relationship to branches is that of coordinator.

message into the community.   In another, the board president may attend as few meetings as possible, never fully comprehending the institution's goals and objectives, and the library may suffer financially and reputationally.   The organization chart cannot capture the institutional culture of the library.

Institutional culture is a flavor, a feeling, an atmosphere that pervades an institution.   It is impossible to see, and difficult to define, but it is there nonetheless and it will be reflected in the attitudes and behavior of the people who work at your library.[11]

Nor can it reflect the that spontaneously generated, loosely structured, but important, *informal organization*.   Organization charts provide insight into how the organization perceives that power is exercised.   In reality, power may be identified with proximity -- whose office sits where.   Specialized knowledge, too, may confer power.   In libraries, both financial officers and technological experts are accorded substantially more power and respect than the organization chart may indicate.   Personal relationships that carry beyond the workplace have the potential to modify the library's formal structure, especially those between supervisor and supervised.

ORGANIZATIONAL PROBLEMS

Small libraries face problems caused by their inability to hire specialized staff and the necessity for all employees to do everything.   Medium and large-size libraries confront different types of problems, particularly as the pressure toward increased participation by all members of the library staff in the institution's administration escalates.

Early twentieth century management thinking held that bureaucracy -- authoritarian hierarchies and rigid task specialization -- was the most rational and dependable method of accomplishing an organization's goals.   Structural rather than human elements were stressed.   Scientific management, with its attention to time and motion analysis, added to the concept the fundamental notion that workers were essentially lazy and required management pressure and a fixed command structure in order to perform efficiently. Not surprisingly, this approach produced efficiencies, but was also responsible for some of the worst excesses of industrialism.

Towards the middle of the century reassessments of the nature of human behavior and potential led to suggestions that people were motivated by desires far different than previously understood. Theorists now argued that after satisfying their basic physiological needs, humans sought self-actualization, that is to maximize their potential and accomplish *something*. Implicit in the theory is an altered role for both management and employees within an organization. The emphasis shifts from controlling the activities of reluctant workers to stimulating the performance of ones eager to achieve their full potential. This emerging view has led to efforts to decentralize decision-making and to incorporate greater employee participation in management. Many of the problems faced by medium and large-sized libraries today stem from vestiges of the traditional bureaucratic model as well as from attempts to incorporate new thinking and participation into a structure ill-suited to house them.

Centralization and Decentralization. Decentralized organizations permit decision-making closer to the level where the most information exists. In a centralized system, authority is concentrated at the top of the hierarchy and exercised downward. For public libraries, ambiguities exist about the appropriate role of experts, the importance of unity of command and the degree of span of control. For example, larger libraries have traditionally employed experts in advisory capacities, as coordinators, for instance. Their positions are not easily described within the authority/command structure of the organization and their roles remain somewhat ambiguous. A coordinator of children's work may act in an advisory relationship to children's librarians throughout a library system. These same children's librarians are expected to report directly to their supervisors at the branch or unit level. Directives by advisors sometimes contradict those issued by supervisors. In actual practice, employees are often uncertain about reporting responsibilities. The chain of command is clearer without the introduction of the children's coordinator, but the expertise is certainly less.

Yet another example of controversy surrounding centralization and decentralization can be seen in the treatment of branches. Typically, branches have been viewed as clones of a main library, reproducing in miniature its services and resources. Alternately, they have been regarded as unique, individual units, each with its own character and flavor. As clones, they are given relatively little flexibility. Branch heads have not been encouraged to identify unique community traits and respond with appropriate services. Increasingly, however, branches are being asked to meet the distinctive needs of the communities or neighborhoods in which they are housed. Materials selection is an example of the conflict between central library authority and branch library autonomy. Centralizing collection development insures uniformity among units and removes haphazard choices. Conversely, decentralized selection permits materials to be chosen on the basis of the local community's character, thereby producing collections that better satisfy user populations. The answer lies in attempting to balance the advantages of large scale operation -- expertise, economies of scale, staff training -- with those of tailoring service to a community's identity and needs, no mean feat.

Among other problems associated with bureaucracies is an elongated vertical line of organization caused by adherence to the theoretical position that no more than five or six employees should report to a single supervisor. This narrowed span of control has resulted in layer upon layer of middle management. Industry, in the 1990s, has elected to reduce management staffs, effectively widening spans of control. Libraries, too, have become wary of top-heavy management, since many professional librarians regard the bureaucratic structure as an impediment to carrying out their mission.

RESTRUCTURING THE LIBRARY

There have been numerous suggestions for ameliorating and/or counteracting the deleterious effects of institutional library bureaucracies. Most experts agree that traditional library tasks -- acquisition, cataloging and classification, circulation and public services -- are best served by hierarchical organizations. However, calls for employee involvement in management have led to committees, task forces and project management groups, temporary work arrangements to achieve specific goals or to accomplish special projects. Research has demonstrated increased commitment to organizational goals when staff are involved in their creation. Lately, libraries have devised formal structures called "parallel organizations" to enhance institutional responsiveness, participation and problem solving. Parallel organizations are charged with constructing rules, policies and procedures. The information age has produced a multitude of problems with far-reaching ramifications. Matters as diverse as online patron database searching, copyright infringements, privacy of circulation records, and the ethics of service fees require careful deliberation and are best addressed innovatively, with flexibility, a diversity of expertise and outlook, and within an institutionalized structure designed to foster participation.[12] Well-structured problems, those dealing with day-to-day questions can be handled by the line, or bureaucratic, organization. Ill-structured ones are amenable to solution by the parallel organization.

Parallel organizations utilize the same people employed in the hierarchic organization, but combine them differently for the purpose of addressing boundary-spanning issues that require solution. They can be designed to include only professionals or a mix of support and professional staff, depending on a library's size and nature. One difficulty that can arise in "parallel structure" organizations is the relationship between members, especially those who work together in the bureaucratic organization as superior and subordinate and in task-force or committee as equal members of a group.

A few small academic libraries have experimented with collegial structures, electing chairs for a period of years from the ranks of professional librarians.[13] In this model, only the professional staff operates collegially. Support staff remain in traditional structures. Contending that a similar organization could work in public libraries, Martin Jaffe suggests an alternate to the linear career path for librarians which he terms *Steady State*.[14] Linear progressions, Jaffe argues, lead librarians away from the actual practice of librarianship into the management hierarchy whose role it is to monitor, control and structure the work of frontline professionals. The Steady State career focuses on honing one's professional library skills, *doing* collection development, reference or reader's advisory work rather than monitoring and measuring the performance of others. Jaffe sees the role of a manager as akin to that of the department chair in a university department: a professional peer who has agreed to free professional colleagues from some operational tasks for a period of time. The assumption that managers are more important to libraries than are librarians is negated by this model, which calls for according commensurate salaries to those offering direct service.

There may be problems associated with full participatory management in public libraries. For one, decision-making about major policies is not considered the province of the library administration, but is vested in the board of trustees. Further, public funds are granted by municipalities for the provision of certain library services based upon a clear understanding articulated through the budget of what will comprise those services. They are not subject to revision by library employees and can only be modified by action of the Board with consent of the municipality. In addition, there are dangers that accountability may be lost as the decision-making process grows more diffuse.[15] Finally, groups arrive at decisions much more slowly than do individuals.

Nonetheless, some employee participation in management is well established in libraries and interest in furthering it is growing rapidly. Most departments, for instance, operate in an egalitarian fashion, making decisions about non-personnel issues collegially.

Teamwork and individual initiative are widely encouraged. Implementation of participation is enhanced when distinctions between advisory and decision-making roles are clear. Failure to distinguish them may lead to disgruntled employees and poor staff morale.

If the decision-making about a matter under consideration is in fact delegated to staff, then the director must be prepared to accept and live with the outcome. The presence of a staff union or an employee organization usually serves as stimulant and aid to participation. Those who have been active in them are often anxious to increase participation and have received good training in functioning together as a decision-making unit.

Among the deterrents to the type of organizational change that incorporates increased participation may be managers accustomed to hierarchical structures who want to maintain a tight rein rather than relinquish some control to ambiguity.

> Managers comfortable with the old structured environment will devote little planning to the new change effort because they are unable and unwilling to envision and seriously consider the contingency of change.[16]

At bottom, participation may be a balancing act between management control and team opportunity; between quick and easy decisions and giving people an opportunity to deliberate; between too little team spirit and too much.[17]

COMMUNICATION IN ORGANIZATIONS

Among the critical factors predicting the success or failure of an organization is the system of communication by which its people are linked. This includes both the message and the way in which it is transmitted. Its importance cannot be underestimated.

> Communication within a library has been defined as the process
> ...whereby attitudes, directives, ideas, information, opinions, orders, etc. are transmitted and shared among and between the

persons working within that organization as well as with users, governing authorities and boards and other relevant external individuals and groups.[18]

Morale suffers when employees are unaware of events or actions that occur in or about the library. All libraries, like other organizations, have formal and informal channels of communication. Formal channels follow paths established by the formal organization. Informal channels of communication follow the grapevine.

Formal communications may be either written or oral. Public libraries generally utilize memos, letters, reports, directives and policies. Most libraries have staff manuals and rule books, some publish newsletters, virtually all produce annual reports. Written communications provide lasting records and ensure uniformity in policy matters. They are also efficient in that large numbers of people can be notified fairly easily. Unfortunately, the ease of duplication often causes too many messages to be sent, a phenomenon as undesirable as the production of too few written communications. The result may be message overload and employee failure to continue reading. Many libraries generate poorly written, unclear documents that give rise to ambiguity and misinterpretation, and written communications provide no opportunity for immediate feedback and clarification.

Among the important written communications are the periodic reports systems require to monitor performance and judge effectiveness. Most public libraries collect monthly statistical and narrative reports of unit activities, with annual summations at the end of fiscal years. They include, among other information, numbers of books and other materials circulated, numbers added, numbers of reference questions posed and numbers of programs conducted and their attendance. The narrative component attempts to interpret the quantitative data and to convey a sense of the effectiveness of services performed. Annual reports in public libraries have taken some dramatic forms in recent years. Summaries of the year's activities appear on shopping bags, posters, calendars and postcards. They tell the story of a year in the life of a library, trying to capture the excitement in a lively fashion. Automation has effected a minor revolution in libraries' ability to manipulate and massage statistical data and to generate reports. Management Information Systems (MIS) provide library decision makers with accurate and timely information on which to base decisions. "The focus of MIS is to capture, organize, analyze, compare, and repeat a range of data describing library activities, services and management."[19]

Oral communications make immediate response possible. Indeed, they offer the best opportunity to resolve rapidly conflict situations. Nonetheless, they can lead to some of the same problems that plague written communications. Lack of clarity of expression carries similar dangers regarding ambiguity and misunderstanding. Further, sending messages verbally can be extremely time-consuming when large groups of people must be informed.

Informal organizational communication is remarkably efficient at moving information. In addition,

> studies of the grapevine have shown that this means of communication is fairly accurate with over 75% of the messages being transmitted correctly[20]

Many librarians report that the janitor holds the key to informing staff about library happenings, emptying wastebaskets while spreading news and gossip. The grapevine is much faster at moving information than are formal channels. It can also cause trouble. The only method found successful in curtailing excesses and misinformation caused by the grapevine is the issuance of clear, concise, complete and up-to-date communications through formal communication channels.

Electronic mail is beginning to establish new communication patterns in libraries. It is rapid, easy to produce, flexible and relatively inexpensive. Messages can be generally distributed or aimed at target audiences, made permanent or destroyed without adding to the paper file. Recipients can provide immediate feedback, can question ambiguities and make suggestions.

TECHNOLOGY AND ORGANIZATIONAL CHANGE

The traditional library's organization structure is built around files; without the files, units begin to disappear and the organization chart shrinks.[21] New methods of document storage and retrieval will inevitably lead to new library organizing configurations. Staff will be less rooted to locations. Catalogers no longer need to be in proximity to a catalog to accomplish their job, nor do those who check in serials or place orders. As communities become increasingly wired, access is less limited to place and more dependent on the user's knowledge of how to gain entry to information and how to evaluate it. Online database searching, online catalogs, electronic mail delivery systems can convey materials directly to homes and offices. Users do not have to appear in person at libraries to receive service. Public service departments responsible for charging and checking in materials may have fewer items on which to exercise their procedures.

Public libraries must be flexible in order to meet the challenges of an environment made uncertain by the new technology. The traditional bifurcated, or trifurcated structure discussed above is undergoing careful scrutiny based on the impact of automation, the implication of other technological advancements and increased understanding of how organizations function.[22] It is possible, for instance that systems units may serve as intra-library centralizing forces given their potential to encompass the work of cataloging, circulation and acquisition. In traditional libraries, departments work autonomously. New procedures for accomplishing work are applicable only to one function -- cataloging, acquisitions, and so on. The interrelationship between departments made necessary by automated systems means that change is likely to affect the entire organization or least a substantial part of it. As a result, alterations in the library's decision-making structure will also be required. The complexity of decisions, their far-reaching implications, means that the risks associated with implementation are far greater and that decisions must be made at a higher administrative levels. Automation leads to other organizational modifications in libraries. Personnel are added and decreased. The ratio of professional to support staff tends to shift in favor of the latter as day-to-day operations become more routine -- tasks of sorting, filing, counting are taken over by computer. New nonprofessional jobs, however, often require increased support staff who have greater skills, experience and training. Automation may deprofessionalize some formerly professional tasks. For instance, many public libraries are forming production-oriented, rapid cataloging units where the tasks are basically clerical, in contrast with traditional cataloging departments whose work is primarily of an intellectual nature. There is some evidence of a gradual shift in personnel resources away from cataloging and acquisitions toward public service activities.[23]

Technology may have an opposite impact on the organization of an information service. Demand for online database searching may necessitate not only additional professional staff, but service delivered through formal appointments. New data bases often require knowledge of the subjects they cover, or, at a minimum, of their protocols. Not all members of a reference department can perform all searches.

SUMMARY

The primary aim of the library's organizational structure is to deliver the best possible library service to a community. Its second goal is to insure the institution's efficient and effective operation. Finally, the administrative arrangement is designed to motivate employees to reach their potential and gain job satisfaction. The internal structure of the library helps fulfill these three roles. However, the formal organization is only as successful as the actions of the administration and staff. How employees work with one another, the degree to which they understand and share goals, the extent to which the library director and staff can articulate the

organization's goals and mount a plan for their achievement --
these are of far greater moment to the accomplishments of the
library.

Changes in organizational thinking during the past fifty years
have led to a flattening of the traditional, hierarchical library
pyramid. Decisions are reached by a broadened population base,
particularly in matters of library planning. Participation in library
management is likely to increase as public library organizations
accommodate to changing societal demands and new technological
developments.

NOTES AND SUGGESTED READINGS

Notes

1. John Pfiffner and Frank P. Sherwood, *Administrative Organization*
(Englewood Cliffs, NJ: Prentice, 1960), 32.

2. Peter Drucker, *Management: Tasks Responsibilities Practices* (New
York: Harper, 1974), 39.

3. See Ernest DeProspo et al., *Performance Measures for Public
Libraries* (Chicago: American Library Association), 1973.

4. Vernon Palmour et al., *A Planning Process for Public Libraries*
(Chicago: American Library Association), 198.

5. Charles McClure, *Planning and Role Setting for Public Libraries*
(Chicago: American Library Association), 1987.

6. See, for instance, Charles McClure et al., or Floyd Dickman, *Long
Range Planning for Public Libraries*. Occasional Paper. Revised Edition,
Series 1, No. 1-6, October 1988. (Columbus, OH: The State Library of
Ohio), 1988.

7. McClure, 28.

8. Dickman, 1.

9. Roles described by McClure and Dickman have been combined.

10. F. William Summers, "Roads Not Taken: Some Thoughts about Librarianship," in Charles Curran and F. William Summers, eds. *Library Performance, Accountability and Responsiveness (Norwood, NJ: Ablex, 1990)*, 128.

11. Paul John Cirino, *The Business of Running a Library* (Jefferson, NC: McFarland, 1991), 167.

12. William Fisher and Beth Brin, "Parallel Organization: A Structural Change Theory," *Journal of Library Administration* 14 (1991): 51-66.

13. Joan Bechtel, "Collegial Management Breeds Success," *American Libraries* 12 (November 1981): 605-7.

14. Martin Jaffe, "The Road Less Traveled: An Alternative to the Bureaucratic Model of Librarianship," *Wilson Library Bulletin* 65 (Dec. 1990): 49-51.

15. Dennis Dickenson, "Some Reflections on Participatory Management in Libraries," *College and Research Libraries* 39 (July, 1978): 253-262.

16. Jennifer Cargill and Gisela Webb, *Managing Libraries in Transition* (Phoenix: Oryx Press. 1988), 22.

17. Robert Stueart and Barbara Moran, *Library Management.* 4th ed. (Littleton, CO: Libraries Unlimited, 1993), 284.

18. Norman Stevens. *Communication Throughout Libraries* (Metuchen, NJ: Scarecrow Press, 1983), 25.

19. Charles McClure et al., "Design of a Public Library Managment Information System: A Status Report," *Library Administration and Management* 23 (Fall, 1989): 192.

20. Stueart and Moran, 233.

21. Richard Boss, *The Library Manager's Guide to Automation.* 3rd ed. (Boston, MA: G.K. Hall, 1990). 130.

22. Peggy John, "Matrix Management. An Organizational Alternative for Libraries," *Journal of Academic Librarianship* 16 (September 1990): 222-229.

23. Charles Martel, *The Client Centered Academic Library* (Westport, CT: Greenwood Press, 1988), 5.

Suggested Readings

Cargill, Jennifer and Gisela Webb. *Managing Libraries in Transition.* Phoenix, AZ: Oryx Press, 1988.

Cirino, Paul John. *The Business of Running a Library.* Jefferson, NC: McFarland, 1991.

Drucker, Peter. *Managing the Non-Profit Corporation.* New York: Harper, 1990.

Lynch, Beverly, ed. *Management Strategies for Libraries: A Basic Reader.* New York: Neal-Schuman, 1985.

McClure, Charles, et al. *Planning and Role Setting for Public Libraries.* Chicago: American Library Association, 1987.

Martin, Lowell. *Organizational Structure of Libraries.* Metuchen, NJ: Scarecrow Press, 1984.

Reed, Sally Gardner. *Small Libraries: A Handbook for Successful Management.* Jefferson, NC: McFarland., 1991.

Riggs, Donald, ed. *Library Communication.* Chicago: American Library Association,1991.

Riggs, Donald. *Strategic Planning for Library Managers.* Phoenix, AZ: Oryx, 1984.

Sager, Donald. *Participatory Management in Libraries.* Metuchen, NJ: Scarecrow Press, 1982.

Stevens, Norman. *Communication Throughout Libraries.* Metuchen, NJ: Scarecrow Press, 1983.

Stueart, Robert and Barbara Moran. *Library Management.* 4th ed. Littleton, CO: Libraries Unlimited, 1993.

Underwood, Peter. *Managing Change in Libraries and Information Services.* London: Clive Bingley, 1990.

Wozny, Jay. *Checklists for Public Library Managers.* Metuchen, NJ: Scarecrow Press, 1989.

CHAPTER 7

TECHNOLOGY

The current public library reveals a dramatic migration from a simple manual culture to an increasingly automated, technological environment. It is rare now to find any library not utilizing some application of computer technology. Similarly, it is uncommon for an information worker to make no use of computers or of products generated by them during the course of each day.

It may be true, as Verna Pungitore contends, that libraries have always utilized technology, albeit of a largely manual and highly labor intensive nature, if the definition of technology in an organizational context is

> the combination of resources and processes that are used to transform inputs (raw materials) into outputs (products or services). Resources would include the skills of the people who work in the organization as well as the materials and equipment that are involved in the transformation process.[1]

But few would deny that the shift to computers and other technologies represents a transformation whose far-reaching effects are only beginning to surface and be addressed.

The tentacles of technology reach into every corner of the library, involving each user and staff member, and multiplying the channels through which information can flow. Advances occur at a pace so rapid that libraries are unable to immediately grasp their ramifications. Harnessing new technology to library processes means altering work practices, work relationships, attitudes and levels of expertise, and effecting technical changes to processes and equipment. Librarians are forced once again to confront and seek answers to profound and fundamental questions regarding the nature of the public library -- its roles, purposes and ethics. They must consider who can gain access, and to what information. They must investigate how the new technology will affect the private lives of individual citizens. They must learn about who owns and controls the information industry and discuss the consequences of limited ownership to free access to information. The recent quandary about whether the Library of Congress can, will or should charge for online access to its collections deeply effects federal information policy, the rights of citizen access to information and the livelihood of private sector information agencies. Simply stated, librarians are forced to come to grips with the changes technology may portend for human life and interaction.

In some quarters, automation is embraced as a larger-than-life panacea to all library problems. In others, it is viewed, in similar grandiose proportions, as a threat to the very foundations of humanistic values on which the public library has traditionally rested. Bringing both positions down to size is achieved by recognizing that technology is simply a tool whose employment and control remain in the hands of human beings. Realizing that automation, for instance, is not always the solution to a library's problems and, additionally, that it remains subject to human error, restores perspective.

A more formidable question is whether new technologies presage the death of public libraries, at least as we know them. Increasingly, libraries face commercial competition from electronic systems like videotext or from information brokers who respond to telephone queries for a fee. People choose communication channels that are easy, fast to use and cost little. Why should users seek help from a public library when searches to remote databases can be made either directly without public library mediation or by a paid searcher who will do it for them? Technology has the potential to provide individual citizens with the tools to satisfy their own information needs. Happily, at least two factors militate against the early demise of the public library. For one, information-related activities are just one facet of a library's service. And second, while skilled laypersons may be able to gain access to the vast networks that are quickly being mounted and developed, most people have little idea about their existence and even less about how to achieve entry into them. The growth of home computers is far slower than had been predicted and the use to which they have been put much more circumscribed -- only word processing, games and spread sheets are common.

HISTORY OF LIBRARY AUTOMATION

Early efforts to automate library functions occurring shortly after World War II centered around mechanizing cataloging and classification, although Vannevar Bush had described his Memex machine, a prototype design of a scholar workstation in 1945.[2] Shortly thereafter the concept of an integrated library system, one based on a single, machine-readable bibliographic master file of the library's holdings that would permit many of the library's tasks, particularly those of a routine nature, to be performed without moving from module to module, was proposed. The two impulses merged in the construction of an automated card catalog which could serve as a central source for cataloging and circulation. Wish lists containing hoped-for sub-systems that would handle acquisitions, manage statistical information and provide public access were compiled by so-called visionaries whose vindication finally came with the arrival of "On-line Public Access Computers" (OPACs) in the early 1980s. These integrated library systems utilized a central data source for all record management and display, one that could be revised by computer keyed-in corrections and was friendly in its search capabilities.

The thrust to automate was a product of both societal and

technological events. Pushing its rapid deployment were needs for accountability, financial considerations, rising expectations of the populace with regard to information access and increased interdependency. Because the history is so recent, distinguishing among and between societal trends to determine which was most influential is difficult. The following must all be considered to have played a major role.

The notion of *accountability* came to public libraries in the mid-1970s as municipalities began to demand documentation about activities and outcomes based on measurable units that could be compared from year to year. The need to be accountable induced librarians to begin to plan for the future, to review their current programs and generally to rationalize their activities. The ability of computers to generate information about who was using what part of the collection provided librarians with a compelling argument in favor of automating -- at least some functions.

A second force was the renewed need for *economic belt-tightening*. Librarians were compelled to review their allocations for materials and services. Automation with its labor-saving promises began to look attractive.

A third factor driving automation was the increased importance attached to information by more *enlightened clientele,* who insisted not only on its potential availability but on its immediate provision. For this group, effectiveness, not economy, was the point.

Finally, new advancements in *networks and other cooperative activities* brought with them requirements for the generation of accurate, shareable information. Computers permitted ease in compiling union catalogs, insured that librarians geographically distant would have access to the same information, and helped monitor cost-sharing among participants in the system.[3]

Bibliographic utilities, an infrastructure invention, made their appearance in the 1960s. The Ohio College Library Center, OCLC's orginal name, was begun in 1967 as an attempt to initiate cooperatively machine-readable bibliographic data bases. OCLC was the brainchild of the Ohio College Association, a group of higher education leaders, and Fred Kilgour of Yale University and Ralph Parker of the University of Missouri. Its goal was to maintain and operate a computerized regional library center that would serve all the academic libraries of Ohio and become part of any national network that might be established. Kilgour became its first president.

OCLC initially sought to produce subsystems for shared cataloging, serials control, technical processes, circulation control and subject and title access for users. By 1970 its online catalog card production system became operational, and in 1971 the shared cataloging system was installed. Membership was opened to public libraries in 1972, and service extended to regional groups outside of Ohio. In 1977, it changed its name to Online Computer Library Center, retaining the OCLC acronym, but reflecting its now national character. As of 1993, OCLC has over 16,448 members world wide and its data base contains more than 27 million records.

New advances in hardware, too, facilitated the rapid spread of technology. Main frame computers, extremely expensive and massive in size, gave way to minicomputers, which were smaller, but still costly, then to microcomputers and personal computers, and finally to supermicrocomputers

> multiuser, multitasking systems that can use the software developed for minicomputers while bringing library automation to libraries with less than $100,000 to spend."[4]

By the turn of the coming century, the majority of libraries will be automated, but not paperless.[5]

EFFECTS OF AUTOMATION ON LIBRARIANS

Initially, librarians greeted automation attempts with skepticism, if not dismay. Computers were user unfriendly, their protocols difficult to understand and follow, and librarians were unschooled in their manipulation. As systems became less complex, librarians soon recognized their potential labor-saving and service-expanding capabilities. Today they investigate each new advancement with interest and excitement.

But each new advancement carries the commensurate demand that librarians attain mastery of it. Librarians must be able to manage information technology based on knowledge of its limits and potential. They must maintain awareness of the state of the art both in libraries and in other settings, and of future improvements. Familiarity with recent research into individual patterns of information-seeking behavior and into knowledge based construction is yet another imperative. Finally, public librarians must be aware of social issues affected by information technologies such as what constitutes violation of copyright, privacy and intellectual freedom.[6]

Librarians have seen significant alterations in job responsibilities and assignments as a result of technology. Some formerly professional positions can be handled by support staff. Technicians, rather than professional librarians, currently complete 86% of library cataloging. On the other hand, professional reference librarians find that searching online demands at least as much skill, judgment and experience as it does in print format, negating the possibility of delegating those tasks to staff with lesser training.

The threat that automation will replace some workers with machines is real and requires diplomatic handling. While it is legitimate to terminate the services of employees when their job assignments no longer exist, the serious effects on staff morale of dismissing workers make this step extremely problematic and worrisome. A far better approach is to depend on attrition rather than termination whenever possible. At the same time, technical assistants whose mastery of automation results in greater productivity deserve increased compensation.

Staff feel the effects of technology through increased public demand. More and more library users, particularly young ones, are "computer literate," comfortable in front of a terminal and encountering little difficulty in understanding basic protocols. This leads inevitably to heightened expectations. Users recognize no boundaries to information. More and more library patrons who own computers and equip them with modems (telephone connectors) demand remote dial-up access to library files. They want to know whether information relevant to their needs exists, regardless of where it is housed or from whom it may be obtained. And they want it as soon as possible, no matter where it is located and what the difficulties are in obtaining it. These same users are more likely to accord increased respect to librarians who seem to have mastered apparently sophisticated technology. Automation empowers staff as well as conferring on them a mantle of expertise that was previously nonexistent or less apparent.

On the other hand, some library users may be technophobics, intimidated and embarrassed by and reluctant to use computers, even expressing anger at the lack of availability of the familiar card catalog. As a result while

> more people have greater access to a larger store of information than at any time in the past...it is incorrect to assume that the depth and breadth of individual access is growing...People do not know that the information is there, or if they do, they have no clear sense of how to penetrate the cryptic maze that surrounds it.[7]

Many library schools have recognized the impact of technology on library professionals and have incorporated advanced training of both a theoretical and practical nature into their curricula. But workers in smaller, more remote libraries are often denied the opportunity to acquire needed competencies. This deficiency, in turn, serves to widen the already existing gap between society's information haves and have-nots.

LIBRARY USES OF COMPUTERS

The computer represents a high speed, reliable method of dealing with routine, day-to-day library calculations and processes. John Cirino maintains that "Anything involving paper can be accomplished more efficiently and stored more rapidly using less space when it is computerized."[8] Its benefits are well-suited to the repetitive procedures that are related to charging and discharging materials and conducting inventories (circulation), with entering, retrieving, and expunging bibliographic records (cataloging and classifying), with acquiring and discarding library materials (collection development), and with identifying sources of materials located elsewhere (interlibrary loan). In addition, activities associated with internal office, personnel and financial procedures are particularly amenable to automation. Finally, computers have enabled libraries to collect more of the information needed to make informed management decisions about the allocation of resources.

Computers increase libraries' abilities to serve directly their publics. They permit large quantities of material to be searched for needed information. Through keyword access techniques, recently devised algorithms and other sophisticated protocols, materials heretofore virtually unretrievable can be rapidly delivered from remote locations as well as from local ones. In many libraries journal citations, encyclopedias, dictionaries, and thesauri are available through the Online Public Access Computer (OPAC). Forecasters maintain that low cost, copyright protected, full text retrieval systems, connected to present bibliographical databases, with user friendly information management techniques are just around the corner. Already available in a number of institutions are library generated data bases containing information about community resources. Libraries have incorporated into OPACs information about voting, demographics, careers, community agencies, clubs, organizations, adult education courses and calendars of community events.[9]

Computers are being employed as in-house and external communication systems. Electronic messaging (E-Mail) though not without drawbacks permits rapid and effective macro and micro mail delivery. Access to public library information through Internet, the electronic network, has burgeoned within the past two or three years. Office automation capabilities have been added to the potential uses of the online integrated system. Ideally, says Richard Boss, office microcomputers would be able to function as terminals to the library system as well as performing filing, word-processing and other office tasks. Records could then be passed back and forth between the two systems.[10]

Within the foreseeable future computer based library systems will include 1) traditional automated library systems; 2) public access terminals; 3) online search services; 4) electronic publishing; 5) electronic delivery; 6) micro-based videodisc services; 7) nonbibliographic databases; and 8) personal computers and scholar work stations.[11]

AUTOMATING THE LIBRARY

While most public libraries today use the output of computers, they remain, nonetheless, at fairly primitive levels of automation. For those who adopted technology early, one generation of computers has already succeeded another. Libraries that came to automation later or are just beginning to plan for it have profited from the mistakes made by their predecessors who learned how complex, time-consuming, and costly the planning processes involved in automation can be.

Budget implications are considerable. Major alterations may be necessary, including organizational changes, revisions in library policies and procedures, changes in the attitudes of staff and patrons and detailed contractual obligations. Richard Boss warns that automation is too complex and costly to be undertaken without first engaging in extensive investigation, discussion and decision making.[12]

Most libraries cannot afford completely integrated systems. The components they choose to acquire vary. It is for this reason that what constitutes an integrated system for one library may be its primitive ancestor for another.

> Automating piecemeal, however, can result in greater expense, public frustration and poor use of staff time. Automation should be based on a logical plan, even if only one application is currently being considered.[13]

As in any planning process, it becomes important to ask what you wish the system to do. The time to determine its characteristics is during the design phase. Making alterations once a system has been installed is tedious and expensive. Subsystems are arranged in order of desirability, and determinations made about which to acquire. College libraries tend to produce their public catalog first and then institute a circulation system. Public libraries often reverse the steps. Small libraries may have to decide whether they will purchase stand-alone systems, or whether their automation will be a cooperative or consortia effort.

Prudence would suggest that before the project advances too far it be sold to funding authorities and to the public. Library trustees must understand the need for automation, particularly in face of its high cost and the potential difficulties that every library faces during the conversion process. While it may be obvious that automation projects cannot proceed without sufficient funds, administrators sometimes forget that without appropriate staff, they can neither be mounted nor continued. Depending on a single employee to provide all the electronic data processing expertise is foolhardy. The entire operation could be jeopardized should that person decide to take another position.

Risk is involved in any computer project. Among the hazards are inadequate resources, negative patron attitudes, a fear of failure on the part of administrators and, finally, the danger that there will be a loss of commitment to the project brought on by financial difficulties of the vendor, administrative realtering of budget priorities leading to funding cutoff, and staff resistance to automation.[14] A number of important decisions must be made after the initial determinations have been reached about the nature of the service to be provided.

Consultants

1. Should a *consultant* be hired? If so, at what stage? Consultants are most valuable when staff expertise is limited, as is frequently the case in public libraries. If there are staff

knowledgeable about the technology and familiar with basic terminology, or if the library has access to specialists working for the municipality, the services of a consultant may be dispensed with, at least at the earliest stages. Consultants are extremely valuable when translating the idiosyncracies of a library's processes into general requirements for subsystems. Automated systems demand a uniformity and internal consistency that differs from a library's current flexible approach to file maintenance and policy interpretation. Consultants can help staff apply specific descriptions of local practices to systems where rules dictate more rigid applications. They can also recognize when protocols are intrinsic to a system and when local modification is possible. Among the other important contributions consultants make is to assist librarians in reaching decisions about performance levels for new systems, and aiding staff to digest technical knowledge. Consultants may be asked to write or review requests for proposals, negotiate with vendors, and, in general, guide the library in its expectations and actions. While their charges range between $400 and $1,000 a day, when properly utilized they may save the library sizeable amounts of money by limiting the possibility of costly error and reducing the amount of staff time spent in becoming knowledgeable. Hiring a consultant does not suggest that staff can relinquish their obligation to learn about automation. At the start of the project it is useful to consult handbooks on computers. They all include some form of activities checklists that specialists leading the project will follow. They also provide clear definitions for generalists who may find discussions with consultants dominated by the language of computer science and, therefore, difficult to follow. Nor does hiring a consultant mean that the library staff can abdicate its responsibility for deciding which system is best for the library. The ultimate choice rests with the administration and the board.

Types of Systems

2. Which *type of system* should be procured? Libraries may

choose from an array of options acquired through one of the four following sources:

a. *Selecting a Turnkey System.* In a turnkey system the hardware and the software are supplied by the vendor who takes responsibility for the installation and training, and offers ongoing support of both the hardware and software. Among the advantages of turnkey systems are low cost, firm prices, firm delivery dates, and known features.

b. *Purchasing software packages and mounting them on a separately procured computer system.* If the hardware is already available, this is the method of choice. Unfortunately, in this situation no one is charged with the responsibility for assuring that the hardware and software are compatible and work together.

c. *Developing In-house Systems.* In-house development permits libraries to control the design of a system. A high degree of staff expertise is required, however. Very few libraries possess the staff skills or financial resources to mount their own integrated systems, but a number have produced modules for single functions, particularly when available software does not satisfy library demands. Fewer libraries are creating their own systems as turnkey systems become more widely available.[15]

d. *Utilizing data-processing facilities and staff of the library's municipality.* There are dramatic cost benefits when someone else's data processing computer is used. However the system's design must be based on broad institutional procedures and priorities rather than on the library's. A major upgrade may be required to accommodate the system to the library needs with expenses so great that purchasing a smaller, stand-alone system may be preferable.[16]

The Automation Team

3. Who should serve on the *Automation Team* and what are its *responsibilities?*

The automation task is usually assigned to a committee composed of representatives from acquisitions, cataloging, reference and circulation. A trustee may meet with the group, either as a non-voting member or as a full participant. The staff member most knowledgeable about library automation may be designated as the committee's leader with the library director acting as overseer, critic, advisor, encourager and enthusiast,[17] until the moment of the final decision when his or her involvement is mandatory.

The work of the committee is tension-producing. Its decisions are far-reaching and involve large financial commitments. Myriad choices are available and vendors make extravagant promises about forthcoming modules. Fears arise about making the wrong decision, particularly since, as a rule, the library must live with the system it selects for at least five years. Systematically comparing the capabilities of various subsystems helps to reduce the options and alleviate anxiety.

Visits to sites where systems similar to the ones being sought have been installed assists in clarifying their relative benefits and disadvantages. Committee members unfamiliar with the intricacies of automation may profit from seeing the print descriptions translated into practice. Face-to-face conversations also serve as opportunities to acquire information about vendors. A company that can boast a cluster of satisfied users in similar public libraries has much to recommend it. Problems with vendors that have been encountered by libraries can be noted and subsequently discussed to avoid misapprehensions and misunderstandings about product performance. It makes no sense to contract with vendors simply because they are associated with user groups whose members are from prestigious public libraries. Nonetheless, the presence of an active user group can help to insure pressure on vendors to produce needed software modules, or to devise methods of achieving particular goals. Current software systems lack the capability to generate some information needed by managers to make decisions and many libraries report dissatisfaction with acquisitions subsystems. These are good topics for user groups.

The automation team sets performance specifications, in outline form, for what the library expects the system to be capable of doing. This includes, among other considerations, minimum capacity, expandability, conformity to standards, software design, hardware configuration, delivery schedule and total cost over five years.[18]

The final contract describes these previously-agreed upon performance specifications, a delivery schedule, terms of payment, a maintenance program for both hardware and software and an acceptance test plan specifying a percent of consistent performance for a period of 30 days. Clauses are generally inserted in contracts that provide penalties should the contract fail to meet the completion target.

Implementation Steps

4. What implementation steps must be taken? The four most time-consuming steps for the library during the implementation process are staff training, record conversion, bar-coding and program promotion, including user instruction.

Without enthusiastic staff, no system can succeed. For this reason alone, it is crucial to transmit information to the staff about the work of the automation committee as it progresses and to begin training as soon as the contract is signed. Training includes a basic orientation to the system's capabilities and in depth practice in its use. Unfamiliarity breeds anxiety, which in turn, has a negative impact on performance.

Transforming the library's bibliographic data base into machine-readable records is time-consuming and complicated. Decisions must be made about how many items will be included. To be effective, circulation systems must incorporate at least 50% of the library's records and online catalogs 100% beginning with a specific imprint date.[19] Libraries must also decide whether to include serials, manuscripts, maps, audiovisual and foreign language materials, all of which are more expensive to input than English language monographs.

Bar-coding, affixing identification symbols that link bibliographic data to physical volumes, may represent the automation processes' largest headache. Librarians either remember the experience as a nightmare or, when it has been well-planned or run smoothly, as a unifying one. Teams that include all staff work in pairs to mark the material and enter the identification into the computer. The work is intensive and subject to considerable human error. It is no wonder that tempers sometimes fray.

No single approach will be sufficient to publicize the program and explain it to users. Different audiences require different orientation techniques. Patrons will want to know both how to use the computer and what its advantages are for them. Newspaper articles, handouts, interviews and displays are all channels through which messages about the systems may be distributed. Demonstrations to groups and individuals are probably the most effective means for disseminating information about online systems. They are time-consuming and labor intensive, but the benefits more than justify the efforts.

Costs

5. How much will the system *cost*? It is expensive to purchase an automated system and to maintain it. In the early days, librarians routinely claimed that automation was linked to cost savings, increased productivity and decreases in staff. By now, however, it is common knowledge

> that automation does not reduce library expenditures. Increased costs are the rule and are justified by the capacity to provide improved and enhanced services...Although successive generations of equipment and software may allow us to access information more effectively and faster than ever before, the need to replace expensive equipment in a three to five year time span is a real challenge and contrasts dramatically with replacement of traditional equipment such as desks, chairs and bookshelves.[20]

The cost of manual operation compared with those of automation are no longer compared because the operational benefits of the latter are so clear. In addition, while the size of the staff may not be diminished, savings in staff time to undertake, for instance, bibliographic searches using on-line databases rather than manual sources, may be applied to other problems which have never before been properly addressed. Automation then, may not result in actual dollar savings, but it greatly expands the value of the service provided.

Computer charges decrease as hardware is miniaturized and use rises. However, there are many additional costs associated with acquiring an automation system that must be taken into account when calculating the required investment. It is important to know the charges that will accrue over a five year period and at what stage payments will be necessary. Up-front charges can destroy the financial stability of an institution if not factored in with sufficient lead time. Further, the ongoing costs to maintain the system can run as high as 25% of the original price, although they typically average 12%.[21]

Some libraries have chosen to fund automated systems with bond issues. Others have attempted to pay for them with operating funds, a difficult task. Most municipalities have held that both software and hardware are legitimate capital costs if included as part of a total system package.

OTHER TECHNOLOGIES

Telecommunications: Allied to the growth of computer technology has been the increased capacity to rapidly process and transmit messages between remote locations. While automation has resulted in the ability of libraries to provide sophisticated entry to and analysis of large amounts of information, enhanced telecommunication enables it to be transmitted from point to point, reducing the need for retention of copious amounts of on-site information. As fiber optics replaces conventional wire, the use of telecommunications is likely to expand still further, reducing the pendulum swing from standalone software -- CD-ROM databases, for instance -- running on personal computers to centrally organized time-sharing systems.[22]

The widespread use of facsimile transmission (FAX) permits libraries to communicate messages instantaneously and rapidly retrieve materials for patrons that heretofore would have required days and weeks. FAX is reliable, cost-effective and by now so pervasive as to be almost universal.

CD Technology: Compact disc (CD) technology provides on-site stored information. Its use in public libraries has grown substantially in recent years, particularly as more and more bibliographic data bases are transferred to that format. Whereas on-line computer technology requires telecommunication to transfer information from point to point, CD data bases necessitate only onsight terminals to provide access. They are generally far easier for the public to search than are on-line data bases. Unlike on-line data bases, however, discs are not constantly updated and must be replaced periodically.

Additional Technologies: Video tapes and other visual and aural technologies have produced decision problems for many libraries. Some refuse to collect them; others see no impediment to imposing charges for them; and still others have embraced them with a fervor that violates all library principles of collection building. (See Chapter 8.) Underlying the conflict is the difficulty some librarians experience in understanding that styles of learning may change and that print is not always superior to other formats. Historically, public libraries have been hesitant to accept non-print materials. Film collections were seldom viewed as more than supplementary. The same held true for pictures and slides and few libraries collected them systematically.

The impact of television is probably far greater than that exercised by film or even by radio. Hollywood had a profound influence on American values, but neither it nor radio served as the primary source of information. Television does. Pictures make people knowledgeable about the world.

As more and more information is available in non-print formats libraries will have to confront the nature of their collections and determine how best to package and disseminate information. Learning in the future seems likely to be based on both print and non-print images, mutually reinforcing one another, and libraries will have to adjust.

Among the still young and developing technologies are Artificial Intelligence (AI) and Robotics. Expert systems and improved computer technology have created machines that perform complex tasks. For instance, we already use AI in helping to diagnose medical problems and in troubleshooting engines. It shows great promise for improving the way in which information and materials requests are handled. Robotics makes Artificial Intelligence mobile and perhaps ambulatory. Its ramifications and applications for libraries have yet to be explored.

In the relatively near future transmission will be speeded and new interfaces and linkages between systems will appear. Circuit chips which today have capacities of slightly over one million components will be able to accommodate 30-100 million. Microcomputers will be able to process 20-40 million instructions per second compared with 1-3 million today. Optical storage density is predicted to increase by a factor of six through data compression and other techniques. End-to-end digital phone systems will carry text, data, graphics, pictures and full-motion video as well as voice. Desktop publishing, electronic mail, voice messaging, teleconferencing, internal and external databases, optical character readers and image scanners will become familiar and much easier to use.[23]

THE LIMITS OF TECHNOLOGY

Reading the literature of technology is an exhilerating, intoxicating experience. Claims made about the transforming powers of technology are convincing, particularly in their promises to provide excellent library service. But knowledgeable librarians know how excessive and misleading they may be. To suggest that technological change is possible does not imply that it is desirable.

Each innovation produces unanticipated drawbacks as it produces benefits. All new technologies create ripple effects on library services. Facsimile transmission, for instance, was originally employed by libraries solely for interlibrary loan and acquisitions tasks. The introduction of low-cost facsimile machines for office and home use now gives individuals the capacity to request delivery of materials from the library directly to them and libraries can anticipate heavy demand for this service. Unfortunately, the very positive aspects of this innovation are partially offset by the increased demands for staff service that it produces. Locating, retrieving and delivering requested materials involves considerable work and few libraries have extra labor readily available.

Past experience teaches us that the easier the technology is to use, the more it will be employed. Motivation to master a more complicated innovation can be generated when a potential user understands the degree to which a task may be simplified by its use. Current practices, therefore, do not necessarily predict those that will follow. For example, libraries of all forms have promoted access to "information" as one of their primary goals. Some library experts, however, agree with Tom Ballard's contention that

> Present assumptions about the future of the public library seem to have little basis in fact. Whatever rate of growth is occurring in publishing and electronic data storage -- the "information explosion" -- it seems to have little effect on public library agencies where use is determined by proximity to the home, educational attainment levels and what is on the shelf at the time of the patron's visit.[24]

These same critics contend that money allocated to technology that supports resource sharing and information retrieval is ill spent. Rather, they argue, the major emphasis should be on collecting library materials locally since it is here that needs appear to exist. Those who take the opposite position point to the large numbers of information seekers using public libraries and maintain that the improved performance provided by new technology will encourage even greater use of information services. At the heart of the argument is a contention that would probably find agreement in both quarters. Patrons' needs should shape technological change, rather than needs being shaped by technological advances.

SUMMARY

As public library technology migrates from manual to automated, the effects on materials, staff and the public are consequential. Work assignments, information seeking behavior, materials acquisition, and document identification and delivery all change. Technology can be harnessed to help achieve library goals and objectives. Unchecked, it may determine them. Because expenses associated with automating are significant, careful planning is required to assure that needs and benefits are justified by so large a commitment of resources. Sensitivity to the potentially deleterious effects of automation and other technologies demands that staff and patron anxieties be handled delicately and with care, and that attention be paid to the larger societal implications of their employment.

Jesse Shera once bemoaned the fact that there was "data, data, everywhere, but not a thought to think."[25] The new technology can make information available, but it can never convert it to knowledge. "The future status of the public library," writes Bob Usherwood, "will depend not on its adoption of hardware and software, but on the quality of its liveware."[26]

NOTES AND SUGGESTED READINGS

Notes

1. Verna Pungitore, *Public Librarianship* (New York: Greenwood Press, 1989), 185.

2. Vannevar Bush , "As We May Think," *Atlantic Monthly* 176 (July 1945): 101-108.

3. Sheila Intner, *Circulation Policy in Academic, Public and School Libraries* (Westport, CT: Greenwood Press, 1987), 9-12.

4. Richard Boss, *The Library Manager's Guide to Automation* (Boston: G.K. Hall, 1990), 2.

5. Boss, 159.

6. Richard Sweeney, quoted in Jose-Marie Griffiths, "Competency Requirements for Library and Information Science Professionals," in *Professional Competencies-Technology and the Librarian,* Linda Smith, ed. (Urbana-Champaign, IL: University of Illinois Graduate School of Library and Information Science, 1985), 5-12.

7. Joseph Rosenthal, "Crumbling Walls: The Impact of the Electronic Age on Libraries and Their Clienteles," *Journal of Library Administration* 14 (1991): 12.

8. John Paul Cirino, *The Business of Running a Library* (Jefferson, NC: McFarland, 1991), 153.

9. Kenneth Dowlin, "Library Automation and Telecommunications Systems," *Public Library Quarterly* 8 (1988): 4.

10. Boss, 159.

11. Ward Shaw and Patricia Culkin, "Systems That Inform: Emerging Trends in Library Automation and Network Development," *Annual Review of Information Science and Technology* 22, Martha Williams, ed. (Amsterdam: Elsevier, 1987): 266-7.

12. Boss, 129.

13. Daniel Sager, *Public Library Administrators' Planning Guide to Automation* (Dublin, OH: OCLC, 1983), 5-6.

14. Ibid., 129-130.

15. Boss, 110.

16. Ibid.

17. John Corbin, *Managing the Library Automation Project* (Phoenix, AZ: Oryx Press, 1985), 5.

18. Boss, 138.

19. Ibid., 140.

20. Rosenthal, 16.

21. Boss, 151.

22. Kenneth Dowlin, "Technology in the Public Library: The Impact on Our Community," *IFLA Journal* 13 (1987): 40.

23. Robert Olsen, "Keynote: The Future of the Public Library," in *The Future of the Public Library: Conference Proceedings* (Dublin, OH: OCLC, 1988), 7-8.

24. Thomas Ballard, "The Best Reading for the Largest Number, At the Least Cost," in *The Future of the Public Library: Conference Proceedings,* 45.

25. Quoted in Bob Usherwood *The Public Library as Public Knowledge* (London: The Library Association, 1989), 90.

26. Ibid.

Suggested Readings

Boss, Richard. *The Library Manager's Guide to Automation.* 3rd ed. Boston: G.K. Hall, 1990.

Clayton, Marlene. *Managing Library Automation.* Brookfield, VT: Gower, 1987.

Corbin, John. *Managing the Library Automation Project.* Phoenix, AZ: Oryx Press, 1985.

The Future of the Public Library: Conference Proceedings. Dublin, OH: OCLC, 1983.

Gaddis, Dale. "Automation of the Public Library." *North Carolina Libraries 47* (Spring, 1989): 26-32.

Gallimore, Alec. "Developing a Microcomputer based Management Information System." *Library Review* 38 (Nov. 2, 1989): 17-37.

Greiner, J.M. "Professional Views: Technology in Public Libraries." *Public Libraries* 29 (May/June, 1990): 145-53

Hernon, Peter and Charles McClure, eds. *Microcomputers for Library Decision Making: Issues, Trends and Applications.* Norwood, NJ: Ablex, 1986.

Intner, Sheila and Jane Hannigan, eds. *Library Microcomputer Environment: Management Issues.* Phoenix: Oryx Press, 1988.

Kolb, Marcia "Moving to the Next Online System: Points to Consider." *North Carolina Libraries* 4 (Fall 1989): 186-9.

Mason, Marilyn Gell. "Library Automation: The Next Wave." *Library Administration and Management 5* (Winter, 1991): 34-36.

Rosenthal, Joseph. "Crumbling Walls: The Impact of the Electronic Age on Libraries and Their Clienteles." *Journal of Library Automation* 14 (1991): 9-17.

Saffady, William. *Automating the Small Library.* Chicago: American Library Association, 1991.

Saffady, William. *Introduction to Automation for Librarians.* 2nd ed. Chicago: American Library Association, 1989.

Sager, Donald. *The Public Library Administrators' Planning Guide to Automation.* Dublin, OH: OCLC, 1983.

Schuyler, Michael. "ISDN to the Rescue-but Whose?" *Computers in Libraries* 12 (October, 1992): 44-47.

Usherwood, Bob. *The Public Library as Public Knowledge.* London: The Library Association, 1989.

CHAPTER 8

COLLECTION DEVELOPMENT

Metaphorically, the heart of any library is its collection, what some have recently come to term the data base. The collection is built to respond to the information needs of a community, that is, to make available materials required by various segments of the population at levels appropriate to their interests and abilities. Collection development is the process by which the library insures that these needs will be met in a timely and economical fashion using information resources located both inside and outside the institution.

The term collection development encompasses a wide variety of activities which, taken together, guarantee that a library owns the books, periodicals and other materials necessary to support the information needs of its community and is one aspect of collection management. Other collection management duties include acquisition of material, maintenance and preservation of the collection, housing, storage, deselection and discarding, all according to a preestablished policy.

Paul Mosher has outlined eight specific functions of collection development:

1. Preparing plans and policy statements for collection development.
2. Developing and allocating materials budgets.
3. Analyzing and evaluating collections with regard to their utility to users. What does the collection contain? Are they the right things?

4. Reviewing the collection management program. What needs preservation? What material is obsolete, undesirable, redundant and, therefore, can be discarded?
5. Conducting use and user studies.
6. Studying the effectiveness, economy and efficiency of the program. Does it do what it is supposed to do? Do bibliographers have adequate training, time and support to do their work effectively?
7. Determining the effectiveness of acquisitions programs. Do vendors and dealers function effectively in terms of time, cost and responsiveness?
8. Establishing which cooperative or coordinated collection development or collection management activities -- with other local or regional libraries -- would allow profitable reallocation of resources.[1]

Certain important assumptions govern this chapter. First, print will remain the most frequent medium for public library materials during the next decade, at least. Second, although books will continue to be published, increasingly information will be available in multimedia and electronic formats. Although for the foreseeable future, extensive collections of print-published materials will remain the mainstay of the public library collection, many new formats will supplement books and periodicals. Librarians will now be compelled to provide access to them as well as make available the traditional printed ones and supply links between all of them. Almost a half century ago, Ortega y Gasset foresaw the librarians of the future "as a filter interposed between man and the torrent of books."[2] Today, the expanded definition of material includes not only books, but alternate types of materials. Tomorrow we will have "virtual collections," electronically browsable libraries available on subscription bases, widening the horizons of even the smallest libraries and permitting them to offer a previously undreamt of depth of material resources.[3]

Collection development is among the most challenging, enjoyable, threatening, difficult, and intellectually engaging of all library tasks. Librarians agonize over every $20 expenditure, often losing sight of the time equals money equation or the fact that there are no right or wrong books, simply some better or worse ones. Every selector makes errors. Only experience helps to predict success. Proponents on each side argue about whether selection is an art or a science. Both are correct.

Public libraries anticipate that the majority of titles purchased will be used immediately, an expectation that differentiates them from other types of libraries. Emphasis is placed on

> identifying popular materials as soon as they are announced for distribution, predicting the volume of local demand, and then buying quickly in appropriate quantities. When public interest in certain authors, subjects or formats wanes, the unwanted materials are removed from the collection to make room for those of rising popularity.[4]

It would be short-sighted, however, to assume that the work of collection development in a public library is solely concerned with materials that are new and of only transitory interest. The integrity of any collection is guaranteed not only by the importance attached to an individual item, but by the relation of that item to its neighbors on the shelf and to the collection as a whole. It is not formed by adding and weeding items in a series of discrete, unrelated decisions, no matter how conscientiously these activities are performed. Rather, a collection is an organic unity that grows from a shared philosophy about collection development, a clear picture of what that collection ought to be, and a plan to achieve it.

Recent shrinkages in public library budgets, coupled with the burgeoning of information and the mounting costs of books, periodicals and other library materials, present dilemmas of unprecedented difficulty for collection development librarians. Further complicating the process has been the recent realization that librarians sometimes make fundamental decisions based on untested assumptions about the materials that different groups of readers come to the library to use.

The vast majority of public librarians consider articulated demand crucial to material selection decisions. The importance of demand in selecting library materials cannot be denied. However, certain borrower habits make total dependence on this approach risky. With few exceptions, public library users select materials from what is available to them on the shelves of the library outlet they regularly visit. Library use is most heavily associated with proximity, ease of access and satisfaction. Most patrons do not ask librarians for help or make extensive use of the catalog in whatever form it exists. They browse on shelves in subject areas and in fiction forms and select from what is there. When librarians help patrons, intra-system and inter-library loans are more likely to result, although time constraints often inhibit patrons' willingness to endure the wait, even a minimal one, necessary to borrow materials from branches, system members or through inter-library loan.

Collection development librarians, responding to what they perceive to be demand, are, in reality, responding to *stated* demand and not to needs that remain unarticulated. The absence of apparent demand results in lack of attention to the collection as a whole and establishes a self-fulfilling assumption: Patrons demand best sellers because they have come to anticipate that the demand will be met. And librarians stock best sellers based on their belief that patrons want them and little else. And then they assume that a collection is adequate because there are no requests for other material.

Carol Hole has suggested that the public library has been "feminized" as a result of lack of articulated demand and misperceptions about needs for material. Contending that men and women often utilize different books, she says that technical materials in the "hard sciences," building trades and automotive repair are unavailable in most public libraries. On the other hand, a wide array of women's technical books -- cooking and interior design, for instance -- are purchased routinely.[5]

A public library's collection is composed of materials for different audiences who use the library for a variety of reasons. Satisfying all of these constituencies is probably impossible. Establishing priorities based on the nature of the community eases decision-making about where to concentrate efforts. Certainly every public library must contain some of the types of materials listed below:

1. a basic collection of reference materials
2. a collection of adult fiction and non-fiction books.
3. a collection of books for children and young adults
4. a collection of general periodicals for adults, children and young adults
5. a collection of audio-visual materials
6. a collection of materials relating to the local community, including local history, local newspapers, and government and other documents

Many librarians have chosen to expand the definition of materials and have circulated such artifacts as toys, tools, trading stamps, and even pet animals. No matter what is lent, however, the principles of collection development remain constant and are based on a continuing reference to the nature of the community -- to who uses the library and for what reason. In a sense, the collection constitutes a statement of how well the library has understood its community.

DEMAND VERSUS QUALITY

Probably the most intense debate in the public library community centers around the question of whether a collection should be based on "demand" or on "quality." Even the framework of the debate is problematic. Some contend that the argument is between *need* and quality, with need referring both to want and to yet unexpressed demand. Quality, itself a difficult concept to define, changes with each context. There is a certain ingenuousness to labeling the debate in this way since demanded books may also be of high quality. It is true, however, that the books currently in greatest demand often do not exemplify the best literary standards and produce collections vastly different from those based entirely on merit, however defined.

The arguments on each side of the debate, no matter how framed, are very complex and heated, calling into account the very meaning of professionalism in librarianship. It is an old controversy, with roots deep not only in early American public library history (see, for instance, Chapter 2 for a discussion of how the mission of the public library has changed over time) but in English literary history, as well. While the argument touches on popular materials of all manner, it is most often posed in terms of works of fiction and may well date to the inception of the novel as a literary form. Fiction has always been suspect since the discovery that Robinson Crusoe was not a real person. The original purpose of literature was didactic and intended to exemplify the moral life. Fiction, on the other hand, was untruth parading as truth and could not hope to fulfill that noble purpose. The great literary critic Samuel Johnson, writing in the periodical *Rambler*, in 1850, said:

> It is justly considered as the greatest excellency of art to imitate nature, but it is necessary to distinguish those parts of nature which are most proper for imitation: greater care is still required in representing life, which is so often colored by passion or deformed by wickedness. If the world be promiscuously described, I cannot see what use it can be to read the account, or why it may not be as safe to turn the eye immediately upon mankind as upon a mirror which shows all that presents itself without discrimination.[6]

Novels differed from their predecessors -- poetry, plays, religious works -- in a variety of ways. First, they made ordinary middle-class people, not aristocrats, heroes. Novels used local, recognizable settings and placed an increased emphasis on realism and realistic interpretation. In other words, ordinary persons' daily activities in ordinary settings became the focus of literary attention.

Fiction reading was a middle-class occupation. Only members of this strata of society had funds either to purchase novels or obtain them through subscription libraries, and commanded sufficient leisure time to read them. Women, in particular, became avid consumers of the new literature. Their thirst for fiction was borne, in part, from lack of sufficient activity to occupy their attention, but more, perhaps, from a desire for new experiences and wider horizons. Virginia Woolf has described the limitations of the sphere in which Jane Eyre and women like her existed:

> and I read how Jane Eyre used to go on to the roof when Mrs. Fairfax was making jellies and looked over the fields at the distant view. And then she longed "for a power of vision which overpass that limit; which might reach the busy world, town, regions full of life I had heard of but never seen: that then I desired more of practical experience than I possessed: more of intercourse with my kind, of acquaintance with variety of character than was here within my reach. I valued what was good in Mrs. Fairfax and what was good in Adele; but I believed in the existence of other more vivid kinds of goodness, and what I believed in I wished to behold."[7]

Women currently comprise 73% of adult library patrons. In general, they read more fiction than do men. Sometimes perhaps for the same reasons as their eighteenth and nineteenth century forbears.

To rejoin the quality/demand argument then, most public librarians, with some notable exceptions, agree with William Wortman's contention that with non-fiction, the librarian has a distinct professional responsibility to identify and select the best and most appropriate materials to meet users' needs.[8] With fiction, he says, issues are less clear.

C. E. Gorman, in distinguishing between the responsive and responsible role, sees three possible stances that public libraries can assume:

1. to provide readers with exactly what they want;

2. to meet the dictates of a socially responsible institution, this approach should be qualified by selecting the *best* material available that meets users' demands;

3. a third path may mandate that the library should select the best there is without worrying about demand.[9]

Other commentators term the debate as one between a supplier-oriented posture and a user-oriented one, or alternately as between "an internally derived judgment of the general good a title is anticipated to contribute to the community to a decision based on an externally derived expression of community demand, either positive or negative."[10] In the former case, the library provides materials that would further its educational cultural mission. Give the public the best and it will be used to advantage. Only in this way can its users be educated and enlightened and thoughts and attitudes constructively influenced. Not circulation, but lives changed by confronting new realities should be the measure of a book's success. Minority rights to information must be protected. The bulk of these arguments rest on the premise that good reading makes people better and, as a corollary, the public has bad taste and will read at the lowest possible level unless presented with better material. Librarians fulfill their *professional* obligation by utilizing their professional training in providing an "excellent" library.

Among the most vocal proponents of the quality half of the equation are those who argue that libraries meet a "need of our society, indeed the world society, for a public sector in information, a set of information agencies designed to meet the public's need and right to know, whether the individual involved is a student, or a working or unemployed citizen, or a scholar or whatever."[11] The importance of balance and diversity in collections is stressed by proponents of this position.

One last argument often advanced against the demand posture is that "efficient provision of recreational reading to patrons able to afford to purchase these books is not an appropriate use of tax money."[12]

User-oriented

The other side of the equation, the demand-driven, user-oriented, "give 'em what they want" school presents equally compelling points in favor of its position. This group argues that libraries exist for their patrons who ought to be able to find what they want -- not what librarians think they *should* want. Quality is a relative and arbitrary term. Librarians have no right to impose their views about what constitutes excellence.

The quality stance is seen as anti-democratic and elitist. Materials are to be used, not to sit on the shelf. Many who make the demand argument continue to contend, as did their 19th century ancestors, that all reading is of value and that users will progress from lesser to higher quality reading matter.

The most compelling, frequently repeated argument rests on the premise that those who pay the piper get to dance. In other words, taxpayers have a right to demand what they want from the library. Those who make this case, advocates such as Charles Robinson of the Baltimore County Public Library, warn that ignoring popular demand carries with it the danger of losing public support.

How are such divergent positions reconciled? Which master -- demand or quality -- is the appropriate one for a public library to serve? Recognizing that the debate is not limited to two mutually exclusive categories, but that the positions are extremes on a continuum immediately softens the shrillness of the controversy. Further, realizing that most libraries approach materials selection with a flexible attitude lessens the pressure to adopt one or the other view. And, finally, careful construction of a collection development policy helps to set priorities and constraints and to rationalize choices based not only on these two considerations, but on all the others such as goals, geographic location and constituency.

FINANCIAL CONSIDERATIONS

The last two decades have witnessed a number of societal events whose impact on public libraries has been substantial. Among them are the very real fiscal problems experienced by municipalities, be they city, county or school district, particularly after revenue-sharing was abandoned by the Reagan administration. Other federal grant funds have also substantially dried up or completely evaporated during the past two decades. New pressures to supply materials for discrete user groups put further strains on library collections. Many college students without sufficient money to purchase their education at high priced institutions have now chosen to remain at home, attend local schools and use the public library as their resource of choice. Burgeoning immigration has resulted in requests for books in Vietnamese, Russian, Polish, Spanish, and countless other languages. Senior citizen groups have become more vocal in their demands for large print materials, magnifying equipment and more programs. Libraries, in accepting the challenge to help meet societal literacy problems, have had to accommodate to the needs of yet another group who traditionally did not comprise the library's public.

Prices of materials have far outstripped inflation (Books, for instance, rose 33% between 1977 and 1981 and there was an appalling leap in journal subscription prices, 60% in the same time period.) At the same time, the print publishing industry experienced no shrinkage -- 700,000 new book titles are produced around the world annually, as well as millions of less trackable items, among which are pamphlets, newspapers, printed documents, technical reports, videotapes, maps, data tapes and bases. And electronic media, many requiring new equipment, burgeoned, placing additional demands on already diminished budgets. There has been a *relative* decline in purchasing value of the library dollar and an *actual* decline in library acquisition budgets during the 1970's and 1980's.[13] Libraries were able to buy far less material for substantially more money.

The combination of declining budgets, inflation, increased publishing, equipment needs and new constituencies are all responsible for the great financial and managerial collection development problems that public libraries are experiencing. Trying both to maintain their traditional role and expand their services to meet new demands is a daunting task. Limited financial resources necessitate decisions that are often painful and lead back to that sometimes acrimonious debate about who most deserves library service.

THE ORGANIZATION OF COLLECTION DEVELOPMENT

There is no routine arrangement for collection development as there is for, say, technical processes. Tradition within an individual institution, more than any other single factor predicts how it will be organized. A recent study of how public libraries are grouped to perform collection development reveals that libraries approach the problem in a variety of ways. The task remains with the head librarian in the smallest libraries. Larger ones tend to distribute the work among a group of individual selectors who report to a single person. Most of these have other responsibilities, as well, serving, for instance, as members of the adult services or reference staff or as branch librarians. Some delegate part or all of the task to a committee. A few of the largest libraries have a unit with full-time staff that is responsible for collection development, sometimes coupled with other duties such as interlibrary loan.[14]

There is a movement toward centralization of collection development among libraries with branches, but currently most branch librarians select from a list of items presented by subject specialists in main or central libraries. A number of libraries utilize a "hot title" approach, centrally selecting and ordering those items destined to become best sellers. Even in library systems where collection development is largely centralized, branches continue to select their own periodicals. Audio visual materials, particularly videos, are more likely to be selected centrally, no matter how other materials are handled.

Libraries of a certain size generally designate a single person as responsible for collection development. These librarians have titles with the words collection development, manager/coordinator in them and they report to second or third tier library administrators, though occasionally their immediate supervisor is the Library Director.

In the absence of its own department, collection development is located in technical services, public services, central services or administration. Sometimes it subsumes acquisitions, other times the reverse is true, it is a function of acquisitions.[15] One major problem with housing collection development outside its own department is that it often becomes an activity relegated to slow times, or is sandwiched between questions at the reference desk. Selectors are typically responsible for a Dewey or LC classification and a particular format. For example, they may be assigned the entire Dewey number of 900 and be responsible for all books in history and travel. Alternately, they may be charged with purchasing all periodicals. Selectors are recruited from among the ranks of professional librarians and are chosen on the basis of experience, interest and education. In some libraries, they volunteer. In others they are assigned.

The key characteristic of good selectors is their willingness to read. Keeping abreast of current developments in their designated field means not only reading professional library literature, but materials in the subject as well. As much as any other aspect of library work, collection development demands a pro-active stance that seeks to remain informed about current developments and to supply materials that are timely.

ALLOCATING FUNDS

Public libraries allocate, on average, about 15-25% of their budgets to materials. There is no single, agreed upon method for apportioning funds. At best, it is a judgment call based on accumulated experience, knowledge of the community and the consensual values of the library reflected in its mission statement. Some librarians who oppose allocated materials budgets consider the activity too time consuming. Proponents, however, view it as an important method of monitoring and controlling collection development and contend that "ultimately allocating is not so much a procedure as it is a policy decision."[16] In small libraries, with single or very few staff members involved in collection development, there is often no formal allocation of the materials budget. Some libraries, particularly those practicing a demand driven philosophy, respond to user requests, purchase from positive reviews and spend until the budget is depleted. Even for these libraries, however, there may be unarticulated allocations and analysis of expenditures, particularly over time, will reveal that distribution patterns do indeed exist. In larger libraries, where allocations are apt to be more precise, they are most often apportioned in four ways, often in combination:

1. by format (books, periodicals, audio-visuals, and so on.)
2. by subject area (in broad or narrower subdivisions.)
3. by user (juvenile, Young Adult, for example.)
4. by use (retrospective, current, replacement.)

Responsibility for allocating the materials budget characteristically rests with collection development, acquisitions, or whichever department has responsibility for the activity after advice of others in the institution, branch heads, reference librarians, and others has been sought. The largest libraries require each selector to submit a request for a specific amount of money each year, along with a justification for it.

Many public libraries now use allocation formulas to distribute their acquisitions budget. Early formulas based new budgets on past spending, allocating to each category its last year's amount plus an across-the-board percent increase. Newer formulas include previous budgets, but also circulation, strength of existing collections and prices of materials by subjects. Contingency funds amounting anywhere from 5-15% of allocated materials budgets are generally reserved for special needs -- unanticipated expenses or exceptional opportunities. Most libraries do not maintain separate funds for replacement of lost or damaged material.

COLLECTION SIZE

Numbers of volumes -- the mere size of a collection -- has a remarkable influence over municipal officials. Librarians are not exempt from the charms of this popular fallacy. Collection size is printed in their annual reports. State libraries and other agencies gather this information. Yet, as sensible people know, the value of a public library is determined by its quality and not by the quantity of its holdings.

Everyone agrees that libraries should be "good," but affixing criteria to "goodness" is extremely difficult, if not impossible. Size has been assumed to be one measure of a "good" collection. Certainly it is true that if enough of what is published is purchased, some of it is bound to be valuable. On the other hand, this approach produces an awful lot of "bad," as well.[17] Beyond this lies the question of "access." Is denying access to what we judge "bad," a benefit, or is the concept of wider access to material in itself "good?"

Throughout much of this century, an important factor in resource allocation decisions for libraries has been the standards drawn up by various professional organizations and state libraries. These standards attempt to define both qualitatively and quantitatively, the procedures and the human and material resources necessary to provide the services expected of a library at an adequate level. They have frequently been used by libraries not only as guidelines in determining budgetary needs, but also as evidence for justifying their budgets to funding agencies. The American Library Association issued new or revised standards for public libraries in 1933, 1943, 1956, and 1966. Their nature has changed over the years. The 1933 public library standards statement, a two page document, was confined to setting minimum resource levels. The 1943 statement ran to 92 pages and "covered the whole range of objectives, government, organization and services, as well as collections, personnel and finance," serving many libraries as a "compact planning and administrative guide."[18]

The 1956 formulation largely played down quantitative measures in favor of broad operational guidelines. Subsequent publications have stressed the importance of "Output Measures" and the community context, based on the realization that one library's minimum standards, represents another's optimal ones when access to financial resources are calculated in the equation. Nonetheless, many state libraries continue to promulgate standards that call for X number of books per capita. These represent base collecting levels below which libraries cannot fall if they are to continue to receive State Aid (see Chapter 5, Governance). Pennsylvania, for instance, demands that independent local libraries have written policy statements covering the selection and maintenance of their collections; that they provide well-balanced minimum collections of 1 1/2 currently useful catalogued and classified items *per capita*, provided that no library shall have a collection of fewer than 15,000 such items; that the library shall receive a balanced collection of currently useful periodicals in accordance with the following minimums:

Less than 10,000 population	30 titles
10,000-24,999	50
25,000-49,999	75
50,000 and more	125

Standards vary for District Library Centers, for System Headquarters, for local libraries that are system members and for branch libraries.[19]

CORE COLLECTIONS

There has been increasing attention to the degree to which libraries ought to contain a core collection. Core usually implies important material. A complete set of Dickens, for instance, or all of the Platonic dialogues ought to be part of *every* library collection, advocates contend. Two factors argue against this position. The first is that the "core" has never been adequately defined and changes from moment-to-moment depending on who seeks to define it. The second reintroduces the demand/quality argument. Should the shelves be stacked with unread items, particularly in light of a scarcity of shelf space?

Conversely, several arguments lend the core concept support.

Libraries without these materials deny the value of browsing and serendipity. Countless famous writers have described, for instance, their local public libraries as havens from sometimes harsh and inhospitable environments that provided them with the mental sustenance to grow and develop. Further, core advocates maintain, without the works that create the intellectual foundations of the society, libraries are not fulfilling their functions.

It used to be assumed that although collections will vary from one institution to another depending upon local needs, core holdings, if compared, would overlap significantly. Studies, however, have revealed less commonality than might have been anticipated.[20]

Research into use of library materials has consistently demonstrated that only a small part of most collections finds its way into the hands of users. Trueswell reported that 99% of the materials needed for circulation in a particular library could be met by between 25 and 40% of its collection.[21]

Unfortunately, the needs of library users are little understood. Library use is difficult to measure. Many library activities leave scant if any material record for analysis. Most library studies are based on circulation statistics, an inaccurate description of use. Coupled with this difficulty has been the reluctance of some librarians to undertake systematic analysis, fearing that the results might somehow be detrimental to the broader humanistic goals of the library or to the willingness of municipalities to continue funding. It is not wise to base library policies on use data alone nor is it wise to let intuition by itself guide collection development. Each path, without the other, invites serious error and poor distribution of resources.

COOPERATIVE COLLECTION DEVELOPMENT AND RESOURCE SHARING

No library has ever been self-sufficient. Recently, however, it has been difficult for most libraries even to be adequate and many have found it judicious to enter into cooperative collection development arrangements. Technology has eased a number of the difficulties formerly associated with cooperation. On-line bibliographic access, for instance, or rapid telefacsimile transmission of materials have made resource-sharing substantially more feasible. Despite the new emphasis on access rather than acquisition, libraries will nonetheless be responsible for providing locally the materials required to meet the routine needs of their users. Public libraries will continue to devote a large portion of their resources to supplying popular fiction and nonfiction. There are, however, difficult decisions to be made about what to collect and what to relinquish to another institution or a system. The following considerations should dictate policy:

1. Public libraries must supply items which are most frequently in demand and provide *access* to other resources and information that cannot be furnished on site. No one with a leaking water pipe wants to wait several weeks to borrow a basic plumbing book from another library.

2. Resource development at the local level should be developed to respond to what users need to meet their recurring educational, informational, and recreational needs. This results in high use collections geared to primary clientele.[22]

Designing organizational structures that support decision-making for substantive cooperation without limiting individual library autonomy is complex. Very often state libraries, or regional headquarters, if they exist, assume the task. Fair and equitable distribution of resources and responsibilities is not easy, but necessary if system members are to function amicably. To ask one library to collect in depth materials not germane to its community, while others are given topics that would be suitable to any constituency is to court resentment and noncooperation. As attractive as resource-sharing arrangements may be, they often carry unanticipated drawbacks. There is always time-consuming and expensive paper-work to complete. Depending on resource-sharing may irritate patrons because no matter how efficient, it is always slower, more cumbersome and uncertain than direct access to materials on hand. There is also a danger of spending too much money on cooperative arrangements. Thomas Ballard has argued that in public and nonresearch libraries, money spent on interlibrary loans and cooperation would be better spent on acquiring additional books and periodicals.[23]

COLLECTION DEVELOPMENT POLICIES

Collection development based on a plan and an understanding of who selects materials, for what purpose, to what extent and for whom is always more effective. Codifying this information into a widely embraced document helps to alleviate some of the misunderstandings and uncertainties of the process, a process which, despite the best intentions is always subject to selector bias. Staff members of libraries that have formulated and written total collection policies tend to share a philosophy of collection development and to be consistent in their decisions about what to acquire and keep. For new selectors, the policy functions not only as a training tool, but as a socializer to the library's values.

A collection development policy should include, as considerations, an overall description of the nature of the community, its past and future, the library's constituency, the levels of material to be collected and the use of library materials. In addition to the collection development statement there should be information about retention, discarding and weeding policies, a preservation policy that includes binding, microforming, restoration, housing, storage and housekeeping statements. Finally, there should be an anti-censorship declaration. Sadly, studies indicate that many public libraries never write policies and many librarians are skeptical of their value particularly when they consider the amount of time and data necessary to produce them. In truth, even when libraries do not have a formal, written selection policy, they most often have formulated unwritten ones that guide them in collection development and management. But an explicit policy serves a variety of functions. Ross Atkinson contends, for instance, that the creation of a unified collection policy is intended to articulate and render consistent criteria which are often already being applied by selectors. The purpose of the policy is to raise those criteria to consciousness, to compare and coordinate them, to adjust them to meet the varied and competing needs of the institution as consistently as possible.[24] The value of constructing a policy far outweighs the drawbacks in demands on time and resources. It is the only way to ensure that a public library collection is based on selectivity, integration and direction rather than a product of haphazard, miscellaneous growth. A collection development and management policy contains the following elements:[25]

1. *Overview.* The collection policy is framed by the scope, objectives, goals of the library, clearly established at the outset. Preliminary material describes the community, identifies clientele, states the parameters of the collection, describes in detail the types of programs or patron needs that are to be met by the collection; includes a section of general limitations and priorities that will determine how the collection will be developed; and discusses in detail the library's participation in cooperative collection development programs.

2. *Scope of collection.* A detailed description of subject areas and formats to be collected. As much as possible, the policy should establish priorities and levels of collecting intensity. Many libraries are now using the Conspectus,[26] a six step numeric system of collection description, to help assess their current collection strength and help them make decisions about desirable collecting levels. These are the steps:

       0. out of scope, not collected
       1. minimal
       2. basic information
       3. instructional support
       4. research
       5. comprehensive

Certain dangers inhere, however, in this classification scheme when applied to public libraries. Its academic orientation does not reflect the nature of such popular collections as hobbies, pets, best sellers, or children's materials. These may, indeed, be collected in substantial depth, but not on an "instructional support" or "research" level.

Most public library collections do not go beyond Steps Two or Three above. In certain cases, however, research or comprehensive levels may be appropriate. For instance, a cooperative collection development plan may result in a library's accepting a fairly intensive collecting level for a particular subject. Many public libraries, particularly those that share quarters with historical societies or which assume responsibility for collecting local history materials, will attempt to gather all published and manuscript materials dealing with their communities. This, then, puts them at "comprehensive" on the Conspectus scale for that category of material.

3. *Collection Responsibility.* A clear statement that delineates responsibilities for selection, for weeding and the guidelines to be used in the process. What material and in what quantity is to be duplicated, an offshoot, in part of the quality/demand debate, is one policy that must be delineated. A rule of thumb used by many public libraries is to purchase duplicate copies of a book for every four reserves on that title. Some libraries solve the reserve problem by instituting rental plans. They lease from a jobber collections of books that duplicate materials they already own, retain them for a period of time and return them when use has diminished. Although there is a cost for rental, it is less expensive than owning the title and less cumbersome to discard. Rental plans permit libraries to meet short-term periods of high demand. Rental fees for leased books are levied on patrons by some libraries, which helps to defray the cost. Few, however, charge fees for books which they do not otherwise own.

4. *Miscellaneous Issues.* These include gift policies, the disposi-

tion of weeded and discarded materials, bases for decisions regarding binding, housing, equipment, microfilming, preservation and/or restoration and/or replacement.

5. *Intellectual Freedom* Every collection development policy should include a statement committing the library to support of intellectual freedom and against censorship and contain the relevant documents including the Freedom to Read statement, the statement against labelling, and so on. In addition, the procedure for registering a complaint, as well as the form should be appended.

Collection development statements are only effective if they represent a collaborative effort of all of those involved in the process. They deserve wide dissemination, and should be frequently reviewed and revised at regular intervals.

METHODS OF SELECTION

Except for the very largest ones, public libraries select materials by using published information -- generally reviews -- rather than by physically examining an item. This is both fortunate and unfortunate. Most often, public librarians are generalists without specific subject expertise. They depend, therefore, on recommendations of reviewers. Unfortunately reviewers' credentials are not always impeccable. Dependence on a single reviewing source can lead to serious defects in the collection. In addition, reviews, particularly in more specialized journals, are often late. Some journals only review recommended titles. But given how few books are reviewed, it is difficult to know whether a title has been evaluated negatively or simply unexamined.

Community need is the dominant factor in materials selection. Most selected titles bear current imprints and retrospective purchasing is limited as a rule to replacements for lost or damaged items. In public libraries premiums are placed on having books available when they are new and being discussed. Anticipating public demand is a challenge for public library selectors. Clues to the upcoming importance of a particular book can be found in both *Publishers Weekly* and *Kirkus* where notations appear about whether or not a title has been chosen as a book club selection, the extent of copies to be issued in the first printing, whether major advertising is planned, or if it is to be a motion picture or a television miniseries accompany annotations. Public libraries can keep in touch with current taste by regularly consulting the *New York Times* best-seller list and by reading reviews in popular magazines such as *Time, Newsweek* and the *New Yorker.*

Few of the books published each year are ever reviewed and no one book source covers more than a fraction of total publishing output. Assuming approximately 50,000 new books in English published each year, the following summarizes how many each of the most widely consulted reviewing journals has been able to evaluate: *Library Journal* 5,819; *Booklist,* 4,719; *Publishers Weekly,* 4,184; Kirkus 4,050; *School Library Journal* 2,430; *west coast review of books* 1,352; *New York Times* 1,186; *Bulletin of the Center for Children's Books* 798; *Horn Book* 429, *New York Review of Books* 314.[27]

Publications from non-traditional publishers, particular small presses, are extremely difficult to locate and assess. They rarely receive adequate reviewing and the lack of access to financial resources prohibits their advertising or aggressively marketing their products. Yet the output of small presses, both literary and nonliterary, are often of extremely high quality and influential. The importance of these publications should not be underestimated and every effort should be made to seek them out.

Approval Plans

Some large public libraries use Greenaway or similar approval plans. Named after Emerson Greenaway, former Free Library of Philadelphia Director, these plans call for libraries to receive, at nominal prices, one copy of each title in advance of publication. Staff can review them early, making recommendations about multiple copies and branch acquisition. Because of their low prices, books acquired through approval plans cannot be returned. Similar plans with more stringent guidelines can be put into place, as well.

Approval plans, though related, are not the same as Standing Order plans where the library agrees to buy groups of titles from a publisher or vendor. Standing order plans are used to purchase series, yearbooks, annuals and may be on a "til Forbidden" basis; that is, publishers and jobbers continue sending the title until further notice.

WHERE AND HOW TO BUY

Public libraries buy most of their materials through jobbers, publishers, local booksellers and subscription agents.

Jobbers or Wholesalers

The best sources of current books for public libraries are book jobbers or wholesalers. A number of benefits accrue from utilizing their services. For instance, by consolidating all library book orders for various publishers to one order, librarians are able to reduce record-keeping and the number of bills to be paid. Second, because they deal in bulk, jobbers are able to offer substantial discounts, particularly on trade books. Third, most jobbers are familiar with library procedures and library needs. As a result they can anticipate requirements and deal with them efficiently as they arise. Fourth, jobbers who have been awarded the major portion of a library's orders can be expected to deal with smaller items on which there is little or no profit, or to make special purchases, such as continuations. And, finally, jobbers can facilitate the return of unwanted materials and make adjustments, two occurrences frequent in all acquisition transactions.

It is legitimate for libraries to expect jobbers to have large inventories of titles; to promptly and accurately fulfill orders; to report regularly on items not in stock; and to give personal service at a reasonable price. Jobbers, on the other hand, can rightfully expect libraries to cooperate by placing orders accurately and in a timely fashion; to keep paperwork to a minimum, that is to keep the invoice procedure as simple as possible; and to make prompt payment for services. Librarians occasionally forget that jobbers are in business to make a profit and are therefore influenced in their relations with libraries by the amount of business placed with them. This suggests that libraries are well-advised to order heavily from a single book jobber whose discounts and service are known to be good rather than distributing them among a group of vendors. On the other hand, the library should guard against permitting the discount size to govern the decision about which jobber to select, since service factors such as turn-around time, receipt time, fill rate and others, are of equal or greater moment.

The following considerations surround the two elements of discounts and service:

1. *Discounts*: Discounts will depend on the volume of library business; the efficiency with which library orders are prepared and sent to the jobber; the type of material bought; and continuity in the library/jobber relationship. As a rule libraries can expect a discount of at least 35-40% on trade books and 10% on short-discount books (reference works, technical books, etc.) A conscientious librarian will check the discounts at frequent intervals to insure that they have not suddenly disappeared or been substantially reduced. Libraries that are able to join forces with other libraries -- a regional consortium or a county library system, for instance -- may be able to take advantage of substantially larger discounts because of quantity purchasing. Agreements to participate in these cooperative buying groups sometimes oblige participants to remain with the group no matter who it selects as jobber. Changing jobbers can be both costly and detrimental to service.

2. *Service*: The discount rate is not the only consideration in selecting a jobber. Service is at least an equal partner. Jobbers must be prompt in delivery, have an acceptable fill rate, make

suitable transportation arrangements, adjust bills and orders as necessary, and be accurate. Of great importance is the "follow-up" pattern -- the accuracy and promptness with which the jobber reports back on "shorts" and out-of-print titles. Time considerations, particularly for public librarians, are very important. Jobbers can be expected to supply 75-80% within 6-8 weeks after the receipt of a purchase request. A jobber with a large inventory should be able to meet this time constraint by supplying a substantial portion of a current book order from the shelves.

Bidding

Some libraries, particularly those supported by public funds, may have their choices of jobbers limited by laws that stipulate that there be competitive bidding for the contract. These libraries must send out *Requests for Bids*, and often are required to receive three proposals before decisions on a jobber can be made. Bidding as a method for selecting jobbers has some virtues. It can result in lower costs and eliminate patronage. Conversely, however, having to choose the lowest bidder relegates considerations regarding quality of service to lesser importance. Any librarian experiencing undue delays or poor handling of service queries will testify about the short-sightedness of this approach.

Publishers

On occasion publishers offer larger discounts that do other book agents. Still, as a rule, it is financially unwise to order directly from them because of the extensive paperwork involved when dealing regularly with numerous publishers. Small libraries, in particular, with minimal staffs who need to be doing more important jobs than placing a multitude of book orders, will find it economically unsound to order books from many agencies. From time to time, however, the most judicious course of action is to order from domestic publishers. When a book is urgently needed and the jobber does not have it in stock, the publisher may be the only recourse. Some publishers do not sell to vendors, or offer such a limited discount that jobbers refuse to carry their books. In this case, also, it may be necessary to deal with the publisher. Public libraries use local booksellers only rarely. Sometimes demand for a popular title is so high and sudden that, in an effort to rapidly diminish the reserve list, libraries will purchase a number of duplicate copies from a bookstore if they are in stock. Discounts are almost always lower, mostly about 10%. However, the purchase offers not only rapid solution to the problem, but contributes certain public relations value, as well. Remainder sales at local bookstores should be monitored, particularly when titles are offered substantially below their original publication price. Good bargains may be acquired in this way, but only if chosen with great care.

WEEDING OR DESELECTION

Weeding, or deselection, the process of reassessing the current value of older material, is as essential as selection to public libraries. Partly it entails restocking the library's inventories. But it also involves evaluating the intellectual content of materials on shelves. Yet weeding is too often neglected. Apparently, decisions about what should remain on shelves are as threatening as initial determinations about whether to purchase items. Librarians fear making mistakes, discarding potentially useful material or retaining useless titles. Weeding is time consuming and only when pressures to create additional space arise are librarians willing to invest the time. Weeding is also expensive. Staff must be trained, records cleared, materials deaccessioned and disposition of unwanted materials arranged for. On the other hand it is expensive *not* to weed. More materials mandate more maintenance. Crowded shelves deter use. Carrying out-of-date materials represents a betrayal of professional obligation. Users have a right to expect that materials on the shelf are currently useful.

There is an extensive literature describing the weeding process and criteria to be used in its accomplishment.[28] Judgments are made on the basis of use, timeliness, physical condition of materials, duplication, reliability (reflecting changing viewpoints), coverage in indexes and so on. Circulation history has been demonstrated to be the best predictor of future use.[29] Books that have not been borrowed after a specific period -- most libraries use a time frame of from 18-36 months -- are considered lively candidates for weeding. Weeding should be assigned to selectors where there are divided budgets and subject or format responsibilities. A collection evaluation schedule, designed to cover the entire collection within a finite period, helps to routinize and normalize the process.

Most materials removed from the public library are either placed in ongoing book sales, reserved for a major book sale or sometimes, when all other alternatives fail, destroyed. In some communities, used book dealers will routinely inspect gifts and discards for items that are unusual or for which they may have some demand. Few public librarians are well-schooled in rare books. A trustworthy dealer with whom a relationship has been established can compensate for this lack of knowledge and guard against selling a rare edition for 25 cents.

PRESERVATION

The 1980's saw a rise in concern about the great numbers of materials in libraries that are deteriorating. Although rare or unusual material is more readily discovered in university or special libraries, unique items often reside on the shelves of public libraries, particularly in local history collections. Where they exist, they must be protected. Methods ranging from photoduplication, deacidification and microfilming should be considered.

General collections, too, demand care. Regular vacuuming, greater attention to issues of heating, ventilating and air conditioning, proper shelving, binding and copying machines designed to handle various types of material will help to protect library materials.

INTELLECTUAL FREEDOM

The problem of what constitutes intellectual freedom and what constitutes censorship is a complex one, requiring long and thoughtful consideration of its nuances. It is relatively easy to be against censorship in its most blatant forms. But it is far more difficult to oppose when two competing values meet head-on. Some feminists, for instance, have sought to have pornography declared illegal on the grounds that it is abusive to and engenders violent behavior towards women.[30] In another example, while no one would defend the extremity of the Iranian response to Salmon Rushdie's novel *Satanic Verses* -- demanding for the author's life -- similar treatment of Judaism, or Christianity, for instance, would undoubtedly provoke outrage and calls for boycotts, if not for outright bans. And finally, is it censorship, as an article in *American Libraries* asked, to remove all copies of *The Joy of Gay Sex* because it advocates sex practices that are now felt to be dangerous in light of the AIDS epidemic?[31]

Charles Osburn warns that although librarians are often taught to defend themselves against the censor in specific kinds of cases, they tend to ignore the *positive thrust* of intellectual freedom.[32] Their written policies, seen as protection from encroachments, are rarely viewed as "instruments of process through which bias and prejudice both within and outside the library can be addressed in a more general context and in the positive spirit of intellectual freedom."[33]

The real basis for intellectual freedom and against censorship is, in Lester Asheim's words, "the defense of access to ideas, to information, esthetic pleasure, to recreation in its literal sense of re-creation, and to knowledge or at least to the process that leads to knowledge."[34]

A brief recounting of the complex history of censorship in the United States may lend understanding to our current situation. The First Amendment to the U.S. Constitution proclaims that "Congress shall make no law....abridging the freedom of speech, or of the press." This has often been applied to political or religious freedom, but the Supreme Court has held that obscenity is not protected under that statute. Over the years, therefore, the Court has sought to define obscenity, a concept whose nature changes with each generation. A few states enacted statutes regarding obscenity in the early 19th century, and the Customs Law of 1842 prohibited importing obscene works from abroad, but the real crusade for control of the nation's reading materials began with the vigorous legislative campaigns of Anthony Comstock. In 1873, Congress passed Comstock's law which prohibited the importation, carriage by mail, or interstate commerce of "every obscene, lewd, lascivious, indecent, filthy or vile article, matter, thing, device or substance," and charged the U.S. Postal Service with its enforcement. At the same time, Comstock's Society for the Suppression of Vice became the citizen watchdog to check on printed material available to local citizens, whether the source be bookstore, newsstand or library, public or private. A third method of ensuring that only "moral" books reached the hands of the American public was the self-censorship of publishers, booksellers and librarians. Prior to the 1930s, librarians usually supported the censors, priding themselves on their ability to present to the public the best materials.

From 1873 to the mid-1950's, the Comstock Law was slowly modified through a number of test cases. One of the most famous was the 1933 litigation in which Judge John Woolsey found that James Joyce's *Ulysses* was not obscene and could be imported into the United States. Other major changes in the interpretation of the Comstock Law began with Roth v. United States which established a three-part test for obscenity. First, the work as a whole had to appeal to the prurient interest in sex; second, it had to be judged to affront contemporary community standards in its representation of sex; and third, it had to be utterly without redeeming social value. Obviously, this represented a substantial diminution in the power of the law. In September, 1973, however, the Supreme Court, whose membership had taken a turn for the right by virtue of several appointments by Richard Nixon, once again modified the obscenity laws. This time the test read, would *the average person* find the work, as a whole, appealing to prurient interests? Would the work depict or describe in a patently offensive way sexual conduct specially prohibited in a *state's law*? And finally, does the work, as whole, lack *serious* literary, artistic, political or scientific value? In effect, the decision denationalized standards, emphasizing, in its place, local or community norms.

Attempts to censor materials today seem to be on the increase. Reactions to grants by the National Endowment for the Arts, the Mapplethorpe and Serrano cases for example or the film "Tongues Untied," and their use by Patrick Buchanan in his 1992 primary battle with George Bush would indicate that fact on a national level. For libraries, too, censorship is not limited to the written word, but applies to audio-visual materials as well. Protests against inclusion of the film, *The Last Temptation of Christ,* for instance, in video collections are legion. Copies routinely disappear or are destroyed. In the best of circumstances, the film becomes a target of formal complaints.

What is the appropriate response to a censorship problem?[35] The first step, obviously, is to formulate a policy and procedure for dealing with complaints, and to have it approved by all levels of authority, including the library's governing board. As G. Edward Evans notes: "There is nothing worse than facing an angry person complaining about some library materials and not have any idea of what to do."[36]

The second step is to ask for a formal complaint. A number of complaint forms are available. The one most commonly adopted by libraries is produced by the National Council of Teachers of English and is included as Appendix A. Often this has the effect of defusing the situation and calming a patron. Each request for reconsideration of material should be taken seriously with the complainant receiving a full-scale explanation of why it was purchased and its use in the collection. Often, libraries will include reviews from outside sources attesting to the quality of the material.

The American Library Association's Office for Intellectual Freedom does not furnish legal assistance to libraries facing complaints, but it does provide telephone consultation and assistance. In the last analysis, however, intellectual freedom depends on librarians running risks and any policy is only as good as their willingness to defend it.

ESSENTIALS IN ACQUISITIONS WORK

After materials are selected, they must be secured by the library. This process is called acquisitions and refers to the technical aspects of order and delivery. Included under acquisitions are: obtaining sufficient bibliographical and cost information to describe an item with precision; identifying an appropriate supplier; preparing and dispatching an order; verifying materials received against orders; and initiating procedures for payment. Avoiding unwanted duplication, a major headache for every kind of library, is another responsibility. Errors are easy to make, and may not be discovered until after the library has engraved its marks of ownership into the book. Experience in searching and ordering are the best antidotes for these mistakes.

In many libraries, acquisitions coordinates collection development and monitors its operations. Publishers announcements, reviews, catalogues and other sources useful to those involved in or responsible for collection development are routinely received by Acquisitions and routed to appropriate selectors as expeditiously as possible. One danger in centering collection development in Acquisitions is that there is a temptation to place efficiency before public needs.

Linda Crismond warns:

> Order lists are prepared and circulated to branch libraries so that a standard of quality can be maintained and so that all desired copies of a title can be ordered at the same time. In addition to delaying an order by weeks, this procedure creates library collections which are all clones of each other and do not necessarily reflect the unique needs of the communities they serve. Receipts from vendors are unnecessarily delayed in order to insure that copies of a title arrive or are sent to processing at the same time.[37]

The Acquisitions Department bears responsibility for insuring that order procedures are clear to selectors, proper forms for placing orders are made available to them and reports are routinely given about fund balances.

Gifts

Acquisitions result from purchase or gift. Purchase, of course, is the most important method, although gifts are also useful. Librarians who are indifferent, or sometimes hostile, to gifts run the risk of deflecting legitimate interest in the library. Gifts can present a major headache, particularly if policies about them have not been clearly established. A statement that the same criteria for judging material will be applied to gifts as to new materials helps to document that only those materials that have clear relevance and value to the collection are to be retained. In addition, the library's right to dispose of unacceptable gift materials in any way it sees fit must be clearly asserted, whether this be selling them to a dealer, placing them in a booksale, exchanging them, or simply discarding them. Gifts are most often rejected because of inadequate physical condition, inappropriateness for the library's collection, or because they duplicate items already owned. Refusing gifts involves great tact in explaining the reasons for the decision to the donor. Appraisals and other matters with tax implications are frequently problematic for public libraries. In most circumstances, it is unwise for the library to appraise materials, although names of professional appraisers to help assess the value of a collection can be suggested. Gifts valued at over $5,000 require appraisal in order for the donor to be eligible for tax deductions. In this case, the library can hire an independent appraiser and charge the donor, or alternately send the donor to one. Gifts materials can be added to a library's book sale, (see Chapter 15) along with the library's discards.

Organization

The organization of acquisitions work is essentially the same for purchases and gifts. A staff member, preferably one with business skills and a thorough knowledge of trade bibliography and the publishing industry, is designated to coordinate acquisitions, establish uniform procedures and create records. Order routines vary with individual libraries and the degree of automation applied to the process. All entail verification, checking against library holdings, ordering, checking against orders, charging appropriate funds and forwarding materials to the catalogue department.

Automating

Acquisitions work entails exquisite attention to detail. Its routines are repetitive and control is difficult to maintain. Fortunately, among the clearest applications of library automation is in acquisitions work. Computers can be used to improve control over funds, increase efficiency, permit multiple access to files, keep better records and generate more accurate reports, speed the production of orders and improve management information. Yet, many public libraries continue to report dissatisfaction with acquisitions modules that database vendors currently offer.

SPECIAL TYPES OF MATERIAL

Content rather than format should govern a library's collection development, as well as its materials allocation budget. Selection and retention should be based on the same criteria, no matter the type of material. Yet, certain categories of material have traditionally been singled out because they represent particular problems requiring individual solutions. Most of these are non-book materials -- periodicals, AV, computer programs, maps, realia, manuscripts -- but also embraced are rare books and other special collections.

Serials

Public libraries acquire four kinds of serials: Periodicals

(including both magazines and journals); newspapers; annuals (almanacs, conference proceedings); and monographic or publishers series. Selection decisions for serials differ from those made about trade books because serials represent a continuing commitment over an indefinite period of time. Cancelling a subscription dictates an action. Inertia may be the culprit in causing libraries to retain titles far beyond the time when they have outlived their usefulness.

For public libraries, magazines and newspapers probably represent the two most important categories of serials. Periodicals serve three functions in public libraries: routine reading, reference and research, and information on the frontiers of knowledge.

Despite the apparent shrinkage in the number of newspapers available as well as in readership, every library has its faithful daily newspaper readers. In fact, some gerontologists have labelled newspapers the bane of senior citizens given their propensity to read several of them daily and to exclude other types of reading matter. And, these gerontologists claim, they are reading the same news services stories, over and over again. To some extent, magazines play a similar role. Some users read *Time, Newsweek, US News and World Report,* as well as other newsweeklies, religiously.

Well indexed periodicals and newspapers are among the most important documents for reference and research. They contain more recent information than most books and cover topics not yet available in monographs. The third thrust of library periodical acquisition -- that of identifying and presenting little known, cutting edge, counter culture or alternate material -- is often neglected by public libraries, particularly those guided primarily by demand.

Selection

Whether a periodical is indexed was once considered the single most important factor in judging that title's suitability for library purchase. Indexing remains a salient factor, but other considerations deserve at least equal weight. Periodical selection, like book selection, is based on community's needs and interests. To what extent would foreign language newspapers and magazines be read if they were made available? Is there a need for scholarly materials in certain subjects? Does a particular avocational community exist that will use specialized materials? Periodical use can be charted and demand for individual titles measured. This is especially important for smaller libraries where each title is crucial.

Prices are another consideration. There has been a tendency in recent years for journal costs to escalate at an even greater rate than that experienced by books. Herb White, in a column called "The Journal That Ate the Library," charges librarians with heavy responsibility for accepting publishers' prices and for acting as periodical purchasing agents rather than as periodical consumers. Subscriptions are continued, he contends, to publications that are never read and there is not a rational approach to periodical collection development.[38]

The criteria by which periodicals are selected include relevance, usage, interest general availability, accessibility (index coverage), cost, format, publisher, reputation and, for larger libraries, citation frequency.

Following are some aids to periodical selection:

1. *Sample Issues*: When in doubt about whether or not to subscribe to a particular title, solicit a sample copy.

2. *Reviews of current journals*: professional periodicals, such as *Library Journal* and the *Bulletin of Bibliography* carry descriptive notes about new magazines and include useful bibliographical and order information.

3. *Guides to periodicals*: In the last analysis the selection of periodicals is a skill that depends largely upon the experience of well-informed, intellectually curious, and knowledgeable librarians. However, given the number and range of periodicals, no librarian can hope to be familiar with all or even most of them. For public

librarians, Bill Katz's *Magazines for Libraries* (kept up-to-date by a column in *Library Journal*) is probably the best single source of information and recommendations about periodicals. The original cost of a magazine is only the first expense. The subscription will probably be maintained over a number of years, with the compounded costs of processing, binding and storage. The decision to drop a subscription should be based on such factors as how easily it can be obtained elsewhere, coverage of subject matter by alternate titles, relevance to local needs and how often it is used. Cancelling a periodical is not as momentous an action as it once appeared to be. It is a substantially less threatening activity given the relatively easy access to articles in unowned journals offered by facsimile transmission, commercial document services, better reprographic techniques and rapid inter-library delivery systems. These new methods do not solve the periodical problem. They do, however, help the library to stretch and make judicious use of its dollars.

Organization

Procedures for handling serials from point of selection to point of use differ considerably from library to library. A common practice is to order and "check in" the serials either in the serials department, or if there is none, in acquisitions. Modules for automated serials check-in have lagged behind other automation efforts and the process still consists of extensive record-keeping and attention to detail.

Complete lists of a library's periodical holdings should be publicly available, some placed in close proximity to indexes and abstracting services. Most libraries place the latest issue of a magazine in a public area. Some also include all unbound, recent issues in the same location. Others utilize a paging system in which periodicals are retrieved by staff and called for at a service desk. Back issues are bound or microfilmed and arranged alphabetically on shelves or in drawers. In many libraries, staff members retrieve and ready microfilm for use, rather than permit patrons to locate and use it themselves. In truth, microfilm is not difficult to use and a roll is now substantially less expensive than most books. Few people would be likely to steal a microfilm given the necessity to view it through a specialized reader. Centralizing serial ordering and receipt within a single department, or section of a department, helps to contain the confusion and mistakes inherent in handling the large quantity of items and records necessary to the periodical process. Serials work depends on good organizational skills, careful attention to detail, and the ability to withstand the perpetual criticism that seems inevitably to accompany the task.

Purchasing

Most public libraries consolidate their serials into a single annual order placed with a subscription agent. Increased postage rates, declining dollar values and few publisher discounts has resulted in a serious diminution of the number of subscription agents. Only the largest remain to compete for library business. Choices are limited and decisions are now more often based on the size of the service fee rather than on a discount although some librarians still manage to command a discount, or at least, not pay a fee. Nevertheless, purchasing through a serials vendor remains the preferred choice for serial acquisition. Attempting to deal directly with each publisher is not only time-consuming, and costly, but inefficient and error-prone. Agents provide a central order and billing service, help with back issues, arrange for common expiration dates and automatic renewal unless otherwise notified, supply detailed annual invoices and secure sample copies on request. Good agents are knowledgeable about reduced rates for multi-year subscriptions.

There are a few drawbacks to dealing with vendors that should be noted. The fee, averaging about 4%, makes the periodicals bill higher than the sum of subscriptions would indicate. Very small libraries, with limited periodical lists, may want to compute time and effort and match it to the increase. Some control may be lost.

For example, it is more difficult to enter a subscription midyear in light of the common expiration date.

Following a number of rules regarding subscriptions may ease the complexities of the process.

--Avoid the immediate closing and beginning of the calendar year in placing subscriptions because several months may be needed to effect a subscription.
--Do not change agents frequently.
--Conversely, maintain a watchful eye on the quality of service being provided.

Monitoring such practices as the promptness with which missing issues are supplied, correcting errors in mailing and billing, and so on, is imperative.

The problem of missing issues is acute. Widespread access to copying machines has, to some extent, ameliorated the ravages of theft and mutilation. Nonetheless, issues still disappear. Unfortunately, librarians are generally unaware of missing issues until a reader asks for them, or as they are being prepared for binding. Libraries that have substituted microfilm for binding have solved the problem in the long run, although not for the current period.

Gifts of Periodicals

Patrons and groups interested in furthering particular social, economic and political viewpoints often contribute magazines and newspapers reflecting their opinions to the library. Their handling presents difficult problems for public libraries. Some librarians have chosen to label them "gifts" and have housed them in a separate section than those that are paid subscriptions; some have interfiled them. Still others have refused to include them in collections.

Here are a few general principles many librarians follow regarding the handling of unsolicited periodicals:

1. A reasonable balance between various political and social attitudes is always desirable in a public library collection. The public should expect to find differing viewpoints represented.

2. For the most part, gifts should meet the same standards that apply to purchased material. It is possible to relax some of them, however, if they are outweighed by other merits. For instance, writing standards, or authoritativeness may be less than adequate, but the viewpoint may be otherwise unrepresented in the collection.

3. Decisions about long-term retention of periodical materials can often be substantially delayed. Most gift periodicals are ephemeral, attracting only short-term interest, and can be discarded without hesitation.

Newspapers

All public libraries carry some newspapers. How many and which ones they choose to own depends on such factors as the nature of the community -- its reading level, its geographic location, its ethnic makeup, and so on.

Libraries subscribe to newspapers on a local-first basis. Any newspaper that covers the neighborhood, the town, the city or the county is mandatory not only to purchase, but to retain. Newspapers of interest regionally are a next priority.

Size dictates the extent to which metropolitan daily newspapers with national coverage are carried. Most libraries except the very smallest will subscribe to *The New York Times*, even maintain a complete microfilm run of it. Long considered the newspaper of record, *The Times* has a reputation for objectivity and broad coverage, and an excellent index. High concentrations of foreign language-speaking constituents may mandate purchase of newspapers in those languages.

Government Publications

Local public libraries have a responsibility to collect locally important documents. All public libraries function, in a sense, as miniature Libraries of Congress for their own communities. Minutes of meetings, reports and information involving locally important issues are vital to collect and make available. Vigilance is required to ferret out, for instance, waste disposal initiatives, flood plain plans and other matters relating to the health and well-being of the community.

Yet another essential group of materials to be acquired are county, state, and national government documents regarding local municipalities. Census materials, for example, or other statistical reports that permit communities to undertake longitudinal or comparative studies are of particular value.

With the exception of a few large metropolitan libraries, most public libraries are not federal depositories, that is they do not automatically receive copies of federal government documents. Yet, to ignore their existence is to overlook an important source of current, difficult to locate material. Smaller libraries may supplement their collections by routinely scanning *Monthly Checklist of Federal Government Documents*.

Pamphlets and Clippings

Most public libraries maintain collections of pamphlet and other ephemeral materials in what are called "vertical files." Designed to contain currently useful information, they are often housed in large file cabinets and arranged alphabetically by subject.

The hallmarks of a good vertical file are currency and subject access. Pamphlets can be a leading source of information. Street maps of cities find a home there, as do maps from county surveyors and ones from precincts furnished by political headquarters. Examples of propaganda pamphlets, presenting a variety of viewpoints can be suitably housed in a pamphlet file.

Unfortunately, few libraries have sufficient time or staff to care properly for vertical files. They are permitted to go unweeded for long periods thereby destroying their effectiveness and value. In addition, few librarians other than reference staff are familiar with their contents, and most patrons are unaware of their existence. A particularly effective way to inform users of the existence of a vertical file collection is to place subject information about it in the public access catalogue, with a note to "see vertical file." Another strategy is to remove the files from their cabinets and place them in Princeton files on shelves either together or with their subjects. If a library cannot properly care for a vertical file, it should be eliminated.

Microforms

Microform is a generic term used to describe any information storage and communication medium containing images too small to be read with the unaided eye.[39] They are photographically reproduced and include microfilm, microfiche, ultrafiche, micro-opaque, aperture cards. Typically, libraries buy microforms of publications not available in print, to duplicate print-on-paper materials, or in place of them. Increasingly, however, new materials never before published are appearing in microform. They are an attractive format because they save expensive storage space, preserve information in danger of deterioration, are relatively durable, cost less than binding, are easily used and replaced, if necessary.

The most frequent use of microformats in public libraries is for newspapers and magazines and other serial publications, although a growing number of reference materials are also being made available. There are a few drawbacks to substituting microforms for print. For one, it is hard to curl up with a microform. Another is that the work of staff who have to load and unload it may be increased. Finally, there is a reluctance on the part of the public to accept microform as a substitute for paper. Users with a very strong information need may suffer the inconvenience associated with using microforms. Those whose motivation is less strong may simply ignore it as an information source. Despite patron hostility, studies indicate that use of microfilm does not produce greater fatigue.[40] Subjectively, however, patrons frequently complain that symptoms such as headache and eyestrain result from intensive use of microfilm.

Other Storage Technologies

The pace of technological development is occurring at such a rapid rate that any discussion or list of new methods becomes obsolete before it is presented.

It is predicted that fully indexed books on optical disc with both video and sound will soon be available. Laser technology is receiving increasing attention because of its versatility. Laserdiscs are capable of storing information in analog form as full-motion video with audio, still-frame video or audio only. Library of Congress (LC) analog discs, for instance, contain 40,000 photographs, posters, architectural drawings, and other pictorial items from LC collections. Exact images of printed text are digitized and stored on the disc at a resolution of 300 dots/inch. Storage capacity is from 10,000 to 15,000 pages of text per disc. Laser discs are one form of media that represent a viable alternative to microforms.

A number of database producers are now making full text available electronically. Many publishers are experimenting with compact disc (CD's) as a storage and dissemination medium. Software packages for computers that contain complete texts of Shakespeare, The Bible and encyclopedias are available in interactive format with random access and voice components.

Audiovisual Materials

The place of audiovisual materials -- sound recordings, films, videos, slides, and photographs -- within the public library has attracted wide-spread attention and controversy as their use and the demand for them has geometrically increased. Some libraries now find that close to one-third of adult material circulation is attributable to videos. Entire new clienteles are attracted by this format. Libraries are being visited by persons who never before set foot in the institution. Some librarians welcome these newcomers. Others resent their presence, terming illegitimate their use only of videos to the exclusion of other library materials.

Accompanying this problem, and strongly related, is the difficulty of deciding what kinds of videos are appropriate to library collections, how much to allocate to their purchase, and how to treat them once they have been acquired. Selection and acquisition of nonprint materials is considered more difficult and time-consuming than selecting and acquiring print materials, due, in part, to the scarcity of selection and acquisition aids and in part to market volatility.[41]

More and more librarians are coming to the position that format is not nearly so salient a factor as was once believed, and that content should govern purchase. As a result, some libraries have begun to integrate their non-fiction videos into their print collections. A patron seeking travel information about Paris can find side-by-side on the shelf not only the traditional guidebooks, but videos, as well.

Non-print formats are integral parts of our personal and professional lives. Movies and television are dominating channels of information and recreation for most people, particularly those under 35. They offer easy and quick gratification. Current events and entertainment are offered on television in short, comprehensible sound bites, often without subtlety or depth, appropriate to the demands of a fast-moving and ever-changing global village. The luxury of available time to dip leisurely into an 800 page book is a scarce commodity to many adults and an intimidating prospect to young people.

Problems with sound recordings -- now primarily in CD format -- are similarly knotty. Librarians fear that purchase of popular music will lead to widespread theft. In addition, the ephemeral nature of many of the titles on the current charts will eventuate in rapid obsolescence.

Special Collections

There are many types of special collections. Some are defined by subject areas, by date of publication, others are collections of books, manuscripts, ephemera and photographs that document a particular time, place or occurrence. A special collection may be composed of materials brought together in some field of knowledge or discipline that includes rare or unusual material. [42] Most public libraries, except for the largest urban ones, do not collect rare or manuscript materials except as they relate to the immediate community because they are costly, difficult to handle and of little use to the library's public.

On the other hand, first editions of recognized authors associated with the region are often retained. Items with relevance to the history of a community are essential to collect organize and preserve. Relationships with local historical societies may help to define the collection development of each vis-à-vis the local community. The absence of a historical society puts further burden on the public library to collect not only items of local history interest, but genealogical materials as well, often a daunting and time-consuming task. Genealogical materials and genealogists are sometimes considered nuisances by public librarians given their voracious appetites for specialized materials. Often they have travelled long distances to gain access and are unwilling to wait their turns or be satisfied with information readily available. As with so many other aspects of collection development, it helps to have a policy to turn to when demands for material or assistance outdistance the capacities of the library to provide them.

SUMMARY

Excellent collection development insures that the materials required by a community to meet its educational, recreational, informational and cultural reading and viewing needs are available. Its achievement can only be reached by formulating a comprehensive collection development and management policy, by rationally allocating available monies and by establishing efficient, timely acquisitions procedures.

Public libraries tend to emphasize the importance of individual titles, but only as they relate to the collection and to the community. The lingering debate about quality versus demand is probably best solved by each individual library and then uniformly applied to collection decisions. Some balancing is always advisable.

A collection is the heart of a library. For librarians, it represents their legacy to the community. For most users, it is *the* reason for the library.

NOTES AND SUGGESTED READINGS

Notes

1. Quoted in Mary Ghikas, "Collection Management for the 21st Century," in *Managing Public Libraries in the 21st Century* (New York: Haworth Press, 1989), 121.

2. Quoted in DeAnna Covinee, *Effective Collection Development: A Unified Approach.* Occasional Paper. Series 2, #5. (Columbus, Ohio: The State Library of Ohio. 1989), 9.

3. Ghikas, 119-132.

4. Rose Mary Magrill and John Corbin, *Acquisitions Management and Collection Development in Libraries.* 2nd ed. (Chicago: American Library Association, 1989, 42.

5. Carol Hole, "Click! The Feminization of the Public Library: Policies and Attitudes Make Men the Great Unserved, *American Libraries* 21 (December 1990): 1076-1079.

6. Samuel Johnson, *Rambler*, 1750.

7. Virginia Woolf, *A Room of One's Own* (New York: Harcourt Brace and World, [1929] 1957), 71-72.

8. William Wortman, *Collection Management: Background and Principles* (Chicago: American Library Association, 1989), 75.

9. G.E. Gorman and B.R. Howes, *Collection Development for Libraries* (London: Bowker-Saur, 1989), 185.

10. C.B. Osburn, "Impact of Collection Management Practices on Intellectual Freedom," *Library Trends* 39 (Summer/Fall 1990): 170.

11. John Berry, "Acquisitions and Collection Development: A Perspective from the Top," in David Genaway comp. & ed. *Acquisitions, Budgets and Collections,* Conference May 16 and 17, 1990. St. Louis, Missouri. Proceedings (Canfield, OH: Genaway and Associates, 1991), 7.

12. Thomas Ballard, *The Failure of Resource Sharing in Public Libraries and Alternative Strategies for Service* (Chicago: American Library Association, 1986), 152-3.

13. Wortman, 47.

14. Bonita Bryant , "The Organizational Structure of Collection Development," *Library Resources and Technical Services* 31 (April-June 1987): 117

15. The information regarding organization of collection development is based on an informal unpublished study of 56 metropolitan or system libraries conducted in Nov-Dec 1990 by Elaine McConnell and Alice Gertzog. The response rate was 77%, with 44 completed questionnaires.

16. Wortman, 134.

17. Elizabeth Futas and David Vidor, "What Constitutes a 'Good' Collection?" *Library Journal* 112 (April 15, 1987): 45.

18. Lowell Martin, "Standards for Public Libraries," *Library Trends* 21 (October 1972): 164.

19. *Pennsylvania Library Laws.* (Harrisburg, PA: State Library of Pennsylvania, Library Development Division, 1989), 75.

20. W.G. Potter, "Studies of Collection Overlap," *Library Research* 4 (1982): 3-21.

21. Richard Trueswell, "A Quantitative Measure of User Circulation Requirements and Its Possible Effect on Stock Thinning and Multiple-copy Determination," *American Documentation* (January 16, 1965): 20-25.

22. Karen Krueger, "A System Level Coordinated Cooperative Collection Development Model," in Luquire Wilson, ed. *Coordinating Cooperative Collection Development: A National Perspective* (New York: Haworth Press, 1986), 50.

23. Cited in Wortman, 139.

24. Ross Atkinson, "Old Forms: New Forms: The Challenges of Collection Development," *College and Research Libraries* 50 (January 1989): 512.

25. Excellent collection development policies have been adopted by Skokie (IL) and Hennepin County (MN).

26. Nancy Gwinn and Paul Mosher, "Coordinating Collection Development: The RLG Conspectus," *College and Research Libraries* 44 (March 1983): 128-40.

27. G. Edward Evans, *Developing Library and Information Center Collections.* 2nd edition (Littleton, CO: Libraries Unlimited, 1987), 124.

28. See, for instance, Stanley Slote, *Weeding Library Collections*, 3rd ed. (Littleton, CO: Libraries Unlimited, 1989) as well as chapters in Evans, Broderick and Curley, and Wortman.

29. Herman Fussler and Julian Simon, *Patterns in the Use of Books in Large Research Libraries* (Chicago: University of Chicago Press, 1969).

30. See, for instance, Andrea Dworkin, *Letters From a War Zone.* (New York: E.. Dutton, 1989).

31. "Censorship in the Name of Public Health," *American Libraries* (May 1986): 306.

32. Osburn, 168-82.

33. Ibid., 175.

34. Cited in Osburn, 168.

35. Assistance in handling intellectual freedom/censorship problems can be found ALA's *Intellectual Freedom Manual*, compiled by the Office for Intellectual Freedom of ALA. 3rd ed. (Chicago: American Library Association, 1989) or Frances Jones, *Defusing Censorship: The Librarian's Guide to Handling Censorship Conflicts* (Phoenix, AZ: Oryx Press, 1983).

36. Evans, 407.

37. Linda Crismond, "Overview of Collection Management in the Public Library," in Judith Serebnick, ed. *Collection Management in Public Libraries*, proceedings of a preconference to the 1984 ALA Annual Conference, June 21-22, 1984, Dallas, Texas (Chicago: American Library Association, 1986), 1-12.

38. Herbert White, "The Journal That Ate the Library," *Library Journal* 113 (May 15, 1988): 62-63.

39. William Saffady, *Micrographics.* 2nd ed. (Littleton, CO: Libraries Unlimited, 1985), 1.

40. Ibid., 147.

41. Charles Forest, "The Nonprint Trades," in Karen Schmidt, ed. *Understanding the Business of Library Acquisitions* (Chicago: American Library Association, 1990), 219.

42. T.W. Leonhardt, "The Place of Special Collections in the Acquisitions Budget," *Library Acquisitions Practice and Theory* 6 (1982): 17.

Suggested Readings

Baker, Sharon. *Fiction Collection Assessment Manual*. Champaign, IL: Lincoln Trails Library System, 1992.

Cassell, Kay and Elizabeth Futas. *Developing Public Library Collections: Policies and Procedures*. New York: Neal-Schuman, 1991.

Curley, Arthur and Dorothy Broderick. *Building Library Collections*. 6th ed. Metuchen, N.J.: Scarecrow Press, 1985.

Evans, G. Edward. *Developing Library and Information Center Collections*. 2nd ed. Littleton, CO: Libraries Unlimited, 1987.

Guide for Written Collection Policy Statements. Chicago: American Library Association, 1989.

Intellectual Freedom Manual. Compiled by the Office of Intellectual Freedom of ALA. 3rd ed. Chicago: American Library Association, 1989.

Magrill, Rose Mary and John Corbin. *Acquisitions Management and Collection Development in Libraries*. 2nd ed. Chicago: American Library Association, 1989.

O'Hara, Frederic. *Informing the Nation: A Handbook of Government Information for Librarians*. New York: Greenwood, 1990.

Shoemaker, Sarah. *Collection Management: Current Issues*. New York: Neal-Schuman, 1989.

Slote, Stanley. *Weeding Library Collections,* 3rd ed. Littleton, CO: Libraries Unlimited, 1989.

Weihs, Jean. *The Integrated Library: Encouraging Access to Multi-Media Materials.* Phoenix, AZ: Oryx Press, 1991.

Wortman, William. *Collection Management: Background and Principles.* Chicago: American Library Association, 1989.

CHAPTER 9

TECHNICAL SERVICES

Among all library departments Technical Services, particularly cataloging and classification, is the most underrated, isolated and least understood. The preponderance of public service librarians know little or nothing about how a catalog is built. Technical Services department members are frequently ignored when library-wide committees are formed. They suffer from what Diane Cimbala calls "invisible anonymity."[1] Sandy Berman comments ruefully that

> librarians have been conned into believing that cataloging (making materials quickly and painlessly accessible through the catalog) is much less important than choosing those same materials.[2]

Ironically, bibliographic organization is the one piece of intellectual property that belongs almost exclusively to librarians.[3]

Yet, those who impeach the work of catalogers and classifiers charge that they have invented systems that over time have grown so complicated that a library school education is needed to find the headings, follow the tracings, and locate the material desired by users. Lionelle Elsesser says that

> The reasons for organizing a collection of any type of materials are generally the same for all libraries. Librarians want to establish control of content for the professional staff's economical information as well as promoting patron ease of access. Most systems serve informed librarians well enough.

But the client must often be a vigorous and undaunted sleuth.⁴

Much of the criticism, deserved or not, has been rendered less meaningful by the wide-spread acceptance of new technology. Few library departments have felt the impact of automation more than has Technical Services. This includes changes in the numbers and qualifications of staff as well as the nature of the work and the methods for performing it. Tasks that used to be termed "professional" are now completed by support or clerical staff. Those jobs that were clerical in nature are now routinely and automatically assigned to the computer. Duties that never existed are now embraced by the few remaining department professionals. Feats of access considered beyond the wildest expectations of the most enlightened catalogers are now, not only possible, but an assumed part of every new automated system. And the difficulties of the systems, sometimes a result of limitations imposed by the *card* catalogue, are now amenable to repair, renovation and improvement.

Technical Services generally refers to the tasks in a library that are concerned with the processing of library materials in order to make them accessible to users. Depending on how a library has chosen to divide its work, this may include acquisitions, cataloging, materials processing, circulation services, automated systems management, materials handling, system-wide support services that maintain the catalog and/or patron files. In this text acquisitions has been placed within Collection Management, Circulation has been treated separately and automated systems management assigned to Technology. This chapter, therefore, deals with organizing and labeling material and providing descriptive and subject designations; the bibliographical information that permits potential users to select the items they need.

HISTORY OF TECHNICAL SERVICES

Even before the turn of the century there had been an inexorable move toward standardization of the manner in which library materials were to be described, and toward sharing the tasks involved in this description. The goal of commercial and cooperative processing was articulated as early as 1876 when the concept of sharing cataloging information was initially mentioned in library literature. But not until 1901 did the Library of Congress begin offering cards for sale. Somewhat unexpectedly, libraries signed up in droves. In 1938, the Wilson Company entered the market with the sale of catalog cards. Book processing made its appearance in 1958. By 1968, over fifty business organizations were selling both processed books and catalog cards.

Attention to standardization of cataloging, too, was an outgrowth of the distribution of Library of Congress cards. Commercial cataloging highlighted the lack of uniform approach applied by both those selling the product and those completing the cataloging themselves. Each company provided its cataloging in slightly different form than did its competitors. In addition, not all material could be catalogued nationally. Far too much of it still required local treatment. Not surprisingly, all manner of description found its way into libraries' existing catalogs.

Four interrelated developments in the last twenty-five years have revolutionized the way in which cataloging, classification and processing are accomplished in most public libraries. The first was the creation of a standard format for entering cataloging data into a computer. In the late 1960's, under the leadership of Henrietta Avram of the Library of Congress, the MARC (an acronym for MAchine Readable Cataloging) format was developed. MARC established a standard arrangement for entering and storing descriptive cataloging information into the computer.

The second event was the adoption of a new cataloging code, a set of rules for describing library materials and for assigning access points (headings) to those descriptions. AACRII (an acronym for Anglo American Cataloging Rules, second edition) was implemented nationally in 1981. It is the authority for descriptive cataloging and, as such, establishes the proper bibliographic record for an item, based on the item itself. While the Library of Congress has published cataloging rules since 1908, it was not until the 1968 publication of AACR that there was generally agreement of a standardized description. Classic bibliographic practice held, for instance, that descriptive data would be given in the order in which they appeared in a book. Current standardized description practice calls for data to be presented in an invariable standard order. Thus descriptive data for books follows the same predictable order of presentation as does data for other media such as films and video or computer programs.

The third important innovation was the inclusion in most published monographs of Cataloging in Publication (CIP), begun in 1971. The Library of Congress agreed to provide classification and catalog entries for those books submitted either in galley form or with pre-publication data so they could be included in the final printing of the book. Currently more than 2500 publishers participate in the CIP program.

The final and perhaps most important development was that of telecommunications-based bibliographic utilities. Networks such as OCLC, RLIN and WLN are formed by agreement of member libraries to use a centralized computer system linked through telecommunications lines to terminals at local sites, thus enabling libraries to coordinate and exchange cataloging data.

These four elements combined to insure that cataloging, classification and technical services would become standardized, shared and less burdensome.

CATALOGING

Catalogs provide access to all books, journals and most other types of material added to the library by presenting brief descriptions of them. The process of creating this description is known as cataloging. Three levels of activity characterize cataloging. *Original cataloging* means creating a new record for an item; *copy cataloging* indicates that another's cataloging, modified to meet the real or perceived local cataloging requirements, is adopted; and, finally, *true copy cataloging* wherein an exact copy of the originating library's work is accepted and used.

Only the largest public libraries today undertake much original cataloging. And only in the smallest library would a cataloger function without using some form of an automated cataloging system. Estimates for the amount of cataloging undertaken locally run as low as 0% or as high as 20%. Expense, speed and expertise are among the major considerations in decisions about the extent to which material can be handled locally. Most public libraries can ill afford to opt for accuracy over speed, quality over quantity. How soon new materials can reach the shelves is crucial. A voracious public demands many fiction and non-fiction titles within days of their publication. Bibliographic shortcuts sometimes help materials reach the shelves quickly, although this may compromise accuracy and consistency. On the other hand, the average life of a cataloged title in a public library is only three to five years before it is withdrawn because of outdated material, because its condition is no longer acceptable or because it has been stolen.[5] Quick fixes, therefore, do not represent permanent mistakes.

Shared cataloging is cheaper than original cataloging in most cases. Although most librarians would hesitate to choose to duplicate exactly records cataloged elsewhere, editing existing records is obviously less expensive than doing it from scratch. One study found that the per-item cost of original cataloging is five times the cost of using provided cataloging.[6]

Barbara Kwasnik describes how cataloging has changed:

> Whereas cataloging used to be somewhat like the performance of a musical composition--that is, there was room for individual style--in form, punctuation, detail--the requirement of shared cataloging is that cataloging be absolutely uniform and standardized. The computer is unforgiving of even slight discrepancies. Thus the cataloger is now less of an interpreter of guidelines for a given set of users, than an interpreter of a mass of rules that are designed for all situations rather than for the individual library.[7]

Similarly, most libraries, public as well as other types, do not routinely engage in *true copy cataloging.* They adopt what is presented and then adapt to their own local uses. The one area in which librarians are encouraged to tinker with standardization is in the assignment of subject headings where the principle of quick and liberal access should prevail. Sandy Berman says:

The purpose of subject cataloging is to make material accessible by topic, to pinpoint items in the collection that either deal with specific themes and subjects or represent particular genres. The instruments of access are subject headings, either independently formulated or selected from a subject thesaurus...Too often however [thesaurus] vocabulary is archaic, inaccurate and unpredictable, compelling often deadly second look-ups. Too often the scheme fails to indicate genuine related headings or to convert common synonyms into cross-references. Too often old and new subjects go unrecognized. And too often not enough subject tracings are applied to make a work properly findable...Individual libraries must assume some responsibility; that is, to whatever degree they can manage, they've got to "tinker."[8]

Most libraries use Sears List of Subject Headings or Library of Congress List as the thesaurus or authority for assigning headings of their own. When card catalogs were the norm, catalogers tended to limit the number of headings assigned to a particular title because an increased number of access points would swell the catalog beyond tenable proportions. In addition, subject headings were routinely inverted so that the most significant word would be in filing position. Today's automated catalogs, however, can supply finding aids far beyond the powers of any manual catalog.

1. They are amenable to *keyword or component word searching.* Titles and subheadings automatically become access points, serving as supplements to controlled vocabulary, or thesaurus, searching, and have the added advantage of providing entry through the authors' own terminology. Searching by keywords provides an antidote to much of the terminological disadvantage provided by controlled vocabulary.

2. Most permit *Boolean Operations*, the capability of using AND, OR or NOT in combinations and exclusions. This powerful methodology which could be achieved only by laborious manual effort in a card catalog makes post-coordinated searching (devised during the search rather than preassembled) feasible.

3. It is possible, because of the fixed field code structure of MARC records to arrange for *limitation* by specified criteria. For instance, the year of publication, the document type, the language or geographic location of the publisher may serve as a demarkation by which items may be searched.

4. A built-in *automatic switching* enables a valid subject heading to be automatically substituted for a "nonpreferred" input term.

5. *Subject browsing* offers users lists of subject headings from which they can choose an appropriate term.[9]

The foregoing developments, coupled with the relative ease of revising catalogs in an online environment, contain the potential to make real and meaningful change to cataloging, to update terminology, to eliminate inconsistent and unpredictable forms and to rectify the dearth of subject headings per record.

Three principles of subject accessibility -- intelligibility, findability and fairness -- are important considerations that underlie all cataloging. The cataloging must be helpful to catalog users, should make sense and access points located where searchers are mostly like to look.

Lionelle Elsesser has described a research project in which public library users were asked a series of questions about terms they would most likely use to seek information on the following subjects:

1. Recent books and films have been about people with "split personalities." What terms would you use to find information about this?

2. A friend has liver disease from drinking too much. You want to learn about this condition. Under what words would you look?

3. You want to know more about why people change [their] behavior when they get older. Under what words would you look for this information?

4. Your doctor has recommended surgery to remove your gallbladder. Under what words would you look for information about this surgery?

5. You are scheduled to have surgery to remove the prostate. What terms would you use to find information about this?

Responses to the questions were compared with terms available in Sears List of Subject Headings and the Medical Subject Headings (MeSH) of the National Library of Medicine.

Obviously, subject headings assigned by specialists are not those that would be chosen by laypersons.

While the principle of accessibility is clearly important, says Sanford Berman, honesty, correctness and human respect are preferable considerations.[10] For instance, it is unfair to use rubrics for ethnic groups that are not their own, preferred names. Similarly, inappropriate age bias may be found in such labels as "adult," "youth," or "juvenile" when "elementary," "intermediate," or "advanced" may better describe contents and in a less offensive manner.[11]

The problem of how to deal with subject access to fiction is beginning to command attention, although it is yet in the early stages of solution. Teachers request stories about drugs or homelessness. Children and young adults, in particular, seek novels about specific subjects or time periods. Unfortunately there is presently no real way to gain access except by recourse to the subject catalogs in librarians' heads.

Question	*Patient Responses*	*Sears*	*MeSH*

#1	Split Personalities
	Schizophrenia
	Psychology
		Personality
		    Disorders
		Mental Health
			Schizophrenia
			Schizoid
			    Personality

#2	Liver Disease
	Cirrhosis
	Alcohol and
	    Effects
		Alcohol--
		    Psycholog-
		    ical Effect
			Liver
			    Cirrhosis

#3	Senility
	Geriatrics
	Aging
		Elderly--Habits
		    and Behavior
		Human Behavior
		Aging
			Psychoses, Senile
			Geriatric
			    Psychiatry
			    Aged

#4	Gallbladder
	Gallbladder
	    Surgery
	Digestive System
		Stomach
		Digestion
			Gallbladder
			    Diseases
			Cholecystitis

#5	Prostate Urology	Glands Men--Diseases	Prostatic Diseases

Figure 10: Patron, Sears and MeSH Search Terms

CLASSIFICATION AND BROWSING

Classification is both a basic human impulse and a necessity to survival. Animals classify, at least to the extent of choosing which foods to eat and which to eschew. Knowledge, itself, is constantly being defined, redefined, categorized and recategorized.

Phyllis Richmond outlines five principles of classification:

1. Every thing, object, notion, has to have a distinct and unambiguous description of its unique qualities.

2. Principles involving likeness and distinctiveness must be used in creating classes.

3. Hierarchies and other relational methods are necessary in order to group fundamental characteristics and to identify fundamental differences clearly.

4. The final system should appear as a logical progression from general to particular.

5. The system must be hospitable to all knowledge, including things that never were (such as Phlogiston); things that never shall be (like utopias); and things that are impossible (like the square root of minus one).[12]

In the context of libraries, classification can be defined as "the systematic arrangement of library materials in a manner which is useful to those who use it."[13] Public libraries generally adopt either Library of Congress or Dewey Classification systems, with the latter most widely utilized. Classification results in a call number identifying the item in that library. It may include some or all of the following: a) location code, b) classification number (by topic and form), c) Cutter number -- that is, a second line in the call or classification number to more specifically designate a book's location on the shelf, d) copy number, e) volume number, f) date.

Classification in libraries has two purposes. One is to act as a location symbol for specific items within a collection, and the other is to provide a method for grouping like materials to permit browsing. Most public libraries are successful at assigning specific locations for discrete items. But their grouping of related material is often less effective. Partially, this is because patrons do not act as we think they will. Librarians sometimes forget that each patron brings a unique set of experiences, needs and approaches to using the library.

Some of the fault does lie in the way we have chosen to classify materials. Hugh Atkinson has described his hunt for certain ethnic cookbooks in his local public library. The subject area of cookery is one of the heavy collection topics in most community libraries. In Atkinson's library, all cookbooks are grouped under 641.5 because of a library policy decision to assign a brief call number to a group of roughly linked materials rather than draw out the number further to enable French, Jewish or Indian cookery to be be grouped together. As a result, users may have to plow through tier after tier of book shelves in their search for a manual of Chinese food cookery.[14] What is important here is that the library staff must know its collections and clientele and act according to that knowledge. An abundance of cookbooks, and an avid readership, require further delineation of the class.

Studies indicate that most people who are not looking for a specific title or author, in other words a "known item," use the catalog as an entry into the hierarchy of the classification schedule. A study at Los Angeles County Public Library revealed that 60% of the people used the subject catalog, but they did not scan entries or write down authors and titles. Most located the subject they wanted, jotted down the first call number that seemed relevant and went to the shelf to browse.[15] An Australian survey revealed that 48% of patrons came to the library to browse.[16] And Fussler and Simon established as far back as 1969 that in a university library, at least, there may be three to nine browsing uses for every circulated use of an item.[17] Clearly, subject classification and shelf arrangement play a major role in making the collection more useful and used.

The most serious drawback to the browser approach is that searchers cannot know what the shelf should contain, only what is available at a given moment. Technology, however, can help to solve this problem, as well as some other vagaries of shelf browsing. It is now possible to browse online among like call numbers, shelf list fashion, as well as to learn the location of an item, be it borrowed, on holding shelves, or in process.

Standard classification, Dewey or Library of Congress, is generally applied only to certain non-fiction monograph collections in public libraries. Biographies are often shelved together under an alphabetical grouping. Juvenile collections are given separate treatment and government documents are organized with Superintendent of Documents (SUDOC) numbers. Fiction is almost always organized in a straight alphabetical arrangement, although genres such as Science Fiction, mystery, romance, short stories, and westerns are frequently called out and grouped. Whether and how to both catalog and classify sound recordings, periodicals, videos or maps requires a decision on the part of each library. The array of control methods adopted by individual libraries strains credulity. At the same time that the amount of original cataloging has shrunk to minuscule proportions in most public libraries, there is major growth in the area of original cataloging and classification of videos. Another major challenge is to bring under bibliographic control new media such as computer programs and CD-ROMs.

Studies indicate that 87% of libraries accept call numbers on cataloging copy, although a majority (65%) make adjustments in order to meet the special needs of a library. This may be

> to add Cutters or prefixes, to avoid shelflist conflicts, bring subjects together, to make the copy fit the latest edition of Library of Congress or Dewey Decimal Classification, to fix errors on the copy, and to use a number that may be equally correct, according to the classification scheme, but better fits the local collection.[18]

THE WORK OF THE TECHNICAL SERVICES DEPARTMENT

Material enters the Technical Services Department from a variety of sources including acquisition, gift, and exchange. It then must be cataloged and processed, that is, prepared for the shelf. What specifically do technical services departments do?

First, despite the decline in materials requiring original cataloging, there nonetheless remain those items which must be specially handled, that is, cataloged locally. These may be local imprints, rare books, or other specialized material. Unfortunately, automation has had little impact on original cataloging. The decisions that made cataloging so intellectually challenging must still be met. In addition, while corner-cutting was common when records were used only locally, participation in a bibliographic network requires absolute fealty to library rules. Vigilance is called for to assure that the need for original cataloging is not a criteria in the selection of material for the library. Some libraries, particularly smaller ones, may be tempted to purchase only books that come with cataloging thereby potentially screening out non-traditional sources of material, those, for instance from small or alternative presses.

Second, the department must produce, either from a bibliographic utility or another source, catalog copy for the remainder of its collections, nonbook as well as monographic. As output this takes the form of catalog cards, magnetic tapes and/or electronic records downloaded into local systems. Although the work itself may be fairly routine, establishing policies and procedures about cataloging and classification that are important for a particular library can be a complex and demanding task. The decision, for instance, about whether to add a Cutter number will depend on the size of the collection, the extent to which it circulates material and the dependability and accuracy of shelvers.

Larger public libraries will probably choose OCLC as their bibliographic utility; middle size ones may subscribe to Bibliophile or another commercial source online or on CD-ROM format. CD-ROM is popular because its price is lower, but it carries the disadvantage of less frequent updating. The smallest libraries that have not yet automated will purchase cataloging from their book jobbers who will supply not only catalog cards, but completely processed books, as well.

Selecting a centralized processing source requires answers to the following questions:

1. To whom is the service directed? What size and type library can best use the service?
2. What exactly is provided in the service?
3. How customized is the service? Will it meet particular specifications?
4. Is the service linked to a book purchase plan?
5. What are the costs and how do they compare with other services?[19]

Third, the technical services department must produce and manage the catalog. In nonautomated libraries, cards must be filed, following ALA or LC Filing Rules, and the catalog maintained -- that is cards pulled for withdrawn materials, changes in main entries made as they occur, and other related tasks.

Janet Hill Swan comments that in the automation age "catalog management" becomes database management.

> "Database correction" involving computer input and invocation of global changes calls for different levels of staff than "catalog correction" which was suitably staffed by clerks armed with erasers and correction fluid.[20]

Linking the public access catalog with commercially available online abstracting, indexing and full-text reference databases as well as locally developed bibliographic databases, full-text resources such as encyclopedias and local directory information may fall under catalog management. This would require the development of a menu allowing choices and the provision of interfaces that allow users to choose among them applying a single set of search techniques.

As libraries become increasingly "distance independent" patrons will grow to rely ever more heavily on catalog information. When browsing is impossible because material is housed elsewhere, patrons will require the kind of information necessary to make informed decisions about whether a particular item will satisfy their information needs. This may involve abstracts, tables of contents, indexes and other helping aids available through the catalog. To some extent the catalog in this situation becomes not a guide to using the shelves, but a substitute for them.

Fourth, the department is generally charged with coordinating for the local library cooperative catalog relations with system member libraries. In order to be functional, participants in shared automated ventures must identify common goals, create operational frameworks, train staff, insure overall management, and resolve issues of standardization, costs and financing. Members then have to accept and comply, not only with strict bibliographic standards, but with the remaining agreed-upon rules and regulations.

Fifth, Technical Services is responsible for processing materials for the shelves. In a public library this may include marking and labeling materials; stamping, posting or otherwise affixing book plates, card pockets, date due slips, identification markings and accession numbers. If books do not come pre-processed, it also may entail affixing book jackets. Here again, automation has substantially simplified the process. Labels, bar codes, and other identifying information are machine-produced through bibliographic networks or larger local library systems, or by the jobber as cataloging is being completed. Not only are countless staff hours involved in matching and affixing labels saved, but less review is required since computers do not make typographical or transcription errors. The flow of material should be uninterrupted if the savings in time permitted by the computer cataloging are to be realized. By batching materials and avoiding unnecessary or redundant tasks, some libraries report that books routinely reach the shelves within seven days of *ordering*. Compared with substantial backlogs in most libraries of up to a year less than a decade ago, this is impressive testimony to the power of technology.

Sixth, most Technical Services departments are called upon to conduct inventories. An Acquisitions or Circulation department is occasionally given the task, but the strong relationship between catalog maintenance and inventory work make Technical Services a likely candidate for the job. The inventory may be *full* -- a complete check of all holdings -- or *partial* -- a survey, for instance, of a heavily used part of the collection. During inventory, the shelf list, in card form or a computer offprint, is used to check holdings on the shelf and those in circulation, being repaired or at the bindery. Items identified as missing are assessed for current usefulness and are either reordered after a set time and a second rechecking of the shelves, or withdrawn from the collection. High loss rates -- more than five percent of a collection -- should lead the library administration to review present security arrangements.

In a more visionary mode, John Corbin considers the role of Technical Services in the coming electronic library in which *all* information will be in digital form, stored as computer-readable files on magnetic disk, optical disc, magnetic tape or other media yet to be invented and developed, rather than on paper or film. No print copies of any information will exist until there is a demand;

no hard copies will be retained even after a demand is met. Information seekers may never physically enter the electronic library they use.

In this environment, Corbin maintains, there will be a need for bibliographic control, for systems planning, development and evaluation and for systems support. A number of technical services -- physical processing of materials, and binding and mending, for instance -- will no longer be necessary. Computer-readable items will require descriptive cataloging just as do print materials and very little change from today's descriptive cataloging rules and practices will occur. But classification will probably be unnecessary. Technical Services will probably undertake the planning, design and implementation of new or improved systems; train staff to acquire and implement new or improved systems; devise gateway access systems and evaluate the systems for effectiveness and efficiency. Systems support will operate and maintain the computer-based systems supporting the electronic library. Since every service and function will be completely supported or controlled by computers and other electronic equipment, the work of the department is vital. In short, Corbin contends that the electronic library will require technical services just as do traditional ones. But their nature will be different.[21]

ORGANIZATION OF THE TECHNICAL SERVICES DEPARTMENT

Implementation of online public access catalogs in libraries requires that catalogers work closely with system librarians and public service librarians. Michael Gorman and Hugh Atkinson have suggested that decentralization of technical services is not only desireable from work flow and expertise considerations, but also because it would give professionals increased job satisfaction, greater mobility, promotability and enhanced status. Predictions abound that there will be a gradual "blurring of lines" between technical and public services In some libraries, client-centered units are being established with selectors, bibliographers, classifiers and information specialists all attached to single units. Several middle-sized libraries have experimented with selectors also doing copy cataloging and revision, but with technical services support staff continuing to complete the processing task. In other libraries, technical service and system offices are being merged into one division. Circulation, sitting between materials and users, has been deemed a public service. Now, however, automation has highlighted the repetitive nature of the work and revealed a new kinship between technical services and circulation. Another departure is the use of acquisitions staff, on receipt of items, to complete copy cataloging.

Janet Hill Swan has discovered four models of technical services organization:

Larger Libraries, centralized technical services: The prevailing organization, which became commonplace about thirty years ago. Jobs are narrowly focused and skills are developed and exercised over relatively small segments of the operation.

Larger Libraries, technical services dispersed: Configuration for dispersal includes distribution of professional functions to branches and collections, but continued centralization of most nonprofessional activities. Nonprofessional jobs are narrowly focused and professional positions are managerial. Dispersal of professional duties divides a library system into a number of smaller entities that behave as self-contained small libraries. Librarians need to be competent in a range of activities, aware of all aspects of librarianship, balancing the needs of departmental clientele against requirements of the system as a whole. The smaller the entities, the greater the potential for inefficiencies and inconsistencies that arise when doing a complex job part-time and from having consultative access to other professionals doing similar work.

Small libraries, technical services retained: Continue to need staff for technical services activities, although the amount of time required should gradually decrease. Staff must be responsible for several phases of operations and are likely not to be limited to technical services performed elsewhere.

Smaller libraries, technical services performed elsewhere: Small, nonspecialized libraries will be able to cede most technical services operations to a central entity and will need only a small staff component to complete the professional steps left to be done locally.[22]

When card catalogs were the norm, the cataloging arm of technical services had to be situated in close proximity to them or they had to be duplicated, particularly in multi-story buildings. The same held true for the acquisitions department. Unlimited access to online systems has made it possible for technical services departments to be placed in remote locations. One benefit of this new-found flexibility is the provision of more central public space. But in the trade off, the technical services department is rendered still more isolated and perhaps more ignored than ever.

Attention to workflow is crucial in technical services. It is possible to track and therefore predict heavy and light periods that interrupt the flow. During less busy times, department members can attend to neglected matters such as processing gifts or learning new protocols. In order for materials to flow naturally and logically through the department, a functional layout allowing for maximum flexibility is best. Less than 120 square feet per person is deemed inadequate. The nature of the work requires good, shadow-free lighting.

Establishing clear routines prevents snarls from developing and flow-charting a process helps clarify paths through which work travels. The work-flow chart on the following page reveals the steps that must be followed before new non-fiction books can reach the library shelves:

STAFF

Professional technical services librarians today are more likely to supervise and plan than they are to catalog. New generation systems accompanied by vastly improved capabilities appear with

Figure 11
Work Flow Chart for Technical Services Department

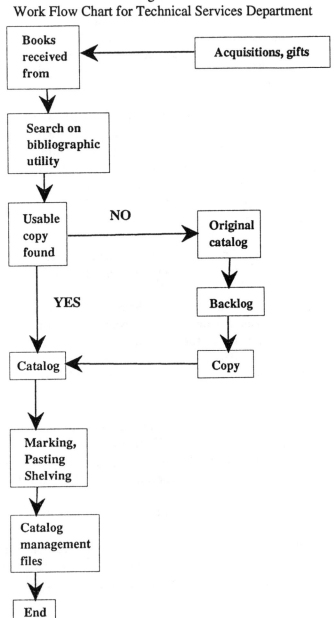

increasing regularity and rapidity. The previously accepted 5-year planning cycle for automation has had to be replaced with more realistic 2-year schedules into which are integrated goals formulated for the longer planning cycle.[23] However, although the amount of original cataloging is substantially diminished, the nature of the work that remains is more specialized and difficult. Today's professional cataloger must have a good knowledge of MARC formats, experience with bibliographic sources, local systems, systems analysis techniques and technical service management, in addition to Anglo American Cataloging Rules II, revised (AACRIIR), Library of Congress Subject Headings (LCSH), Dewey Decimal Classification (DDC) or Library of Congress Classification (LCC).[24]

What comprises the work of *professional* catalogers? They create catalog cards, develop and review procedures, maintain knowledge of standards, plan the departmental work flow, train support staff, oversee equipment operation and maintenance, act as liaison with other library staff. The Department Head must insure that there is release time for experimenting with new systems and equipment, that employees are free to attend network training sessions and user and discussion groups. Without continuing education and staff development, the Technical Services Department will rapidly fade into obsolescence.

The technical services head is faced with a welter of workflow decisions, many of which must be coordinated with other departments. Elizabeth Nichols outlines the following as examples:

---whether pre-order searching will be performed in Cataloging or Acquisitions

---whether order records will be entered in full-MARC format, downloaded from a bibliographic utility or entered in brief format from reviews and publishers blurbs. Who will maintain quality control for records entered online?

---how materials entered online "on-the-fly" will be assessed for discard or inclusion in fully cataloged format;

---whether approval plan materials will be cataloged and available for request online prior to an order or after added

copies, or all copies, have been received; and
---where a specific title with more than one possible call number
will best fit collection needs.[25]

With the diminution of cataloging duties, the problem of
finding librarians for technical services has been exacerbated.
Library school curricula has deemphasized cataloging and offerings
are very thin. And students are discouraged from entering that
branch of librarianship.

The roles of paraprofessionals and clerks in Technical Services
have changed dramatically. Under automation, the Library
Technical Assistant (LTA) acts as the technical expert on OCLC
production, as the copy cataloger and as the supervisor of clerical
staff. Automation has also resulted in a narrower definition of
clerical duties, most of which are performed online. These tend to
be repetitive and wearying. Some medium-sized and larger
libraries have formed Technical Services clerical pools, a move that
permits sharing jobs in a free-floating arrangement, thus preventing
some fatigue and burn-out. Variety should be built in to each
department member's work. No one can or should be asked to sit
at a terminal for eight hours every day.

REPORTS AND STATISTICS

The work of Technical Services is more measurable than are
public service activities. In the catalog department statistics are
kept about the number of titles and volumes cataloged, cards filed
or data entered, retrospective conversions completed, volumes
withdrawn or sent to the bindery, and materials processed. Staff
members maintain individual records of their activities which are
compiled monthly by the head of the department and forwarded to
the director for analysis.

One recurring question centers on production levels and costs.
Unfortunately, no generalizable authoritative data currently exists.
Most studies that have been conducted are place and personnel
specific. Training, type of material being handled, other respon-

sibilities all have impact on output. Charges for outside processing may at first glance seem high, but in the long run represent substantial savings. Among the factors to consider are an honest assessment of total staff time, supplies and equipment required by the operation. Local salaries, choices of processing materials, and decisions about the level of quality in cataloging, may alter cost figures. Data can be generated to provide benchmarks for analysis and comparison. Changes in productivity and costs can then be monitored and procedures altered, if necessary.

SUMMARY

Technology has substantially altered the methods and tools for accomplishing technical services, but the aims and goals remain the same: to make materials accessible by describing them, to determine where materials belong within a library's current scheme of arrangement and to prepare materials for shelving by technicially processing them.

Professional cataloging, once a solitary, site-specific activity, has become cooperative and standardized through the use of bibliographic utilities, the MARC format and AACRII. As a result, public library professional catalogers today are more customarily engaged in management tasks and system development than in original cataloging.

The ability to routinely carry out formerly difficult and time consuming tasks has liberated technical services librarians and challenged them to develop better and more powerful methods of providing access not only to in-house collections, but to those in remote locations.

NOTES AND SUGGESTED READINGS

Notes

1. Diana Cimbala, "Technical Services in the Mission of the Library: The 'Back Room' Performers," in Jennifer Cargill ed., *Library Management and Technical Services* (New York: Haworth Press, 1988), 7.

2. Sanford Berman, *The Joy of Cataloging* (Phoenix, AZ: Oryx Press, 1981), 3.

3. Sheila Intner and Janet Swan Hill, eds., *Cataloging: The Professional Development Cycle* (New York: Greenwood, 1991), 22.

4. Lionelle Elsesser, "A Case of 'Cirrhosis': The Subject Approach to Health Information," in Sanford Berman, ed. *Subject Cataloging: Critiques and Innovations* (New York: Haworth Press, 1984), 63.

5. Kenneth John Bierman, "Technical Services in Public Libraries," in Dres Racine, ed., *Managing Technical Services in the 90's* (New York: Haworth Press, 1991), 118.

6. Leslie Bliel and Charlene Renner, "Copy Cataloging and the Bibliographic Networks," in Michael Gorman and Associates, *Technical Services Today and Tomorrow* (Englewood, CO: Libraries Unlimited, 1990), 99.

7. Quoted in Caroline Coughlin and Alice Gertzog, *Lyle's Administration of the College Library,* 5th ed. (Metuchen, NJ: Scarecrow Press, 1992), 275.

8. Sanford Berman, "Tools for Tinkering," in Berman, Sanford, ed., *Subject Cataloging: Critiques and Innovations* (New York: Haworth Press, 1984), 213.

9. Adopted from Lois Mai Chan and Theodora Hodges, "Subject Cataloging and Classification: The Late 1980's and Beyond," in Gorman, 77-82.

10. Berman, *Joy of Cataloging*, 83.

11. Lionel Elsesser in Berman, *Subject Cataloging*, 64.

12. Phyllis Richmond, "General Theory of Classification," in Betty Bengston and Janet Swan Hill, *Classification of Library Materials* (New York: Neal-Schuman, 1990), 17.

13. Hugh Atkinson, "Classification in an Unclassified World," in Bengston and Hill, 7.

14. Ibid.

15. Mary Ghikas, "Setting Classification Policy," in Bengston and Hill, 128.

16. Reported in Jennifer Younger, "Classification and the Library User," in Bengston and Hill, 177.

17. Herman Fussler and Julian Simon, *Patterns in the Use of Books in Large Research Libraries* (Chicago: University of Chicago, 1969), 115.

18. Elizabeth Dickinson Nichols," Classification Decision-Making in California Libraries," in Bengston and Hill, 165.

19. Donald Foster, *Managing the Catalog Department.* 3rd ed. (Metuchen, NJ: Scarecrow Press, 1987), 48.

20. Janet Swan Hill, "Staffing Technical Services in 1995," *Journal of Library Administration* 9 (1988): 97.

21. John Corbin, "Technical Services for the Electronic Library," *Library Administration and Management* 62 (Spring 1992): 86-90.

22. Hill, 89-91.

23. Irene Godden, ed., *Library Technical Services: Operations and Management.* 2nd ed. (San Diego, CA: Academic Press, 1991), 3.

24. Sheila Intner and Janet Swan Hill, eds., *Cataloging: The Professional Development Cycle* (New York: Greenwood Press, 1991), 22.

25. Elizabeth Dickinson Nichols, "Automation and the Renaissance Librarian," *Journal of Library Administration* 13 (1990): 151.

Suggested Readings

Bengston, Betty and Janet Swan Hill, eds. *Classification of Library Materials.* New York: Neal-Schuman, 1990.

Berman, Sanford. *The Joy of Cataloging: Essays, Letters, Reviews and Other Explosions.* Phoenix, AZ: Oryx Press, 1981.

Berman, Sanford, ed. *Subject Cataloging: Critiques and Innovations.* New York: Haworth Press. 1984.

Berman, Sanford. *Worth Noting: Editorials, Letters, Essays, an Interview and Bibliography.* Jefferson, NC: McFarland, 1988.

Cargill, Jennifer, ed. *Library Management and Technical Services.* New York: Haworth Press, 1988.

Carpenter, Michael and Elaine Svenonius, eds. *Foundations of Cataloging: A Sourcebook.* Littleton, CO: Libraries Unlimited, 1985.

Corbin, John. "Technical Services for the Electronic Library." *Library Administration and Management* 62 (Spring 1992): 86-90.

Foster, Donald. *Managing the Catalog Department.* 3rd ed. Metuchen, NJ: Scarecrow Press, 1987.

Fox, Beth Wheeler. *Behind the Scenes at the Dynamic Library.* Chicago: American Library Association, 1990.

Godden, Irene P., ed. *Library Technical Services: Operations and Management.* 2nd ed. San Diego, CA: Academic Press, 1991.

Gorman, Michael and Associates. *Technical Services Today and Tomorrow.* Englewood, CO: Libraries Unlimited, 1990.

Hill, Janet Swan. "Staffing Technical Services in 1995." *Journal of Library Administration* 9 (1988): 87-103.

Intner, Sheila and Janet Swan Hill. *Cataloging, the Professional Develop-*

ment Cycle. New York: Greenwood, 1991.

Intner, Sheila and Janet Swan Hill. *Recruiting, Educating and Training Cataloging Librarians.* New York: Greenwood, 1989.

Nichols, Elizabeth Dickinson. "Automation and the Renaissance Librarian." *Journal of Library Administration* 13 (1990): 139-55.

Racine, Drew, ed. *Managing Technical Services in the 90's.* New York: Haworth Press, 1991.

CHAPTER 10

ACCESS SERVICES

How the broad undifferentiated mass called "the public" views the library is frequently a product of the relationship that has been established between users and the circulation staff. That department's members are the first users meet when they come to the library and the last they encounter before they leave. The circulation staff bears responsibility for welcoming newcomers and punishing those late returners of library materials. The complicated interplay between user and staff is rendered yet more complex by the rules all libraries find it necessary to impose on borrowers.

And circulation staffs, on the line, overworked, underappreciated, sometimes lose sight of their main purpose -- to place materials in the hands of patrons. They assume rule-enforcing postures, acquire rigid stances and create yet more restrictive policies. Users become the enemy. A we-they attitude develops and eavesdroppers might overhear staff making such comments as *"They'll* take as much advantage as you'll let them get away with" or *"They* are irresponsible and must be punished" or, as one trustee was heard to exclaim about a proposed rule, "We shouldn't make it too easy for people!"

The final step in the process of making library materials available, once they have been acquired, cataloged, and identified as needed by a user, is circulation. The procedure is built on answers to the following questions:

-- Who can borrow library materials?

-- What materials will be lent?
-- For how long may they be borrowed?
-- What will happen if they are not returned?

To underestimate the importance of the circulation experience is to risk support for the entire library operation, particularly as funds become less readily available and competition for what remains intensifies. As a result, attention must be paid, not only to streamlining processes and designing judicious and equitable policies, but to the treatment conferred on patrons while both are being applied. Circulation is concerned with maximizing the investment that the library has expended in acquiring and organizing its collections and therefore should provide every assistance feasible to both the library and the user.[1]

Increasingly, circulation services have come to be known as "access services," those functions that facilitate patrons' access to libraries' collections in all formats -- non-print, sound, video, print, electronic, or graphics.[2] How this differs from past practice rests partially on the older assumption that a library's lifeblood, its own materials, travelled, that is circulated, through its system. Today the term has been enlarged to encompass, in addition, both materials the library does not possess but will borrow from elsewhere, or those it owns but does not choose to lend, i.e. those it permits to be photocopied. Access, then, describes a much broader service.

The functions of circulation/access services include responsibility for registering borrowers, charging and discharging materials, overdue processing, and stack maintenance. In most public libraries today, circulation manages Interlibrary Loan, has custody of copying equipment and maintains library security. The objectives of circulation include facilitating the use of materials, knowing which materials are being used, how frequently they are being used, and by whom. Circulation systems must also permit borrowers to learn when their materials are due.

CIRCULATION POLICIES

Circulation is one of the few library services where policies, procedures and rules are developed, written down and made available routinely to the public. Indeed, the codified policies of circulation are interpreted as quasi legal documents and their acceptance, which occurs every time borrowers agree to abide by library rules, can be considered tantamount to a signed contract. Most circulation policies made by administrators and managers are presented to library boards for approval and are subject to scrutiny by the library's legal counsel. These policies, though, are never created in a vacuum. The size of the library, the arrangement of its collection, the nature of its community, the extent of its circulation and its aims and goals all influence circulation decisions. Successful circulation policies rest on clearly defined objectives and a cohesive set of procedures that satisfy them.[3]

The purposes of circulation rules are to enable libraries to keep track of their materials, to ascertain borrowers' eligibility, and to ensure the equitable and free flow of material through the system. No more controls than are clearly necessary should ever be imposed, and the rules should be reviewed frequently, with patron comments seriously considered, particularly those that are unsolicited.

Unfortunately, research into optimal circulation behaviors -- the best loan periods, for instance -- is sparse, and libraries base their practices on tradition and an instinct for what seems to work.

Registration - Who May Borrow?

Many aspects of the registration process have been simplified in recent years. Nonetheless, its basic intent remains the same -- to permit those eligible for library service to borrow materials and to bar those who are not, nonresidents or abusers of library policies, for instance.

The primary constituents of most public libraries are their residents. Yet even clarifying a geographical borrowing area is fraught with difficult questions. Are those who work in cities, but who reside elsewhere eligible for free library cards? Should those who own property, but live in other communities be afforded free service? Can temporary residents borrow library materials? What must their tenure within the community be in order for them to qualify? Does the library have cooperative arrangements with other institutions that include reciprocal borrowing?

Further, most libraries distinguish among different types of borrowers based on age, educational level, persons with special characteristics or needs (for instance, teachers, handicapped persons, government officials), and institutional or nonpersonal borrowers (school, business or other community organizations).

Differing age levels have often been the basis on which libraries discriminate between children and adults, although sometimes grade level is used as the determinant. Children are generally deemed eligible to apply for a library card when they can write their name. In some libraries, entrance into kindergarten may be the decisive factor. Children's cards routinely require parental or caregiver signature in order to insure the library that a responsible adult not only is aware of a child's intention to borrow library material, but accepts the obligation implied in the transaction. The most popular transition point into full adult borrowing status seems to be fourteen years old,[4] although some libraries use twelve and others sixteen. If grade levels are the discriminant, sixth frequently marks the cut-off point. Occasionally, children's cards carry limitations on what they can borrow. Video, in particular, has been subject to restriction. Most libraries, on the other hand, give children the right to borrow anything without discrimination, refusing to act "in loco parentis," that is, in place of parents.[5] Some libraries walk a middle ground and are willing to bar children from certain materials if their caregivers have specified that their privileges be limited. The Montgomery County (Ohio) Library System has recently adopted a policy of refusing adult videos to children whose parents have notified the library in writing that they wish this action to be taken.

A number of states have instituted statewide borrowing programs in which the library cards of any public library in the state are honored at any other public library. Pennsylvania's "Access, PA," for instance, permits users to borrow materials from any cooperating library in the state and return them to their local libraries. The vast majority of public and school libraries and libraries in state academic institutions have agreed to participate in this program. Most private college and university libraries have not joined, however. Sample periods test the degree of non-resident use of particular libraries and the state library confers monetary rewards based on its findings.

Other libraries have entered multitype library cooperative arrangements which include direct reciprocal borrowing. Few public libraries discourage non-residents from purchasing library cards. How much to charge is problematic. Fees are generally set at or slightly above the average taxpayer's contribution. Some charge substantially more. Most libraries have a system of "deposit" cards for temporary residents, those who intend to remain in the community for only a limited period of time. Summer residents, migrant workers, temporary employees all fall within these categories.

What constitutes identification when new patrons apply for library cards is yet another area that generates debate among libraries. Users at one time had to wait weeks between the time they applied for library cards and when they were permitted to borrow materials. It was common practice to send a new library card to the address on the application in order to verify that the information supplied was correct and that the applicant lived at the address given the library. Today, libraries typically accept almost any document with the applicant's name and address -- a telephone bill, an envelope sent through the mail, a report card -- and allow immediate, although often limited, borrowing privileges.

Information collected during the registration process can supply much-needed management information. Age ranges are interesting. Even addresses can be utilized to learn where borrowers do and do not live in a community.

Probably the most important part of the registration process is the way in which new patrons are welcomed, the verbal and non-verbal messages communicated while information is being solicited and provided. Rules imparted without explanation become onerous. Those explained, justified with supporting reasons, are more willingly accepted. Offers to help use the library are remembered with pleasure. New borrowers can be reluctant users, can have difficulty navigating the catalog, sometimes are unable to discriminate amongst potentially relevant materials, and become tongue-tied in the face of expertise. If the tone set at the initial encounter is positive, the patron may become a regular user. The reverse is, unfortunately, equally likely.

Loans - What Materials?

As a rule, public libraries distinguish between circulating and non-circulating materials. Reference books, those required for consultation, though shelved in open stacks to permit public access, rarely leave the library. In addition, very expensive materials that libraries can ill-afford to duplicate are labelled "for reference only" and not permitted to circulate. Materials that are fragile, invaluable because of rarity or uncataloged -- those included in special collections -- are also non-loanable and may even be subject to restricted use. Archives, historical papers, correspondence, manuscripts, drawings, paintings or photographs may all come under this category of material. The latest issues of current periodicals almost never circulate. The borrowability of back issues is not subject to generalization. In some cases, they routinely circulate; in others they never do.

Materials that may be borrowed are also broken down into various types. Most public libraries house New Books on special shelves where patrons seeking "something to read" rather than specific information can browse among recent arrivals. Not only are they housed separately, but new books are often accorded differential loan periods. Reserve materials in public libraries refer to those titles specifically requested by patrons and set aside for them for a period of time. Reserve materials in public libraries are, for the most part, new books for which there is a current, heavy demand. Post-cards or telephone notification systems apprise patrons of the availability of their reserves with some libraries levying fees for providing the notification service. The books are then held separately for a specified period of time before being passed on to the next reservation, or replaced in the collection. Four reserves are generally assumed to justify purchase of an additional copy.

Loans - How Many and for What Period of Time?

Most contemporary public libraries loan materials. In fact, for many it is their most important function. In ages past, libraries were not only uninterested in having their materials leave the shelves, but made positive efforts to prevent them from exiting the library. During the middle ages, libraries *chained* their books to the walls and desks to dissuade users from borrowing them. In colonial and post-revolutionary times in America, when library holdings represented an institution's wealth, books were regarded as treasures to be admired and placed back in treasuries, that is libraries.

Today, libraries eager to see their materials circulate frequently experiment with varying borrowing periods. As with other questions regarding library behavior, answers lie in such consideration as the location of the institution, its traditions, the nature of its constituency and their reading habits, the ease of use and the demand for the material. There is no uniformity in practice, although two weeks is probably most common. Loan periods are often tied to the relative popularity and/or the demand versus availability of various kinds of material. Heavy use material -- those with long reserve lists, new adult fiction, popular non-fiction, and videos -- are likely to be borrowable for shorter loan periods. Older adult fiction and non-fiction, and children's books can be borrowed longer. A short loan for videos is a twenty-four hour period and for books one week. A long loan is three weeks.

Most public libraries, especially those with two-week loan periods, allow patrons to renew books at least once for the same loan period as the first time if there are no other calls on the material. Many permit more than one renewal. Those with automated library systems are far more likely to accept telephone renewal since the number of times materials have been renewed is easily trackable. Renewals comprise about 3% of circulation -- almost 6% for those libraries who have two-week loan periods and only 2% for those with four-week loans.[6]

Some libraries establish common due dates each week. In other words, they require that all materials be returned on a Thursday or Wednesday. In others, there is a grace period between the time materials are due and when fines are imposed. Extended borrowing periods are often granted to patrons going on vacation, to teachers or to homebound students. Almost all libraries that circulate framed art works, circulate them for long time periods, as much as six months.

Overdues - What happens when materials are not returned in a timely fashion?

Libraries worry a great deal about unreturned materials. According to Carlton Rochell, the number of items that are overdue are about four to five for every hundred borrowed. Those never recovered amount to about two to three for every ten thousand lent.[7] Donald Sager considers the loss to range between 1 and 2 percent of total circulation.[8] Even if the latter figures are accurate, complicated systems designed to retrieve materials are far more expensive that what is gained by attempts to recover them. On the other hand, making the effort to reclaim borrowed materials is viewed as a public trust. Most libraries have instituted procedures for the timely return of their materials. These include notification agendas and sets of contingency actions. Observers have noted that recent thinking about overdue notices has shifted from considering them obligatory to merely regarding them as a courtesy. Borrowers are considered fully responsible for materials and for payment of late return penalties, whether or not the library has seen fit to notify or remind them about their delinquency.

The overwhelming majority of libraries continue to send out one or more notices at standard periods. Sometimes these are followed by telephone contacts and then a final notice or bill. The Fort Worth Public Library has installed a computerized phone notification system to contact delinquent borrowers. The greater the time between the due date and the first notice, the more materials that will be returned and the fewer first notices that will have to be mailed. Decisions about whether to make the final step a collection agency, the police or the threat of litigation cannot be made with impunity. Negative public relations and discouragement to use the library will surely ensue. Yet, the costs of not pursuing this course should also be weighed and determinations reached within the context of which actions are most appropriate to the community and to the problems involved.

What kinds of punishment to impose on delinquent borrowers is yet another matter that requires predetermined policies meted out evenhandedly, but tempered with mercy. Most libraries withdraw library privileges from those who do not return materials. Some also refuse to loan materials to those who owe large overdue or replacement fees. Borrowers who consistently contravene the rules, now easily identified through the computer, also are similarly penalized.

Dire financial times carry with them a strong temptation to use overdue fines to help finance the library. Fines should never be considered a source of income, only a method for encouraging the prompt return of library materials. For this reason, fines should be set fairly low and at rates consonant with the practices of a particular area and type of library. High charges will discourage library use, but may encourage return of materials. Conversely, low charges may not serve as an incentive, but they will not deter library use. Daily overcharge fees in most libraries are nominal -- two to five cents a day for children's materials and five to ten cents for adults -- as are the ceiling amounts that can accrue.[9] Special materials such as videos, periodicals and other audiovisual software and hardware are subject to daily or hourly fines, but even they rarely accumulate to more than $10.

In the late 1960s and early 1970s a number of experiments were implemented to test what would happen if fines for overdue materials were eliminated. The movement never took hold despite slightly more reports of successes than failures. Those pleased with the experiment noted increases in circulation, reduction of clerical tasks, and improved public relations as part of the benefits from embarking on such a program.[10] Other public libraries who experimented with no fees reimposed fines after experiencing very large increases in numbers of overdue books. Libraries have also declared amnesty periods where no fines are collected on overdue materials, and have experimented with substituting donated items for food banks in lieu of fees.

Virtually all libraries charge patrons the cost of a lost book. Most also impose fees in addition to replacement cost for processing. Here, too, it is judicious to consider the transgression, potential damage to future relations, and the nature of the material that has been lost. Older material of questionable value may not be worthy of replacement. New material that has been widely duplicated may also not merit purchasing a new copy. Tempering punishment with reason is always a wise course, particularly in light of the rapid increase in cost of replacement. Charge something, but not an astronomical fee.

CHARGING SYSTEMS

The quantity of detail required to maintain control over borrowed materials and the error-laden state of most existing files impelled many public libraries to automate circulation functions before subjecting other aspects of the library operation to computerization. This contrasts sharply with college libraries who considered cataloging in acute need of quick relief. It is predicted that a substantial majority of libraries will have automated systems within the foreseeable future. The only exceptions will be those libraries whose circulation statistics are low, whose materials do not circulate, who have small numbers of patrons or who are financially unable to support automation.

Manual systems employed prior to installation of computers were based on the use of a "book card" for identification. Transactions were recorded directly on the book card or on a third card called a "transaction" or "T-card." It was impossible to tell without going through all files whether a book had been checked out or when it was due. Other libraries adopted microfilm transaction systems. With this method, records were only retrieved when materials were overdue. This system's drawbacks lay in the fact that patrons could *never* be told when particular items were due or whether they were checked out or lost, although it was faster than its predecessors. Depending on the system employed, keeping track of returns was also time-consuming and error-prone. These errors were costly in a variety of ways, not the least of which was patron-library relations regarding overdue and lost material, and in calculating and recording fines paid and owed.

What librarians find most attractive in an automated charging system is the potential to rid themselves of the endless number of paper files associated with circulation. They also seek to lower the costs of the overdue billing operation, reserve and hold systems, and to speed up the recall system, if one exists. While initially libraries were content to learn who could borrow materials, soon they demanded to know the borrowing status of an item, as well.

Ann Paietta outlines appropriate expectations from a circulation control system:

--availability whenever a library is open and running continuously with no down time;
--charging. The systems should link authorized borrowers, books and date due together fast and correctly, letting staff know patron identity;
--determine location of an item rapidly;
--identify, hold and recall items;
--prepare overdue notices;
--prepare lists of items out on loan to any borrower;
--detect delinquent borrowers at time of check out;
--discharge: the system should update returned materials in files and forgive or add fines to account;
--prepare management information such as statistics and

report;
--register patrons;
--handle different due dates;
--permit book renewal;
--indicate, calculate and account for fines;
--provide search capabilities;
--display status of item and number of copies;
--interface with other library functions.[11]

The impulse to automate circulation may have been a product of four congruent factors:

1. The thrust towards *accountability*. The furor over accountability in the public sector caused people to ask for more than mere generalities in annual reports. Libraries had been accustomed to summarizing the numbers of books added to their collections and the number of people who passed through their doors (whether or not they required service). Now, however, factual data was sought as a basis for budget allocations and as benchmark information for annual comparisons. Some librarians realized that accountability could be turned to their benefit as a way of pointing out effectiveness in providing service.

2. The *economic crunch* of the late 1980s and the 1990s. In creating a list of priority services for public libraries, circulation appeared near the top. This made automation's promise of labor-saving procedures look extremely attractive.

3. Libraries' acceptance of *broadened goals*. The increased recognition of information's importance in the lives of people increased expectations of what the library would contain and could supply. The importance of having materials expeditiously circulating through the system rather than hindered by bureaucratic roadblocks dictated a level of control heretofore unpracticed.

4. The new emphasis on *cooperative ventures* brought about

by broadened goals and the capabilities of computers meant that local libraries had to build files compatible with those of others, ones that could quickly and easily manipulate data in order that the interlibrary loan subsystem could be effective and enable participating institutions to circulate materials held by other libraries almost as easily as it could circulate its own holdings.[12]

Ironically, despite the obvious and deep advances in circulation systems, most still require substantial manual operation. Materials that have been barcoded can be automatically recorded with a light pen or other devices, but making patrons aware of when their material is due back requires hand-charging, whether in the form of a transaction card put in a pocket or a date-due stamp either on an outside flap or inside the book.

INTERLIBRARY LOAN

Libraries have traditionally delivered documents to patrons in one of two ways: by acquiring and circulating them or by obtaining them temporarily from other sources, usually other libraries who join together in cooperative groups in order to share their materials. This temporary acquisition is commonly known as interlibrary loan. Today's libraries cannot possibly own all materials their patrons want or require without recourse to interlibrary loan.

The interlibrary loan system has been standardized in most states. State Library agencies establish networks, inform constituents about required procedures, describe how and where to forward requests for materials not in local library collections, and work out formulas for rewarding net lenders. Delivery is carried out through mail, United Parcel Service, phone, local area delivery systems, electronic mail and facsimile machines. Facsimile delivery, used primarily with periodical materials, has reduced delivery time from days to minutes. State library agencies work out sets of principles, codes, based on the one that governs national interlibrary lending. These usually state:

--that interlibrary loan is not a substitute for buying the materials needed by one's clients:
--that the requesting library is responsible for encouraging clients to go to another library in person to obtain the desired material, eliminating the ILL request, if possible;
--that the list of responsibilities of the lending library absolves it from lending anything it does not wish to share;
--that the lending library publicize its ILL policies, process requests promptly and report failure to fill requests;
--that the lending library should not count time spent in transit in its loan period and is permitted to charge fees for its material.

It has been traditional to discourage the interlibrary loans of certain materials, including out-of-print books, best sellers and ephemera such as light romances. Libraries sometimes use "newness" as a defining barrier.

Each library handles its own interlibrary loan processes differently. And interlibrary loan librarians learn to work around such road-blocks as non-cooperative institutions. As a result, interlibrary lending is fraught with headaches. Libraries with rich collections can expect to receive substantial numbers of requests that, in turn, remove large amounts of materials from shelves, thereby increasing the pressures of shelving work and decreasing the "fill rate." Wear and tear on interlibrary borrowed materials can be considerably greater than on locally owned ones. In-house users may be inconvenienced when staff members utilize copying equipment to fulfill interlibrary requests. Some libraries charge fees for service and others designate only a single staffer as able to initiate interlibrary loan requests.

Public libraries have been far less successful than have academic or special libraries in instituting well-oiled working interlibrary loan systems. Some librarians contend that resources allocated to ILL redound to the disfavor of the majority of library users whose needs for materials are undifferentiated and satisfiable on a local level. Interlibrary loan accounts for a very small (perhaps 1%) and not rapidly growing percentage of library circulation.[13] That fact, however, may be more a product of the reluctance of public librarians to commit resources to ILL or willingly to lend materials to other institutions than to lack of public interest. While academic libraries often deliver solicited materials to patrons in less than a week, it is not uncommon for a six-month hiatus to occur between an initial interlibrary loan request and its fulfillment in a public library. Few small public libraries own OCLC databases that permit them to search easily or verify wanted titles or institute electronic searches. Regional public libraries find demands so heavy that they often impose severe restrictions on borrowers -- one book request at a time, for instance. Interlibrary lending is further impeded when library staffs are reluctant to accord importance to borrowing materials from other sources that are not in their collections. Some administrators discourage purchase of fax-machines on the grounds that their current staffs would be insufficient to meet requests for copies of periodical articles from branches or other libraries if they were to be installed.

Critical funding, however, has caused some librarians to look with increasing favor at interlibrary loan. According to Intner and Fang, for the first time librarians have begun to depend on ILL for materials they know will be needed locally.

> Although no one talks openly about making such decisions, clearly the stage is set for each individual library in a group to buy titles its partners need but will not buy, planning instead to interloan them for their clients. Publishers have warned that these decisions can have disastrous effects on the production of low-demand materials. They believe increased ILL will mean that a small scholarly press will be able to sell only a few dozen copies of a title instead of hundreds or thousands of copies.[14]

Problems with interlibrary loan, both practical and conceptual, should diminish as computerized bibliographic networks become ever more widespread.

SHELVING AND STACK MAINTENANCE

Ultimately, says Fred Kilgour, only the electronic library, where all materials can be accessed directly and copies given to requesters, can eliminate all causes of user dissatisfaction and guarantee 100% availability of requested materials.[15] To date, technology has had little impact on stacks.

Three categories of reasons have been identified to explain the failure of users to leave the library with the books they are seeking. These are: User error at the shelf, materials in circulation and library mistakes. Within the first category are such errors as miscopied call numbers, confusion about proper collection location, and failure to find correctly shelved book. Books may, of course, be on loan, in use in the building or being held for another borrower. Those failures attributed to library error include materials awaiting shelving or photocopying, misshelved books, materials in process of transfer to another location, ones missing and known to be missing by the library, and finally, those not accounted for. The process of planning, organizing and controlling materials in the library stacks is among the most critical functions of access services. The words "not-on-shelf" have been identified as the number one cause of patron frustration and anger.

Collection arrangement, too, is bothersome to patrons. Unfortunately, no one solution has yet been devised to help determine an optimal grouping for materials. Circulation policies directly affect physical arrangements. Classification systems make subject browsing possible. However, fiction collections are usually arranged in alphabetical order by the author's last name, and further divided into genre -- science fiction, detective, western, romance, mystery -- or by audience -- children, young adult or large print. Journal collections may be shelved by call number or alphabetically. The former is better for browsing by subject, the latter facilitates locating known items without having to learn call numbers. Government documents are often housed separately, and arranged by Superintendent of Documents number. Certain materials that disappear with regularity -- financial services, consumer reports, automobile manuals, to name a few -- are kept behind desks. Staff and patrons need guidance in shelf locations. Appropriate signage, dummies for location or title changes, range finders, aisle indexes are all helpful if kept up to date, but worthless if they are not.

The most time-consuming circulation routine is shelving materials returned by borrowers. Until the electronic library becomes a reality, human error is inevitable. Books will be misshelved and the necessity to "read shelves" that is, make sure that books are in their proper spaces, will remain. In larger libraries, a shelf-reading log ensures orderly progression from one section to another.

Many libraries employ high school students as "pages," the name dating from the time when stacks were closed and materials had to be retrieved -- paged -- by library employees. (In the New York Public Library, pages wore roller skates to traverse the vast aisles in order to find materials.) Mercurial and unpredictable, teenagers who act as pages require close supervision.

Senior citizen volunteers or those in special job programs make excellent stack workers. They are conscientious and proud of their performances. No matter who does the shelving, careless or poorly trained staff can negate a well controlled stack environment.

PROTECTION OF LIBRARY MATERIALS

Theft in libraries has been a problem since their inception. Ann Paietta quotes a poem found on the door of an ancient monastic library in Barcelona, Spain:

> For him that stealth a book
> From this library
> Let it change into a serpent
> In his hand and rend him.
> Let him be struck with palsy
> And all his members be blasted
> Let him languish in pain
> Crying aloud for mercy and

> Let there be no surcease to his
> Agony 'till he sink in dissolution
> Let bookworms gnaw his entails
> In token of the worm that ideth not,
> And when at last he goeth to
> His Final judgment
> Let flames of hell consume him
> Forever and aye.[16]

Though contemporary librarians might be loathe to admit that they wish that such a fate be visited on those responsible for the theft and mutilation of library books, missing materials are, indeed, a matter of great concern. The circulation department bears primary responsibility for securing the collection. Public libraries attempt to control the flow of traffic so that patrons entering and exiting have to pass a circulation desk. In this way, material can be easily returned and circulated in an environment that permits staffs to keep a watchful eye on what is being carried out of the library.

Patrons steal material for a variety of reasons. Sometimes they forget to check it out. They may wish to own it, or to add it to a personal collection. They may have trouble using the library and find it more convenient to simply leave with the materials. Most often, however, theft stems from patrons wanting to use material above or beyond the library's willingness to loan it. For instance, they may have borrowed a book, renewed it once, and be unable, because of library rules, to renew it a second time. Sometimes a book or periodical is non-circulating and the patron wishes to use it at home. If certain books are regularly stolen, it may be wise to duplicate them and permit copies to circulate. Unaccommodating library hours, shortened loan periods, limited or non-existent renewal policies and many noncirculating items all contribute to increased loss.

A number of larger libraries have found it necessary to install gates that permit egress only by action of a staff member, to hire security guards who check bookbags and other packages or to install electronic tracking devices. All of these approaches have drawbacks. The first two contain the potential to slow the pace of traffic. The third, which works with a "target," an implanted device that sets off a detection system, can send off false alarms or may be insufficiently sensitive to detect targets. Targets must be desensitized during check-out, another procedure leading to delay. Patrons learn how to circumvent security systems. They cut out theft detection tags, throw books out of windows, conceal materials, hold them above sensors or otherwise sneak them out of the library. The decision to introduce any of these security measures requires careful cost-benefit analyses.

Mutilation of library materials seems to have diminished as a result of the widespread availability of photocopying. Nonetheless, the problem remains. Most often, the target of mutilation is a popular magazine article or one which is useful to a number of high school students fulfilling a paper assignment. Lazy students tear out the pages because they don't wish to take notes; competitive ones are intent on preventing other students from gaining access to the information. Sadly, mutilation generally remains undetected until another patron wants the article. By this time the periodical or book may be out-of-stock or print. Then the library has no recourse but to borrow it on interlibrary loan, copy the pages and "tip" them into the bound book or periodical.

Circulation staffs are in strategic positions to discover books needing repair or binding when they are returned to the circulation desk or when they are being shelved. Although not generally responsible for a final decision about whether the materials are to be replaced, conserved, or simply discarded, staff members can determine which ones need attention and forward them to the proper department.

COPYRIGHT AND COPY SERVICE

Next to the computer, the copy machine is probably the technological development that has had the greatest impact on libraries. It is hard to imagine a library today being able to fulfill its service goals without on-site copy capability.

Access staff are generally responsible for photocopying

equipment. This means supplying machines with paper, clearing jams, adding dry ink, routinely cleaning the machines and performing minor repairs. Because photocopiers have been identified as a source of ozone, they should placed, if possible, in well-ventilated, air-conditioned rooms, with air vented to the outside.

A full and sometimes acrimonious debate between publishers and librarians regarding copyright began after copying machines achieved widespread use. Under copyright law, libraries are permitted to make photocopies at the request of a patron provided that the copies become the property of the user and are within "fair use" guidelines. In other words, individuals are permitted to copy factual, educational, scientific, or informational works for their own use. Copyright was designed to protect the *expression* of ideas, not the idea or thought itself. Creative, fictional or entertainment works are less likely to be covered by the "fair use" exemption, as are items copied in larger quantities. The determination of "fair use" also depends on the extent to which the copyright owner has been harmed by the copying, whether royalties should have been paid, and subsequent use of the material by the copier.

Libraries are responsible for displaying warning signs, such as the one below, about copyright restrictions near the copying machine.

Notice: Warning Concerning Copyright Restrictions

The copyright law of the United States (Title 17, United States Code) governs the making of photocopies or other reproductions of copyrighted material. Under certain conditions specified in the law, libraries and archives may furnish a photocopy or other reproduction. One of these specified conditions is that the photocopy or reproduction is not to be "used for any purpose other than private study, scholarship, or research." If a user makes a request for, or later uses, a photocopy or reproduction for purposes in excess of "fair use," that user may be liable for copyright infringement. This institution reserves the right to refuse to accept a copying order if, in its judgment, fulfillment of the order would involve violations of the copyright law.

On May 1, 1990, the U.S. Senate passed S198, a law which prohibited the commercial rental, lease, or lending of computer software. Nonprofit libraries and nonprofit educational institutions were excluded from the bill's provisions. However, they must affix to each software packet the following notice:

> **Warning:** This computer program is protected under the copyright law. Making a copy of this program without permission of the copyright owner is prohibited. Anyone copying this program without permission of the copyright owner may be subject to payment of up to $100,000 damages and, in some cases, imprisonment for up to one year.

STATISTICS OF LIBRARY LOANS

The circulation department is responsible for keeping statistics of library loans. Tracking borrowing is helpful to understanding the activity of a library over time. Although uniform national reporting is not currently the rule in public libraries, most states require local public libraries to report statistics within defined categories in order to receive state aid. In this way, benchmark figures can be established and year-to-year variations tracked. Typically, primary statistical data includes the total number of items lent for home use, broken down by material format and by class of borrower. Additional statistics include registrations of service area borrowers, paid memberships, and number of interlibrary loans borrowed and lent. Many states require that libraries report fines and fees collected and lost and missing materials.

Interpreting and lending meaning to circulation statistics is not easy. There is a danger to using out-of-building circulation inter-institutionally as indicators of a library's effectiveness in reaching its community without referring to relevant community statistics. Community traditions, attitudes, socio-economic conditions, proximity to other libraries, geographic setting, loan periods, and the rest of the ingredients that factor into the nature of a public library have an impact on circulation. Ignoring these variables leads to misperceptions and unjustified claims.

Most circulation statistics overlook the use of books and other materials inside the library building, thereby omitting a substantial area of library activity. Present in the library, but invisible in statistics, are patrons who read current magazines, browse in the stacks, consult microfilm, use CD-ROMs and videos, and look up information in reference books without asking for assistance. Compiling complete records of this kind of use is virtually impossible without allocating substantially more resources to keeping statistics than could be gained by having the results.

Sampling is one way to learn about library activity without committing excessive resources to the endeavor. Subject, author and title fill-rates can be tracked during one week periods using patron questionnaires. The number of people using the library can be counted on a group of "average" days during the calendar year. Patterns of use by types of borrowers can help determine collection development imperatives. Shelving studies can be conducted to reveal in-house use of library materials. Chapter 20 describes a number of statistics gathering, evaluative methods to help track needed information Statistics do not reveal the uses to which library materials are put, but they often help administrators to support budgets, to improve service, or to explain the library's contribution to the community.

SUMMARY

Many users are introduced to the library through their encounters with circulation staff. That experience may predict a continuing mutually successful relationship or one that has already ended in disaster. Circulation staffs are charged with the difficult and demanding task of enforcing library regulations about who may borrow which materials and for what purpose, and are constantly faced by patrons who believe their needs are unique. Automation has brought order to circulation files, diminishing the opportunities for error, and has also permitted the generation of management information particularly useful in collection development work.

Circulation policies can be adjusted to improve the extent to which users find the materials they are seeking. Even with improvements, however, user and library error continue unabated and are a major cause of frustration. The terms access and acquisitions are gradually coming together as users are increasingly able to borrow items locally and from far distant places without distinction. Interlibrary loan activities in public libraries have been the subject of harsh debate, with some librarians adamant in their contention that the services are of negligible value and that allocating scarce resources to them is foolhardy. Others assert with equal vehemence that straightened conditions promote interlibrary loan to paramount importance if libraries are to succeed in meeting the needs of their users.

NOTES AND SUGGESTED READINGS

Notes

1. Barbara Evans Markuson, "Automated Circulation Control Systems: An Overview of Commercially Vended System," *Library Technology Reports* (July/September, 1975): 6-7.

2. Ann Catherine Paietta, *Access Services; a Handbook* (Jefferson, NC: McFarland , 1991), 1.

3. Ibid., 110

4. Sheila Intner, *Circulation Policy in Academic, Public and School Libraries* (New York: Greenwood Press, 1987), 131.

5. The American Library Association's policy regarding service to children, Rights of Minors, clearly spells out public library consensus on the matter. See Chapter 13.

6. Herbert Goldhor, "Statistics of Renewals in Public Libraries," *Public Library Quarterly* 10 (1990): 63-68.

7. Carlton Rochell, *Wheeler and Goldhor's Practical Administration of Public Libraries* (New York: Harper & Row, 1981), 364.

8. Donald Sager, *Managing the Public Library*. 2nd ed. (Boston: G.K. Hall & Co. 1989), 164.

9. Intner, 132.

10. January Adams, "A Year of Living Dangerously: Implementation of a No-Fine Policy at Sommerville Free Public Library," *Public Libraries* 11/12 (1991): 346-349.

11. Paietta, 15.

12. Adopted from Intner, 7-12.

13. Thomas Ballard, "The Unfulfilled Promise of Resource Sharing," *American Libraries* 21 (November 1990): 990-3; Sager, 165.

14. Sheila Intner and Josephine Riss Fang, *Technical Services in the Medium Sized Library* (Hamden, CT: Library Professional Publications, 1991), 116.

15. Frederick Kilgour, "Toward 100 Percent Availability," *Library Journal* 114 (Nov. 15, 1989): 50-3.

16. Paietta, 75.

Suggested Readings

Boucher, Virginia. *Interlibrary Loan Practices Handbook.* Chicago: American Library Association, 1984.

Buckland, Michael. *Book Availability and the Library User.* New York: Pergamon, 1975.

Hubbard, William. *Stack Management: A Practical Guide to Shelving and Maintaining Library Collections.* Chicago: American Library

Association, 1981.

Intner, Sheila. *Circulation Policy in Academic, Public and School Libraries.* New York: Greenwood Press, 1987.

Intner, Sheila and Josephine Fang. *Technical Services in the Medium-Sized Library.* Hamden, CT: Library Professional Publications, 1991.

Paietta, Ann Catherine. *Access Services; a Handbook.* Jefferson, NC: McFarland, 1991.

Strong, W.S. *The Copyright Book; a Practical Guide.* 3rd ed. Boston: MIT Press, 1990.

CHAPTER 11

INFORMATION SERVICE

At the New York Public Library recently, an irate patron demanded the famous book *Oranges and Peaches* which he could not locate in the catalog. It was a relief to the harried librarian, when, after careful question negotiation, she discovered that what was being sought was Darwin's *Origin of the Species*.[1]

Only rare reference librarians remain untempted to match that search question with an exceptionally challenging one that they have encountered. The endless variety of reference work both in content and in the people for whom the work is performed is what attracts its practitioners and the intellectual content is what lends it prestige within the field. In virtually no other profession, can practitioners deal intellectually with people at almost every social, economic and educational level.

"Numerous and complex are the problems which confront a reference librarian who conscientiously desires to make her work a power for good," wrote Ida Rosenberg in the March 1904 edition of *Library Journal*. She continued,

all reference work should have one unvarying end and aim: to furnish to each and every applicant, the readiest, easiest, and surest method of obtaining any information sought...If our efforts are crowned with a fair measure of success, that, and a consciousness of duty well performed will be the reward with which an earnest worker will be best satisfied. He who looks for such reward in the praise and appreciation of those for whom he works and studies must be disappointed and discouraged, for except in a few rare instances, people are too busy, too engrossed with their own interests, to consider ways and means after they have obtained that for which they are seeking.[2]

The temptation to assert at such a moment, as did Alphonse Karr in 1849, that the more things change, the more they are the same is indeed great. Reference or information librarians have the same ends and goals today as they did when Ida Rosenberg penned her statement -- to provide users who seek information with a referral to a likely source of information, or to the information itself. On the other hand, the nature of the service has altered dramatically following the introduction of powerful new information technology and information locaters -- online databases and CD-ROM products, to mention two. Not only have they led to alternate routes for information retrieval, but they have given rise to questions about the very nature of the service. Considerations about what should be provided, and for whom, have few ready answers, and present complex problems that are intensified by the unprecedented demands on reference and information service, both in quantity and scope.

Every day, 3500 people climb the main steps of the New York Public Library, past the two stone lions, aptly named Patience and Fortitude, to pursue a fact or a fancy. More than half of that number request assistance from a librarian. At least a thousand will ask a reference librarian to help them locate information on topics ranging from bizarre and obscure to indecipherable. Couple this number with the additional 700-900 telephone reference questions posed daily -- one every ten seconds -- to the New York Public Library and some indication can be seen of the extent to which reference librarians ply their trade.[3]

The demand for reference service in public libraries appears to be increasing at a rate far greater than is being experienced by circulation. Linda Crismond reports, for instance, that in Los Angeles County reference has increased at the rate of 8-10% annually while circulation has increased at 3%. The number of reference questions handled by American public libraries in recent years hovers at about 10% of total circulation, or more than 100 million a year, representing about 1/2 question per capita. Small libraries, those serving fewer than 10,000 people, average approximately 5% of their circulation and about .1/4 question per capita, while large libraries with service constituencies of more than 200,000 persons report reference question totals at about 20% of circulation -- one question per capita per year. A steady increase over time in the number of reference questions, in the number per capita and in their percentage of total circulation has been registered. How much is real increase or simply a reflection of more care in counting the questions asked is problematic and requires further research.[4]

Despite this growth in use, maintains Samuel Rothstein, only a small minority of the general public is even aware of the existence of reference services. Reference, he says, is indeed the secret service. By far the greater part of information work in libraries is done, not by librarians, but by patrons themselves, and most of librarians' efforts are expended on enabling patrons to help themselves effectively. Not surprisingly, the public is far less successful than are librarians in locating information. Patrons are likely to spend about nine times as much time as librarians in finding information.[5]

WHAT CONSTITUTES REFERENCE?

In general, reference and information services seek to 1) provide answers to inquiries requiring specific information; 2) teach patrons how to use a public library in connection with their work; 3) provide bibliographical and other reference assistance; 4) locate material for users wherever these materials may be in a library system; 5) make available material not in the library through interlibrary loan; 6) organize uncataloged material for effective reference use; and 7) build reference collections to support community information need and provide knowledge in all relevant areas. Librarians try to

simplify or make more effective the means whereby people find out what exists, relate what exists to what they need, find some way of identifying where the information is, and then create a means of bringing that information to the individual, group or community that has need for that kind of information.[6]

Reference service has been described as connecting people with the information they want, showing them the possibilities and the routines. Simply stated, reference librarians help people find resources by functioning as the living mind and human presence in this world of technology.[7]

The philosophy of reference service has evolved from conservative to a more activist approach in recent years. Librarians initially saw themselves as custodians, collectors and catalogers. The primary audience for reference service was inexperienced users. By the turn of the century librarians were recommending the appointment of special assistants to answer questions, and by 1915, "reference work was ordinarily accepted as necessary service of the individual library and in many cases invested with the prestige of departmental status."[8]

Research on the nature of information began in earnest in the 1950s. At that time, information was viewed as a way of reducing uncertainty, describing and predicting reality and helping people better cope with their lives.[9] Most people assumed that information existed independently of the user. Researchers today are more likely to accept a relativistic view in which the importance of information depends on the observation and situation of the users. The focus of research then is on the user and in identifying situations in which the information is valuable.[10] Many commentators predict an increased need for skilled information specialists to assist users with search strategies, interpretation of information, and selection of appropriate databases.

Public library reference librarians today may function for their communities as mini Librarians of Congress, may sit with municipal officers at meetings and hearings as Chief Information Officers, may engage in a program of Selective Dissemination of Information (SDI) to watch for books, articles and other materials that will aid in the governance and well-being of a community.

Darlene Weingand considers SDI to be a tool of "incredible impact that dramatically influences the opinion makers of the community, and that establishes the library as a key resource and as an agency that produces personal benefit."[11]

Subject specialization is not usual in most public library reference departments which have sometimes been called the last stronghold of generalists. Larger libraries organized along divisional or departmental lines often do employ subject specialists, or, alternately, members of those departments become experts, *de facto*. Even without departmentalization, it is not unusual to find one member of the reference staff characterized as the "online searcher," another as the government documents expert. Libraries that encourage staff specialization within a single reference department may serve the interests of the average reader and at the same time render specialized service.

While there are good arguments for specialization, too much subject concentration can jeopardize the more peripatetic approach most successful with the public library's constituency. More important is a breadth of knowledge and human understanding that permits a librarian to recognize the core of the question and to have a real interest in it as well as in the person who posed it.

A recent survey of library school students revealed that the type of library position perceived as most desirable was reference services.[12] The allure of reference while substantial is fragile and requires librarians to balance the pleasures they receive against the significant demands put upon it. Anyone, argues Paul Frantz, who has worked a regular shift at a public service desk, who has indicated, for the tenth time that hour, where the telephone directories are; who has three telephone calls on hold and four people queued up to ask questions; and who, at that moment learns that the CD-ROM printer has again jammed knows that the pleasures of reference are delicate and exist in a potentially hostile environment. There is, on the other hand, instant gratification when the librarian, after posing one or two short questions to an information requestor, walks over to the 30,000 book reference collection and "selects the one, the precise one, that will answer the patron's question"[13] to the awe and gratitude of the patron. Few others in the library world have the opportunity for such positive and immediate gratification.

Reference librarians have little control over the nature of the questions they receive. The randomness of the reference desk carries with it the psychic relief of temporarily letting go of control, as well as the anxiety of wondering whether this time they will fail to understand the question, or retrieve the answer.

One difference between public and college reference work is the extent the latter see teaching users how to acquire information as part of the process of answering questions. Another is that patrons at a public library are more likely to demand specific and definite information for immediate use, while college students more typically seek subject material, rather than a single fact.

REFERENCE AND THE NEW TECHNOLOGIES

New technologies bring with them fresh problems. Reference departments in public libraries have often attempted, without benefit of additional staff or funding, to launch innovative programs while maintaining existing ones. This situation invariably leads to stress and perhaps to poor service unless good planning, including job analysis and reassignment of duties, has occurred in tandem with the introduction of new technologies.

Ironically reference librarians have been by-passed by the work-saving elements of the computer revolution. Online catalogs are computer-based reference tools that may improve reference productivity, but OPACs merely exchange one end-user tool for another, the card catalogs they are replacing. Online database searching, another computer-based reference activity, has actually transferred to librarians work that was formerly done by library users -- that is manual searching of printed indexes. The trend toward user independence is being encouraged and there is no doubt that end-user searching will become more common. However, the time when end users are the norm is still far distant given most users' dearth of knowledge about the content of databases and about system features and limitations; wide-spread computer illiteracy; lack of patron skill; limited understanding of terminology and search modifiers; lack of comprehension of Boolean logic, file structure or how command languages operate.[14]

Librarians agree that automated retrieval systems have changed the shape and scope of reference service. They recognize that people require, expect and demand more from their libraries because information needs have become more complex. However, integrating automated retrieval systems into reference routines is not easily accomplished. Many reference librarians still offer excuses not to regard automation as integral to reference service. They contend, for instance, that it is:

1. *Expensive.* That it will lead to increased demand and put further strain on already insufficient budgets in addition, the plethora of new systems makes it impossible to satisfy all patron demands.

2. *Too time and labor intensive.* Already straitened staffs when faced with the welter of new questions would find it impossible to properly service people with traditional reference questions, who would inevitably be shortchanged.

3. *Takes no account of user's age.* School kids ask frivolous questions. With technology integrated into reference services those too young for serious research would nonetheless have to be helped.

4. *Does not permit librarian's personal judgment about its use.* People will have queries that are insignificant, not "serious."

5. *Inappropriate for telephone callers.* Requests for sophisticated methodology, they contend, should only be made in-person. Too often librarians assume that people calling on the phone are frivolous or that their question does not represent a serious information need.

6. *Misleading in that it connotes that access is a right* while it is really a privilege.[15]

Not only are these arguments of limited validity, but they imply values that are antithetical to user-oriented service.

INFORMATION SERVICE USERS

Reference or information work in public, college and university libraries is similar. Librarians answer questions, prepare bibliographies and provide telephone service. Many of the source materials consulted are identical. To some extent, even the users overlap. And certainly, the procedures followed in defining and answering questions are the same. Yet, substantial differences characterize the services offered by academic and public libraries.

Probably the most salient difference lies in the nature of the information service public. College libraries cater to undergraduates and faculty whose needs are fairly circumscribed. Public libraries serve that great, undifferentiated mass called the "general public." The range of questions, therefore, is likely to be broad, but perhaps, in the majority of cases, not as deep. Phrased differently, public librarians are the "kamikaze pilots of the war against ignorance." They have the most difficult job...taking on all who request information. Other librarians face expert clients. [16]

> The reference librarian meets the hostile patron, for whom no service is ever performed adequately; the gracious patron who never forgets to thank us; the stuttering patron, for whom the act of asking a question is an ordeal; and the gushing patron, who wants to tell us her life story as a prelude to her question. The reference librarian meets the introvert and the extrovert, the gifted and the disabled, the curious and the indifferent. And although many of these individual contacts may not be pleasant, the sum of a librarian's experience with the public provides a gestalt of human nature that has the power to enrich or embitter.[17]

Yet libraries are not the most frequent source of information. Studies of communication patterns and information seeking behavior reveal that most people resort to "back fence" or "invisible college" methods of gathering information. Information needs are met by friends or colleagues -- people in close proximity to the inquirer. The second most common source of information is a personal library. A formal library is the third, or last, recourse. Convenience and ease govern information seeking behavior. Most people turn first to what they can find with the least amount of trouble.

One of the great challenges in contemporary reference service is meeting the information needs of an ethnically, culturally, socially and economically diverse population. This includes persons with various disadvantages and handicaps -- language problems, reading difficulties, mental and emotional problems. Recently deinstitutionalized persons are among the new users of libraries. Often they are people who have been or would be in other times, out of sight and locked up for most or all of their lives; and they are people librarians are unaccustomed to dealing with. Special populations require different handling.

Frances Allegri suggests some general guidelines for working with special populations.[18]

1. pay attention to body language or nonverbal cues, especially when the person exhibits communication disorders;
2. focus on the person, not the disability;
3. avoid pity;
4. offer assistance when appropriate;
5. know the collection and services in terms of special needs of disabled patrons;
6. design services, where necessary, to accommodate special needs;

The homeless in this group are particularly difficult to deal with. Estimates are that as many as 25-40% of the homeless single adults are mentally disabled.

TELEPHONE INFORMATION SERVICE

Among the most numerous and fastest growing segments of users of public library reference services are telephone callers. Unfortunately, a great many libraries are either ambivalent about or hostile to telephone inquiries. The service they provide, therefore, is at best uneven, at times actually derelict.   The assumption prevails that those willing to make a trip to the library are more worthy of assistance than those who merely make a phone call. Consequently, telephone reference services often take a back seat to "real" reference. Called-in questions are considered of low priority, and too often remain on a pad, unanswered. Some reasons for librarian equivocation in handling telephone questions may be illuminated by the following scene.

> The phone rings, and an apparently slurred voice at the other end asks for information about the number of home runs hit by Mel Ott in the 1942 season. Voices in the background indicate that yet another barroom argument has led to a telephone call. In front of the reference desk appear a fourteen year-old waving an assignment, a middle-aged man gesticulating to the place under the desk where *The Value Line,* an investment service, is kept, an older woman waiting patiently, and a young mother and her acting-out pre-schooler.

At best, it is difficult to be civil to the probably inebriated baseball questioner when confronted with the other, apparently more pressing, problems. What the librarian does not know, however, is that the telephone question may have been posed as a matter of survival. Suppose that the telephone questioner is not drunk, but a stroke survivor whose vocal chords have been damaged, that he is close to indigent, that he has discovered a Mel Ott baseball card from 1942 and wishes to verify its authenticity, knowing that if genuine it will fetch $4,000 on the open market, money he sorely needs, and that the sounds in the background are from a television set.

Telephone reference is offered in three ways in today's public libraries, depending, in part, on the size of the library.

--First, it is given its own separate department with no relationship to "general reference."

--Second, and probably most commonly, it is offered concurrently with other reference services. The phone is on the reference desk, and calls are handled simultaneously with answering in-person questions. Generally, library staffs are admonished to help those who are at the desk before answering the phone, a policy which enrages those who call on the phone and disconcerts both in-person patrons and reference librarians.

--Third, telephone reference is segregated from, but is an integral part of, the reference department. The staffs are common and serve in both places. Telephone questions which merit further handling are given to the Reference Desk to be pursued when time allows.

The same qualifications necessary for general reference staffs (described below) apply to telephone reference, with a few exceptions. Telephones are faster media and carry with them even more pressure; there is a premium placed on speed. Patrons are reluctant to wait more than two to three minutes for answers. In addition, question negotiation is far more difficult without the non-verbal signals that patrons exhibit during a face-to-face interview. Further, in responding to telephone questions, the burden of doing the actual looking is placed much more heavily on the librarian. A telephone caller can't be told to look at the green book on the third shelf, or to check the catalog.

In the past few years there have been a number of new telephone advancements with strong implications for improving and enlarging public library reference service. For all of the familiar reasons -- expense, insufficient time and staff, and so on -- reference departments have been reluctant to experiment with such exciting innovations as:

1. automatic call sequencing, where the phone is answered automatically, a message relayed to the caller, the call held until the appropriate person can respond and the librarian informed about which calls have been waiting longest.
2. call forwarding and call waiting.
3. hands free feature.
4. voice amplifying headsets.

5. cordless phones that allow patrons to "come along" on the search as the librarian consults various sources.[19]
6. messaging so that 24 hour service can be provided.

The optimum telephone reference collection is full of facts, up-to-date and conveniently arranged. Care must be taken to keep it from becoming too large. The design of furniture, and order of books will have ramifications for service. If placed in circular fashion, the most important books will be at the center with the remainder around the periphery. Some other matters that must be addressed in the course of establishing the telephone reference collection are: the percentage of the reference collection that should be duplicated; the extent to which on-line and CD-ROM be utilized as a matter of course; what policies will be adopted by telephone reference regarding depth and breadth of questions taken on the phone.

INFORMATION AND REFERRAL

The degree to which a library commits itself to offering Information and Referral (I & R) is one reference policy decision that requires specific description. I & R can be thought of as "facilitating the link between a person with a need and the service, activity, information or advice outside the library which can meet the need."[20] Designed for "people who do not know that certain information exists and are therefore unaware of their rights,"[21] I & R aims to reach those not ordinarily helped by traditional reference service.

Libraries generally offer one of two types of I & R service -- "steering," that is, providing information and pointing patrons in a particular direction, and "referring" actually trying to make contact for clients, sometimes expanded to include advocacy and problem serving. Most libraries can be classed as "steerers," which they carry out by developing and maintaining up-to-date resource files about social and governmental agencies and institutions within communities to which patrons can be referred.

The more liberal I & R policies associated with advocacy,

those that require work to overcome obstacles that inquirers encounter while trying to secure help from outside resources agencies are entered into with more reluctance by reference librarians who are more comfortable with the role of information dispenser.[22]

I & R has had a varied history in public libraries. Baltimore's Enoch Pratt Free Library is crediting with initiating, in 1970, the first program called *Public Information Center* (PIC) an unfortunately short-lived program that closed in 1974. Detroit's TIP (The Information Place), inaugurated in 1971 was probably, and remains, the most successful of these undertakings. By incorporating I & R into already existing services, not isolating it, the program was able to be integrated into the entire library program. TIP shifted the focus from printed matter to services. The New Haven (CT) Free Public Library established Neighborhood Information Centers, branch libraries, staffed jointly by social workers and librarians which functioned as ombudsmen in their communities. Recently, Nassau (NY) Library System joined with the Palmer School of Library and Information and the Nassau County Department of Senior Citizen Affairs in "Senior Connections" designed to get elderly persons information on needed services -- tax assistance, housing applications, medicare, medicaid, transportation. Branches are staffed by social work and library school interns who train and supervise volunteers.

Those libraries who, for want of funds, or staff, or a variety of other reasons have chosen the passive "steerers" path have nonetheless generated useful community information files. Pikes Peak, for instance, has CALL (lists social service agencies); CLUBS (clubs and associations in Colorado Springs); COURSES (adult education & recreation); and CALENDAR (cultural events) in its main database and made available to the public through its OPAC.

REFERENCE POLICIES

Reference policies, including reference values and behavioral expectations, require clear definition and description in a reference staff manual. Reference departments fail without a shared sense of aims and goals. A useful staff manual delineates the purposes of the operation and describes how it is organized to deliver service. More important during times of transition and change, such as are currently being experienced by reference departments, staff manuals require continuous revision as new approaches and new ideas are developed.

Many of the analysts who argue that patrons often receive incorrect answers to reference questions blame the structure of reference and the lack of policy orientation. Clare Beck, for instance, describes librarians as resistant to making distinctions between and among questions. They

> can be seen scurrying about at all hours of weekday and weekend, anxiously rifling through book after book to settle a phone caller's bet or satisfy an imperious student whose term paper, assigned two months ago and begun two hours ago, is due first thing in the morning.[23]

Indeed, one article of public library faith has been to treat equally the apparently frivolous and the apparently scholarly, despite the intense pressure of logic to discriminate between them. To adopt a hierarchy of question importance would represent a substantial danger to the concept of equal access.

On the other hand, to consider appropriate reference behavior, to set limits and parameters is essential. The following is a list of questions requiring policy responses:

-- Are all patrons equal?
-- Are all questions of equal importance?
-- Do in-person patrons rank higher than telephone patrons?
-- Can answers be without authority (i.e. established by outside expert, either in print or verbally)?
-- How should medical and legal questions be handled?
-- What is acceptable behavior at the reference desk.
-- Which types of questions are suitable for response;

-- To what extent are patrons expected to participate in the search for answers;
-- Should librarians accompany patrons to shelves or is pointing the way acceptable.

The Reference Staff Manual should contain, among other elements, a statement of the library's philosophy of service; a description of the physical arrangement of the room and of the collection; a list of outside resources -- other libraries, co-ops, networks and community agencies -- and discussion of referral policy. The organization and supervision of the department with clear delineation of lines of authority and responsibility also need to be included.

In view of its relative newness, it is advisable to specify policies surrounding automated systems and services.[24] These include: procedures to be followed in conducting online searches; patron residency requirements; limitations (i.e. time spent per search, numbers of records, numbers of searchers per request); turn-around time per request; necessity of appointments; whether patron presence is required or may the question be posed on the telephone; the method of delivery to patrons; evaluating service; the reference interview; and fee collection, if applicable.

ORGANIZATION OF REFERENCE

Staffing

How to staff the reference department is an intrinsically difficult problem, complicated by online database searching. The end product of staffing should be the formation of a team all aiming toward the same goal. The staffs of most reference departments are arranged hierarchically, mirroring their parent institutions. Recently some academic libraries have experimented with collegial structure for their reference departments, electing chairs for specific terms, and conducting departmental business on a peer basis. Still considered visionary, a number of public library directors have expressed interest in testing such a structure.

Two hour desk shifts are the current mode in public libraries. During evenings and weekends shifts are longer, usually 3 or 4 hours. Normally a librarian provides a total of four hours of public service for 4 days, with one day completely off the desk. Most reference staffers serve 19 to 21 hours weekly on the desk. Public library reference librarians work a larger portion of the week on desk than do academic librarians.[25] These are behaviors currently practiced by libraries and do not represent optimal number of hours on duty.

A multitude of time periods and assignments must be woven into the fabric of reference service, a fact that causes scheduling, particularly in larger reference departments, to be a major headache. The task is compounded when the Reference Department is also responsible for staffing an information desk, a periodicals section, or a separate telephone reference service.

Resentments among staff accrue more rapidly in conjunction with the schedule than with almost any other facet of reference work. In general, the schedule should remain flexible, but be sufficiently standardized so that librarians can assume they will work on the same evenings, or have the same day off each week. Equity is essential. The position of schedule maker/keeper is a powerful one and requires great sensitivity. It should always be occupied by a senior level librarian. While soft-ware scheduling packages are available and can be manipulated by support staff, variations and exceptions are best left as the province of the person in charge.

Another potential source of conflict and misunderstanding in reference staffing is inattention to the expertise of various department members. For reasons such as friendship or convenience, it is not unusual to find three or four junior librarians working together on one evening and three or four senior ones on another.

Too little use of management information is utilized when devising the schedule. It is relatively easy to track hourly, daily and seasonal shifts in patron load. Work planned to conform to the calendar can be more effectively completed. Schedulers can easily institute systems of "on call," minimizing desk staffing until demand is greater.

A further impediment to making generalizations regarding the optimal numbers of reference librarians that should be available is the variability in what is assigned to the reference department, even in similar institutions. In some libraries, the absence of a collection development unit may imply reference staff responsibility for that function, or, at least, reference department responsibility for selection and weeding of materials.

How a library handles its periodicals has an effect on how a reference department is organized and staffed. A large public library will have a separate serials department. A small one makes no distinction between its handling of any types of material. The middle-sized institutions that describe most public libraries may assign periodicals to any of a variety of departments. The Ocean County (NJ) Public Library, for instance, handles periodicals through a section of the reference department. In other libraries, the task is assigned to collection development, and in still others to acquisitions.

Periodicals represent some of the most difficult problems that reference librarians *and* patrons encounter. Consider the following possibilities for transaction error. After discovering a reference in a periodical index, the patron may find that: the library does not own the needed title; the library has the title, but not the issue; the title and issue may be owned, but it is not on the shelf because it has either been checked out or sent to the bindery; the issue may be located, but the pages may be missing; and finally the issue may be located, but the index reference was erroneous.[26]

When online database searching first appeared in public libraries, there was a tendency to view it as separate from other library functions and to house and administer it apart from the reference department. Most librarians have now realized that online databases are simply another type of reference source and have integrated the use of them into the reference department, along with CD-ROM services, and other forms of reference material. Patrons coming to the library want information about certain subjects. They are not generally concerned about the form in which the material appears -- book, microfilm, journal, tape, or CD-ROM. If assistance is required, it is more easily provided at a single reference desk where help is available from all sources regardless of the medium. It is both more efficient and effective. Patrons do not have to cross boundaries or reexplain their problems.

But integrating the new technologies into the reference department and insuring that there are professionals prepared to utilize them and, at the same time, ready to instruct end users in their application, is one of the great challenges of contemporary reference departments. Systems vary. Search command structures differ from producer to producer. New products appear at a dizzying pace. Electronic mail is now commonplace for sending and receiving reference questions; telefacsimile transmission makes instant response possible. The pace has quickened; the demands become more intense. Keeping up may become the ultimate test of a good reference librarian.

Advances in our understanding of the information transaction have led to a realization of the necessity to probe during the reference interview, of the importance of verifying that a patron's problem statement has been properly understood and addressed, and of the need to ascertain that the question has received sufficient negotiation. The new understanding of the complexities of the entire process, shaped as it is by ambiguities in human communication, cause us to reaffirm the truth of Karen Markey's assertion that:

> Question negotiation is an illustration of a complicated interaction between two individuals in which one person tries to describe for another nothing he knows, but rather something he does not know.[27]

There has been a sharp increase in the number of workshops offered that teach reference transaction behaviors, particularly question negotiation. Many of these were constructed following publication of the dismal results of a group of unobtrusive measures studies (described in Chapter 20) which contended that reference librarians answered correctly only 50% of the questions asked of them. These workshops utilize "Model Reference Behaviors," peer coaching, and effective listening to improve the quality of reference service. The results of follow-up unobtrusive testing after training have been encouraging. Test scores reveal far better percentages of correctly answered questions.

Physical Arrangements

The physical organization of a reference department is an important element in providing quality service. The information desk or counter should be centrally located, accessible, and inviting. Studying the behavior of users as they approach the counter or handle reference materials may suggest rearrangements of materials and equipment. For instance, while it may be acceptable to present circulating collections in rows of stacks, to organize reference collections in this fashion establishes a barrier to use given the heft, cumbersomeness and difficulty of handling most of this material. Lack of proximity to seating or counter space militates against their effective use. Providing counter-height shelving, placing some stools for seating in the aisles and consultation space for users in one area of the information desk all promote use of the reference collection and services.

Experimenting with appointments for more complicated reference questions helps to prevent long lines from forming or from giving short shrift to patrons.

The placement and size of the desk may also have implications for the nature of the service performed. A counter-type desk in front of a ready reference collection facilitates use of reference materials by reference librarians while assisting patrons. Whether to place it waist-high in order for the librarian to maintain eye-contact, or to structure it at desk height to permit reference librarians to sit and consult is a matter of some contention.

ELEMENTS OF A GOOD REFERENCE LIBRARIAN

There is a real joy in reference work. It is considered by many to be the best job in the library. Reference librarians help people directly on a person-to-person basis. Approaches and responses can be tailored to specific needs. Ironically, most reference departments eschew a personal relationship with clients. Staff members are instructed not to reveal their names, probably because of scheduling exigencies. Yet, asserts Herb White, "one-to-one bonding is the ideal way to establish professional communication."[28]

Reference librarians help people to grow while expanding their own horizons by using their own intellects and discretion. "Each reference question is an opportunity to learn more about information sources, about our clients, and about the world at large."[29] Reference librarians require broad general knowledge. Everything ever learned or encountered becomes grist for a reference librarian's store of knowledge. A good memory is beneficial; a hunger for chewing through facts helpful, imagination certainly desirable, intuition useful and a sense of humor indispensable, particularly today when more and more patrons are difficult to deal with. Some of the personality traits or qualities that have been recognized in good reference librarians are inquisitiveness, confidence, a sense of ethics and tenacity. Reference librarians seem able to live with ambiguity and the unexpected.

No day is like any other at the reference desk despite seasonal trends. The questions vary, the patrons vary. Artistic and creative leaps of thought become necessary to link and interpret disparate clues. While librarians have often been accused of being part of a rule-bound profession, no set of rules has yet been devised that adequately describes the reference process or satisfactorily teaches new reference librarians how to make the kind of associations necessary to the work. Despite good, solid research into information seeking behavior and retrieval techniques, there is some doubt that reference service will ever be a codifiable science.

Cecilia Stafford and William Serban have suggested a group

of core competencies needed by reference librarians in an automated environment. These include:

1. User/staff interfacing skills.
2. Traditional and automated reference skills.
3. Data retrieval skills
4. Information technology skills, including computer literacy, knowledge of hardware and software, analysis of hardware/software needs, and so on.
5. Organizational skills.[30]

Though it may be difficult to pinpoint the qualities of an ideal reference librarian, it is relatively easy to distinguish the weaknesses of poor ones. Their most obvious fault is a lack of appreciation for the reference process. They also lack thoroughness and persistence. Their knowledge of bibliographic and library resources is less than adequate. They are abrupt in dealing with patrons, a trait that springs from lack of sympathy and patience. When asked for assistance, they are too quick to jump to conclusions and fail to get all the facts or to evaluate the ones they have. Because they hold positions where even a slight amount of personal assistance often brings profuse thanks, they have no conception of their own shortcomings, no healthy uneasiness about the quality of their work.

> Good reference librarians become frustrated because of their perception of a gap between the way reference librarianship should be and the way it is day-to-day and question-to-question across the desk. The gap between the ideal of joy-filled reference service...and the reality of the kind of service the librarian is able to provide on an hourly basis...[is] intensified by an increasing lack of confidence in our professional and technical knowledge.[31]

Overwork, being stretched to the breaking point, has led to suggestions for alternate ways of providing reference service. Paraprofessionals are now widely used to screen out obvious inquiries. Linda Crismond has suggested that

Perhaps we will begin to build a team in the information center
where a librarian manages a group of paraprofessionals doing
preliminary research and highly educated subject specialists
doing subject analysis.[32]

Reference librarians have been reluctant to use nonreference
department personnel as well as other support staff at the reference
desk. Unfortunately, the increased demand for longer hours and
insufficient numbers of reference librarians to cover these hours has
rendered the discussion mute. Librarians are simply unable to do
without assistance. Much of a reference librarian's time is spent in
accomplishing clerical work or work that could be equally well
performed by others -- answering directional questions, helping
patrons to learn whether the library owns a specific known item.
These can be handled by support staff providing adequate staffing
levels and professional backup are provided. The success or
accuracy of non-professional staff in handling questions increases
when a reference librarian is also present. They do least well when
handling subject questions, due, in part, to the complex nature of
these kinds of questions and the necessity for interviewing skills.[33]

THE REFERENCE COLLECTION

Selecting reference materials has been made more complex by
the appearance of resources in varying forms and by the new
emphasis on access. During the past decade there has been a
substantial increase in the number and kind of heavily illustrated
reference tools, of *printed* access tools, of widely available
computer-readable databases, and systems of networking and
cooperation. The new tools tend to be very expensive and are often
complicated to use. In addition, decisions are made based on
technology which is virtually obsolete on the day it is marketed.
Taken together, reference librarians are faced with a welter of
choices, all of which have far-reaching consequences for their
ability to provide service and for their cost.

Reference collections, like the remainder of a library's stock, should be based on rational policies that have been codified and written down. Unfortunately, few public libraries have written reference selection and weeding policies. Older materials in a reference department are a particular danger especially when they are used by unsuspecting patrons who trust that what they find on the reference shelves will contain the most recent, up-to-date material. Weeding the collection of older works is not merely desirable, but essential to the provision of good information service.

In view of the great cost of purchasing reference books, it behooves librarians to study reference material use with the same care that they give the rest of the collection. Rarely do reference staffs track the utilization of materials, nor do they establish guidelines about what represents sufficient use to acquire or retain a title. The tendency of those who provide reference assistance is to consider more material better. And there is some justification for doing this. Studies have shown that there is a significant causal relationship between reference collection size and the percent of test reference questions answered correctly.[34] On the other hand, in light of the expense of reference materials, librarians must assess the value of each item. Those referred to by only a small number of people; those consulted once or twice annually; those with good information for whom there is no audience ought to be reconsidered. Putting pencil marks in the back of reference books when they are utilized by a patron or staff or when found on a table helps to provide needed information.

Online database search service, mediated or not, should be normal, pervasive and expected. The old argument that online searches are of an add-on or auxiliary nature is no longer defensible. Once thought an expensive extra, online reference service can now be regarded as basic to comprehensive library service. More and more, reference departments are considering the availability of a source online in their decisions about whether to purchase a title in paper form, particularly when space is short or where use of certain titles is so limited that ownership seems unnecessary. CD-ROM index products, a middle ground between online database searching, microform and traditional print indexes, hold great promise for reference, primarily because of their comparative economy. By purchasing complete access with a single annual -- sometimes very costly -- subscription, rather than paying for each individual use, every search can decrease rather than increase the per-use cost and produce efficiencies of volume not possible with online searching as it is currently practiced. Cost per search, in other words, can be much lower with CD-ROM than with online, although there is the commensurate danger that low usage of a particular index may eventuate in substantially higher cost. The absence of telecommunication connection charges also reduces CD-ROM expenses. And the possibility of eliminating the services of the librarian/mediator to conduct the search can also help to offset the initial cost.

In addition to acquiring books, periodical guides, and other information sources traditionally associated with reference service, the reference department is responsible for organizing and making available certain types of generally uncataloged materials. These include vertical files, although their use is diminishing, and self-organizing collections such as college catalogs.

An important information source, often overlooked by reference librarians, is the telephone. According to Ken Kister, a strong argument can be made that the telephone is currently the most effective and exciting telecommunications tool available to reference librarians. Depending on the type of question or information sought, the telephone can provide answers as quickly or more quickly than an online search. Telephone costs are usually less than those incurred for online searches. Wide Area Telecommunications Service (WATS) lines and similar systems now provide reasonably priced, unlimited long-distance telephone service to virtually all libraries that wish it.[35]

FEE OR FREE

Technological change challenged and continues to challenge and modify the value structures in librarianship to the consternation of some members of the profession and the delight of others. Perhaps the most important of the issues raised is whether the principle of free access to information can continue to prevail as an article of faith. Arthur Curley contends that "The newness [of certain informational formats] has served as an excuse for at least contemplating the imposition of user charges on access to this information."[36] Initially the debate raged around the extent to which libraries could or should offer database searching without a fee. As further additional technologies became available, new dilemmas continued to surface concerning who should pay for them, who might benefit and whether they should be adopted. American librarians generally agree that access to information in a barrier-free manner is an important occupational value and that any inhibiting factor is to be negatively viewed. Yet, when online database searching became possible in public libraries, questions surfaced about who could or should pay for the new service and led to a major controversy within the profession.

Those who favored or at least accepted the notion of charging fees offered a number of convincing arguments. Fees, they asserted, are not a late 20th century innovation. Libraries have always imposed some fees, whether it be for rental books, photocopying, reserves or fines. In the 1930s, straightened budgets caused the levying of such charges to readers as 25 cents per hour for use of dictionaries after the first 15 minutes and $1 per hour for research work.[37] Fee advocates pointed to the add-on nature of online services. Database searching, they contended, was something innovative and extra, not a service traditionally available in the library. In addition, they noted that an online search is patron specific, with the result useable only by a single consumer. They also stressed the need to control the demand for the services; the financial reality of funds not being available from other sources; and the supposed acceptance of fees by library patrons as justification for charging. Charles Robinson of Baltimore County Library alleges that "the controversy over 'fee or free' is made in libraryland, not in the real world"[38] where no one finds the fees problematic.

Librarians opposed to fees suggested that fees have a significant effect on information demand. When fees are levied for online searches "the result is to discriminate in favor of acquired as opposed to accessed material, and to discriminate in favor of the haves as opposed to the have nots."[39] Fay Blake argues that fee based information changes the very nature of information. The specific kinds of information poor people need are least likely to be collected for commercialized databases. Where, for instance, she asks, are the customers who can and will pay for a national, regional, or even local job training database or a database of jobs that under-educated or unskilled workers can fill? Who is interested, she continues, in collecting and distributing up-to-date information about free child care services or free well-baby clinics or available free shelters or free hot meals. Those who need such information can't pay for it, so it ceases to exist.[40]

Those opposed to fees argue further that it is possible to offer free searches; that online services will become so integrated into reference departments that fees will be unjustifiable. Further, they place the argument in larger terms. The decision is not merely one of fees, but one which effects the institution as a whole. The choice is ultimately about who the public library will serve, about which citizen needs will be answered and which will be left to the private sector to meet or not meet.

Legally there are few impediments to imposing fees; economists find fees efficient; and there has been no evidence of the erosion of public support for those institutions who have instituted fees for database searching or videos. But, in an impassioned argument, Peter Giacomo insists that *justice* is the first virtue of public institutions. And justice is not served by charging for library services. Fees confirm the practice of conferring on the most aggressive, most talented, most gifted, most able to contribute to society the benefits of knowledge and the fruits of social cooperation, such as income and wealth. And yet doing more for the disadvantaged to facilitate their access to knowledge resources may be requisite in a just society if citizens are ever to achieve true equality of opportunity. Giacomo concludes:

> The public library is not an institution devoid of identity exactly because librarians have not been willing to abandon their beliefs in deference to the pressures of the moment -- whether for morally "correct" books, for opening the library's circulation records to police officers, or for charging fees. The public library's identity as an institution dedicated to fostering the freedom of inquiry among free citizens in a democracy is imparted to it by librarians committed to that principle and other related principles such as equal access and the right to read. As the commitment of librarians changes and wavers, the identity of the public library will correspondingly change and weaken. In time, a community may discover that in gaining either of these, it forfeited, with the aid and encouragement of librarians, something it valued deeply which it let slip away gradually and with conscious intent. It may discover that it has lost its *public* library.[41]

Recently, a number of libraries have reallocated funds from the materials budgets to cover the cost of searching, basing their action on the belief that library budgets should reflect online searching as part of standard reference service. The acquisition of CD-ROM technology has vitiated, to some extent, the argument since access is offline and hourly and connection charges are not levied.

Other fee-based issues will emerge with new technologies. As access to libraries becomes possible from increasingly remote stations, such questions as who can use online catalogs from dial-up ports will become important. When widespread access to electronic texts is available, will patrons have to pay for every use of an item, including browsing? Who owns information? The now popular conception of information as a commodity is currently being challenged, based, in part, on the argument that a great deal of information is generated from taxpayer funded government reports.

We can anticipate the debate to continue to test the values we have traditionally shared as librarians.

PRIVATIZATION OF INFORMATION

A related, equally nettling, problem has been the recent governmental practice of turning over to the private sector publication and operation of many of its basic information and collection activities. One of the fundamental beliefs of a democratic society is that the need to know and freedom to know are at the root of the social contract and that when government creates information, it has a duty to make it available to citizens at the lowest possible cost, even if that means subsidized publishing.[42]

Yet, as a result of concerted lobbying efforts by the information industry and the Reagan administration's policy commitments, for the first time in American history even the information produced directly by government agencies is being regarded as a commodity for sale rather than as a public or social good.[43]

Since 1982, one of every four of the government's 16,000 publications has been eliminated. The chief culprit, according to F. William Summers, has been the Office of Management and Budget using powers granted by the Paperwork Reduction Act of 1980.[44] This diminution in publication has led to a concentration of private information in fewer and fewer hands and to mounting expense. Five database vendors account for over 90% of the sales and uses of database services in the U.S.; nine firms account for 50% of all trade book sales. Prices of government publications have jumped. The *Congressional Record* rose from $75 to $208 and the *Monthly Catalog* from $65 to $215.

PROVISION OF MATERIAL NOT IN THE LIBRARY

Assistance in locating and securing material not available in a particular public library has become an increasingly important and labor consuming job. At times, members of the public may require information and advice about the location of special collections or nearby libraries with strength in certain subject fields as they plan visits in connection with research. By virtue of the reference librarian's knowledge of bibliography, research activity in different fields and the holdings of other libraries, the Reference Department has become a partner in the interlibrary loan transaction. Technology has removed some of the geographic barriers associated with use of other collections. The small library, by necessity, must depend on resources outside itself to better fulfill the information needs of its community. The strengths and weaknesses associated with local libraries no longer represent the constraining factor it once did. Some library, some database, will help answer the question. With the emergence of bibliographical utilities, and the vast number of bibliographic records converted to machine-readable form, much of the electronic structure is now in place to identify where material is located.

Unfortunately document delivery systems have not kept pace with systems of bibliographic access. We can determine exactly who owns a desired book or journal by depressing a few keys at a computer terminal and then we can tell the patron not to expect the material for a substantial period of time.

ETHICS

The moral stance with which librarians approach the reference transaction, their protection of client confidentiality, and the possible conflict of client interests with those of the society are ethical considerations which have occupied increasing attention in recent years.

Respect, impartiality, objectivity, honesty, and candor are all attributes of ethical professionals. Charles Bunge comments that

> reference librarians develop coping mechanisms to deal with [such] circumstances, including truncated reference interviews, hurried use of information sources and rationing time among users -- sometimes treating different types of users or questions differentially.[45]

Difficult as it may be, librarians have an obligation to overcome personal prejudices, to treat the unattractive kid whose nose is running with the same respect accorded the clean, apple-cheeked polite child.

Client confidentiality has been established as a principle value of reference service. Distinctions between professional consultation and gossip are not always easy to make. It is important to confer about difficult questions, to ask for help from peers when sources are not readily apparent. Yet the temptation to discuss the questioner as well as the question has to be avoided. Several years ago, the FBI launched a program to track the library research and borrowing habits of certain foreign nationals who they contended might be engaged in subversive spying activities. The ALA, basing its position on every library user's right to privacy, was outspoken in its opposition to the FBI's undertaking and the attempt was abandoned.

The neutrality with which librarians handle reference questions has posed one of the more complex ethical dilemmas. An important tenet of public library faith has been that reference staffs are obligated to provide any and all patrons with full and complete information, no matter the topic, and without consideration of the uses to which the information might be put. Yet, a number of critics have recently suggested that adopting this stance may in reality be abandoning ethical responsibility. Two types of queries with ethical implications occur in libraries. In the first, the interest of the client conflicts with the library as an organization. An illustration of the results of this dilemma is the policy of most libraries to bar their staffs from answering medical and legal inquiries, in order, among other reasons, to protect the library from lawsuits engendered by faulty responses. A second type of question is one in which the interest of the client conflicts with the interests of the society. For example, what are the ethics in assisting a patron search for the means to make a pipe bomb, or to put LSD in a city's water supply? Gillian Gremmels asserts that there are instances when community interest may overweigh individual needs. "Protecting and advancing the free flow of information is commendable, but there may be times when it is ethically unacceptable."[46] On the other hand, warns Charles Bunge, surely merely the potential that the information might be used for illegal purposes or to injure someone, or even the vague suspicion that this will be the case is not sufficient reason to limit one's obligation to one's client to assist in finding requested information.[47]

SUMMARY

The new technology has produced profound and far-reaching effects on reference services in public libraries. Access is now possible to information in every recess of the globe. On the other hand, privatization of governmental information, trends toward charging for online database services, and bottom-line mentalities of information producers has further widened the gap between the information haves and have-nots. Public reference librarians have obligations to protect the rights of all constituents to gain information and further to help them to utilize it. They sustain that commitment by guarding free access to information and by maintaining up-to-date skills.

NOTES AND SUGGESTED READINGS

Notes

1. Lynda Richardson, "At Library, No Inquiry Is Too Odd," *The New York Times* (February 13, 1992): B11.

2. Ida Rosenberg, "Problems of a Reference Librarian," *Library Journal*, March 1904. Reprinted in *Library Journal* 116 (June 15, 1991): S14.

3. Joseph Deitch, "Portrait: Barbara Bowsher Shapiro," *Wilson Library Bulletin* 65 (April 1991): 47.

4. Herbert Goldhor , "An Analysis of Available Data on the Number of Public Library Reference Questions," *RQ* 27 (Winter 1987): 195-201.

5. Samuel Rothstein, "The Hidden Agenda in the Measurement and Evaluation of Reference Service, or, how to make a case for yourself," in William Katz, comp., *Reference and Information Services,* (Metuchen, NJ: Scarecrow Press, 1986), 65.

6. Arthur Curley, "Obstacles to Information Access," in *Unequal Access to Information Resources: Problems and Needs of the World's Information Poor* (Ann Arbor, MI: Pierian, 1988), 2.

7. Mabel Shaw, "Technology and Service: Reference Librarians Have a Place in the '90s," *Reference Librarian* 33 (1991): 51-8.

8. Samuel Rothstein, *The Development of Reference Services Through Academic Traditions* (Chicago: American Library Association, 1955), 29.

9. *Adrift in a Sea of Change* (Sacramento, CA: California State Library Foundation, 1990). 11.

10. Ibid.

11. Darlene Weingand, *Administration of the Small Public Library* (Chicago: American Library Association, 1992), 27.

12. Paul Frantz, "The Fragile Allure of Reference," *Reference Librarian* 33 (1991): 23.

13. Ibid., 24-5

14. Rosemarie Riechel, *Personnel Needs and Changing Reference Service* (Hamden, CT: Library Professional Publications, 1989), 52-3.

15. Ibid., 2-4.

16. Barbara Quint, "Real Research for Real People," *Wilson Library Bulletin* 65 (March 1991): 97.

17. Frantz, 30.

18. Frances Allegri, "On the Other Side of the Reference Desk: The Patron with a Physical Disability," *Medical Reference Services Quarterly* 3 (Fall 1984): 65-76.

19. Rochelle Yates, *Telephone Reference Service* (Hamden, CT: Library Professional Publications, 1986), 24-5.

20. Thomas Childers, quoted in George Hawley, *The Referral Process in Libraries, a characterization and exploration of related factors* (Metuchen, NJ: Scarecrow Press, 1987), 2.

21. John Banigh, "Community Information and the Public Library," *Journal of Librarianship* 16 (April 1984): 79.

22. Rosamund Tifft, "The Growth and Development of Information and Referral in Library Services," in *Information and Referral in Reference Services,* ed. by Bill Katz and Marcia Middleton (New York: Haworth Press, 1988), 2229-2259.

23. Clare Beck, "Reference Services: A Handmaid's Tale," *Library Journal* 116 (April 15, 1991): 33.

24. The following is summarized from Reichel, 1989, 15.

25. Charles Bunge, "Reference Desk Staffing Patterns: Report of a Survey," *RQ* 26 (Winter 1986): 178.

26. Joseph Puccio, *Serials Reference Work* (Englewood, CO: Libraries Unlimited, 1989), 8

27. Karen Markey, "Levels of Formulation in Negotiation of Information Need During the Online Research Interview," *Information Processing and Management* 17 (1981): 23.

28. Herbert White, "The Variability of the Reference Process," *Library Journal* 116 (June 15, 1991): 55.

29. Charles Bunge, "Potential and Reality at the Reference Desk: Reflections on a 'Return to the Field,'" in William Katz, *Introduction to Reference Work* (New York: McGraw-Hill, 1989), 4.

30. Cecilia Stafford and William Servan, "Core Competencies: Recruiting, Training and Evaluating in the Automated Reference Environment," *Journal of Library Administration* 13 (1990): 81-97.

31. Bunge, *The Reference Library User*, 4-5.

32. Linda Crismond, "Information Services in the Public Library," in *The Future of the Public Library: Conference Proceedings* (Dublin, OH: OCLC, 1988), 77.

33. Beth Woodward, "The Effectiveness of an Information Desk Staffed by Graduate Students and Professionals," *College and Research Libraries* 50 (July,1989): 455-464.

34. Frances Benham and Ronald Powell, *Success in Answering Reference Questions: Two studies* (Metuchen, NJ: Scarecrow Press, 1987).

35. Ken Kister, "Making the Connection: The Telephone as a Creative and Potent--but Underutilized--Instrument for Reference Service," *Reference Librarian* 33(1991): 103-9.

36. Curley, in *Unequal Access*, 3.

37. Pete Giacoma, *The Fee or Free Decision* (New York: Neal-Schuman, 1989), 3.

38. Ibid., 4-5.

39. William Britten, "Supply Side Searching: An Alternative to Fee-Based Online Services," *Journal of Academic Librarianship* 13 (July 1989): 147.

40. Fay Blake, "Information and Poverty," in *Unequal Access,* 12.

41. Giacomo, 159.

42. The Washington Office of ALA publishes "Less Access to Less Information About the U.S. Government" every six months (Jan. and June) as an attachment to its *Washington Newsletter* or as a separate publication.

43. Bryan Pfaffenberger, *Democratizing Information, Online Databases and the Rise of End-User Searching* (Boston: G.K. Hall, 1990), 10.

44. F. William Summers, "Introduction: The Need to Know," in Al Trezza, *Effective Access to Information* (Boston: G.K. Hall, 1989), 4.

45. Charles Bunge, "Ethics and the Reference Librarian," in F.W. Lancaster, ed. *Ethics and the Librarian.* (Urbana-Champaign, Ill: Graduate School of Library and Information Science, University of Illinois, 1991), 50.

46. Gillian Gremmels, "Reference in the Public Interest: An Examination of Ethics," *RQ* 30 (Spring, 1991): 368.

47. Bunge, in *Ethics,* 57.

Suggested Readings

Auster, Ethel, ed. *Managing Online Reference Services.* New York: Neal-Schuman. 1986.

Bunge, Charles. "Ethics and the Reference Librarian," in Lancaster, F.W., ed. *Ethics and the Librarian.* Urbana-Champaign, IL: Graduate School of Library and Information Science, University of Illinois. 1991.

Childers, Thomas and Cheri Krauser, *Information and Referral in Public Libraries.* Norwood, NJ: Ablex, 1984.

Cleveland, Anna. *Building the Reference Collection.* New York: Neal-Schuman, 1991.

Crismond, Linda. "Information Services in the Public Library," in *The Future of the Public Library: Conference Proceedings.* Dublin, OH: OCLC Library, Information and Computer Science Series, 1988.

Giacoma, Pete. *The Fee or Free Decision.* New York: Neal-Schuman, 1989.

Hernon, Peter and Charles McClure. *Unobtrusive Testing and Library Reference Services.* Norwood, NJ: Ablex, 1987.

Katz, William, ed. *The Reference Library User: Problems and Solutions.* New York: Haworth, 1990.

Katz, William, comp. *Reference and Information Services. A Reader for Today.* Metuchen, NJ: Scarecrow Press, 1986.

Lang, Jovian, ed. *Unequal Access to Information Problems and Needs of the World's Information Poor.* Ann Arbor, MI: Pierian, 1988.

Pfaffenberger, Bryan. *Democratizing Information. Online Databases and the Rise of End-User Searching.* Boston: G.K. Hall, 1990.

Puccio. Joseph. *Serials Reference Work.* Englewood, CO: Libraries Unlimited, 1989.

Riechel, Rosemarie. *Personnel Needs and Changing Reference Service.* Hamden, CT: Library Professional Publications, 1989.

Trezza, Al. *Effective Access to Information.* Boston: G.K. Hall, 1989.

Yates, Rochelle. *Telephone Reference Service.* Hamden, CT: Library Professional Publications, 1986.

CHAPTER 12

FACILITATING LIBRARY USE

Efforts to reach and to serve the needs of disparate publics have induced some libraries to provide the kinds of outreach services described in Chapter 14, as well as to find creative ways to market and publicize the library's activities (see Chapter 15). For most librarians, enhancing the quality of *in-house* library use and encouraging the reading habit are among the library's fundamental goals. These they accomplish through activities as varied as providing reader advisory and learner services, offering bibliographic instruction, generating or making available live programs of interest to adults, and guaranteeing a safe and desirable place in which these activities can take place. Libraries are not immune from the problems caused by homelessness, delinquency and aberrant behaviors that plague American life in the 1990s and administrators have been forced to protect their institutions by adopting policies and taking measures to safeguard both their publics and their employees.

UNDERSTANDING USERS

People differ in their uses of the library. Many typologies have been constructed to help librarians understand the uses to which their collections are put. The Phoenix Public Library recently identified following four basic user types:

Browsers or Readers, the largest group, rely on the library to supply them with leisure and recreational reading. Their interaction with staff tends to be minimal. They help themselves either by consulting the catalog or going directly to shelves to browse among familiar materials. It is this group, however, that is most likely to be affected by formal or informal reader advisory assistance if that service exists in the library.

Researchers come to the library to locate information that supplements an occupational or scholastic concern. Their target is to gather information suitable to a particular inquiry. They are not necessarily regular library users, but utilize its services, primarily reference, as needed.

Independent Learners use the library as their primary educational institution. They aspire to become conversant in an area of particular interest or to attain a level of competence sufficient to qualify for a position or occupation. They may be drawn to the library by a research need, but their commitment is a long-term one, rather than merely occasioned by the necessity to secure a fact or a piece of information. Substantial library involvement can be required in adult learning projects. Self-education is an expanding field and many library users recognize the public library as an alternate source of education.

Group Participants or Associates use the library to participate in special programs held on the premises. Their contact with the staff may be insignificant, but for library personnel planning and carrying out the program consumes significant amounts of staff time and expertise.[1]

Three of the above groups utilize the services described in this chapter: those who come to the library to find "a book to read," those who seek to learn something and those who come to participate in a program. Differentiating groups by use may result in more rational allocation of resources based on better understanding of client behavior, but the distinctions are often less apparent than their descriptions would indicate. It is probable, for instance, that both independent learners and participants in group activities desire to acquire new knowledge about a subject. What differs is their method of obtaining it. Similar difficulties arise when distinguishing between reader advisory activities and those associated with adult learning. For purposes of this chapter, reader advisory work is more closely identified with recreation or leisure and adult learning related to the mastery of a particular skill or body of knowledge. Recognizing that both endeavors exist as a continuum rather than as ends of a spectrum offers a solution to some definitional problems.

READER ADVISORY SERVICES

The imminent demise of the novel and of serious nonfiction has by been prophesied by scores of post-modern literary commentators. It may be, however, that the fault lies more with the reading public than with the writing sector. As Philip Roth notes:

> There's been a drastic decline, even a disappearance of a serious readership. That's inescapable....By readers, I don't mean people who pick up a book, once in a while...I mean people who when they are at work during the day think that after dinner tonight and after the kids are in bed, I'm going to read for two hours. That's what I mean...There is a change in the mental landscape having to do with concentration, and that is what's responsible for the declining readership.[2]

No matter the cause or who bears responsibility, serious reading has indeed decreased. Adults read to sharpen their work skills, to prepare a report, or to pursue a hobby or avocation. For many the joy of reading for its own sake is an unknown or long forgotten experience. Most public librarians, along with their colleagues in academic and school libraries, consider reading to be an essential attribute of culture and a pursuit that deserves their deepest commitment. They willingly promote reading in their libraries, fully realizing the restrictions imposed on them by an institution whose clientele is limited. Libraries can influence people who are reached by their services -- users and recipients of information about activities. A display of recent intellectually challenging books, for instance, can stimulate reading, but only of those exposed to it. A library generated newspaper book column has the potential to reach a wide audience, including nonusers, but it too communicates within a limited sphere. Despite these handicaps, public libraries play an important role in helping to preserve a humane and cultured civilization in the face of increasing mechanization. They do this by fostering and furthering positive attitudes toward reading and learning. One librarian, echoing Holden Caulfield, reported that she became a librarian because she wanted to

> be a sort of *Catcher in the Rye* for readers. I wished to share with them what I had experienced as I read particular books or authors, to have community with them. I, myself, relish the recommendations of those I respect and I think others feel similarly. My most fun is in picking out books for good readers whose tastes I understand.[3]

History of Reader Advisory Services

Reader advisory work in the public library has led a checkered career. From the inception of the institution, librarians advised users about good books. Their selections were based on the notion that reading changes behavior and that the positive influence of good literature counteracts evil impulses on the part of the reader. Sometimes they dispensed their wisdom from a separate department; sometimes from a reference or circulation desk. The ambivalence about where to locate reader advisory services stems from questions about the best way to achieve the goal. Supporters of separate units maintain that institutionalizing the service promotes its importance and therefore its effectiveness. Those who oppose segregated departments maintain that advising readers is an integral part of all library work, rather than the province of the few who would staff them.

Reader advisory services were energized by the Library War Service Program which supplied library service to soldiers and sailors during World War I. During a twenty year period in the first half of this century, the pendulum inched toward formalizing advice to readers about books. From 1922 to 1926, reader advisory endeavors began to develop structure. Reading guidance, covering both fiction and nonfiction, was conveyed through a separate department. Advisors met with patrons in private interviews to determine appropriate plans for them and prepared "individualized reading courses for persons who wished to read systematically to meet the practical needs of daily living."[4]

A major growth spurt in reader advisory activities appeared during the years 1927 to 1935 when the ALA's Education Roundtable was formed and libraries began publishing annotated lists on special topics. The practice of conducting extensive interviews with patrons about their reading interests in order to ascertain their reading levels and develop individualized lists continued. Expansion in reader advisory services during the period has been attributed to three factors: 1) the growing number of professional workers in public libraries; 2) increased idleness and leisure caused by the Depression; and finally, 3) the beginning of systematic research relating to the problems of adult reading.[5] Douglas Waples' landmark study concerning the reading habits of library users in 1931 gave testimony to the new importance attached to understanding reading behavior.[6]

From 1936 to the start of the Second World War, reader advisory activities remained at an intense level. Subject specialists worked with reader advisors to formulate reading lists. One study identified seventy reader types, classified by occupation, race, sex and personality traits. Among these could be found: "The Timid and Inferior Feeling Person," "The Low Brow," "Tenement Dwellers," "Ambitious Persons," and "Sophisticated Women." Reading suggestions were then matched to these traits. Unskilled workers were advised to read *Of Mice and Men* and people judged as cowardly directed to *Lord Jim.*[7] The implicit assumption of these activities is that reading has a direct effect on behavior and following these recommendations would result in dramatic self-improvement.

By 1949 reader advisory services were no longer quite so fashionable. Public libraries are flexible organizations whose services fluctuate with changing societal needs and economic conditions. The kinds of advice proffered to readers during those decades had been pedantic. Readers were expected to better themselves, to move toward "classic" literature, not toward recreational reading. Librarians *knew* what was good for them and they were expected to follow directions. Expanded publishing, a steady influx of new kinds of users, the lessened availability of discretionary or leisure time, the increased access of populations to post-secondary and specialized institutions of learning, the new importance attached to "information" resulting from Sputnik, the Cold War and the Arms Race, the beginnings of multi-culturalism and lessened adherence to the "canon" -- those books which were said to be seminal to cultural literacy -- all combined to distract attention from Reader Advisory services. In addition, libraries began to turn away from the individual services lavished on readers toward group programs which they saw as more cost effective since substantially larger numbers of people could be reached at one time. (See below, Programming.)

Current Practices

Only a few libraries today maintain separate reader advisory departments. The advisory role has been dispersed and is assigned to all librarians who serve adults. Advisors no longer aim to "elevate the masses," but to be knowledgeable about library holdings in order to help readers find materials that interest them. That said, however, the task remains a formidable one requiring vast stores of information about books, their topics, their styles and their reading levels, as well as how to interview and probe in order to be able to match readers with books. The absence of reader advisory departments sometimes represents a lacuna in library services with no individual or group accepting responsibility for promoting reading, that is for mounting book exhibits, creating bookmarks, publishing annotated book lists or giving booktalks to organizations and associations.

Recently, there has been a resurgence of interest in providing the kind of one-on-one service that characterized earlier reader advisory attempts, though the philosophic position that was then embraced -- that reading directly influences behavior and that the more a person reads, the "better" his or her taste will become -- no longer holds dominion. The demand-driven library that supplies great quantities of bestsellers, but does not market interesting, lesser well-known fiction and non-fiction titles may feel even greater need for staff to be knowledgeable about reading material. Furnishing individualized reading advice is labor intensive, both in practice and preparation, and should not be undertaken unless there is administrative willingness to allow sufficient time for its practitioners to develop their skills and exercise them. Reader advisory services lack the immediacy of reference, circulation or other library transactions and may receive short shrift in the face of other demands.

A sign of the new found interest in reader advisory services has been the variety of new finding guides that have come onto the market to help reader advisors. Among these are *What do I read Next?*, *Good Reading Guide*, *Genreflecting* and *Olderr's Fiction Index*.

The new technology can be harnessed to assist reader advisory services. Subject access to fiction online, not yet a widespread practice, will enable the creation of bibliographies based on specific types of reading materials. A number of libraries have already or are contemplating integrating annotations to fiction into their Online Public Access Catalogs (OPACs), another boost to reader advisory services.

ADULT LEARNERS

We have, perforce, become a "learning society" in which rapid change requires a lifetime of learning in order to survive.

According to recent studies, between 79 and 98% of the population learns *something* during the course of a year, only 17% in classes and less than 1% for credit.[8] Learning activities are undertaken for a variety of reasons among which are to prepare for a job, or update skills; to cope with job-related problems; to deal with home and personal responsibilities or upgrade broad areas of competence; and to satisfy curiosity about a particular subject.[9]

History of Adult Education in the Public Library

From its inception, the public library has been associated with universal education. Lee suggests that it was

the first tax-supported agency established in the United States for the informal education of adults. It was organized specifically to provide a means by which mature individuals could continue to learn through their own efforts.[10]

American idealism held that even ordinary people could advance through self-education and improvement. Workers, for instance, could help themselves by using the mechanics' and apprentices' libraries. Evidence to support the continuing interest over time of public libraries in an educational role can be found in periodic reports issued from time-to-time by influential librarians. E.A. Hardy's "The Special Activities of the Library in Relation to Education," published in 1911, outlined the steps toward constructing an individualized plan of study for readers, with advice on how to refer them to formal classes and educational institutions. William Learned's 1924 influential treatise *The American Public Library and the Diffusion of Knowledge* contended that the educational objective of the library be paramount and proposed a plan for achieving that end. By 1926, the American Library Association Commission on the Library and Adult Education issued *Libraries and Adult Education* which held that libraries had an obligation to assume an active role in adult education.

Much of adult education activity in the 1930s was

indistinguishable from that of Reader Advisory Service. The vocabulary changed in 1938 when Alvin Johnson, under the auspices of the Carnegie Corporation, wrote *The Public Library -- A People's University*. Reader advisor work was on the wane, due perhaps to a decrease in leisure time, to a lessened demand for the service, its costly nature, and the lack of prepared staff to render it. Johnson proposed a dynamic plan to establish the educational prominence of the public library. Its acceptance in the library community was limited, but the conceptualization of the "People's University" became fixed in the library lexicon. The *Public Library Inquiry* appearing in 1947 reaffirmed the educational mission of public libraries, but suggested that the institution should focus their educational energies on the small but select segment of the population who would appreciate them.

During the 1950s the public library's adult education goal assumed a secondary role after recreation and information, although the ALA Fund for Adult Education supported and generated many important adult education activities. Its Library Community Project, for instance, which ran from 1955-1960 aided long-term adult education programs based on community needs analysis. By 1956 minimum standards placed education before information and recreation in the list of main objectives.

The thrust toward nontraditional study and independent learning was, in part, an outgrowth of 1960s student activism and the declining student population base, as well as increased federal support and concern, perhaps generated by the space race and the cold war. In 1966, an amendment to the Elementary and Secondary Education Act of 1965 created the Adult Education Act and in 1976, the Life-Long Learning (Mondale) Act was passed. By the 1970s, the conventions regarding the terms, places, mechanisms and content of postsecondary education had been loosened. Schedules and locations now included evenings and weekends, and remote sites. There were even opportunities for self-paced learning. In addition, adults participated in community-based continuing education opportunities. Private vocational, trade and business schools suddenly appeared; churches, synagogues, and Y's offered courses, most non-religious in nature. Cooperative extension services, afforded varieties of opportunities to continue learning, as did hospitals and medical centers.

Libraries, too, began to experiment with adult education programs. The College Board, the Council on Library Resources and the National Endowment for the Humanities conducted the Dallas Public Library Independent Study Project, in which the Dallas Public Library and Southern Methodist University joined forces to help adults acquire formal credit for independent study. Other programs followed and forms of Lifelong Learning Centers were established at Reading, Philadelphia, Westchester and Winston Salem. Despite a recent diminution in formal programs in lifelong learning, the Public Library Association's *Planning and Role Setting* lists "Formal Education Support Center" and "Independent Learning Center" as two of its eight proposed library roles. The description of the latter role includes a broad range of activities to further those who desire to pursue a sustained program of learning independent of an educational provider. The recent focus on adult literacy has reinforced the public library's traditional aim to supply unlimited knowledge and unlimited opportunity to acquire it.[11]

Independent Learners Today

The largest group of life-long learners would appear to be those involved in independent, self-initiated learning projects. Research has identified a number of reasons why adults prefer to pursue their own learning, rather than enroll in a formal class. For one, they want to proceed at their own pace and use their own style of learning. Another, related reason is that they want to retain control of the structure, and thereby keep the activity flexible and easily changed. Sometimes they are unaware that classes in the subject they desire to learn can be obtained. Many do not possess the discretionary time or capital to take a formal course. Finally, a number of independent learners have been found to dislike classroom settings, a carryover from unhappy childhood experiences.[12]

No matter whether adults are engaged in formal classroom learning or independent education, it seems logical that they would turn to the public library to support their aspirations. It is the "only major educational institution with a mandate covering the entire lifespan of its clients."[13] It is a free institution where individuals have access to vast resources of material. Librarians, with their historic concern for the individual and their neutral and non-punitive demeanor, are experienced in making connections between people and resources. Involvement in adult learning can range from information provision to information and referral services to advising and counseling. At the traditional end of the spectrum, the one requiring the least active intervention in the learning process and least personal contact, is the simple provision of materials for the learner. More activity is required of the librarian who supplies support services for the education activities of other community agencies. This might include making available materials, meeting facilities and bibliographies or study guides. Librarians increase their participation when they organize services to groups, or perhaps when they conduct programs. Libraries that maintain information and referral services (see Chapter 11) take putative learners a step further, by linking them directly with agencies that will help them achieve their learning goals. The final commitment, one that librarians are least willing to make, is dynamic participation in the learning project itself.

The major obstacle to librarians' acceptance of this role seems to be their discomfort with dispensing advice and counseling. Traditionally neutral, librarians have been trained not to interpret, only to locate and tender information. They do not judge, for instance, who is the best writer on a subject, or which product is best. They only report that critics suggest that X is said to write more authoritatively than Y, or that a consumer group reports that its tests reveal one product to be superior to another. Librarians feel unqualified to be counselors. Van Fleet attributes this insecurity to a poor understanding of adult learning theory.

...librarians, influenced by traditional concepts of teachers and

students, tend to assume too much responsibility for the planning
and the outcome of learners' projects.[14]

They are far more enthusiastic and confident about personalized
learning services when they recognize that they are facilitators, not
instructors, in what is essentially an equal partnership.

Another reason for librarians' reluctance to assume a more
activist role with independent learners is that while programs may
be started with special funding, they are expected to be continued
after the additional moneys have ceased to exist. Most librarians
feel overworked and unable to absorb even moderate increases
either in time or in dollar expenditures.

Those librarians willing to make a commitment to independent
learning require skills in interviewing, similar in nature to those
necessary for reader advisory and reference work. They must
understand how to probe, to be able to gauge a patron's reading
ability and level of knowledge about a subject, to be sympathetic
and certainly to be non-judgmental. Some libraries will view work
with independent learners as a departure from traditional library
activities. Others may consider that it is simply doing the same
things that have always been done, but with more care, true
planning, dedication and enthusiasm.

BIBLIOGRAPHIC INSTRUCTION

Bibliographic instruction, the process of producing information
literate library users, has for some time attracted substantial
attention in academic libraries. Recently, some public librarians
have wondered whether their users would respond to and profit
from similar service. Learning society imperatives dictate that
learners possess not only bodies of information, but knowledge of
the process of attaining them, as well. Becoming information
literate means acquiring the skills to gain access to information;
that is constructing information-search strategies, locating
information, and evaluating and using it effectively for a given
need. Being able to apply appropriate information-seeking behav-

ior to whatever tasks are encountered or maximizing the use of information in problem-solving are among the characteristics of information literate people. Critical thinking about information is yet another.

Few would deny the potentially salutary effects of group and classroom bibliographic instruction. Instituting the service in a public library, however, is difficult to accomplish. Academic libraries have captive audiences when entire classes are herded into the library for orientation and training in the use of library materials. Public library users may perhaps respond to a training proposal, but probably only when they are motivated by direct need. The problem, then, becomes identifying the need and the audience that will most profit from the instruction.

Of course, public librarians have been providing bibliographic instruction for years, but only informally on a one-to-one basis with limited aims and aspirations. Among the indirect bibliographic instruction steps that are easily managed in a public library are:

--Properly preparing and conspicuously hanging appropriate signage including notices, displays and location guides.

--Orienting new users to libraries when they register for cards.

--Creating readable materials describing library procedures and policies such as "How to Use an OPAC," or "Checking out a Book."

--Constructing pathfinders about subjects for which there is substantial demand. Pathfinders combine bibliographic instruction with methodology. They are commercially available, but can also be locally generated.

--Installing systems of Computer Assisted Instruction (CAI). CAI holds great promise for public libraries in that it presents opportunities in programmed instruction that no other format can offer. Among its benefits are interactivity -- it can provide immediate and appropriate feedback -- flexibility, ability to accommodate to varying skill levels -

- to adapt to changing end user requirement -- and availability any time the library is open. On the other hand, CAI is more expensive than other formats because it requires costly equipment and time-consuming programming. Interactive video is potentially a useful public library medium for bibliographic instruction. Its costs, too, are considerable and librarians lack expertise in devising appropriate programs for this new technology.

PROGRAMMING

The term library programming, as used in this chapter, refers to group activities, sponsored or cosponsored by libraries, that utilize live presenters or nonbook formats. Programs might include book and public affairs discussions, poetry readings, concerts, lectures, demonstrations, health information fairs or art exhibits. Librarians today are ambivalent about whether or not to present programs and if so what the nature of those programs should be. Do they wish to act as cultural centers for their communities? To what extent is adult education a focus of their program? Affirmative responses lead to yet another group of questions. Must programs relate directly to library materials -- that is be tied to attempts to stimulate use of the collection -- or can their aim be to impart culture, no matter if it promotes increased reading? Finally, libraries must address the knotty problem of whether culture can be broadly defined or must be linked to what is known as "high" culture. How librarians define their goals, and how they hope to achieve them, may help to answer these queries.

Among the early indications of American desire to further culture and education beyond the confines of schools and museums was the nineteenth century growth and spread of lyceums and similar institutes. Sinclair Lewis, in his *Main Street*, immortalized the Gopher Prairie lyceum which he called "The Thanatopsis Club." (Ironically, Thanatopsis means study of death.) At the turn of the nineteenth century and into the twentieth, tent Chautauquas carried culture and new learning into the furthest reaches of the nation. The famous muckraker Ida Tarbell described how the first Chautauqua Assembly, in 1874, was a revolutionary event that upset the old order and enabled attendees to experience challenging contacts with current intellectual life. Libraries allied themselves with these and similar cultural movements, frequently sharing quarters and staff. The Meadville (PA) Public Library still bears as its official name The Meadville Library, Art and Historical Association. Many associations that later became Friends groups were originally organized to pursue culture in one form or another. Literary clubs that sprang up throughout the nation often associated themselves with libraries, either directly or in fund-raising capacities. The linkages were clear.

Other library activities contributed to legitimizing library programming. The drive to socialize immigrants led to Americanization courses being offered by public libraries. There were English classes as well as sessions in hygiene and appropriate behavior. By 1910, the professional literature indicates, libraries were being urged to promote access to the collection through lectures and exhibits. The uses of meetings rooms, where they existed, were expanded to programming that included live performances for both children and adults, meetings of civic organizations and municipal departments and neighborhood gatherings.

As group programming gained popularity, there was a commensurate decline in individualized services. Programming was cost effective, efficiently utilizing resources to reach a much larger clientele. The *Post War Standards* for libraries issued in 1943 described the uses and guidelines for meeting rooms. It clearly specified that live and group programs though acceptable were peripheral to the library's program, and, by implication, simply means of introducing users to the library collection. Rooms were

desirable for such educational activities as discussion and book review groups, film forums, radio and record listening, and story hours...less closely related activities as a general rule should be

included only when...the administration of such activities will
not divert time and attention to the library staff from its primary
responsibility.[15]

The notion of the public library as an intellectual meeting place
was articulated in 1948 when it was described

as a community center to which the citizen turns as he
seeks expression of his interests and desires through group
affiliation and which might include...film forums, poetry
readings and symphony performances.[16]

And in 1956, ALA's *Public Library Service* affirmed that

the library should facilitate the use of materials by verbal, visual
or other interpretive means but...all group activities sponsored or
cosponsored by the library should be clearly related to the further
use of library materials.[17]

Inclusion of libraries in the National Endowment for the
Humanities plan to bring humanities to local communities, much
as the Chautauquas had done a century before, institutionalized the
legitimacy of live library programming. NEH programs entailed
hiring scholars in residence for public libraries. Their purpose was

to encourage public understanding of the humanities, an interest
in academic and public library humanities resources through
thematic programs, exhibitions, publications and other library
activities to stimulate the use of resources.[18]

The level of funding was never more than a trickle, but libraries
justified applying for NEH grants on the grounds that the programs
could attract new library users, increase the community's
awareness of library services, help the library become a cultural
and information center and act as a forum for consideration of
current events.   They argued that the library's universal
accessibility and essential neutrality made it a perfect place for such

programs to be instituted.

Some scholars and librarians doubted that public libraries were the appropriate sites for NEH programs. They claimed that the activities required to produce the program were extraneous to librarians' main purposes and required more in time and money than the grants could furnish.

Other dissension centered around the dispute between those who wished the programming to be "high culture" and those who supported the notion of "popular culture." The phenomena of the rise of cultural pluralism and the academic study of popular culture led to a heightening of the debate. Those who supported popular culture championed the assumption that "popular culture reflects and expresses the aesthetic and other wants of many people, and that all people have a right to culture they prefer."[19] They contended that a truly democratic culture must be driven by an appreciation of cultural relativism. Both "high" and "low" culture were said to be motivated by the urge to bring beauty into people's lives.

> The choices people make, whether indicative of high or low culture, are appropriate if they reflect the values and standards meaningful to them...viewed in isolation, apart from the people whose lives they serve, some cultures may seem superior to others in their scope and depth, but cultures evaluated apart from their consumers are meaningless. [20]

The early history of public library programming had been guided by the premise that its proper audience was educated users capable of participation in high culture. By the 1960s providing popular culture programming was deemed appropriate for libraries. Librarians worked not to change the tastes of clientele, but to give them wide exposure to alternative cultural models, to expand life experience. High culture programming tended to be located in central libraries, while programs devoted to folk and ethnic culture were frequently found in branches of the same system.

In one of the most radical conceptual shifts, libraries began to view programs not simply as mere enducements to further use of the library's book collection. They now preferred to make available "a wide range of traditional or innovative aesthetic experiences for the sake of the humanizing experience itself." [21] The ALA's *Public Library Mission Statement* of 1979 read:

> Information includes not only the sum total of recorded human experience...but also the unrecorded experience which is available only from human sources.[22]

The global recession of the late 1970s greatly reduced special funding for innovative programming. Several other societal factors also influenced the decline of library programming. Competing demands on the time and attention of potential attendees, the numbers of working women and of moonlighters, the pervasiveness of television and the unprecedented growth of video home entertainment all contributed to the lessened demand for public library programming. So too, did the rise of community arts organizations that grew in response to the availability of National Endowment for the Arts funding. They assumed much of the responsibility for cultural programming and became outlets for local artists.

The library as a focus point for community activities, meetings and services continues to be accepted as appropriate to the library's mission. It is, in fact, specified by the Public Library Association as one of the twelve possible roles a library may play. By providing a central location for cultural, civic and recreational activities, "community members [have] opportunities to explore common heritage, discuss divergent views on issues and current topics."[23]

Critics of contemporary library programming, even those who support the concept, accuse libraries of lack of definition of appropriate goals for the activity. Programs are not targeted to need and do not take into consideration competing ventures. Some libraries have confined their adult programming to book discussions. Others, as a result of the planning process, limit their programming to activities attractive to children. On the other hand, libraries in developing areas, support active cultural programs because alternate cultural opportunities have not yet emerged.

Meeting Room Use

In addition to conducting their own programs, libraries often allow community groups to use their meeting rooms if they qualify and abide by a policy that establishes eligibility criteria and conditions of use. As simple as that may sound, meeting room policies are complicated to write and subject to debate, contention and criticism. Before a meeting room policy can be set, libraries must determine the reasons for permitting the room or rooms to be used. Justification can lie, for instance, in giving the community a place in which to share special knowledge or discuss beliefs in an open forum. Or it can be offered in the name of providing a convenient, central meeting place for community organizations.

Many libraries permit all groups whose meetings are open to the public at large and who do not charge entry fees to meet in the library. Some libraries bar those groups whose orientation is political or religious. However, the distinction between religion and philosophy is arguable and denying access to these groups raises the specter of censorship. On the other hand, if religious groups are not rejected, libraries may be accused of not properly separating church and state. Whatever the position taken by the library, care is required that the policy is applied equally to those wishing to use the room. Privileges are sometimes refused to organizations that repetitively request space or who meet regularly and at intervals of less than a month. Libraries also must decide whether to charge for meeting rooms. Customarily, fees are imposed when meetings extend beyond normal library hours and special custodial help is required.

A recent case in San Francisco exemplifies some difficulties of applying library meeting room policy. A group of men calling themselves NAMBLA gathered in a branch library to "look at pictures of children." What library officials did not know was that the acronym stood for North American Man-Boy Love Association. The men were violating no criminal law, nor any library policy.

However, parental complaint and media attention caused the library to redefine its policy, while safeguarding the right to assembly. Among the policy revisions were procedures that mandate that all groups must file applications for the meeting room at least one week in advance, with full names and missions of the group clearly spelled out, and that the library reserved the right to change the meeting site if it felt the action necessary.[24]

CREATING AN ENVIRONMENT THAT FACILITATES USE

Public libraries, in order to facilitate use, must be readily accessible, have good signage, have comfortable chairs, and space set aside for study and quiet. Users have the right to feel that libraries are safe places, where they can pursue their interests without threat of bodily harm.

Problem Patrons in the Library

Among library stereotypes is the pervasive one that they are quiet, safe havens away from the bustle of contemporary life. Many famous writers have written of the escape   from the vicissitudes of harsh street life they found in libraries.[25] From time to time librarians have tried to distance themselves from the "quiet" stereotype by introducing varieties of activities into the library's programs. Recently, society itself has contradicted the traditional conception of the library, and librarians are unclear about an appropriate response.

During the last two decades, a number of the safety nets once provided by American society to its less fortunate citizens have been removed resulting in increased poverty, homelessness, and, some feel, drug addiction and criminal behavior. Among the newly homeless are countless persons with mental problems. At one time, people considered to be severely psychologically disturbed were routinely incarcerated and cared for in institutions. Today, however, civil liberty and economic considerations have emptied mental hospitals. Many former patients now deemed no threat to the society or themselves roam the streets and other public spaces seeking safe haven. Libraries, warm, comfortable, often welcoming, are among their most likely destinations. Public libraries have always been frequented by patrons who were obviously troubled. They looked odd, were disheveled and sometimes smelled. Generally, they could be categorized as needy, isolated and attention-seeking, rather than dangerous, and could be safely ignored or redirected. Today, however, the presence of deviant patrons may, at worst, present a safety hazard and, at best, stand as a major impediment to the delivery of library service. Problems of actual and tangible threats to patron and staff safety are now legion; library literature routinely reports incidents in which library workers have been physically harmed. Weapons are common, as is intoxication. Larger libraries and those in reputationally unsafe neighborhoods have found it necessary to hire security guards to monitor the behavior of patrons. Some directors have found it difficult to hire employees for inner-city libraries without financial incentives and guarantees of, often costly, safeguards -- taxi transportation, escort services and parking lot attendants, for example. A few libraries have even cut back to daylight hours as a defense against late evening incidents.

In the face of patrons who exhibit anti-social behavior, are threatening, or emit a smell so repulsive as to prevent others from using the facility, what rights does a library have to protect the majority of those who use the building? How should that protection be manifested? At what point is the library's traditional allegiance to first amendment civil liberties issues put at risk by actions taken to make the institution comfortable for its more conventional users?

Unfortunately, people disagree on the range of appropriate behaviors. An odor offensive to one person, may go unnoted by another. "Much disruptive, but non-criminal behavior that affects libraries may be a problem of different standards being used by different people." [26] Most "nuisance" conditions or actions, while annoying both to staff and patrons, are not sufficient grounds for legal action.

Recently, a number of test cases have been adjudicated in the nation's courts regarding the rights of libraries to set limits on patrons exhibiting atypical behavior. Decisions have been ambiguous; reversals are frequent and the questions remain without decisive answers.

The Morristown Case

The case that probably attracted greatest attention surfaced in May, 1991 in New Jersey. The library had, at times, barred a user, Richard Kreimer, because his demeanor in the library made patrons uncomfortable and his lack of hygiene rendered him malodorous. Federal District Court Judge Lee Sarokin ruled that the Morristown Public Library had erred in adopting regulations governing conduct in the library and in applying the following ones to Richard Kreimer's behavior:

1. Patrons shall be engaged in activities associated with the use of the public library while in the building. Patrons not engaged in reading, studying, or using library materials shall be asked to leave the building...

5. Patrons shall respect the rights of other patrons and shall not harass or annoy others through noisy or boisterous activities, by staring at another with intent to annoy that person...

9. Patrons whose hygiene is so offensive as to constitute a nuisance to other persons shall be asked to leave the building.[27]

The regulations were found to be too broad, vague and drawn so as to deny equal protection and due process under the law. Judge Sarokin noted "that in establishing regulations for use, the conditions imposed must be specific, their purpose necessary, and their effects neutral."[28] Further, he wrote, "If we wish to shield our eyes and noses from the homeless, we should revoke their condition, not their library card."[29]

The Morristown Library appealed the decision and requested support from the American Library Association. ALA found itself in a quandary, caught between upholding First Amendment principles expressed in the opinion and helping its member libraries with the very real problem of creating policy for behavior in public buildings.[30]

Reactions of the profession were mixed. Intellectual Freedom Committee Chair Gordon Conable suggested that the Sarokin decision "is consistent with the ALA intellectual freedom policies," does not deny the right of local libraries to adopt appropriate non-discriminatory policies; and contains an "extremely useful affirmation of the First Amendment right to receive information..."[31] Conable recommended that any ALA involvement in the appeal be in support of Judge Sarokin. He later stated that one of his major concerns had been the "loss of recognition of the library as a public forum and the rejection of the legal concept of the right to receive information will be used against libraries effectively by censors who would find a precedent in this case."[32] Some found the Morristown regulations ad hominem, proposed specifically to address the Kreimer problem rather than broad general policy.

Opposing these views were those who saw the conflict not as a first amendment issue, or even one of homelessness, but rather in terms of the fundamental right of an institution to adopt regulations dealing with the maintenance of order and the protection of the rights of all patrons to use the library without harassment. This position was supported by the New Jersey Library Association, local newspapers and many individual members of the profession. Will Manley, for instance, writing in *Wilson Library Bulletin* said

> To those of us who actually have to work in a library, the regulations seem not only reasonable but necessary. Isn't it our job to create a library environment conducive to study, learning, thinking, reading, and writing? Isn't it our responsibility as administrators and trustees to protect the health and welfare of

our employees and users?...I thought so, but apparently the judge
has some other weird view of the purpose of libraries...[33]

Obviously, legitimate concerns exist on both sides. Public
libraries rely on basic constitutional guarantees governing free
expression and free transmission of information. Effective exercise
of these guaranteed rights depends on the maintenance of public
order, and the protection of individual rights of citizens. Judge
Sarokin's decision recognized the existence of both needs, but
weighed them differently than might have been done by others.
Morristown Public Library appealed Judge Sarokin's decision and
found the upper court more sympathetic to its position. The
decision was overturned on the basis that the library's policy was
grounded in "well established constitutional privilege" and had not
infringed on the rights of Richard Kreimer.[34] The Court held
unanimously "that a library is a limited public forum and is
obligated only to permit the public to exercise rights that are
consistent with the nature of the library."[35]

ALA and New Jersey Library Association are both currently
wrestling with the twin problems in order to articulate a policy that
protects intellectual freedom and freedom of information while still
asserting the legitimate rights of libraries to safeguard their staffs
and public from disruptive behavior.

SUMMARY

Public libraries play an important role in achieving a humane
and cultured civilization. They do this by fostering positive
attitudes toward reading, by helping people to accomplish the
educational goals they set for themselves, by presenting programs
that introduce the public to new ideas and experiences.

Changing societal priorities, among other factors, cause
libraries to alter their methods of facilitating library use and
furthering self-learning. Library programming, for instance, has
diminished in recent years, due, in part, to increased competition
from other activities. New importance is attached to making people
information literate, teaching them how to gain access to library

material and how to evaluate and utilize it once located.

Patron behavioral problems have lately plagued libraries and given rise to a lively and important debate regarding the rights of patrons to use the library without the unwanted interference of other users while safeguarding the rights of those who exhibit deviant, but not criminal behavior.

NOTES AND SUGGESTED READINGS

Notes

1. T. D. Webb. *Reorganization in the Public Library* (Phoenix, AZ: Oryx Press, 1985), 56-58.

2. Esther Fein, "Roth[1] on Roth[2] and Roth[3]: They're Real. *All* of Them," *New York Times* (March 11, 1993): C13+.

3. Anonymous librarian in conversation with Alice Gertzog.

4. Joyce Saricks and Nancy Brown, *Readers' Advisory Service in the Public Library* (Chicago: American Library Association, 1989), 3.

5. Ibid., 4.

6. Douglas Waples and Ralph Tyler, *What People Want to Read About* (Chicago: American Library Association, 1931).

7. Ibid., 5.

8. Connie Van Fleet, "Lifelong Learning Theory and the Provision of Adult Services," in Kathleen Heim and Danny Wallace, *Adult Services* (Chicago: American Library Association, 1990), 168.

9. Allen Tough, *The Adult Learning Project.* 2nd ed. (Austin, TX: Learning Concepts, 1979), 32.

10. Robert Lee, *Continuing Education for Adults through the American Public Library, 1833-1964* quoted in Heim and Wallace, 206.

11. Summarized from Van Fleet in Heim and Wallace, 170-182.

12. Tough, 39.

13. Van Fleet in Heim and Wallace, 198.

14. Ibid., 102.

15. Connie Van Fleet and Douglas Raber, "The Public Library As a Social Cultural Institution," in Heim and Wallace, 472.

16. Ibid., 477.

17. Ibid.

18. Ibid., 465.

19. Ibid., 482.

20. Ibid.

21. Ibid., 485.

22. Ibid.

23. Charles McClure et al., *Planning and Role Setting for Public Libraries* (Chicago: American Library Association, 1987), 32.

24. "Man-Boy Love Association Spurs San Francisco Public Library Changes," *Library Journal* 117 (March 15, 1992): 16.

25. See Susan Toth and John Coughlan, eds., *Reading Rooms* (New York: Washington Square Press, 1990).

26. Bruce Shuman, *Foundations and Issues in Library and Information Services* (Englewood, CO: Libraries Unlimited, 1992), 139.

27. *Library Journal* 116 (August 1991): 20.

28. Ibid.

29. Ibid.

30. Ibid., 15.

31. *American Libraries* 22 (July-August, 1991): 610.

32. *Public Libraries* 31 (Jan-Feb, 1991): 2.

33. Will Manley, *Wilson Library Bulletin* 66 (October, 1991): 51.

34. *Wilson Library Bulletin* 66 (May, 1992): 13.

35. Ibid., 13.

Suggested Readings

Birge, Lynn. *Serving Adult Learners.* Chicago: American Library Association, 1981

Brown, Barbara J. *Programming for Librarians: A How to do it Manual.* New York: Neal-Schuman, 1992.

Carlsen, G. Robert and Anne Sherrill. *Voices of Readers: How We Come to Love Books.* Urbana, IL: National Council of Teachers of English, 1988.

Davidson, Cathy N. *Reading in America: Literature and Social History.* Baltimore, MD: John Hopkins, 1989.

Heim, Kathleen and Danny Wallace, eds. *Adult Services: An Enduring Focus for Public Libraries.* Chicago: American Library Association, 1990.

Lubans, John, comp. & ed. *Educating the Public Library User.* Chicago: American Library Association, 1983

Monroe, Margaret, "The Cultural Role of the Public Library." *Advances in Librarianship* 11 (1981).

Reilly, Jane. *The Public Librarian as Adult Learners' Advisor.* Westport, CT: Greenwood, 1981.

Saricks, Joyce and Nancy Brown. *Readers' Advisory Service in the Public Library.* Chicago: American Library Association, 1989.

Toth, Susan and John Coughlan, eds. *Reading Rooms.* New York: Washington Square Press, 1990.

Weibel, Marguerite Crowley. *The Library as Literary Classroom.* Chicago: American Library Association, 1992.

Wilson, Patrick. *Second Hand Knowledge.* Westport, CT: Greenwood, 1983.

CHAPTER 13

YOUTH SERVICES

Robert Cormier, the noted author of books for young adults, commented to a group of youth services librarians present to witness his receipt of the Margaret A. Edwards Award that:

> We are a sweet gathering of gentle forces in a world that is not always gentle or sweet. We form a unique outpost of civilization in a world that is not always civil. We revere the written word in a world where the image dazes as well as dazzles and leaves us feeling strangely wanting.[1]

Traditionally, children's departments, their services and staffs, have held an enviable position within public libraries. Robert Leigh, in his largely critical 1949 assessment of the public library, singled out children's librarians for praise. "Not only are the children's librarians expert, but also in the community they are recognized as such. Thus children's rooms and children's librarians have been the classic success in the public library."[2]

Echoing Leigh's findings two decades later, Lowell Martin observed:

> The notable success in the public library has been children's services...It works in the slum as well as the suburb...And in the public mind it is thought of as one of the most natural and significant activities of the public library.[3]

Children's librarians bore the responsibility and the pleasure of introducing children to the joys of reading unrelated to school or work. Their enthusiasm and dedication were models of the missionary zeal that characterized early library work. Frances Clarke Sayers, a pioneer of children's librarianship, called the opening of public libraries to children "one of the most gracious and humane acts of faith in this great and fumbling democracy."[4]

Unfortunately, by the end of the 1960s, the most favored status of children's librarianship began to wane and in the 1970s it fell casualty to budget shortfalls, indifference and changing societal priorities. Children's librarians became scarce commodities and many libraries adopted generalist, non-age-level approaches to providing service.

Today, however, new exigencies have once again catapulted children's librarianship to the forefront of public library attention. Among these have been the realization that learning takes place very early; the new premium placed on the learning society; the imperative to educate Americans so they can compete in the Global Village; and the maturing of "Baby Boomers," reared in Children's Rooms, who are now themselves parents. The myriad problems that afflict contemporary society -- poverty, illiteracy, single parenthood, immigration, homelessness, dual career families and latchkey children, sexual and other physical abuse, drugs, rootlessness -- have spilled over into the Children's Room carrying broad implications for service need and delivery. In addition, such difficult conundrums as equal access for young people to online information sources, to interlibrary loan and to audiovisual materials have caused children's librarians to once again examine their missions and obligations and to reaffirm their time-honored principles. The importance to children's librarians of examining and understanding what they are doing, framed against the background of library as well as social demands has never been greater. Pressures to justify programs and expenditures are made necessary, first by library administrators determined to be accountable, but second, and perhaps more significantly, by the society which cannot afford to squander its scarce resources when the stakes are so high. Barbara Rollock warns that:

> In order to be viable, library service to children must be nourished by adequate resources, properly respected and neither taken for granted nor smothered with benign neglect. A community's future, a nation's future are its children and young people, and we shortchange or ignore library services to them at our peril.[5]

CLIENTELE

In this chapter, the comprehensive term "Youth Services" is employed to include both what we have come to term children's services and those directed to Young Adults. Grouping them into a single chapter is problematic and the coupling here is a matter of convenience rather than a theoretical stance. Where Young Adults rightfully belong has occupied substantial attention in library literature. To isolate or segregate them is to perpetuate the distinctions society already makes. As Mary K. Chelton notes, "It is difficult to figure out what kind of adult you might like to be when no institution provides conditions under which you might interact with many different kinds of adults."[6] To group them with children is to continue the elongation of childhood that has characterized this century. This chapter includes both children and young adults, but is divded into two sections with the YA discussion following the one about children.

In general, the term "children" refers to those under the age of twelve or thirteen and Young Adults range from thirteen to eighteen, although some place the bottom limit of this latter category as low as ten. Obviously, a flexible approach to the age question is preferable to fixed parameters. The tendency, for instance, on the part of library administrations and children's staff to operate children's rooms separately from the rest of the library, rather than the eminently more desirable complementary or integrated model, continues the arbitrary barriers between adult and children's services.

In reality, children's departments serve a number of distinct age groups:

> --*Adults*--parents and other caregivers, as well as teachers and other social agency personnel comprise an increasingly large portion of children's room patrons.

> --Younger and younger *pre-school children*--toddlers and even infants are using the library in great numbers. Many libraries report that preschoolers form the largest distinct category of library borrowers. In Baltimore County, for instance, 14% of the entire library's circulation is accounted for by preschool materials.

> --*School-age children* are those below what Barbara Rollock terms the magic preteenage of twelve and above seven. This is the after-school crowd who make heavy demands on resources and staff late in the afternoon, weekends and during holiday periods. They are the target of most Children's Room materials.

> --A final age-related group may be termed *transitional users*, those who have trouble shifting from children's to adult collections. Among their ranks are children who are developmentally disabled, have limited reading ability or are non-native speaking.

Age groupings are delineated only to point children in a particular direction, not to exclude them from any part of the library's collection. An important tenet of the contemporary library faith is that it does not operate "in loco parentis." Freedom of access to the entire library is guaranteed by ALA's Library Bill of Rights and its Freedom to Read Statement. (See Appendix A).

The "Free Access to Libraries for Minors" ALA statement adopted in 1972 and amended in 1981, reads:

> The American Library Association opposes libraries restricting

access to library materials and services for minors and holds that it is the parents -- and only parents -- who may restrict their children -- and only their children -- from access to library materials and services. Parents who would rather their children did not have access to certain materials should so advise their children. The library and its staff are responsible for providing equal access to library materials and services for all library users.[7]

The path to free access for children has never been smooth. From the inception of the public library there have been questions about whether or not a child could enter a library, could ask staff members for help and could use various sections of the collection. It was common to restrict reading rooms to adults only, to limit circulation of some materials and to have closed, adult-only collections. The question of equal access to library materials for children has not entirely disappeared. Most libraries no longer discriminate their circulation of books on the basis of age, but new technology has brought with it fresh questions regarding the extent to which youth can and should be served and are discussed in the section on reference service.

GOALS OF CHILDREN'S SERVICE

Children's departments, in miniature, do what the rest of the library does. They provide basic collections of materials that are educational and recreational, and mount programs that make the collection accessible. That includes cataloging and classifying material, offering reference service, affording access to extra-library information (online databases, interlibrary loan), and presenting programs for younger and older children that will stimulate interest in reading.

In 1987, the Youth Services Section of the New York Library Association issued a comprehensive -- and courageous -- ten point set of responsibilities that libraries serving young people should be fulfilling. The following is a summary of those points:

1. Stimulate, encourage, support and nurture the young in their efforts toward literacy. Introduce and motivate youth to read for enjoyment. Give guidance to children, teens, parents and teachers in their choice of books and other materials.

2. Recognize and serve the needs of young people -- identify and meet diverse educational, cultural, intellectual, social and information needs.

3. Build strong local collections of materials. Provide access without censorship. Support school curricula.

4. Provide library staff who are responsive to, responsible for and trained in youth services -- who will act as youth advocates and catalysts for change.

5. Serve all young people through outreach.

6. Create networks of all types of libraries and community agencies, communicate with peers, share programs and resources.

7. Articulate to administration the need for library service for youth.

8. Stimulate, nurture and support the ability of youth to become their own information managers.

9. Market library service for youth -- at every level.

10. Actively work for legislation and adequate funding.[8]

Serving children well ensures the future of public libraries by creating an informed, taxpaying library-using citizenry that will support the library as adults.

THE SOCIAL CONTEXT

The gradual, but steady decline in the number of parent-accompanied preschoolers at story hour surprised some children's librarians. They would have been more prepared for that eventuality had they monitored closely demographic and other societal trends. Children's librarians, like all public librarians, can ill-afford to ignore those factors that impinge so heavily on the services they have offered, the ones they are currently providing and those they may be required to furnish in the not-too-distant future.

The litany of societal ills has become all-too-familiar. Statistics describe the situation in dimensions even more terrible than we are led to suspect by merely intoning such words as homelessness, AIDS, drug addiction, and so on. On the other hand, librarians know better than most others that knowledge means power. Below are some facts about and implications of societal trends that have great moment for service to children in public libraries.

Demographics. The birth rate has decreased while other groups -- senior citizens, for instance -- have grown larger. This adds to the political and economic powerlessness of children. The population is highly mobile. Children are subject to constant geographic dislocations. About 12 million of them move annually, making it difficult for them to set down roots and to have close, extended family relationships. Friendship becomes more problematic, both for parents and children.

Immigrants. There have been massive waves of immigration from Latin America, Asia and the Middle East. The number of immigrant children of school age ranges between 2.1 and 2.7 million. They face special hurdles, including the ethnic distrust of Americans and possibilities of cultural alienation from their parents because of competing value systems, among which may be education for women and new patterns of socializing. Immigrant children experience difficulties in acquiring language. The librarian has a sensitive role to play in helping to bridge the gap between immigrant children, their families and the dominant society. Supplying appropriate materials is extremely difficult.

New Family Configurations. More than one-half of mothers with children ages three to five now work outside the house. Two-thirds of working women are either sole wage earners or have husbands earning less than $15,000 a year. The number of parents affected by divorce has more than tripled in the last thirty years. Over twelve million children live in female headed households and over half of these children are poor. One out of five children live in poverty. So-called *latchkey* children -- those left alone before and after school each day for periods of time while parents are at work -- are one result of new family configurations. Children are often dropped at the library as a safe place and told to remain there until picked up. They are a group who would much rather be doing something else and as a result can become noisy, boisterous and troublesome, frequently demanding far more than their fair share of attention. Whether the library should accept responsibility for them becomes a matter of grave concern. Some libraries have welcomed the challenge, working with other community agencies to provide services and programs for latchkey children. Others have instituted rules that demand that children under ten be accompanied by an adult. While understandable, the rules may result in denying independent visits to the library by children under ten who live in the library's neighborhood and can come by themselves.

Homelessness. More than 3 million families are homeless. Children with no fixed address face real hurdles when they attempt to use a library. They are ineligible for library cards. They probably can't care for library materials. The library *can* serve at least some homeless children, those in shelters. Sheltered children can be invited to the library as a field trip. They can be made aware of library programs. Displays on homelessness to educate children with homes about their less fortunate peers can be mounted in the library. Small, in-house collections of reading materials can be placed in shelters. And, finally, librarians can assist homeless parents to acquire the information they need to locate lodging, jobs, and other social services. Unfortunately, the small number of shelters means that relatively few homeless are housed in them and, therefore, reachable by libraries.

Health Problems. Physical, mental and emotional illnesses among children have burgeoned. Poor nutrition, inherited addictions, depression and alienation have all increased at an alarming rate. Like other professionals dealing with children, librarians need to be alert to evidence of abuse and take appropriate steps to report the situation to proper authorities.

Illiteracy. The drop-out rate is at about 25% nationwide, but as high as 50% in some urban centers. There are 700,000 functionally illiterate students who graduate from United States high schools each year. The incidence of functional illiteracy and semi-literacy has worsened in the past several decades. Parents who cannot read, and millions who can, but don't, cannot be expected to set an example for children. Head Start serves 43,000 -- less than 20% of the eligible population. The burden becomes even heavier for children's librarians.

Influence of Electronic Media. The average child spends thirty hours weekly (one-third of waking hours -- 1500 hours per year) in front of television. Proliferation of nonprint media has worried children's librarians since they first made their appearance. Movies, some contended, would cause children to lose their ability to concentrate on print. Today, television cartoons, professionally produced videotapes of classic children's stories and computer games "which allow children to destroy the forces of evil themselves instead of hearing about someone else doing it," all compete with library programs.[9]

Television has had a strong impact on children's literature. Non-fiction books are shorter, and more heavily illustrated. Fiction, like television, has briefer scenes which end more abruptly. Vocabulary has been limited and altered as have concepts of sequence and passed time. Images of the human condition and human relationships, death and its finality, violence, crime, urban decay, cruelty, drug addiction, rape and suicide are delivered daily into people's homes. Children have shorter spans of attention and a need for instant gratification. Subjected to constant sales pitches, young people are trained to become voracious consumers.

Benefits can accrue from watching television. Children can be exposed to live performances, ballet and theatre, to far off places, to recreations of historical events, and so on. Salutary effects, however, occur only when caregivers monitor what is being watched, when and for how long.

Mixed Messages. Today's children are pulled in a variety of directions. They are commanded to be high achieving students, while given latitude to make a variety of decisions that may create the opposite result. Their television watching is unlimited and unmonitored. Society is alarmed by the extent of sexual activity and number of adolescent pregnancies, yet advertisements in the media for jeans, sneakers, cosmetics and even cereals hype sexuality and the fast life. At the same time, childhood and adolescence have been so prolonged that children remain economically and sometimes emotionally dependent on their parents until late teens and early twenties.

HISTORY OF CHILDREN'S SERVICES

Since they were first introduced into American libraries, children's departments have had to deal with the youngest victims of societal malfunctioning. Health considerations have always been present, though they were more likely to manifest themselves as tuberculosis and malnutrition than as AIDS, or drug dependence. Newly arrived Americans, in particular, have been a presence since the early days of children's libraries when fears of the immigrant invasion resulted in an educational and moral crusade to socialize and "Americanize" the newcomers. The reform movement of which the library was a part, concentrated its efforts on children.

It should be no surprise that children's libraries were slower in making an appearance than were those for adults. For centuries, children in western society were considered as possessions whose value rested in their contribution to family labor. From the time they left childhood, often as early as age seven when speech developed, they worked full time, usually as apprentices. Portraits of eighteenth and nineteenth century children pictured them as small adults.

Puritan theology held that children came into the world as sinful creatures and in need of salvation. There was no indulgence, no sparing the rod and no differentiation was made between parent and child. Both were subjected to the same sermons regarding Hell, Satan, eternal damnation and everlasting torment.[10]

Ironically, though children entered the work force at an early age, they were not considered sufficiently mature to choose the books they read, or to utilize their own moral standards. Adults, primarily parents, maintained hegemony over the non-work lives of children and adolescents. They set firm boundaries of behavior and children were expected to adhere to them.

A group of social developments, as well as the realization, in the 19th century, that children have special needs began to alter treatment and attitudes toward children. Among the societal forces were child welfare laws; shorter work days and weeks for parents; growing expectation of high school and even college levels of education; changing structure of family and home; and, wide availability of contraception resulting in reduced family size.

In the late 19th century, John Dewey, sometimes called the father of progressive education, began to stress the importance of educating the *whole* child. Child development researchers and theorists helped to further understanding of the stages of mental and psychological growth through which children pass.

Against this background, librarians attention began turning toward children. It is difficult to pinpoint the first children's department in a library. Perhaps it was West Cambridge, or Brookline, Mass., or, alternately, Minneapolis. By 1896, over a dozen libraries had children's rooms. What seems to have pressured libraries to segregate and relegate children to their own department was the presence of so many young people. In 1906, one library reported that "its reading room tables were occupied with one man, one woman and 51 children."[11]

At the turn of the century public library service to school-aged children had become fairly well established. Story hours were introduced in Pratt Institute as early as 1896 and by 1900 Carnegie Library in Pittsburgh had begun a weekly story hour based on 16 stories from the *Iliad* and *Odyssey*.

Service to preschoolers is a relatively recent development in public libraries, coming substantially later than library service for older children. In 1928, Wanda Ga'g wrote and illustrated *Millions of Cats*, and by the mid 1930s there was a sizable selection of good picture books for children available. Just as the presence of so many school-aged children in the library had guaranteed that attention be paid to them, so too, the sheer numbers of preschoolers assured that they would receive service. Librarians complained that "preschoolers were ruining our school-age story hours by their continual presence."[12]

A series of position papers issued in the 1970s and early 1980s proposed that school libraries be given complete responsibility for satisfying all or most of the library needs of elementary school children. A New York State Report by the Commission of Education's Committee on Library Development in 1970 suggested that the elementary school media center should have the responsibility and capacity to meet *all* library needs of children pre-school through grade six. This, the report asserted, would be economically more efficient, would avoid duplication of funds and give the public library more latitude to improve services to Young Adults and adults.

NCLIS (The National Commission on Library and Information Services) issued a report in 1975 agreeing with the earlier findings, but acknowledging severe deficiencies in school libraries, most of which were (and continue to operate) at levels below ALA/AASL[13] standards with inadequate staffing, space, and book and AV collections too small to support curriculum needs. In 1981, Lowell

Martin, in his study of the Philadelphia Free Library, also concluded that the schools should be the sole source for study materials, but reaffirmed the public library's role in promoting reading enjoyment and the habit of leisure reading. Despite great strides in the condition of school libraries, they are scarcely nearer to reaching a goal of providing for the information needs of all their students than they were when these statements were promulgated. The public library remains an equal or greater partner in the process, and its preeminence in the field of pre-school materials and services is firmly established.

COLLECTION DEVELOPMENT

Children need materials that will stimulate their physical and emotional growth. Children's books today are the fastest growing segment of publishing. Over 70% of all new children's and young adult titles sold each year go to schools and public libraries. Profits are booming, a somewhat ironic development when many librarians fear that the ability to read is a fast-disappearing skill.

In addition, children's rooms now collect great varieties of non-print materials -- recordings, toys, games, videotapes and computer software. Indeed, library pages who once spent their time reading shelves and mending books are now responsible for assuring that puzzle pieces are accounted for, that records and cassettes are free from damage, and that computer diskettes are in their proper sleeves.

Books

Print remains the mainstay of children's library collections. In most public libraries, the children's department is allocated between 20 and 30% of the materials budget. The figure will vary by how much of the total population and circulation is accounted for by juveniles. Not unexpectedly, picture books are most heavily used, and most often in need of replacement, explaining their relatively large allocation.

The following allocation of funds among juvenile categories has been suggested:

Books	80-90%
Picture	30-40%
Fiction	20-25%
Non-Fiction	35-40%
Nonprint	10-20%[14]

The quality/demand argument is less salient in selecting children's materials than it is for adult books. Children are not likely to demand the latest title and more willing to read anything that looks interesting. On the other hand, materials of more questionable quality may have a place in the collection as well. In the years when women were relegated to subordinate professions (nurses, not doctors; secretaries, not lawyers), the one independent heroine who inspired generations of young women, Nancy Drew, was barred from the library on the grounds that the books about her were poorly written.

Children's librarians most often learn about recent books from *Horn Book, Booklist, Journal of Youth Services* (formerly *Top of the News), School Library Media Quarterly, School Library Journal, Wilson Library Bulletin, Kirkus Reviews,* and *Bulletin of the Center for Children's Books.* Each year ALA issues *Notable Children's Books.* Libraries routinely purchase Newbery and Caldecott medal books as well as many other award winners. One interesting source of information is *Children's Choices,* a reviewing publication that reflects the votes of children about their best-liked books.

While most children do not ask for help, they may be needier than adults in making selections for themselves. Children's librarians, therefore, are fortunate in having a remarkable opportunity to influence and guide the reading of their users.

Intellectual Freedom

Children's books, like magnets, attract censorship, both from librarians and from the external community. Librarians, in the guise of "literary censors" have fallen back on such phrases as "objective judgments, discriminating taste and sensitivity" when they choose not to include certain materials in their collections.[15] Self-appointed individual and group censors are most likely to criticize materials in four categories. Those dealing with family values and sexual behavior, political views, religious beliefs and minority rights. Books about witchcraft, Satanism and the occult often are considered questionable; those which do not portray minority groups in a particular light may also be protested. But other materials, too, have been the objects of scrutiny. Non-fiction books, including encyclopedias, which depict in detail human anatomy routinely attract complaint. Animal rights activists are becoming more vocal in their disagreements about the way in which their concerns are addressed in children's literature. As with adult books, the best defense against the censorship is a well-prepared collection development policy, and an established policy for dealing with complaints. (See appendix.) Jane Connor admonishes librarians

> to avoid precensorship...Parents have full rights to control their children's reading, listening and viewing, but the library cannot allow a few parents to decide what is or is not appropriate for all children in the community.[16]

Non-Print Materials

Unfortunately, there is a tendency to view non-print materials as peripheral or adjunct to the total children's collection, rather than as an integral part. Children's librarians have been among the most vociferous critics of the mindless passivity of television and the harmful effects of its content, perhaps accounting for the antagonism a number of children's librarians have voiced toward non-print material in general. Considered shortsighted by most librarians, this approach ignores the latest research on learning styles. Approximately 10% of the population has been labelled "learning disabled," and 25-30% are classed as auditory learners. Helping a child enter the magic world of fairy tales and literature through a listening experience is certainly preferable to barring him or her entirely from that world.

In libraries that have decided not to separate out videos from the rest of their collections, the children's department is responsible for the selection and dissemination of children's videos. Libraries are shortchanged when the librarian refuses outright to purchase them, or alternately neglects or ignores them. A far better course is to accept the reality that videos are now part of the American culture and that the choice is not between whether or not to collect them, but whether to build a collection that furthers the aims and goals of the library or one that panders to unselective taste. How children's access to R and X rated videos is handled represents a new test of minor's rights to library materials. In this case, an outside group, the Motion Picture Industry, has labelled materials and set standards.

Computers are another of the non-print materials the library can offer to its public, particularly to children and their families who have no access to them at home. Rollock cautions that "unless all children are taught to use this new technology, we are in danger of creating a whole new disadvantaged class of people."[17]

Libraries that have chosen to collect toys offer a number of justifications for their decision. Good toys, they argue, are expensive for individual families to purchase. By sharing them among a community's children, everyone can have access to the best educational toys. In addition, borrowing and returning toys helps to establish the library habit in the very youngest children.

REFERENCE SERVICES

It has been estimated that 90% of a children's librarian's public service time is spent in reference.[18] Empirically, we know little about the information needs and information-seeking behavior of children and young adults. Some children ask questions, others never do. We do know that parents and other adults concerned with children require information on child development, educational theory and practice, nutrition and health. In other words, about the environmental, social, intellectual, cultural and medical needs of children.

Questions elementary school children most frequently ask are school-related. They also request information about pop-culture -- TV, movies, sports, space, media stars. Societal concerns are reflected in queries about drugs, violence and family situations. Information sought by the gifted, by physically or developmentally disabled children, by those with special difficulties, by ethnic minorities and non-English speakers is often unique and difficult to locate.

Rosemarie Reichel deplores the current state of reference service to children and young adults, attributing its poor quality to the nature of assistance offered, staffing shortages, attitudes toward children, deficiencies in professional training, inadequate collection development, fees for online searching and lack of access to resources housed elsewhere. In short, she says "...the state of library service to children and young adults does not seem to have moved significant or fast enough toward information ages requirements." Children will simply not have the skills they need for the new century.[19]

Among the issues facing those who provide reference services to young people is the degree to which librarians are responsible for providing information in contrast with teaching the skills to gain access for themselves. "The liberal view," says Gertrude Herman,

is that the professional response to any user's request for information is to provide the information. The conservative reprise may be as dogmatic as "look it up in the card catalogue" or as supportive as "I'll show you how to look it up."...The need to instruct the young seems to run strong in adults' blood, so that the library skills lesson often takes precedence over giving the child what he came to the library for.[20]

The best library service is both or all of the above. Children should never leave the library without the information they have come to obtain, but no reference question should be answered without, at least, some informal instruction in how to search for information and some attention to showing children how to analyze the value of the information. Carole Marie Hastings remarks, facetiously, that if children are taught to find all their own sources, librarians would miss questions like "If we want to have twins, do we have to do it twice?"[21] The heavy emphasis placed on instruction leads some librarians to deny telephone reference service to students, demanding instead that they come to the library in person if they wish assistance. They assume that all school assignments are designed to teach library research. But this ignores other motives which may have precipitated the assignment, as well as the inability of some children to get to the library.

Correlated to questions about the extent to which bibliographic instruction should be practiced in the public library is the far more difficult matter of the degree to which children who, theoretically, have been taught are successful in their quest for material. The results of studies of how children use online catalogs for materials have been chilling.[22] The hit rate is almost negligible. Catalogs are not as user-friendly as people have been led to believe; children cannot alphabetize beyond the third letter, and cognitive skills are less sophisticated than previously thought. Alternate screens for elementary age children which present catalogue information at simpler levels, for instance KIDSCREEN (INLEX) have been developed, but they are controversial and some librarians find their uniformity and utility questionable.

A final, and perhaps most crucial question, is the degree to which children are granted access to online information sources and to interlibrary loan. While the profession continually affirms the rights of children to access, libraries routinely discriminate against them when they refuse to borrow material from another library, to do a database search or to answer a telephone reference question from a young person.

Both online searchers and interlibrary loan networks assume

a hierarchy of legitimacy to help them determine whether or not to do a search or request ILL material. A number of years ago, a librarian reported serious troubles with adult newspaper microfilm machine readers who complained bitterly that children were reading their own birth announcements in newspapers while they were waiting to read about those of their ancestors. A case could be made that the children were learning an important history lesson while the genealogists were merely filling in blanks on a form. No such argument is advanced here. The only point is that children's needs are no less than those of adults, and are sometimes even greater. The most legitimate reason for denying an ILL to a young person is that the material will not be available in time for use with a particular paper or project, which is the reason why most children request special loans.

Charging fees for online searching, another practice which discriminates against children, once again penalizes those least able to afford the service. Offspring of relatively wealthy and well-educated parents who can afford to improve their children's competitive edge will have access to sources through their home computers. Those who are educated in well-funded districts will have electronic data available at school. Children who are disadvantaged by lack of access to information expand the gap between society's haves and have-nots.

Too often, online database searching, interlibrary loan and access to special collections are available only during daytime when most children are in school. This represents yet another way in which they are effectively denied use of information and services.

PROGRAMMING

The purpose of library programming is to communicate to children the joys of reading. Unfortunately, the practice of traditional programming has diminished during the last decade. Libraries consider that expending funds for that purpose to be less cost-effective in the face of staff shortages and financial limitations.

Pre-school Story Hours

Some libraries still program heavily, with their primary audience largely pre-schoolers, followed closely by whole families. Head-Start classes are perhaps the first target since children who attend them have already been identified as being "at risk." Next, attention is turned toward children in day care. A third target is the family unit. Finally, some children's librarians privately admit, are those in nursery school who seem to be recipients of many privileges and are therefore least needy.

Story hours are not frills, not merely ways to occupy the attention of children. They are a

> mind and imagination stretcher, a beginning of relating, thinking, listening and absorbing an idea -- skills to be greatly needed in later life. The habit of inquiry feeds on itself: the more one knows, the more one needs to know; the more one reads, the more one needs to read. This pattern forms the basis in later life for leadership, creativity and competence on which our kind of society depends.[23]

The most common story hours are for children ages three to five. They are usually composed of storytelling, puppetry and creative drama. One and two year old story hours target early language, movements and easy books. Once jeopardized by budget cuts, they are reemerging as an important activity, particularly in light of the large group of teenagers who are becoming mothers and electing to keep their children. The number of grants awarded for early intervention programs give testimony to the importance presently placed on reaching at risk parents.

Parents need to be shown that reading is important for both themselves and their children. Among the reasons for sharing books with preschoolers is the widely held belief that reading and writing behaviors and attitudes are established long before children start elementary school. Termed "emergent literacy," the concept is based on the premise that children learn written language by interacting with parents and other adults in reading and writing situations, and by exploring print on their own and by watching how the adults around them read and write. While reading readiness assumed that neural ripening or environmental experiences led to reading, emergent literacy holds that "any child who comes to school at five without certain kinds of literary experiences is a deprived child in whose growth there are deficiencies already too difficult to make good."[24]

Ann Carlson presents the following rationale for sharing books with preschoolers:

> Preschoolers who have experienced books have acquired not only a taste for them but also a knowledge of basic conventions about books such as beginning and end, front to back, left to right and top to bottom. They understand that print needs to make sense; that there is a relationship between print and speech; and that book language differs from conversational language. They learn something about a story, that it has a plot, dialogue and sequences. In addition, book experiences create "habits of mind," they bring order to thinking. They may help meet the needs of preschoolers for secure loving relationships, for adequate achievement, to belong to a group, to be free from fear, anxiety or guilt, and the need for a variety of experiences in one's world.[25]

Older Children

Older children also enjoy being read to, even those who read well for themselves. Booktalking gives librarians a chance to share their enthusiasm for a particular work and perhaps to pass it on to a curious listener. Incentive programs such as summer reading are widely offered, but not universally admired. Those who oppose their use contend that competitiveness is encouraged and primacy given to quantity of material read rather than to the quality. In addition, they maintain that it discourages slow or poor readers and perhaps communicates the message that reading is not "fun" but rather something one is paid to do. Defenders of incentive programs assert they can attract children and parents to the library and provide an effective, albeit admittedly external, incentive to reading beyond required books.[26]

Mounting programs for older readers can be stressful, and some librarians, finding them burdensome, burn out quickly. Volunteers can be a wonderful programming resource, one which helps dilute demands on the paid staff. Seeking out and discovering expertise within a community not only enhances the library's program, but helps to solidify the library's relationships with the community.

OUTREACH, COOPERATION AND NETWORKING

Schools

Typically, children's librarians have sought to strengthen ties with school librarians and teachers. They do it as part of their outreach and for their own protection as well. One of the nagging annoyances children's librarians face is having to satisfy the large numbers of students seeking the same information for school assignments. Collections of materials become rapidly depleted and students and parents often assume that public library resources are inadequate.

Most public libraries have developed a parent/teacher notification form that states the reasons why they were unable to fulfill a student's request for information. This can help, though students are still left frustrated, dissatisfied and anxious. Eminently preferable is for the school, teacher or school librarian to notify the library of a forthcoming assignment to enable the staff to, if necessary, ration materials or hold them on reserve.

A more positive homework-related form of cooperation has been the establishment in some libraries of a "Homework Hotline" which enables elementary school students to call someone at the library for assistance. In the first two months after Brooklyn Public Library established its service, 3,800 calls were received, primarily from fourth to sixth graders, over 50% of whom requested assistance in mathematics.

The principle goal of cooperation and networking between schools and public libraries is to provide access to information for youth during and after school. Neither school nor public library can hope to satisfy completely the reading and research demands of its clientele. Staff and financial shortages as well as recent technological advances have given new impetus and urgency to these joint efforts. Cooperative ventures have experimented with formal, complex and structured multitype library arrangements using shared catalogs, shared databases, document delivery systems, cooperative collection development policies and other electronic inter-connections. There are barriers, however, to easy cooperation. One is the difficulty in surmounting differing institutional missions and mandates. Another is the complexity of political and fiscal arrangements. Finally, and the one which seems to loom largest of all, is the negative attitude of some participants.

Class visits from the school to the public library should be encouraged. Conversely, public librarians may visit schools, although such trips tend to be less successful because identification with the building itself is weaker.

Other Agencies

The traditional ambivalence toward children's outreach however defined remains. According to Margaret Mary Kimmel and Jill Locke:

> There is a profound contradiction between a professed philosophy of service to all and the fears and attitudes that prevent them [children's librarians] from actively reaching out to all.[27]

Ervin Gaines, for instance, calls the social work role obsolete and suggests that libraries focus on books and information. He urges librarians to resist the romantics who see the library as savior of the illiterate and as a daycare center for the child of the working mother.[28] Others, however, feel that we have to go where the kids and/or their caregivers are.[29]

Service to schools, of course, is the most basic and most enthusiastically promoted outreach program. But as far back as 1901, the American Library Association was suggesting cooperation with playground departments, juvenile courts, detention homes and settlement houses. Today, this list would be expanded to jails, to homeless shelters, and centers of all kinds for pre-schoolers. Increasingly, librarians are joining with professionals in other non-school institutions to plan cooperative programs and expand children's horizons.

STAFFING

The vast majority of public libraries, some 80%, serve populations of 25,000 or less. Over half of American public libraries (58%) have no trained children's librarians. Branches of large libraries are often staffed by one professional who provides all services. Children's librarians are even less frequent in urban libraries than they once were. Enoch Pratt in Baltimore, for instance, now has no more than four or five trained children's librarians for the entire system and Chicago has about 40 children's librarians for its 85 branches.[30] There has been a steady erosion over the past 20 years in the ability of libraries to provide service to children.

A number of factors have been blamed for the dearth of children's librarians. Accurately affixing the reasons seems almost impossible, so intimately are they bound with each other. Financial conditions, the high cost of children's programs, shortcomings of children's librarians, dead-end career paths, low pay, and the failure of library schools to attract and train people into the children's library field all bear part of the responsibility.

Early on, the tasks of children's librarianship were relatively less complex, although by no means easier. Book selection and knowledge of literature were the two most important components of the job. Heavy emphasis on "the book" and its quality led to the perception that some children's librarians were inclined to be "precious" elitists, more interested in their own reaction to books than in those of the children for whom the books were intended.[31]

With the new attention to pre- and after-school programming, children's librarians were seen as cutters and pasters, not "serious" librarians. In a devastating and oft-quoted description, Regina Minudri outlines the negative images of youth services librarians. They

1. are childlike, overly identified with their client group.
2. are incapable of seeing "the big picture."
3. don't see beyond their services.
4. are emotional.
5. live in an ivory tower.
6. are inflexible.
7. fluster easily.
8. don't understand budgets.
9. don't know how to justify requests.
10. can't estimate or forecast.
11. won't set priorities because *everything* is important.[32]

Children's librarians were called petty, trifling, compliant, inept managers who refused to justify their services. They were advised to abandon their nurturing roles, to dispense ideas instead of goodness.

Not surprisingly, after a barrage of this intensity, many children's librarians internalized the criticism and the field, always low-paying, and of low status, began to attract fewer and fewer recruits. Those who wanted to work with children, became school librarians -- the pay was better as were the hours and working conditions.   Those who sought higher status followed the automated information handling route that led to private sector jobs at far higher salaries and rank.

One response to the shortage of children's librarians and to decreasing budgets was to eliminate, as did Charles Robinson at Baltimore County Public Library, age-level specialists and create a pool of generalists -- a group of librarians able to handle a full range of services. Robinson justified this approach by assuming that any librarian given some in-service training can work with children. Robinson admits that he is not convinced that *better* service is offered with generalism, but insists it is the way in which the best service can be offered given the present budgetary circumstances. Many, probably most, librarians view Robinson's experimental approach as short-sighted and ill-advised. Without excellent, well-trained staff, they maintain, children's services would probably remain ineffective, an outcome we can ill afford.

A major casualty of the funding crunch were Children's Coordinators or Consultants, those charged with coordinating children's services within larger libraries and in systems. Among the work they performed was writing grant requests, responding to legislative initiatives and lobbying, representing children's services to schools and other community groups and for staff training. A move toward decentralization in the 1970s based on the premise that the needs of a particular community could be best understood locally gave branches more authority to make decisions about their collections and programs, further deteriorating the coordinator role and function.

Straws in the wind seem to point toward a rejuvenation of children's librarianship. Despite budget cuts, children's circulation is on the increase. A sample of 53 public libraries revealed a rise of 20% compared with a rise of 9% in adult circulation. Some library systems have made conscious efforts, not only to recruit excellent children's librarians, but to insure their career path. At Columbus (Ohio) Metropolitan Library, for instance, Assistant Branch heads are almost always children's librarians, a classification from which they have the same access to management positions as do any other public service librarians.

Children's librarians today enter the field as full-fledged professionals in the information age. They have been trained in the new technology as well as in management; are equipped to set goals, to make plans and to evaluate; are adept at training staff, implementing programs and selecting and evaluating materials; and have been schooled in child development and learning theories.

ORGANIZATION AND ADMINISTRATION

It is not unusual for children's departments in public libraries to exist in isolation from the rest of the library. Traditionally, they had been separated -- placed upstairs or downstairs -- thereby creating both a psychological and physical barrier. The new imperative for children's librarians to justify their services, as well as the recent systems approach based on the interdependence of all library departments, has forced an integration heretofore unpracticed. In many small libraries, nonfiction adult and children's materials have been interfiled. Proponents claim that users can more readily find the material they require at a level that best suits their needs. It is a way to mainstream learning disabled and newly literate persons. And, finally, it avoids needless duplication. Opponents argue that the practice may be insulting to adults and young adults and confusing for children; that children's librarians may be drawn away from their clientele by having to use the integrated collection; that certain non-fiction designed to be read rather than consulted will be overlooked -- fairy and folk tales, for instance, and biographies. Studies of this approach have thus far produced ambiguous results.

Among the administrative tasks that must be accomplished in order for the Children's Department to run smoothly is a certain amount of rule-setting. When, for instance, are children eligible for a library card? When they can sign their names? Report their address and telephone number? Enter school? Are the fines for overdue children's materials the same as those for adult's, or should they be non-existent, as some suggest? What is the borrowing period? Are there limits to the numbers of items that can be checked out at one time? How are lost library cards handled?

Discipline

Will Manley reminds us that children "are not the cute, kind, innocent and naturally loving creatures portrayed on television.

They are loud, uncompromising, cantankerous, obstreperous, selfish and very difficult to communicate with."³³

Consequently, it is imperative that behavioral guidelines be set for the children's room. Children's librarians report new types of discipline problems requiring different responses. Growing numbers of children, though accompanied by adults, are ineffectively supervised. Preschoolers are routinely deposited in the children's room while their caregivers go to the adult department or out of the library for a brief period of time.

On occasion, every librarian -- children's or adult -- has to eject an older, disruptive child from the library. More rarely, a child may have to be barred for a period of time. These actions, however, should be utilized only sparingly. First, they send the wrong message. Public libraries want to encourage, not discourage, use. Second, sometimes children who are ejected or barred are "latchkeyers" who have been told to remain in the library until their parents call for them and who have no place to go.

Serious delinquency may require calling the police. The use or distribution of drugs, for instance, should precipitate this response, as should questionable behavior on the part of adults with young children. Pedophiles and exhibitionists are often attracted to children's rooms.

The best way to minimize behavioral problems is to maximize security. Staff should be able to observe bookshelves and seating areas. Some librarians have chosen to keep restrooms in children's areas locked, to give keys to individuals on request and to limit use to one person at a time.

Publicity

It is easier to garner publicity for children's services than for virtually any other department of the library. The media love to carry stories -- and pictures -- of children. Book lists and book marks are very popular and useful. Placing them strategically throughout the community expands the audience for children's services. Highlighting children's books through newspaper, radio and television reviews and notices also produces salutary results.

The attractiveness of children's programs makes fund raising from private sources relatively simple. The dangers, however, are equally great. Children's services are an important part of a library's program and should be publicly supported. Private funds are only appropriate for special, non-routine programs, not for operating expenses or staff.

The Children's Room

The size and composition of the children's room depends on the community it serves. The atmosphere and furnishings must be appropriate to children whether the department is an entire floor, a separate room or a section. There has been a tendency to, like 19th century paintings of children, create children's rooms that are miniature adult ones. Colors suitable for adults, are not those that children find attractive and exciting. Tasteful signs that discreetly direct adults are useless for children who need oversized and eye-catching ones.

Patterns of children's activity within a room help to predict its space and furniture needs. Certainly there must be various size seating and programming spaces for differing age-level audiences. Heavy use by adults may suggest the need for adult-sized furniture. Study tables, carrels, hangers for outerwear, different height and size shelving, display and exhibit areas and terminals must all be provided. Story areas -- steps, pits, separate rooms -- are also necessary.

YOUNG ADULTS

Much of what appears earlier in this chapter applies equally to children and young adults. There are, however, special considerations about adolescence that merit attention. The mercurial nature of young adults is captured in the following passage:

Adolescence is an ill-defined developmental period. Teenagers, like quicksilver, shift back and forth between adulthood and childhood with...sometimes charming vigor; and the age group as a whole, with its changing fads, language and concerns, seems almost to reinvent itself every few years.[34]

Coupled with the unpredictability of youth are the relatively new societal pressures that greet them at almost every street corner and perhaps in every darkened room.

As a group, young adults are the most ill-served of all library constituencies. In part, this stems from economic considerations. But perhaps even more from what Eva Martin terms frustration, confusion, fear and indifference on the part of public libraries over services for young adults.[35] Certainly they are harder to reach and to satisfy than, say, senior citizens or preschoolers. But this does not justify the fact that only slightly more than ten percent of public libraries have trained YA librarians. Most young people are served either by generalists, adult services librarians or, at times, children's librarians.

Young adult public library services were designed, initially, to provide a non-school-related option in the lives of adolescents. Unfortunately, much of the information-seeking that brings young adults into the public library today is in conjunction with schoolwork. Reference rooms are brimming over with students completing literary criticism and science assignments.

Physical Space for Young Adults

As early as 1948, the American Library Association proclaimed the importance of giving young people, if not a room, at least a place of their own in the public library. While some might disagree with this age segregation, the balance of opinion seems currently to favor separate though contiguous quarters where teens will feel more comfortable and welcome. The designation of a special space may help to ensure continuity in service through the vicissitudes of budget ups and downs. A YA area should be in near the adult collection and a staffed reference desk. It is suggested that for a YA population of 2,000 or more, there be a minimum of thirteen sections of shelving (150 books per section) and at least three tables with 15 to 20 chairs.[36] As with the children's room, color, furniture and signage should be age appropriate. A significant amount of space for display is vital.

Collection Development for Young Adults

Little Women published in 1868 may be the first young adult novel. But it was not until the 1960s that the kind of "problem novels" that characterize so much of modern young adult literature came into existence. The new realism probably dates to 1967 with the publication of S.E. Hinton's *The Outsiders*, Ann Head's *Mr. and Mrs. BoJo Jones*, and Jean Thompson's *House of Tomorrow*. In 1968 came Paul Zindel's *The Pigman*, and in the following year Vera and Bill Cleaver's *Where the Lilies Bloom* and John Donovan's *I'll Get There, It Better Be Worth the Trip*.

Today's young adult collections are composed primarily of fiction. A great many YA heavy readers are drawn to science fiction and fantasy, and the collection should include a generous offering of this genre. Romance, too, holds an important place in the hearts of many teens and their needs must also be met. Among the other categories of importance to young adults are biography, personal development, vocational and career information, collecting, sports, as well as information on sex and sexuality (contraceptives, venereal disease, pregnancy, abortion, homosexuality); about drugs and alcohol; and on family problems including child abuse and runaways. Many of the topics listed are controversial. As Marion Paper reflects, however

> Instead of cowering in our corner hoping the censor won't notice us, why not take the stand that an inoffensive library collection is a waste of money, that libraries exist to provide the materials that will allow the people who want to grow to do so.[37]

Among the decisions which must be made about what will constitute the YA collection are whether to include only paperbacks or a mix of hardback and paperback; there should be a separate record and cassette collection (this will depend to a great extent on whether the parent institution has chosen to separate media or to integrate it into the collection); to provide a separate YA vertical file; the extent to which there should be magazines and reference material; and, finally, how much to duplicate resources available elsewhere in the library.

Young adult librarians sometimes distinguish between information and enrichment, holding the latter to be their province. The distinction, says Mary K. Chelton, is an invidious one. Typically, a student might be assigned to read a story set in the United States from 1860 to 1900. The librarian must find material which meets the needs of the assignment, as well as the needs of the student requesting the information, that is, the proper level of reading difficulty, the degree of reading interest and so on.[38]

Programming for Young Adults

The few libraries with sufficient staff to work with Young Adults may find programming for and with them simultaneously rewarding and frustrating. It is not unusual for adolescents to show enormous enthusiasm about a topic for two days running and to completely lose interest on the third.

On the other hand programs can be an effective deterrent to the self-absorption caused by television, video recorders and stereo equipment. Those programs that stimulate discussion can bring teens from different areas together and provide them with alternatives. Baseball cards, comic books, information on car engines and bike repair, hair styling, film showings, are all grist for the YA programming mill. The one important fact to bear in mind is that the success of most programs is unpredictable and that failure to attract a large audience is not shameful.

A young adult advisory board has proven successful in many libraries, particularly if a broad net is cast in recruiting to fill slots on the board. There are myriad uses of such a group. They can facilitate young adults helping other young adults as tutors; can arrange for teens to assist older or handicapped people. They can function as a resource when planning programs or as an aid to collection development. And, of course, these same children grow up, put away their childish toys, become taxpayers and concerned citizens and, sometimes if the job has been done well, Friends of the Library.

SUMMARY

The recent checkered career of children's services in public libraries tends to obscure the challenging, crucial, exhilerating and satisfying nature of the work. Introducing children to the joys of literature, intervening with an "at-risk" population, facilitating the adjustment of young immigrants to a new society are all fulfilling undertakings.

While the library community and the public sector loudly proclaim the importance of children's services, financial support does not seem to verify their sentiments. Library efforts to economize have disadvantaged children's librarians and programs and are partially responsible for the present dearth of professionals trained to carry on children's work. Current shortages of children's librarians have led some libraries to adopt controversial generalist or non-age-specific models of staffing. Such an approach shortchanges not only children but the society as well. Will Manley heralds the child as our future:

> the perception of society's goals, objective and ideals is dependent upon their transference to children. We may not realize it, but our futures are in the hands of our children's librarians.[39]

Or as the Nobelist Bernard Lown reminds us, "The world was not left to us by our parents, but lent to us by our children."

NOTES AND SUGGESTED READINGS

Notes

1. "Robert Cormier's 1991 Edwards Award Acceptance Speech," rep. in *Joys: Journal of Youth Services in Libraries* 5 (Fall, 1991): 49.

2. Robert Leigh, *The Public Library in the United States* (New York: Columbia University Press, 1950), 99-100.

3. Lowell Martin, *Baltimore Reaches Out: Library Service to the Disadvantaged* (Baltimore: Enoch Pratt Free Library, 1967).

4. Dorothy Anderson, "From Idealism to Realism: Library Directors and Children's Services," *Library Trends* 35 (Winter 1987): 393.

5. Barbara Rollock, *Public Library Services for Children* (Hamden, CT: Library Professional Publications, 1988), 4.

6. Mary K. Chelton, "Young Adult Reference Services in the Public Library," in Bill Katz and Ruth Fraley, *Reference Service for Children and Young Adults* (New York: Haworth, 1983), 36.

7. *American Libraries* 12 (September 1981): 493.

8. *Libraries Serving Youth: Directions for Service in the 1990s.* Proceedings of a NY State Conference, April 16-18, 1986 (New York:Youth Services Section, New York Library Association, 1987), 9-10.

9. Adele Fasick, "Carrying on the Tradition: Training Librarians for Children's Services," in Adele Fasick et al. *Lands of Pleasure: Essays on Lillian H. Smith and the Development of Children's Libraries* (Metuchen, NJ: Scarecrow Press, 1990), 21.

10. Harriet Long, *Public Library Service to Children: Foundation and Development* (Metuchen, NJ: Scarecrow Press, 1969), 9.

11. Rollock, 5.

12. Ann Carlson, *The Preschooler and the Library* (Metuchen, NJ: Scarecrow Press, 1991), 17.

13. See *Information Power: Guidelines for School Library Media Programs* (Chicago: American Library Association, 1988).

14. Jane Gardner Connor, *Children's Library Services Handbook* (Phoenix, AZ: Oryx Press, 1990), 18.

15. Kenneth Donelson, "Literacy and Moral Censorship" in Zena Sutherland, ed. *Children in Libraries: Patterns of Access to Materials and Services in School and Public Libraries* (Chicago: University of Chicago, 1981), 4.

16. Connor, 17.

17. Rollock, 96.

18. Ruth Gordon, "On Children's Librarians: Some Observations and a Wish List," in Katz and Fraley, 94.

19. Rosemarie Reichel, *Reference Services for Children and Young Adults* (Hamden, CT: Shoe String Press, 1991), xiii.

20. Gertrude Herman,"What Time Is It in Antarctica? Meeting the Information Needs of Children," in Katz and Fraley, 81.

21. Carol Marie Hastings, "Doin' Da Missin' Books Boogie: Thoughts on Axioms, Flexibility and Attila the Hun," in Katz and Fraley, 94.

22. Leslie Edmonds, *School Library Journal* 36 (October 1990): 28-32.

23. Rollock, 63.

24. Carlson, 65.

25. Ibid., 66-70.

26. Connor, 83-4.

27. Jill Locke and Margaret Mary Kimmel, "Children of the Information Age: Changes and Challenges," *Library Trends* (Winter, 1987): 408.

28. quoted in Anderson, 396.

29. Patrick O'Brien, quoted in Anderson, 395.

30. Connor, preface.

31. Rollock, 8.

32. Regina Minudri, "The Management Perspective," in *Libraries Serving Youth* (New York: New York Library Association, 1987), 50-57.

33. Quoted in Anderson, 407.

34. Andre Gagnon and Ann Gagnon, *Meeting the Challenge: Library Service to Young Adults* (Ottawa, Ont: Canadian Library Association, 1985), 3.

35. Eva Martin, "Goals and Objectives for Services to Teens," in Gagnon, 17.

36. Kenneth Setterington, "The Physical Layout and Set-up of the YA Area," in Gagnon, 79.

37. Marion Paper, "Breaking Down the Barriers to Services for Young Adults in Public Libraries," in Gagnon, 23.

38. Chelton, in Katz and Fraley, 34

39. Quoted in Anderson, 395.

Suggested Readings

Amey, L.J. ed. *Combining Libraries: The Canadian and Australian Experience.* Metuchen, NJ: Scarecrow Press, 1989.

Anderson, Dorothy. "From Idealism to Realism: Library Directors and Children's Services," *Library Trends* 35 (Winter 1987): 393-412.

Benne, Mae. *Principles of Children's Services in Public Libraries.* Chicago: American Library Association, 1991.

Broderick, Dorothy. *An Introduction to Children's Work in Public Libraries.* New York: Wilson, 1965.

Broderick, Dorothy, ed. *The Voya Reader.* Metuchen, NJ: Scarecrow Press, 1990.

Carlson, Ann. *The Preschooler and the Library.* Metuchen, NJ: Scarecrow Press, 1991.

Competencies for Librarians Serving Children in Public Libraries. Chicago: Association for Library Service to Children, American Library Assocation, 1989.

Connor, Jane Gardner. *Children's Library Services Handbook.* Phoenix, AZ: Oryx Press, 1990.

Ellison, John and Patricia Ann Coty, eds. *Nonbook Media: Collection Management and User Services.* Chicago: American Library Association, 1987.

Fasick, Adele et al. *Lands of Pleasure: Essays on Lillian H. Smith and the Development of Children's Libraries.* Metuchen, NJ: Scarecrow Press, 1990.

Fasick, Adele. *Managing Children's Services in the Public Library.* Englewood CO: Libraries Unlimited, 1991.

Gagnon, Ann. *Guidelines for Children's Services.* Ottowa, Ontario:

Canadian Library Association, 1989.

Gagnon, Andre and Ann Gagnon. *Meeting the Challenge: Library Service to Young Adults.* Ottawa, Ontario: Canadian Library Association, 1985.

Katz, Bill and Ruth Fraley, eds. *Reference Service for Children.* New York: Haworth Press, 1983.

Libraries Serving Youth: Directions for Service in the 1990s. Proceedings of a NY State Conference, April 16-18, 1986. Youth Service Section, New York Library Association, 1987.

Rollock, Barbara T. *Public Library Services for Children.* Hamden, CT: Library Professional Publications, 1988.

Sutherland, Zena, ed. *Children in Libraries: Patterns of Access to Materials and Services in School and Public Libraries.* Chicago: University of Chicago, 1981.

Willett, Holly. "Current Issues in Public Library Service for Children." *Public Libraries* 24 (Winter 1985): 137-140.

CHAPTER 14

OUTREACH SERVICES

The face of America is changing rapidly. It is now multi-hued, multi-aged and multi-tongued. Streets made for walking are presently home to countless Americans of every generation and complexion. Burned out buildings, littered sidewalks, graffitied walls testify to the conditions of poverty that surround urban dwellers whose lives are played out against a background of drugs, gangs and violence. Many of the nation's residents are older, less empowered and poorer than ever before. Responding to the needs of these nontraditional clientele -- at risk populations -- may be the most compelling challenge facing the public library today.

Interest in providing social services has fallen victim to diminished funding, increased costs and a decade-long and growing disengagement from tax-supported agencies. Reclaiming for the public library the mantle of an institution that provides "service to all" from one whose current practice is more properly described as "service to a select few" is a daunting task. Yet the seminal question of who public libraries should serve and benefit is once again in contention. Is outreach, the term most often applied to activities involved in fostering library use by the disadvantaged, merely a vestige of the sixties that will disappear from disuse? Or will it find new definition in the countless mission statements and roles being generated in the nation's public libraries?

THE PROBLEMS

That some people -- middle-class, college educated, English-speaking, young -- benefit more than do others from public library services has been documented in study after study. Although library doors are rarely closed to individuals seeking entrance, certain sectors of the public may find the institution cold and less than welcoming to their needs. As Claire Lipsman comments:

> The disadvantaged do not use the library; the reasons why they do not use it include illiteracy, ignorance, apathy and hostility. To overcome these powerful obstacles, the library must actively, energetically and physically seek out and involve the groups they wish to reach. The responsibility of the library is extended from that of supplying information to that of actively seeking to modify individual behavior and attitudes.[1]

Services to non-traditional clienteles involve not only more staff, more per capita expenditure and more time, but also a commitment to change existing patterns of service. Recent studies have revealed that public libraries may, themselves, be part of the problem.

> They can be disorganized, overly bureaucratic, frequently humiliating in treatment of clientele, often unresponsive to more difficult needs and uninformed about the lifestyles of their users.[2]

Three avenues of library service compete when decisions about the nature and extent of service that should be provided for special clientele are made. Following the first implies that libraries should serve well their traditional patrons. Supporters of this path maintain that focusing attention on those whose needs are so much greater will invariably detract from the benefits currently enjoyed by those who now utilize the resources. They contend that people who know what they want, or who can quickly be shown where to find it, are the appropriate clientele for librarians who are merely custodians and dispensers of information, not social activists. Libraries already fulfill an important social role by providing information, something they know how to do. They are not "social work" agencies, but rather places for books and material. Dollar for dollar, providing service to the middle class family produces the best return on investment.[3]

The second road stresses principle, not expediency. Those holding this position argue that libraries as social institutions cannot in good faith turn their backs on social problems.

A moderate position favors uninterrupted service to the children, students and middle-class persons who make up the library's traditional clientele, in recognition of both their needs and the library's need for their continued support, while at the same time structuring special services for the dispossessed.[4]

Librarians who walk this route understand that special groups may have the most need and that their problems demand long-term intensive commitment and may, realistically, produce only marginal success. These librarians are willing to try to balance demands from traditional clientele against those from special groups. Some argue forcefully that

...where the public library service has been willing to make the necessary effort, local communities have responded with often embarrassing enthusiasm, be these communities of the unemployed, of deprived youth or of people resident in deprived neighborhoods.[5]

The final course, currently followed by very few, is one of advocacy, that is, of advancing the causes, interests and rights of people in need. The aim of advocates is enfranchisement -- social, political and economic -- of constituent groups who are alienated from the mainstream resources and services.

Community development-oriented librarians are aware that the disenfranchised must have reliable, current information if they are to effect the transfer of power that will improve their life chances.[6]

The most compelling argument for providing service to groups not generally associated with heavy library use is that they are, in reality, the emerging majority. America is greying at a rapid pace, becoming increasingly multicultural, more frequently institutionalizing its citizens, and raising a larger and larger underclass. That is why, in truth, there is no choice but to provide services and materials that meet the needs of these diverse constituencies.

Poverty is a factor associated with many of the special groups described in this chapter. It is related to sex, age, race, educational level and institutional condition. Those of Hispanic origin are three times as likely to be poor as are families headed by whites, and those headed by blacks are four times as likely. The incidence of poverty doubles for people over 65 years of age. Eight or fewer years of formal education increases the likelihood of poverty by six times over families headed by persons with one year of college.[7]

The poor have as little access to information as they do to the other advantages of the society. Moreover, they do not understand that lack of information about, say, adequate housing, education or income, is a barrier to their securing these benefits. In other words, they are unlikely to see information as an instrument of their salvation, rendering the task of providing service to them far more difficult.

In recent years, economic considerations have caused taxpayers to be reluctant to support public services that do not benefit the majority. In 1983, Nauratil found the priorities for outreach to be ordered in the following manner:

> 1) children's services; 2) regular school visits; 3) service for shut-ins; 4) service to the physically handicapped; 5) special services for racial minorities; 6) services to the aged; 7) literacy training; 8) services to institutionalized.[8]

THE AGING

Older adults are generally thought to be at least 65 years of age. This definition may have originated with the Social Security Act of 1935 which entitled people to claim retirement benefits at that age. Now, however, gerontologists categorize those 65 to 75 as "young-old," those over 75 as "old-old." Definitions of age are influenced by:

Sex. Women, though biologically aging more slowly than men, are often considered old much earlier; and

Social class. Professionals, for instance, generally continue their lifestyle well into their seventies.

There are currently more old people than ever before. A measure of the aging population can be seen in the numbers of today's retirees who are caring for their aged parents. The size of the aging population has been accounted for by high fertility rates in the late 19th and early 20th centuries; by the fact that immigrants in the early part of the century were young adults and children; and by the decline in mortality rates because of improved living standards and medical advances.[9]

The tendency to lump together the aging population, despite its significant diversity, may be misguided. Nonetheless, older people do share certain common experiences induced by changes in their financial, health and social status.

Students of social gerontology point to three theories of aging that influence how people treat older persons:

Disengagement theory. In this model, individuals gradually withdraw from society and society withdraws from the individual. Society, it is contended, must distance itself from individuals as they age, shifting them out of positions of authority, in order to insure that the holders of such key positions will be younger and thus less susceptible to illness and death. While older persons are sometimes relieved from shouldering the responsibilities they willingly assumed when younger, there is a great danger of their being isolated from the society, and that the society is unable or unwilling to intervene in their behalf.

Activity perspective. Activity is defined as any regular action or pursuit beyond those required for basic maintenance. Older people whose central roles have been lost are less likely to engage in activities and a loss of self-concept results. Compensatory activities must therefore be substituted.

Developmental approach. This theory holds that old age is not the end of life, but a normal phase of it, with its own challenges and opportunities for growth and satisfaction. Though many day-to-day considerations involve coping and compensation, there are nonetheless challenges and opportunities.[10]

The third approach to aging is particularly amenable to program planning in libraries. It avoids the indifference of the disengagement theory and the "keep them moving" attitude of the activity perspective. The profession has strongly advocated increased library interaction with older adults. The Reference and Adult Services (RASD) Division of ALA published in 1975 "Guidelines for Library Services to an Aging Population" and small numbers of exemplary programs have been instituted. Among these has been Brooklyn Public Library's Services to Aging Program (SAGE) which offers continuing education, an augmented reference service, a lecture series, films, discussions, musical performances, senior assistants program and includes activities such as reading and reminiscence therapy, as well as oral history. SAGE provides services in-house as well as maintaining large print deposits in key locations throughout Brooklyn and bringing programs into local hospitals, community senior citizen centers and nursing and residential homes.

Unfortunately, most public libraries have advanced little beyond the traditional service offered to most patrons. Typically, libraries stock large print books, deliver materials to institutions and housebound people, install deposit collections in nursing and senior citizen homes and supply talking books and reading aids. Little attention is given to developing lifelong learning activities or to establishing active Information and Referral (I & R) Centers.

Marcia Nauratil has outlined a ten-point approach by libraries to serving senior citizens in a way that widens their horizons, rather than merely permitting them to become disengaged or simply to keeping them busy. Libraries, she says, serve their communities by

1. Contributing to a positive attitude toward aging and the aged;
2. Providing information and education on aging and its problems for older adults as well as professionals and laypersons who work with this group;
3. Facilitating the use of libraries by aged through improved library design and access to transportation;
4. Providing library service appropriate to the special needs of all the aged, including the minority who may be homebound and institutionalized;
5. Utilizing the potential of older adults as liaisons to reach their peers and as a resource in intergenerational programming;
6. Employing older adults in the provision of library services;
7. Involving older adults in the planning process when designing services and programs for the entire community;
8. Developing working relationships with other agencies and groups concerned with these needs and problems;
9. Providing programs, services and information for those preparing for retirement;
10. Continually exploring ways to making these services more effective, aggressively seeking sources of funding and assigning a portion of the regular budget to meet the needs of older adults.[11]

Are the aging really in need of special services? Some contend that they are no different from any users, simply older. Indeed, senior citizens often complain that librarians tend to think that once a person has passed that 65 year old threshold, his or her brains turn to mush. If this were not the case, they ask, would large print collections not contain serious fiction and non-fiction rather than only inspirational materials, light romances and other books of lesser intellectual quality. Yet the information requirements of older people *are* more specialized. Changing health requirements, for instance, produce demands for materials dealing with fitness, exercise, diet, cooking, care and control of certain conditions,

medical information and   doctor credentials. To those who
maintain that serving older persons is the problem and province of
social workers, not librarians, the best response may be that the
majority of library programs for older adults are informational in
nature, certainly a library responsibility.

Librarians are often reluctant to program for older adults,
fearing that segregating them from the general adult population will
have deleterious effects. On the other hand, older adults have
discretionary time that can be utilized in library-related programs
and activities and they are often loathe, because of age-related
problems, to attend those offered, say, in the evening.

ILLITERACY

The measure of literacy/illiteracy is generally associated with
a grade level equivalency. Those deemed *illiterate* are unable to
read the easiest children's picture books, advertisements, signs,
menus or instructions.   Common words are sometimes
recognizable, but only as symbols. Competency here is placed
somewhere between 0 and 4.5 grade level. *Functional illiteracy*
refers to those able to read and write at a "primitive" level, to read
simple instructions, manuals, want ads and common signs. These
people normally read at a grade level of between 5 and 8.9.
Standards of literacy have changed over the years. Years ago, the
criterion for determining illiteracy was simply whether a person
had completed fewer than six years of school.

About 10% of the adult population never entered high school
and about half of that number have fewer than five years of formal
education. An additional 10% of the population cannot read or
write well enough to be considered functionally literate. The
illiteracy rate in the United States is put at somewhere between 15
and 20% of the population depending on how the problem is
measured. While substantially lower than the overall world literacy
rate of 28.6%, it is among the highest in the developed world and
only slightly better than Latin America where the rate is 20.2%.

Lack of other literacies also prevent adults from succeeding in contemporary society. Among them are:

cultural literacy -- knowledge of the history of civilization and of the great political, philosophical, religious and scientific trends that helped to shape our society;
mathematical literacy -- a certain level of competence in arithmetic and elementary algebra. People who lack this are called "innumerate."
computer literacy -- familiarity with processes and procedures associated with using new technology.
scientific literacy -- the ability to understand and put to use medical and other scientific developments and concepts.
information literacy -- the ability to recognize when information is needed and how to locate, evaluate and use it effectively once acquired.[12]

Illiteracy in all its forms is a severe and growing problem. It is particularly concentrated among the poor and minorities, and is exacerbated by immigrant populations who are considered functionally illiterate despite their abilities to read and write in languages other than English. The causes of illiteracy, other than those prompted by developmental problems, are relatively easy to pinpoint, but far more difficult to eradicate.

Television, in and of itself, is not associated with illiteracy even though the average pre-schooler spends 28 hours and 6 minutes weekly in front of it, and the average 6-11 year old watches it for 23 hours and 31 minutes each week, more time than in school, reading or pursuing athletic goals. Yet children who spend more time reading are less likely to be illiterate.

Poverty, like television, does not produce illiteracy, but the conditions of life are often so burdensome that little time is left to develop reading skills.

Parents as Models.

The role of parents as models may mediate between poverty as a causative factor and illiteracy as an outcome.

High illiteracy rates among poverty-stricken parents means their children miss the early stimulation toward good literacy which is provided by literate parents who read to their children and provide literacy role models by being regular readers.[13]

Education. While schools do not cause illiteracy, most people agree that they are not as effective as they should be and consider the dropout rate -- about 30% -- as indicative of the lack of quality.

Illiterate people have difficulty negotiating contemporary society. They are barred from full participation in the economic, political and social life of the community and are at great psychological risk. The dramatic effects of illiteracy on their lives is almost incalculable. Without reading skills, it is impossible to obtain a driver's license, to vote, to fill out an application, or send a letter.

Ironically, though librarians long espoused the benefits and joys of reading, they ignored the tens of thousands of children and adults who were not equipped to participate in, or reap the products of, this activity. The ability to read was taken for granted and services to all citizens actually meant services to those able to use to them, effectively overlooking those who were unable to read and write or who possessed limited English literacy skills.

In 1983, a report condemning our educational system, *A Nation at Risk*, was issued. The library community responded with *Alliance for Excellence* which summoned libraries to become dynamic partners in the "Learning Society." Many librarians perceived this as a call to begin to address the problems of literacy. But others argued with equal vigor against the notion of librarians *teaching* reading. That is not our business, they contended; nor is it our business to waste money on adult reading material that aims at the lowest common denominator. In addition, they continued, the reading public is the voting public. Diluting service to them jeopardizes future funding. And finally, they asserted, literacy is a societal responsibility, not a library one. Even those who see a role for librarians in literacy, fear their libraries cannot handle the task. There is too little time, staff are untrained and will do the job poorly; there is insufficient space available for students, reading tutors, or new collections; and funding to undertake a new program of major proportions is inadequate. Few library issues have stirred as much literature, emotion, controversy, and effort.

Libraries that have chosen to make literacy efforts do so on one of four levels of involvement. First, they have facilitated access to materials, providing appropriate reading at required levels. They have also sought to reduce institutional barriers. Second, they have made instructional materials available. Third, they have afforded actual reading instruction. And fourth, they have instituted outreach programs in the form of family literacy, workplace literacy and tutoring to incarcerated felons. While participation at the first and second level is relatively widespread, few have taken the third and fourth steps.

Providing access to materials for literacy students is itself a difficult task. The books geared to this audience differ from those in the library's general collection. It is crucial to the success of any program that the materials be appropriate and able to hold the interest of adults whose attention readily strays. Some librarians have been reluctant to add Adult Basic Education (ABE) materials to their collections on the grounds that they are difficult to evaluate or that they do not meet the library's quality standards. Yet book selection training renders librarians singularly equipped to fulfill the selector role, and the argument about quality disregards the library's responsibility to make information accessible to every segment of the community. "...rejection of materials intended for adult new readers may be a sign of unconscious disrespect for the materials' audience, rather than disapproval of the material itself."[14]

Census reports provide some indication about the extent of illiteracy in communities. Studies have indicated that 38% of undereducated adults live in rural areas. Most public libraries that have mounted more extensive literacy programs are located in big cities.

A full scale literacy program means hiring at least a full-time coordinator, recruiting volunteer tutors, training them, evaluating student skills, matching students with teachers, purchasing appropriate materials, publicizing the program in ways that reach those who do not read, no mean feat. Non-literate persons are often embarrassed or ashamed of their disability and make every effort to hide it. Newspapers, pamphlets, posters and other print media are useless. Television, radio and word of mouth are far more effective. Other supports for literacy education include bibliographies of adult new reader materials and software programs that provide interactive drills and other forms of computer assisted learning.

Among the stumbling-blocks in any literacy programs are the inconstancy of both tutors and students. The former become frustrated when the results are discouraging. The latter often have short attention-spans, or of greater moment, problems encountered at home or on the job. Since literacy is so often associated with poverty, simply arriving at a tutoring session may represent a major accomplishment. Learning to read as an adult is difficult. Imagine, for a minute, picking up a Russian, Greek or Chinese newspaper if you are not literate in those languages. Suppose, then, that an authority figure enjoined you to read the first line, and when you had difficulty commented that any fifth grader could read that. Patience and understanding are key attributes required from anyone associated with teaching reading, especially to adults.

Another difficulty in mounting a literacy program lies in the reliability of funding. Many libraries entered the literacy field spurred by the willingness of the federal government to lend some tangible support to programs. The main funds came from Title VI of the Library Services and Construction Act which authorized grants to state and local public libraries for literacy. In addition the Department of Education gave start-up funds to the Coalition for Literacy an organization spearheaded by the American Library Association whose main purpose was public information and advertising. Literacy is currently a "hot issue" for which competitive grants are available. In 1990 Congress produced two acts affecting literacy programs: The National Literacy Act and

Literacy for All Americans, part of an omnibus education bill. Both of these are awaiting funding. The Library Services and Construction Act (LSCA) supported 237 library literacy programs in 1990. Programs have also been funded by state and local governments. However, grants are never sure, long-range, and are rarely for operating funds. They may help to establish a program or fund new undertakings such as family or work-place literacy. But they are short-lived and undependable.

Family literacy programs are based on the premise that reading parents or caregivers produce reading children and conversely, that children whose parents are functionally illiterate are twice as likely as their peers to be functionally illiterate. Tutors teach parents how to read to their children. Adolescents, too, have been targeted because illiteracy in that group has been associated with other problems including crime, pregnancy, unemployment, drug and alcohol abuse and school failure. Programs for them include after-school and summer literacy programs, homework help sessions, peer tutoring and peer-group reading sessions.

Workplace literacy generally implies a cooperative program between a literacy training supplier and an employer and involves release time and encouragement. American businesses currently spend more than 25 billion dollars teaching remedial literacy to their employees. Literacy programs in jails and other correctional institutions are particularly effective and are believed to have a major impact on recidivism rates. Literacy programs have also been designed for people for whom English is a second language. Success rates for this group are far greater than for English speaking illiterates, although the initial language problems may be intimidating.

MINORITIES

While there are many minority and immigrant groups in the United States, in this section the term is used to describe Asians, Hispanics, Blacks and Native Americans. White immigrants who belong to various ethnic groups have hastened their assimilation into American society by changing their names, religion, appearance and by learning English. The racial minorities listed above have no such option. Libraries have been slow to serve non-white constituencies.

> In the mid-nineteenth century, which saw the beginnings of the public library movement, most black Americans still had the legal status of chattels, and American Indians were widely considered vermin worthy only of extermination. Both Asian immigrants and chicanos born in U.S. territories were objects of hostility and scorn.[15]

Today, these groups can scarcely be overlooked, so substantial are their numbers. Carl Harb, a demographer at the Population Reference Bureau, states that

> cultural diversity probably accelerated more in the 1980s than any other decade and will be seen as a period of remarkable ethnic change even when compared to the high immigration period early in century by southern and eastern Europeans.[16]

Approximately 46 million minority individuals reside in the United States. By the year 2,000 the figure is expected to be 77 million, or 29% of the total population and by 2025, 35%.[17] Legal immigration in 1992 surpassed 700,000. In California alone, during the past two decades, total minority populations have grown to comprise over 40% of the total state population and by 2,000 will comprise 46%. Needless to say many communities are predominantly minority members. Yet a study of California libraries reported that

> In the main, the state's public libraries appear unable to mount serious, systematic changes in their operational patterns, resulting in severe dislocations between the new types of library patrons and traditional services offered.[18]

Libraries may, in fact, be guilty of *institutional racism* in which "the very institutions of society operate to maintain existing inequalities between members of different racial groups. This can occur even where the individuals in charge of these institutions are not themselves racist in their beliefs."[19]

The term "special services," often used to describe library services to minority groups is obviously a misnomer particularly when applied in communities in which the prevailing population is one or another ethnic group. In this case, "special services" means providing everyday service relevant to the needs and interests of the majority ethnic population, a task that suggests a less taxing effort than it is in reality. A number of factors contribute to the difficulty of the task:

1. As a profession, librarians are predominantly white. Often they are uncomfortable with members of ethnic groups. Sometimes they espouse overly racist ideas. No matter where on the continuum their attitudes or uncertainties lie, how they feel cannot help but influence the philosophy and practice of library service. A first, imperative step is to become cognizant of our biases, stereotypes, values and assumptions. "As we work to undo racism, we must confront it in ourselves."[20]

2. Many librarians argue that it is the responsibility of minorities to become part of the predominant culture and "situate the reasons for nonuse in the minority cultures themselves, thereby absolving the library of both past culpability and future responsibility."[21]

They say, for instance, that reading is not part of Native American culture and that adult tribal members do not utilize library facilities already available to them. Hispanic and African-Americans are characterized as reluctant or indifferent users. Current literature suggests that the information poor are that way because of the character of non-users -- poor, disadvantaged, unacculturated, illiterate and minorities. Recent research indicates that the fault may lay closer to home, with public librarians themselves, whose institutions may be uninformed about the needs and life styles of their users. If librarians accept the challenge of providing services to a multicultural clientele than the library must be seen as an institution where all people, regardless of race, creed, color, or sex will be warmly welcomed and treated with dignity and respect. "Multiculturalism," says Nauratil,

> seeks to afford all members of society equal opportunity to realize their fullest potential, to have equal access to services and to be able to maintain their own culture without prejudice or disadvantage.[22]

3. Some librarians claim that to provide special services is to segregate or "ghettoize" minority populations. It is true that

> information needs do not differ primarily because of race or ethnicity, but rather because of an individual's life situation, which may include factors *associated* with race or ethnicity, such as cultural experiences, language, level of literacy, socioeconomic status, education and level of acculturation.[23]

For this reason, the library's collection should be able to provide information on how to file a discrimination complaint, or about sickle-cell anemia, as well as non-English language books. Mary Lee Bundy maintains that

> Failing to provide service to the poor and to minorities is not an option which should be open to public libraries. If any public library in the United States does not want or cannot render viable library and information service to [them], then whatever is their share of the library budget should be turned over to community-based groups who do want and can render services needed and wanted by the community.[24]

Perhaps the most difficult task is determining community needs and interests. Few libraries undertake careful needs assessments, but rather make assumptions based on scanty evidence. One California survey of minority groups revealed some surprising information about differing goals and needs of various ethnic groups. The following table presents the findings.

Figure 12

1979 INFORMATION NEEDS BY MINORITY GROUPS

Rank	*Statewide*	*Asians*	*Blacks*	*Hispanics*
1.	Money Matters	Consumer Issues	Health	Job-Related Issues
2.	Consumer Issues	Education	Consumer Issues	Money Matters
3.	Housing/ Home Care	Transpor- tation	Housing	Education
4.	Health	Job-related Issues	Job-related Issues	
5.	Job- related Issues	Money Matters	Transpor- tation	
6.		Housing		

Source: *Information Needs of Californians,* California State Lib., 1979

Once needs have been identified, a plan to provide service must be developed. Kravitz suggests that a phased program similar to one followed when automating may be the most effective path, and outlines the following plan of action

    1. In a multiethnic community, improve service to the ethnic group or groups already serviced and add additional ethnic

groups in subsequent years.

2. Add children's services first, adult-reference second, and then adult circulating materials.

3. Set priorities according to the staff and community expertise available.

4. Work closely with the target audiences and market the joint successes to build trust and support for increased budget needs.

5. As a traditional strategy, use bookmobile services to introduce the library to nonusers, highlighting the works, records, and posters of people of color.

6. Reorder service priorities to concentrate on the most underserved groups.[25]

Attempts to reach special clientele always fail when they are underfunded and lack community involvement. Understanding the life experience of community persons is key to designing successful programs. Community leaders need to be involved in designing the program and in creating ethnically sensitive publicity and flyers and in translating library brochures and forms into appropriate languages. Any perceived barriers to serve, whether real or imagined, must be dismantled.

Among the two most important steps in serving the emerging majority are the recruitment of minority librarians and the sensitizing of existing ones. There must be staff who know, identify with, appreciate and respect the values and aspirations of the community. All staff who meet the public will require sensitivity training, training in dealing with diverse clientele, training to meet the information needs in a variety of languages and information about new collections and available services.

The Queensborough (New York City) Public Library has supported a New Americans project, and conducted such programs as "Living in America," "How to Deal with a Landlord," "How to

Get a Green Card," and "The Rights of Immigrants." Branch libraries are intended to be a

> comfortable link between the lands they left and the new one they are tentatively discovering, offering them classes in how to cope with American life while providing books and magazines in languages they know. To learn English, an immigrant in Queens may go to just about any branch in the library system.[26]

THE INSTITUTIONALIZED

Nearly six million Americans live in group quarters. Of these, almost 2 1/2 million are institutional inmates and the numbers are growing. Institutions include prisons and jails, juvenile detention centers, mental hospitals and residential treatment centers, nursing homes, homes for the aged, schools and residences for the mentally and physically handicapped, homes for dependent children and homes for unwed mothers.

A turning point in service to prison populations came in the 1960s. Nauratil describes how a riot at the Tombs Prison in New York City included a vicious attack on the prison library. What was first deemed wanton violence, in a later reassessment was thought to have been prompted by the library's contents. Its holdings included books in German and French, 300 copies of the *Autobiography of King Farouk,* and 500 copies of the *Coin Collectors Handbook.* The importance of libraries to inmates has once again been highlighted in Spike Lee's film *Malcolm X*, where the reading he did in prison changed the direction of the Black leader's life.

Most public library service to institutions takes the form of delivering materials to inmates, although, in a few cases, inmates are brought to the library. Unfortunately, despite the new consciousness of the importance to prisoners of reading material, most library service available to incarcerated people is substandard at best.

What responsibilities do public libraries have for supplying materials to those who are institutionalized? There are those who contend that through their actions prisoners have earned their second-class status. Punishment should include lack of access to the benefits of society, including libraries.

Librarians who choose to provide library service to people in institutions adopt one of four courses:

1. They provide *deposit collections* only, staffed by institutional personnel or volunteers who are responsible for circulation of materials within the institution. Often collections are paperback discards that have been approved by prison authorities.

2. They set up a *library unit* within an institution to serve both personnel and patients, providing walk-in and book cart service.

3. They may extend *bookmobile service* to institutions within their service area.

4. The public library may offer *interlibrary loan service* to established libraries maintained by personnel attached to the institution's staff and funded by the institution.

OTHER GROUPS

Among the other groups which may require special services are the handicapped or disabled, or as some preferred to be called the "differently abled" or "physically challenged." This includes, according to the Rehabilitation Act of 1973, those with physical or mental impairment that substantially limits one or more major life function such as caring for oneself, performing manual tasks, walking, standing, hearing, speaking, breathing, learning and working.[27] As with the poor, there is a strong coincidence of differently abled among the other special clientele that have been discussed above, especially among the aged, the illiterate and the institutionalized.

The federal government participates in library service for the disabled. LSCA provides

> library service to physically handicapped persons (including the blind and physically handicapped) certified by competent authority as unable to use or read conventional printed material as a result of physical limitations.[28]

The National Library for the Blind and Physically Handicapped, a division of the Library of Congress, maintains an extensive collection of books on tape that it supplies to individuals who meet the qualifications.

Among the other services that many libraries have offered to blind and physically handicapped users are Kurzweil reading machines that convert printed matter to sound using electronic scanners with speech synthesizers. In addition, libraries will often purchase magnifying devices of various strengths for those with sight problems. Services for the deaf are still relatively undeveloped. Few library members are literate in sign language. However, a number of libraries have purchased telecommunications devices (TDDs) that provide video or printed communication over telephone lines. Utilizing this technology, librarians can perform telephone reference for hearing impaired clientele

Another group whose members have increasingly turned to libraries for assistance is the unemployed. Most Americans, it is reported, are four paychecks away from being without a roof over their heads.[29] Help to the unemployed has included establishments of business and job centers in the library, making available personal computers with resume software and conducting such programs as "How to Get a Job."

BOOKMOBILES

Bookmobiles extend library services to user populations who have difficulty making regular visits to permanent library facilities. Often they travel to remote or rural parts of a library's service area.

But they are also valuable in giving service to urban populations whose members are reluctant library visitors.

Bookmobiles were started before the turn of the century when canal boats, pack mules and railroad cars were all harnessed to provide library service. The first traveling bookmobile has been traced to Hagerstown, Maryland in 1905. A converted spring wagon, its black box-like body could hold 250 books. It served an area of 500 square miles and required four days to complete one round trip.[30] By 1937 there were 60 bookmobiles and 919 in 1956, the majority travelling southern routes. LSCA furthered their use and they reached their largest numbers in the 1970s. The dramatic increase in gasoline prices caused libraries to reconsider the cost effectiveness of the service and many dropped it.

Many factors make bookmobiles less than optimal library outlets. They are small; their reference materials inadequate. There are no facilities for sitting and programming efforts are limited. They are rarely serviced by professional librarians. Breakdowns make them unreliable and the initial investment plus the prices of continued maintenance make them fairly expensive, less cost-effective some say than a "books by mail program."

On the other hand, bookmobile collections can be kept up-to-date and without large numbers of obsolete, unused volumes relatively easily to reflect better the needs of patrons. If their schedules are well publicized, well planned and consistently maintained, people will use them to meet their reading needs.

Bookmobiles are most common in libraries with large geographical areas to cover. Twenty-five percent of public libraries operate bookmobiles; only seventeen percent supply books by mail. Their flexibility makes them particularly valuable as interim service providers when new branches or facilities are being constructed, especially in areas experiencing population growth or shift.

Special user populations well served by bookmobiles are groups that might otherwise have no access to library services the elderly, migrant workers, foreign born, those living in areas cut off by freeways and complex terrain. Minority communities are attracted to their informality. They have no high columns, fancy archways or carved doors.

> They roll into the neighborhood, fling open side panels and blend into the surroundings just like the bread trucks and fruit vendors people remember from their youth.[31]

New technologies enhance the ability of bookmobiles to provide quality service. Remote access computers allow easy access to online catalogs from bookmobile units. Cellular phones make possible communication with reference collections and online databases from remote locations. Facsimile (FAX) can instantly transmit material. In view of their flexibility, it is probable that bookmobiles will continue to be viable channels of library service, at least until the turn of the century.[32]

WHAT IS TO BE DONE?

Clearly, serving the special groups mentioned above is no easy task. New commitments and reaffirmations of old ones are required. Developing a coherent program of service to both individuals and groups entails establishing priorities, short and long-term expectations and appropriate outcomes amenable to evaluation.

Library budgets will be forced to reflect new service goals; library funds must be reallocated to mirror new priorities and public relations programs informing potential constituents of new services undertaken. Coalition-building with groups who share objectives makes work with special clienteles eminently more effective.

The library profession itself has a number of difficult issues to confront. As Nauratil asserts,

> the gap between our rhetoric and our practice has become entrenched in the library's organization. The public library, as a bureaucratic oligarchy, is less susceptible to transformation than are individual librarians...We can no longer afford to think

in terms of "what is best for my branch" but, rather "what is necessary to meet human needs."[33]

Library schools need to recruit minority members to the profession. But they are also obligated to encourage their traditional student bodies -- white females -- to be sensitive to and aware of society's problems. In addition, more information research and investigation about the best ways to utilize information and the library in order to strengthen the quality of life for all citizens is needed.

SUMMARY

The middle class, well-educated population who are the library's traditional public require little encouragement to utilize the institution's services and programs. People who are undereducated, illiterate, aged, institutionalized, non-English speaking and physically or emotionally handicapped may meet or, alternately, construct behaviors that deny them access to information.

Librarians have a responsibility to communicate in creative and innovative ways with those who are not reached through normal channels to inform them of the potential benefits to them of using the library's services and, further, to assure that those services are appropriate to this constituency.

NOTES AND SUGGESTED READINGS

Notes

1. Claire Lipsman, *The Disadvantaged and Library Effectiveness* (Chicago: American Library Association, 1972), 11-12.

2. *Adrift in a Sea of Change* (Sacramento, CA: California Library Foundation,1990), 11.

3. For a discussion of this position, see Ervin Gaines, "The Large Municipal Library as Network," *Library Quarterly* 39 (January 1969): 47.

4. Marcia Nauratil, *Public Libraries and Nontraditional Clienteles* (Westport, CT: Greenwood Press, 1986), 37.

5. William Martin, *Community Librarianship* (London: Clive Bingley, 1989), 76.

6. Ibid., 41.

7. Nauratil, 21.

8. Ibid., 155.

9. Ibid., 52.

10. Ibid., 57-59.

11. Ibid., 63.

12. Jeffrey Salter and Charles Salter, *Literacy and the Library* (Englewood, CO: Libraries Unlimited, 1991), 2.

13. Ibid., 7.

14. Nauratil, 93.

15. Ibid., 109.

16. Rhonda Rios Kravitz et al., "Serving the Emerging Majority: Documenting their Voices," *Library Administration and Management* 5 (Fall 1991): 184-8.

17. Charlene Cain ,"Public Library Service to Minorities," in Kathleen Heim and Danny Wallace, *Adult Services* (Chicago: American Library Association, 1990), 212.

18. *Adrift in a Sea of Change*, iii.

19. Nauratil, 116.

20. Kravitz, 185.

21. Nauratil, 110.

22. Ibid., 118.

23. *Adrift in a Sea of Change*, v.

24. Mary Lee Bundy, "An Advocacy Perspective: The Public Library and the Poor," *Catholic Library World* 53 (April 1982): 383.

25. Kravitz, 186.

26. Ingrid Lesley, "Library Service for Special User Groups," in *Bowker Annual Library and Book Trade Almanac*. 37th ed. (New Providence, NJ: Bowker, 1992), 31.

27. U.S. Code 706(7)B, Supplement V (1981), quoted in Kieth Wright and Judith Davie *Serving the Disabled* (New York: Neal-Schuman, 1991), 1. See also P.L. 101-335, Section 1(b), Section 3 Americans with Disabilities Act of 1990,

28. Janice Simpson ,"Service to the Handicapped," in Heim and Wallace, 373.

29. Ingrid, 26.

30. Bert Boyce and Judith Boyce, "Bookmobiles and Adult Services," in Heim and Wallace, 315.

31. Ibid., 322.

32. Ibid., 320.

33. Nauratil, 165.

Suggested Readings

Allen, Adela Artole, ed. *Library Services for Hispanic Children: A Guide for Public and School Librarians*. Phoenix, AZ: Oryx Press, 1987.

Heim, Kathleen and Danny Wallace. *Adult Services*. Chicago: American Library Association, 1990.

Lesley, J. Ingrid. "Library Services for Special User Groups," in *Bowker Annual Library and Book Trade Almanac*. 37th ed. New Providence, NJ: Bowker, 1992. 25-37.

Lovejoy, Eunice. *Portraits of Library Service to People with Disabilities*. Boston: G.K. Hall, 1990.

Nauratil, Marcia. *Public Libraries and Nontraditional Clienteles*. Westport, CT: Greenwood Press, 1986.

Pungitore, Verna. *Public Librarianship*. New York: Greenwood Press, 1989.

Rubin, Rhea Joyce and Gail McGovern. *Working with Older Adults: A Handbook for Libraries*. 3rd ed. Sacramento: California State Library Foundation, 1990.

Salter, Jeffrey and Charles Salter. *Literacy and the Library*. Englewood, CO: Libraries Unlimited, 1991.

Schamber, Linda. "The Role of Libraries in Literacy Education," *Emergency Librarian* 19 (1991): 34-5.

Turock, Betty ed. *Information and Aging*. Jefferson, NC: McFarland, 1988.

Wright, Kieth and Judith Davie. *Serving the Disabled*. New York: Neal-Schuman, 1991.

Zweizig, Douglas et al. *Evaluation of Adult Literacy Programs*. Chicago: American Library Association, 1990.

CHAPTER 15

MARKETING, PUBLICIZING AND INTERPRETING THE LIBRARY

Public librarians share both a profound faith in the value of the services they offer to their publics and a major frustration in the fact that not more of them are used. Further, they hold firm convictions that those not currently using the library would certainly respond if only the library's message -- a description of resources and services -- were to reach them. This basic assumption has impelled library directors to call for enhanced "public relations" efforts as the best avenue to reach potential patrons. This development is not without irony. Historically, librarians have seen public relations as "tainted information used to manipulate consumers." [1]

Unfortunately, the term public relations itself has become problematic under the weight of conceptual and definitional ambiguity. Viewed in its simplest terms, public relations can mean "creating or changing the attitudes, beliefs, and perceptions of people by influencing them -- primarily with information disseminated through the media." [2] *Publicity, promotion* and *advertising* are all methods used to achieve the goals of public relations. Modern media -- radio, television, newspapers -- are the primary vehicles by which publicity, promotion and advertising are delivered.

Recently the phrase *external communications* has been substituted for public relations in an effort to broaden the concept and suggest some of its complexities. A sound program of *external communications* based on a smooth-running operation and a well-developed internal communication program

   --helps to improve and strengthen the role of the library in the
   community;
   --informs people about the library's programs and services,
   policies and procedures;
   --gathers support for the library;
   --interprets and explains the library to those who are charged
   with its oversight and direction;
   --reports to a variety of people with differing interests about the
   library and its operations;
   --brings to the library a range of information and opinion from
   those outside the library that can aid in the planning and decision-making process.[3]

External communication -- public relations in its best sense
-- is a system of mutual influence and understanding involving a
two-way exchange of information dissemination and feedback
between the library and its publics. It fulfills an educational role
essential in a democratic society when it honestly, but thoroughly
reports on its goods and services.

In yet another departure from the traditional view, *marketing*
has come to be considered the overarching activity under which
public relations is subsumed; and *marketing* itself is deemed to be
an outgrowth and companion to *strategic planning.* The defining
difference between old-style public relations and contemporary
marketing seems to lie in the latter's focus on customer need. The
object of marketing (and of the current interpretation of public
relations) is to insure that the institution offers what the customer
wants in contrast with, say sales, whose object it is to insure that
the customer wants what the institution has.[4]

Following a marketing concept entails:

Analyzing user need. This may involve collecting new
information, utilizing existing data -- published statistics, for
instance -- conducting focus group and individual interviews, and
administering surveys.

Segmenting the potential market into smaller sub-markets. For libraries this might mean special users, children, ethnic groups, nonliterate persons, and so on.

Matching services to users. For instance, reference services, home delivery, large print books, etc.

Developing and implementing a marketing plan. This requires intimate knowledge of the service, its costs, its distribution mechanisms and the best means for making it known to its public.

Evaluating its effectiveness.

Some judge that distinctions made between public relations and marketing are merely semantic. However, as we have stressed throughout this book, satisfying a community's information needs, no matter the definition of information, is the main object of a public library.

THE PUBLIC RELATIONS EFFORT

The Public Relations Budget

Suggestions about the amount of library budget needed to sustain a successful public relations program range one to seven percent of total expenditures.[5] This includes funds for supplies, materials, film, equipment, cassettes, tapes and required services such as printing, duplicating, videotaping, recording or photocopying. In truth, a budget for public relations in most small and medium-sized libraries is either non-existent or so small that funds must be scavenged from other dedicated library accounts.

The level of support accorded public relations will dictate the nature of the program a library is able to mount. A library with a $200,000 annual budget that dedicates two percent of its expenditures to public relations would have $4,000 available to spend. That amount, spread throughout a year, and over all activities can only purchase a minimal program, one that utilizes in-house personnel and allows no use of outside expertise. The larger the library, the more it is able to afford a sustained public relations effort. Options may include hiring skilled staff specialists or farming out the work to consultants. Among the attractions to smaller libraries of joining regional systems is that some services closed to them by virtue of their straitened circumstances are now obtainable. That benefit certainly is applicable to public relations.

Staffing Public Relations

Experts recommend that a local library public relations program serving a population of less than 40,000 be supervised by the director with some part-time or volunteer assistance. For a library whose service area is between 40,000 and 100,000, a half-time public relations specialist and a part-time library display artist are desireable. Libraries with populations around 100,000 should have a full-time public relations director and a full-time staff artist. Those with populations of 500,000 or more can use a public relations staff of at least eight persons.[6]

The question of whether to utilize a professional librarian to conduct the public relations program or to secure the services of a public relations expert without library training has no ready answer. Most librarians lack expertise and professional public relations competence to undertake the job. In addition, they may be reluctant to surrender their professional work either with the public or with materials. Conversely most public relations specialists have little understanding of the objectives and functions of public libraries, except, perhaps, as users. Hiring either has drawbacks. Workshops, courses and seminars can help to ameliorate background deficiencies, at least to some extent. Librarians, however, have little choice when insufficient funds are available to staff public relations. Then they must accept responsibility for mounting and implementing any program, in addition to fulfilling their duties as librarians.

The primary skill essential to success in public relations is the capability to write copy clearly and quickly, followed closely by an ability to speak in a clear and engaging fashion to an audience of strangers.[7] Other attributes include familiarity with print media, methods of working with press, radio and television, principles of graphic communication, and knowledge about coordinating special events.

The Public Relations Plan

A public relations library program is not a campaign but a continuing relationship with various segments of the population who use and support the library. It is internal as well as external, "enhancing the library's image among the staff who then collaborate to promote the public's awareness and use of resources."[8]

A written plan defines the program's purposes, sets goals and measurable objectives listed in priority order, describes the methods by which it will be evaluated, and provides an indication of when projected periodic reviews that assure the continued relevance of the program will be held.

Successful public relations undertakings are initially modest in scope, targeting only the top few priority objectives. They are carefully designed far in advance with ample time allowed both for maximum impact, and to permit them to be terminated if the results are minimal.[9]

The object of a public relations message will determine the medium chosen to carry it and the form it will take. Presentation style must fit the subject, the audience and the occasion. Some messages are institutional, devised to promote the library's name and keep it in of front its public. Others highlight specific programs or services and are directed at discrete constituencies. A press release to the popular media -- radio, television, newspapers -- serves best when the aim is to reach a broad cross-section of the public. Identifying the less well known publications with limited readerships or locating organizations and groups with particular interests requires more effort, but carries the promise of substantial reward in interest and/or attendance. Often personal letters can be more effective than can press releases. When Woodbridge (NJ) Public Library launched a new service to assist adult independent learners, they publicized the effort with news releases, paid advertisements both in newspapers and on area billboards, spot radio announcements, posters displayed inside and outside the library, direct mail to all community households, and flyers carried home by every schoolchild. A random sample of 1000 community residents revealed that the most effective means, by far, had been direct mail.

Staff and Board Public Relations Activities

Intrinsic to any public relations effort is the myriad important roles played by the library staff and board. Staff support excellent public relations when they present the library in a favorable light in their over-the-counter exchanges with users. Further, staff and trustees also strengthen the public relations program by making specific contributions of special skills. Finally, library board and staff further public relations goals by becoming involved in the community.

> An effort must be made to see that lines are established with various social, cultural, religious, economic, ethnic and business circles in the community. The library board of trustees, if properly selected, should provide at least some of the mix of lines into the community.[10]

FRIENDS GROUPS

A strong active Friends of the Library group is one of the most valuable assets a library can have. Organizations vary from city to city, but are generally composed of people who share an interest in helping the library fulfill its mission. Often these are men and women who love books, reading and libraries and are willing to help by publicly proclaiming the library's virtues and by helping to add to its resources. They function in a number of areas crucial to the library's well-being, with advocacy, fund-raising and cultural endeavors heading the list. Friends can

--build public awareness and stimulate public support;
--enrich the cultural life of the community by sponsoring programs as varied as author talks, children's parties, concerts, exhibits, film festivals, flower shows, lectures and book discussions;
--fund raise to provide equipment and materials not available through the regular library budget by conducting the annual direct mail appeal for funds, by running the library book sale, or by holding special fund-raising events;
--encourage the use of library resources and services;
--maintain cooperation and open communication between the library and other civic and community groups.

In some communities, Friends groups accept responsibility for library beautification, for supplying literacy tutors, or even for providing a cadre of library volunteers.

Friends groups require clear communication, specific goals and objectives and a formal structure for the organization, with a designated liaison between it and the library. Friends' organizations do not require elaborate machinery to be successful. Most have by-laws, officers and an advisory council. Some Friends groups collect dues; others do not. Occasionally Friends groups generate interest by publishing a bulletin or by producing a brochure describing the organization.

Too often, librarians ignore Friends groups who then begin to act autonomously and to promote their own goals and objectives which may diverge from those of the library's current administration. The danger is particularly great if a Friends group has been in existence over a period of time or through a series of directors. The two most harmful Friends problems are the possibility that, first, in their roles as "library ambassadors," they will decry the library's current program and, second, they will seek to influence policy by controlling the use of funds they have raised. Both problems arise when the Library Director does not attend Friends meetings, does not assure that the group is acting within the framework the board has adopted, permits members to remain unclear about library goals and objectives and does not articulate the library's appreciation for the work of the Friends. In addition, controversy over the expenditure of moneys raised by Friends are easily resolved when the Board adopts a statement to the effect that "All fundraising by Friends will be in accordance with library policy and all gifts to the library will be made with the approval of the library director." In some libraries a board seat reserved for the Friends President represents an additional avenue to the promotion of both harmony and shared goals.

Information about organizing Friends groups is readily available. The Friends of Libraries, U.S.A. publishes *Friends of Libraries National Notebook* and *Public Relations Handbook,* as well as a newsletter. Assistance may be solicited from the American Library Association which publishes *Friends of the Library Sourcebook.* By joining national Friends groups, local friends organizations can insure support of libraries at the legislature, telephone networks to further library causes and other joint endeavors.

Book Sales

Most libraries sponsor ongoing or periodic book sales as a way of disposing of unwanted books that have either been donated or weeded from the collection. Rarely unsuccessful and environmentally sound, these recycling sales further public relations by giving the public an opportunity to secure a varied group of books at little cost. In some communities they are one of the year's "events." Librarians, tempted to wonder who might want such beat-up, outdated materials, would do well to remember that one person's junk is another's treasure. Book sales lend Friends a common purpose, a reachable goal and a cooperative process between them and library staff. It sometimes represents the cement that binds them and keeps them working for a common cause.

Book sales require decisions about who should be responsible for evaluating materials, how books should be priced, how to publicize the sale, and how to handle the money raised. Few people, even most professional librarians, have the expertise to recognize rare books when they appear or to appraise the value of unfamiliar ones. For this reason, all materials should be carefully examined for autographs, indications of first edition, rare imprints, or other distinguishing marks. Those suspected of having more than routine importance should be segregated and kept for the scrutiny of a local rare book dealer. Pricing books to sell always makes a more successful sale, although some distinction may be made between those in lesser supply -- children's, travel and cookbooks are always in demand -- and those such as old copies of *National Geographic* or *Heritage* Magazine which are always plentiful. The sale should be well-publicized sufficiently far in advance to allow people to plan to attend and held at such time that it least interferes with the library's operation, a Sunday for instance if the library is generally closed. Holding booksales in sites other than the library is sometimes necessitated by lack of appropriate space within the building, but is probably less desireable since it discourages associating the event with the institution.

Lobbying

As the need for human and financial resources grows, lobbying efforts by volunteer groups in behalf of the library will continue to grow. Lobbying, defined as "interaction with politicians to secure specific objectives as an appropriate point in the legislative, policy-making or budget process,"[11] involves providing information and education to a legislator on a topic about which he or she may not be fully informed either by phone, by mail or in person. Successful lobbying always demands a broad base of community support and a strong relationship between the library and key individuals.

The goals of lobbying are 1) to increase library funding, 2) to create public goodwill in order to generate pressure on decision makers when it is needed, 3) to avoid onerous and uninformed, though well intentioned efforts by decision makers, and 4) to ensure an "ear" for a problem when necessary.[12]

Active Friends groups with large numbers of members are particularly valuable in the political arena. They provide a "bulk" that library staffs and boards, acting alone, cannot. They can be utilized to promote budget proposals, work on bond issue campaigns and join efforts to charge state statutes affecting public libraries. Friends groups write letters, make phone calls, pack meetings when large showings help and pass petitions when required. In this role, Friends activists need to be well informed about the issues, need to be truthful and accurate and positive in their approach.

UNDERSTANDING MEDIA

Learning the local media means understanding the goals, objectives and demands of television stations, newspapers, magazines and radio stations. It also implies establishing personal contact with editors or news directors as well since each organization observes its own rules and customs, and sets its own deadlines and format requirements. In small or medium-sized communities, the newspapers and radio or TV stations generally assign one person to local news. Making contact with the reporter charged with covering local stories, giving him or her a packet of information about the library, offering to provide assistance in securing data about stories being covered, promotes a relationship that may later prove valuable and enhance the library's chances of receiving extensive coverage. Other publicity outlets should also receive routine attention. Among them are PTO newsletters, church bulletins, club and service organization publications and public services releases disseminated through periodic statements issued by utilities and banks.

From time-to-time every librarian issues press releases and media advisories, has press conferences, prepares book columns and appears on radio and TV. Some helpful hints about handling them successfully follow.

Press Releases

A well-prepared well-written press release, the primary tool of public relations, is designed to generate or stimulate media coverage. Fashioned in *pyramid* style, the story presents essential information -- who, what, where, why and when -- in its initial paragraph and adds detail and "color" as it proceeds. Librarians sometimes have difficulty learning how to write press releases because the approach differs markedly from the one they followed when writing school papers and theses where the topic is introduced, explained, analyzed, conclusions defended and summarized. Producing only a limited number of short press releases, assuring that copies are clear, without typing or spelling errors and easily readable increases the chances they will be used.

Media Advisories

A media advisory is an announcement designed to call attention to a high visibility event that the library would like to have covered. A mayor and city council's announcement that they will support an expansion of the library is an example of a statement that the library hopes will receive widespread attention. If the announcement is made at a press conference, it should be brief; there should be time provided for questions and refreshments should be served. If it is possible to videotape the statement, footage can later be provided to television stations.

TV and Radio

Commercial TV coverage of library events has been sparse. Had the TV world remained one of networks with a few regional independent stations and non-commercial channels in each market area, this lack of attention would undoubtedly have continued. The advent of Cable TV with its smaller, more segmented markets, and local origination telecasting on local channels, has increased opportunities for educational and public relations efforts of libraries. Some public libraries have even assumed operation of entire local access channels. The marriage between libraries and local TV program origination has much to commend it, particularly when a community library counts among its important roles the presentation of information about broad issues of local concern. For the library, the benefits can be substantial since the operation of a channel places the library at the center of the local scene, in contact with every local official who has an interest in a local issue.

Access to local radio is often more attainable than is access to commercial television. The radio market is more segmented, inclined to think locally, rather than globally. Public service announcements (PSAs) prepared by ALA, state library associations or self-generated are more likely to be carried by radio at times when they will reach the public. TV stations that agree to use PSAs generally run them at two AM when advertising revenues are unavailable.

Book Columns

Local newspapers without skilled book reviewers are often willing to publish a library book column. What the column involves, the kinds of materials it covers and how often it appears are all factors that help to determine whether the effort to produce it is worthwhile. Critical book reviewing is an art that requires time and skill. On the other hand, book columns that simply describe a set of materials in the library can be constructed rapidly without the type of development needed in reviewing. Some libraries use the column to highlight materials about which the public may be unaware, for instance, new auto repair manuals, medical handbooks, travel guides and self-help materials rather than fiction and non-fiction best-sellers which are amply publicized in other sources.

Cable TV and the radio may provide libraries with

opportunities to construct electronic book columns, an activity that coincides with changing commmunity communication patterns, and extends the possibility of reaching a segment of the population untouched by newspapers.

PUBLIC APPEARANCES

Community Talks

Speaking to civic and social groups about the library permits the library to interpret itself to people who may currently be unaware of its services. Videos and slide shows, narrated by the presenter, can give visual documentation to what otherwise might simply be a litany of library statistics. Filming a child in the act of reading a book in the library is far more interesting and meaningful to non-librarians than an aggregate report of circulation transactions. Library staff are also requested to give book talks, to discuss contemporary literature, or to speak about developments in libraries and the information world. It is a golden opportunity to introduce people to the riches of the library's collections and services.

However, short-handed, over-worked librarians are loathe to commit time and effort outside the library when in-house demands by current users loom so large. Consideration of possible outcomes helps to determine whether the merits of an aggressive public speaking agenda outweigh those of attending more conscientiously to internal considerations.

School and Library Visits

Librarians have traditionally called on schools during the course of a year to encourage students to visit the library. Typically, a librarian tells a story or two and passes out information about the library. Conversely, during the school year, librarians schedule visits to the library by classes of school children. Older children, those of junior high school age, are often introduced to non-school associated reference materials -- *Consumer Reports,* or a Rock and

Roll Encyclopedia, for instance -- to set them on the road to lifelong learning. Not only do these exchanges prove fruitful from a service point of view, but the public relations benefits are incalculable.

IN-HOUSE MEDIA OF INTERPRETATION

Annual reports, handbooks, booklists, exhibits and signs are media commonly used to interpret the library to the community.

Annual Reports

The annual report has wide public relations potential. It serves to record the year's achievements and is an indication of what the library hopes to accomplish in the future. Most reports document collection growth, reader services, staff, library use and include a brief narrative summary that takes stock and suggests areas in which the library could be improved. The best annual reports are written in straightforward, factual style without technical terminology or jargon and accompanied by clear, understandable, simple statistical charts.

Handbooks

Although handbooks are more common in academic libraries, some public libraries do publish brief ones describing how to gain access to the library and its materials and setting forth the library rules, including hours, borrowing periods, fines, access to interlibrary loan and database searching stipulations. Hallmarks of successful handbooks are clear writing, good graphics, no jargon and an upbeat tone.

Booklists

Library patrons love book lists of all kinds be they about new acquisitions, on specific topics or ones devoted to particular genres.

They love annotated lists best. Unfortunately, staff and time constraints, plus expense, have led to partial or total abandonment of the practice of routinely devising them, even those designed for children where the need is even more crucial. The ease of desktop publishing and the rise of commercially produced lists may help to reverse the trend.

Displays

Although libraries, from time-to-time, place displays outside the building, most exhibits are mounted in-house and aim to stimulate the use of certain collections and services. Often community groups will request display spaces to promote themselves. A policy that stipulates who may use exhibit areas and for what purposes helps to insure appropriate displays. Many older libraries have fixed display cases that when unfilled are unsightly and communicate lack of attention. As a result, display programs require careful planning and scheduling so that the cases are constantly in use. Newer demountable systems are storeable when not being used and are flexible enough to adjust to a variety of display types.

Exhibits of subject selected books, or of recent prize winners -- for example, National Book Awards, Pulitzers, Caldecotts, Newberys -- are always popular and well received. Lesser used parts of the book collection can be promoted by book displays. Many libraries distribute monthly responsibility for book exhibits among their public service staffs.

Signage

The library should be a house of welcome. Appropriate signage helps to transmit that message. The multiplicity of signs needed in any library gives staff the opportunity to plan a coherent and attractive approach to presenting basic information. Range finder letters, directories of collection locations, eating, drinking or smoking regulations, and schedules of library hours are common to all public libraries. The Americans with Disabilities Act (ADA) regulations also require such special signage as raised lettering for use of those with visual impairments.

Newer public libraries that have benefitted from the attention of a graphics designer stand in sharp contrast to older ones with visually outdated and badly coordinated signage systems. Handwritten signs communicate a poor image and should never be permitted to remain for more than 24 hours. The tone of a message can be as important as its design. A hint of humor helps to soften the categorical nature of most rules. A sign that reads "In this library please eat, smoke, read, sleep, browse, enjoy yourself," with eat, smoke and sleep crossed-out, adds a touch of whimsy to the need for regulations.

Newsletters and Direct Mail

Sending a message to every household in the community, one that says exactly what the library wants, in the way it wishes to say it has virtues. Some libraries produce newsletters, mail their annual reports, or use this communication channel to inform residents of an important new service.

SUMMARY

The many publics housed in the community in which the library operates are often unfamiliar with its services and resources. A rigorous public relations program, based on the library's overall plan of service, can help to inform community members about the library and to change erroneous public perceptions. Many formal and informal channels of communication are available to be utilized in pursuing publicity and spreading the library's message. Press releases in the media and public appearances call attention to the library's program. Staff, board members, and volunteers all participate in the public relations effort. Friends of the library are particular sources of financial and advocacy strength and deserve careful nurturing.

A common tenet of public librarians' faith is that their institutions are crucial to democratic society. Yet they are loathe to embark on a public relations program, considering the activity somehow dirty and demeaning. Only recently have librarians realized that public relations need not be deceptive, can be pursued with integrity and is crucial to a library's success.

NOTES AND SUGGESTED READINGS

Notes

1. Ann Roberts and Susan Blandy, *Public Relations for Librarians* (Englewood, CO: Libraries Unlimited, 1989),4.

2. Charles Mallory, *Publicity Power; A Practical Guide to Effective Promotion* (Los Altos, CA: Crisp, 1989), 4.

3. Philip Kotler, *Principles of Marketing*. 3rd ed. (Englewood Cliffs, NJ: Prentice-Hall, 1986), 757.

4. Neil Findlay, "Am I Marketing or Am I Selling," *Pacific Northwest Library Quarterly* 55 (Spring, 1991): 19.

5. Carlton Rochell, *Wheeler and Goldhor's Practical Administration of Public Libraries* (New York: Harper, 1981), 275-6, suggests 1% to 2%; Alice Norton, "Public Relations -- Its Meaning and Benefits," in Ellen Altman ed., *Local Public Library Administration*, 2nd ed. (Chicago: American Library Association, 1980), 48, suggests 4% to 7%.

6. Norton, 48.

7. Patricia Latshaw, "The Janus Profession: Public Relations--Looking out and Looking in," *Library Administration and Management* 3 (Summer 1989): 118.

8. Roberts and Blandy, 16.

9. Darlene Weingand, *Administration of the Small Public Library* (Chicago: American Library Association, 1992), 57.

10. Rochell, 274.

11. Lisa Kinney, *Lobby for Your Library* (Chicago: American Library Association, 1992), 22.

12. Ibid., 24.

Sugggested Reading

Grunenwald, Joseph. *Developing a Marketing Program for Libraries.* Clarion, PA: Clarion University of Pennsylvania,1989.

Harris, Thomas. *The Marketer's Guide to Public Relations.* NY: Wiley, 1991.

Hill, Dennis. *Power PR.* Hollywood, CA: Fell, 1990.

Kies, Cosette. *Marketing and Public Relations for Libraries.* Metuchen, NJ: Scarecrow Press, 1987.

Kinney, Lisa. *Lobby for Your Library.* Chicago: American Library Association, 1992.

Kohn, Rita and Krysta Tepper. *You Can Do It; A PR Skills Guide for Librarians.* Metuchen, NJ: Scarecrow Press, 1981.

Kotler, Philip. *Strategic Marketing for Nonprofit Organizations.* 3rd ed. Englewood Cliffs, NJ: Prentice Hall, 1987.

Leeburger, Benedict. *Promoting and Marketing the Library.* Rev ed. Boston: G.K. Hall, 1989.

Norton, Alice. "Public Relations -- Its Meaning and Benefits," in Altman, Ellen, ed. *Local Public Library Administration.* 2nd ed. Chicago: American Library Association, 1980.

Roberts, Anne and Susan Blandy. *Public Relations for Librarians.* Englewood, CO: Libraries Unlimited, 1989.

Sherman, Steve. *ABC's of Library Promotion.* 3rd ed. Metuchen, NJ: Scarecrow Press, 1992.

Weingand, Darlene. *Marketing for Libraries and Information Agencies.* Norwood, NJ: Ablex, 1984.

CHAPTER 16

THE DIRECTOR

Library directors face both the internal world of the library and the external one that is the community. Through the head librarian flow directives *from* the *municipality* that funds it; the *community* that uses it; and the *board* that sets its policies *to* the *staff* that mounts and offers library service. Reversing the process, the head librarian must carry messages *from* the library staff *to* the *municipality* about funds the library requires to carry out its program; to the *community* about the possibilities and limitations of library services; and to the *board* about its plans, programs, operations and conditions. Lynch pin is only one of many roles that library directors play. They also act as visionaries, institutional value setters, mentors and as ultimate exercisers and bearers of authority and responsibility for the operation of the library.

The twentieth-century shift in organizations from autocratic to participative has begun to effect fundamental changes in the relationship between library directors and employees. One oft-repeated cautionary tale about the rigidness of library administration-staff relations describes the response to a request from a New York Public Library branch worker for several days leave in which to marry. The branch librarian, it is reported, took the young woman by the arm, walked her to a large window facing the city hall area, noted that the marriage bureau was within walking distance and suggested that two hours would suffice to complete the procedure. Librarians no longer exercise hegemony over their workplaces though hints of authoritarian behavior remain in the bureaucratic structure most public libraries still follow.

CAREER PATTERNS

Only recently has the profession begun systematically to study the roles, work and nature of library directors. The little research, although limited by geography, small samples, and public library size, has produced some interesting findings, particularly in gender-related matters. An investigation into directors of Northeastern medium-sized public libraries, probably generalizable to similar-sized libraries across the nation, reveals that 57% are directed by females.[1] This compares with the 21% figure found to be directing libraries with budgets over $1 million[2] and leads to the conclusion that "the larger the library, the less likely it is to be directed by a woman."[3]

More than half of the directors of medium sized public libraries are between the ages of 35 and 44.[4] Those of larger libraries average about 52.6[5] and have had 16 to 28 years of experience.[6] Women directors tend to be somewhat older than men[7] and to have attained their directorships at a later age.[8] More women than men remain single.[9]

Females are more likely than males to have advanced within a single system. Males move in increasingly higher positions from one library to another.[10] Medium-sized public libraries recruit their directors regionally.[11] Large ones cast wider nets.

In medium-sized libraries about a third of the men and a tenth of the women hold graduate degrees in addition to the MLS.[12] For larger libraries, the figure is closer to 50%.[13] Heads of large libraries are active publishers in the professional literature.[14]

Directors of large libraries have "a deep and intense belief that what they are doing is not only satisfying, but deeply significant."[15] Directors of small or medium-sized libraries also find librarianship satisfying although many complain of being underpaid and overworked.[16] Some commentators have worried that too much job satisfaction can lead to stasis. Mech warns, for instance, that

> many directors have very comfortable situations. A marriage, family and satisfying career in a community that is home to them and their family and friends can be a very secure and lulling

environment. This environment combined with limited mobility may create an unconscious situation where the last thing directors want to do is "rock the boat."[17]

to which Boss might add the corollary

...the manager who makes relatively fewer mistakes may actually be declining in managerial effectiveness and sidestepping the very administrative and supervisory responsibilities that are the essential content of his or her work.[18]

More than half the directors of large public libraries report having benefitted from mentors who helped them along the way. Mostly white, middle-aged males, mentors played critical roles in providing career opportunities, instilling confidence and acting as models for their proteges.[19]

THE WORK OF DIRECTORS

Library directors are charged with delivering the best possible library service, consistent with preestablished policies, that can be purchased with available funds . Among their duties are:

to staff the library; to plan and carry out the library's programs;

to assess its progress and success and report periodically about it to the staff, board and community;

to market the library's services and programs to its public;

to gauge the library's funding needs and articulate them through a budget; to assure an adequate collection of materials to support community needs;

to provide professional library leadership to the staff and the community; and to manage and administer the operation of the library.

A number of typologies have been devised to describe the work of library directors. Mech divides the external and internal roles as pictured on the following page.

Directors of middle-sized public libraries spend more time and effort on their internal managerial roles than on their external ones.

External	Internal
Figurehead	Leader
Liaison	Disseminator
Monitor	Entrepreneur
Spokesperson	Disturbances Handler
Negotiator	Resource Allocator[20]

Independent solitary pursuits such as administrative paperwork, correspondence, reports, planning and evaluation occupy significant amounts of their attention as do building and maintenance problems, and dealing with vendors. Too many directors, unprepared educationally and psychologically for managerial positions, never learn to delegate or leave behind day-to-day operations.

Directors of larger libraries, those with more robust administrative staffs that include associate and assistant directors, emphasize their relations with individuals and organizations outside of the library to a greater extent.

Paying excessive attention to internal problems, even of the larger kind, can be detrimental to public libraries. Some directors avoid dealing with municipalities in their efforts to remain apolitical. Others find external managerial roles that take them into areas where they have no control very stressful. It is in the public arena, however, where libraries must compete with other agencies for limited and ever-shrinking resources.

> Unfortunately there are winners and losers. Losers are not necessarily the organizations that have least to offer; they are often the organizations least prepared to express their value and contribution in terms understood by their funders.[21]

As the most visible representative of the library, directors cannot afford to lose any opportunity to state positively the library case to the outside world, particularly to members of the political structure. Regular contact with politicians strengthens the library's position, but carries the potential danger of cooptation, of becoming the person who can always be counted on to do the bidding of those in power. In this situation, learning to say "no" is crucial.

Directors who pay too little attention to the internal organization run a commensurate risk. The buck, to paraphrase Harry Truman's famous admonition, does not stop at the assistant or associate director's desk, but at the library director's. While managerial talent in staff can help lessen the burden of demands on the director, no head librarian can abdicate his or her responsibility for running the organization. Knowledgeable directors never lose touch. They move around the library frequently, learn the names of employees at all levels, periodically "work" a desk, find methods of communicating with staff. Directors whose public service staff members routinely ask them, "How may I help you," because their faces are unfamiliar are receiving a very important message.

Joanne Euster, in her study of academic library directors, isolated four main types of head librarians whose counterparts are easily located in public libraries. She named them *Energizers, Sustainers, Politicians* and *Retirees. Energizers,* she found, are most closely associated with change; *Retirees* are most content to sit on their laurels, while *Sustainers* and *Politicians,* respectively, concern themselves with existing processes or with cultivating people. While good directors combine characteristics of all types except *Retirees,* Euster maintains that certain times and situations call for particular management styles and approaches.[22]

LEADERSHIP AND MANAGEMENT

All successful libraries demand competent managers, people who understand the nature of the organization, how it works, how its parts mesh. Smooth-running operations have been well-oiled by efficient and effective managers who deliver day-to-day service in an orderly fashion.

There has been a tendency in library literature to equate management with leadership. However, one can be a manager without being a leader, just as one may be a leader and not be manager. Among the distinctions made between the two are the source of the power to influence. Managers are vested with authority by persons outside the organization. Leaders are willingly accorded authority by group members. Headship and leadership are neither mutually exclusive nor are they mutually coincidental.

Another discriminant used to differentiate the roles of leaders and managers is that the former focus on change and the latter on the use of resources. Leadership, according to this distinction, is more than effective management.

> The critical writings are clearly asking for something more. They are seeking behaviors which will enable organizations to adjust to social and technological change, to develop meaningful goals, to design and implement the systems necessary to implement those goals, and to marshall the necessary resources.[23]

Among the most difficult questions that have plagued leadership theorists over time is whether leadership can be learned or whether it is innate. Contemporary thinking holds that people can learn or teach themselves the skills of leadership. Based on this premise, it seems possible to increase leadership skills by:

1. Improving *selection* and placing more appropriate persons in director positions;

2. *Training* them in conceptual skills, creativity, and -- the most difficult of all -- human relations.

3. *Engineering situations* to improve their compatibility with available leaders.

4. *Developing organizations and improving leadership* which may necessitate intervention by consultants -- specially trained change

agents -- who help with communication, decision-making and interpersonal relations, as well as with goal setting, training sessions and team building.

VALUES AND VISION

All competent library directors recognize what would comprise excellent library service if optimal conditions -- generous financial support and talented, able staff -- obtain. It is this vision, clearly articulated both internally and externally, that creates the social character of the institution and sets its values.

Directors communicate a shared interpretation of organizational events so that members know how they are expected to behave. They generate a commitment to primary organizational values and philosophy and serve as a control mechanism, sanctioning or proscribing particular kinds of behavior.[24] Without this shared vision, the library staff is unlikely to exhibit a high degree of commitment. The visions and values of any library director are contextual, forged in the crucible of personal and professional experience. Those with limited backgrounds may bring this same limited orientation to the library.

Clarity of purpose -- vision -- is easily lost in the myriad daily preoccupations that confront library directors. Without it, directors risk manipulation. The life of a head librarian is made up of dozens of decisions each day, some of such immediate nature that little time is available for prolonged consideration. The culmination of an entire budget negotiation may be reached with a sudden offer by a politician to settle for a particular figure -- to take it or leave it. The director must calculate instantaneously what the budget figure means in terms of service implications as well as whether the library can afford the settlement and still meet community needs. The offer must be calculated and filtered through a firm value system to avoid damaging, perhaps disastrous results.

Returning to the important texts of librarianship, reading the new literature, attending workshops and continuing education courses, and participating in professional organizations can serve to remind librarians of their lost vision and can broaden limited horizons.

It is not only permissible but desireable for librarians to hold alternate opinions about many issues. However, U.S. librarians should accept and be committed to the precepts of the First Amendment of the U.S. Constitution, to the *Library Bill of Rights* and to the *Freedom to Read* statement. The basic assumptions of these documents represent litmus tests to govern how controversies involving library materials, staff, policies and services are resolved. It is a tenet of library faith that all users must have equality of access and opportunity to use information without regard to differences in race, culture, religion, ethnicity, economic status, education or sexual preference. These are the principles that guide operational definitions of access.

Directors transmit to staff the belief that good libraries make a difference, that societies are better because libraries and librarians exist, and what it means to provide excellent library service in a pluralistic society.

POWER AND DELEGATION

In order to discharge the assignments that form the substance of head librarians' positions, directors must acquire or be granted the powers to sustain their actions. When directors accede to office, it is assumed that they also gain power. Many new library CEOs take bold action only to face quick repudiation because what they thought was power was simply authority. Real power in libraries, like leadership, is earned and conferred over time and by the library constituency -- its governing authority (trustees and local government), its staff, the library's public, and to some extent the professional community. These forces confirm a director's real power and capacity to act on behalf of the institution. In normal circumstances, new executives are wise to move cautiously during the first six months of their tenure. However, when a previous executive has been removed because of institutional abuses, a new director must move quickly to relieve the situation. To do less may forfeit permanently staff and governing authority confidence. "Consistent misuse of authority or demonstrated incompetence will necessarily lead to diminished status and loss of legitimate authority."[25] Unless staff support is gained, the director may endure but the library will never thrive. Nor can public library directors succeed without the support of the governing authority, local politicians or the public.

Power in libraries exists to serve the needs of the institution rather than the personal ones of its executives. Even when pursuing organizational goals, power must be exercised within a framework, a social compact, mutually understood by members and governors of the organization. In the library world this compact demands greater participation in management by employees. Power wielded for its own sake threatens to fracture the organization's harmony and makes the achievement of goals virtually impossible. Unfortunately, abuses of power in libraries are not unknown.

In order for the director to concentrate on essential activities, some power, control and authority must be delegated to staff. Decisions about which tasks to delegate might be reached by directors determining the ones they are being *overpaid* to perform. Successful delegation dictates that the right people be selected and trained to do the jobs and the results monitored and evaluated frequently. Library directors are never completely divorced from responsibility for delegated jobs and must not hesitate to reclaim the tasks that are not being successfully handled.

WORK PATTERNS

Research has revealed that most library directors do not manage their time well and that meetings, telephone interruptions, drop-in visitors and attempts to do too much are among the major causes of mismanagement.[26]

A number of factors have been identified as contributing to the poor use of time:

1. Librarians who become directors have typically emerged

from the ranks of public service personnel where frequent interruptions were not only expected, but welcomed. Restricting interruptions is not easy for this group.

2. Many librarians feel insecure and overwhelmed by the rapid developments in information technology and the necessity that they remain knowledgeable about them.

3. As a group, librarians formalize methods and channels of communication, sometimes resulting in excessive numbers of meetings they must plan and attend.

4. Library work is never done. Most activities continue and librarians are rarely able to celebrate the closure of a project.

Among other specific time management problems that library directors face are committee work, problems in delegations, undertaking too much work, and failing to identify goals and priorities.

Setting good work patterns is a personal, individual undertaking. Library administrators differ in management styles; staffs differ in their needs for supervision. "Effective time management exists when administrators' styles match the needs of employees."[27]   Some universally practiced techniques for managerial success are setting personal and professional goals and objectives; helping staff set them for themselves; learning how to delegate; mounting a plan of action that enables rational organization of tasks; and, above all, investigating how time is regularly spent.

Continually reviewing activities may bring to the surface time wasting endeavors -- excessive paper shuffling, daydreaming, perfectionism, unnecessary attention to routine detail or inability to establish priorities. Among the major time-wasting problems librarians face is the tendency to procrastinate. Complex factors lead to delaying important actions and decisions. Among these may be fear of failure, fear of success, avoiding judgment, feeling of hopelessness, avoiding unpleasant work, feeling overwhelmed, personal control, habit and lack of information.[28] A number of techniques have been suggested to deal with procrastination, the most important of which is realizing and acknowledging its presence. Training can help with procrastination as well as other problems associated with inadequate use of time, and poor work patterns.

RELATIONS WITH THE LIBRARY'S BOARD

The pages of public library literature are littered with case histories of boards of trustees and library directors engaged in power struggles or discordant and confrontational relationships. Directors accuse boards of wishing to administer and manage the library; boards accuse directors *de facto* of setting policy, of usurping their powers.

A continuum of relationships exists, strewn between the poles of unshared-autocratic and shared-delegated exercising of power; the adversarial approach versus the collegial or "team" mode of operation.[29]

Boards unarguably are the formal sources of power, power which they must limit in order to exercise it well. The best relations are established through good communication, mutual respect, shared goals and clarity about roles and responsibilities. Substantial advantages accrue to directors and trustees when relationships of a less formal nature than the once-monthly meeting are established.

Performance Evaluation

The performance of library directors requires regular, mandatory, consistently applied evaluation. The degree to which boards currently appraise directors probably ranges from none to totally. Some head librarians receive annual evaluations from the board, although they can be informal or perfunctory in nature. Trustees without supervisory experience can find the appraisal process uncomfortable, if not unpleasant.

The lack of a tradition of peer or subordinate review in public libraries means the director is evaluated only by the trustees. A number of progressive libraries now ask staff to evaluate a library director's performance. All managerial functions are amenable to staff assessment. Among the considerations may be for instance, the director's willingness to delegate; to give commensurate authority; to act quickly and decisively when resolving problems and the extent of objectivity utilized while addressing personnel problems. Evaluations by staff members can shed fresh and different light on a director's performance and they should be heard by both the director and the board. Administrators who resist evaluation from below, claiming that subordinates lack sufficiently broad perspectives to make useful judgments, may be shortsighted and imprudent. The purposes of performance evaluation are to provide useful information to the library director about how he or she is doing and where improvement is necessary, and to insure that the board meets its accountability responsibility by assessing how well the director has fulfilled the mission of the library and expended the public's funds.

The director's evaluation should encompass the following categories:

Administration - the efficiency and effectiveness of the library operation;
Leadership - the tone and direction of the organization;
Budget and Finance - the ability to develop a realistic budget, to administer the wage and salary system and to obtain outside funding;
Communication - with staff, board members and the public;
Decision-making and Problem Solving - the logic, objectivity, correctness and appropriateness of decisions;
Public Relations - relating effectively to the public or other agencies and creating a positive image of the library;
Development of Human Resources - hiring, evaluating, disciplining and terminating staff, as well as building morale, and recognizing high performance;
Professional Development - both of the director and the staff.[30]

Directors prepare for evaluation by reviewing the events of the intervening period between the last evaluation and the current one. They may update their vitae and briefly summarize the period's accomplishments, both personal ones and those of the library. During the evaluation itself, conversation between directors and board members will progress from accomplishments to new goals and to areas where improvement is desired. If performance is judged unsatisfactory, directors are entitled to be so informed, to learn the areas of substantial dissatisfaction and to have a date given for reconsideration of their efforts. Though potentially stressful, when approached positively performance evaluations almost always produce salutary results that redound to the benefit of the library and the director.

Termination of a Director

Though not frequent, from time to time library directors must be fired. Serious dissatisfaction with performance mandates immediate and firm handling. If reviews have repeatedly revealed negative performance and if there has been no improvement, then the director's relationship with the library must be severed, either by forced resignation or outright firing. Written documentation, gathered over time, provides justification of the action. Due process is further satisfied by holding a termination hearing at which all documentation leading up to the action is reviewed, the reasons for the termination are explained, and the ground rules for departure, including when the termination will be effective and any severance benefits that will be awarded, explained. Indeed, lack of such a "due process" hearing, or any other "due process" procedural steps, can leave a library vulnerable in the event legal action were to follow a dismissal.

RECRUITMENT OF A LIBRARY DIRECTOR

The recruitment of a new public library director is among the most important responsibilities that face the board of trustees and also among its most difficult. The selection process can be a factor in determining how a new director is accepted by the staff. A legitimate process serves to confer legitimacy on the person selected. One that is conducted unethically or is inconsistently administered may throw doubt on the choice.

Before embarking on a search, the board must answer several important questions. It must establish a search schedule that includes a time line and budget. It must clarify for itself what it is seeking in an administrator. Not every talented candidate is suitable for every vacancy. Choosing the best person means matching an applicant's strengths with the needs of the library and the character of the surrounding environment.

Trustees must also decide who will participate in the search. Generally a subcommittee of the board is appointed, to which is added staff representatives, members of the lay public and perhaps representatives of local government. Including the former director is never advisable, although there seems to be a natural tendency to do so, particularly if the previous head librarian has been successful and is respected.

Many experts recommend that boards consider the assistance of an external advisor or consultant. Although board members may be willing to commit the time and effort necessary to locate a new director, they may lack appropriate knowledge to undertake a successful search. Governing authorities often depend on the position's former occupant to describe the vacancy. Previous incumbents, however, may be limited by their concept of the position and be unable to broaden its dimensions. An outsider, particularly one knowledgeable about contemporary public libraries, can assist, not only in checking recommendations and setting up procedures, but in the basic work of helping to define the job and update or rewrite the position description based on a new understanding of what it entails.

The search team develops the details of the search strategy, conducts the search and narrows down the field to the three to five most suitable candidates.

Finally, the board must decide whether the search will be local, regional or national and must establish the remuneration it will offer to and credentials that it will demand from an applicant. The board should ask for, at a minimum, a Master's Degree in librarianship from an ALA accredited graduate program. It should also recommend an amount of experience appropriate to the size of the library and the job's responsibilities. Potential excellence can, on occasion, substitute for specific experience and boards may find it wise to suggest rather than require a specific number of years of professional work experience. Candidates need not be limited to those with previous public library experience. Other library work environments can provide relevant organizational experiences.

The choice of a new executive is significantly restricted when libraries are governed by local or state civil service systems. In this case there may be a list of eligible candidates based on some kind of examination from which a selection must be made. Fortunately, a number of states have exempted the library director from civil service eligibility.

In order to generate applications, the vacancy must be clearly and succinctly advertised in those places where candidates would be most likely to see it. For public libraries this would include the nearest metropolitan newspaper, one or two professional publications such as *Library Journal, American Libraries, Wilson Library Bulletin* or *Library Hot Line*. In addition, notices sent to telephone joblines and placement centers can produce lively candidates. Recruiting at national library conferences is effective because it allows for personal interviews.

Advertising the position is also advertising the library.[31] The broad picture painted of the library with the few brief details can encourage or dissuade applicants. Applicants who become candidates should be sent a full packet of information about the library, including annual reports, long range and master plans, and other statistical and narrative in house and external documents in order that they may become knowledgeable before any visit to the library is scheduled.

After the list has been narrowed, finalists all receive interviews.

References are checked prior to their arrival at the library. Written recommendations are likely to be far less revelatory than those communicated orally when candor can prevail after a guarantee of confidentiality. When the list has been narrowed to just a few, it is legitimate to call other people in the candidate's former work place who do not appear on the list of references.

The interview can be predetermined, but not rote. It is wise to formulate a set of objective questions related to the library's needs, desires and concerns to pose to the candidates. The committee can then evaluate and compare the approach taken by each potential director to the challenges of the position. Personal matters such as marital status, age, religious practices are not appropriate topics for interviews. Interviews that extend longer than two hours become nonproductive. Candidates should be assessed by the search team as soon as their interviews are terminated. A formal evaluation schedule is useful as a springboard for discussion.

The final decision should be reached on the basis of who has the ability to best perform the director's position. In the past, and occasionally today, directors are chosen because they belong to the right group, or because they don't belong to the wrong one. Obviously competence is and should be its own recommendation.

Other considerations that may help to narrow the decision include whether a finalist is overqualified; whether a candidate will be comfortable, yet challenged by the position; and whether the potential director simply represents stasis or whether he or she will bring a new perspective to the job and the library.

Directors should never be hired simply because they are the best of a bad lot. It is far preferable and cheaper in the long run to reinstitute the search than it is to settle for a lesser candidate.

THE NEW DIRECTOR

New directors invariably both bring and attract anxiety. They generally come from lesser ranks and must learn on the job, particularly if they are inexperienced in management. Unfortunately, during this bumpy honeymoon period, they are scrupulously observed by older staff members for portents of the shape of the new administration. New directors, therefore, must exercise great restraint in their words and actions at the beginning of their tenure.

The two most important objectives of a new director should be to put the staff at ease about the incoming administration and to learn everything about the organization and the way it functions. The following list, culled from a number of library experts, outlines useful steps and strategies to adopt during a first year in office:

1. Hold periodic meetings with top and middle managers in order to begin to understand their capabilities and how to influence them.

2. Meet both informally with the library board or governing authority. Formal meetings occur routinely. Informal ones must be arranged.

3. Know by name both elected and appointed local officials. They hold great power over libraries. This may entail attending meetings of the local governing body or becoming part of the executive team that administers local jurisdictions.

4. Establish a presence with major educational, cultural and social groups and institutions in the community. This involves contacting PTA's, service organizations and social clubs. Seek out every opportunity to speak to them about the library.

5. Get to know representatives of the local media, reporters, editors, publishers and station managers.

6. Make friends with the people in the "Friends" group. It is vital that they feel a part of the total library effort. They can be invaluable if properly treated and divisive if ignored or mishandled.

7. Call and introduce yourself to directors of other libraries in the area and state. Share data, visit sites and gain insights and assistance from them. Later, there may be opportunities to develop new service partnerships with them.

8. Become familiar with relevant data concerning the local library and the local community.

9. Spend time in all agencies and departments of the library.

10. Have the staff go on a retreat and work on the tasks of

team building and goal setting.

   11. Attend community events.

   12. Decide which programs the library does well and begin to brag about the library's strengths to the staff and the community.

   13. Listen to all parties involved for at least three months before taking actions that affect individuals or programs.

   14. Plan a vacation and take it.

   15. Thank people as you go along for their help and their work.

   16. Try to establish one new program for one group within the first year of a new directorship.

   17. Strengthen or begin staff development programs for librarians and support staff.

The most important recommendation offered by seasoned directors -- implicit in all the others -- is to use library, board and community colleagues as mentors, friends, resources, stimulators and sounding boards. The honeymoon period whether it lasts three, six or twelve months, is a time for information gathering, developing relationships and beginning to plan for the process of change which a new administration usually brings.

RELATIONS WITH STAFF

Staff deserve to be challenged, encouraged and rewarded for work well done, as well as to receive constructive criticism when performance is less satisfactory. Good work experiences often form the basis for future career choices, and influence the delivery of service to the public. Directors, as the staff's voice to the board, must assure that staffs are well compensated, paid a salary at least commensurate with peer institutions, and are given professional opportunities. Staff have a right to expect that they will know what is happening in and to the library and that they will have opportunities to participate in it.

Recruiting New Librarians

Directors are charged with properly staffing the library. They also bear some responsibility for recruiting new members to the profession. Some people are attracted to librarianship because they perceive the work to be routine and non-demanding. If these beliefs are reinforced by the libraries they experience as support staff, the profession will suffer. Directors must assure that professional librarians are not performing clerical tasks, but are engaged in planning and evaluating work. Stimulating library directors make librarianship attractive and exciting. Mentoring and recruiting for the profession are among a director's most important jobs.

SUMMARY

As organizations are evolving from authoritarian to participative, so too are library directors' positions undergoing restructuring. Nonetheless, the broad latitude to shape the institution's value system and to provide a vision of excellent library service remains. Sharing that vision with members of the user community, the library board and the staff helps gain acceptance of the library's program and instills commitment.

New directors face special problems. A wide, thorough search for the best person, one whose qualities mesh with the library's needs legitimates the appointee in the eyes of the community and the staff. However, new directors must take the time to learn about the institution, its traditions, its strengths and weaknesses before imposing change. Library boards and staff have a right to expect a quality performance from the director and the director, in turn, has the right to expect ongoing evaluation and recognition for a job well done.

NOTES AND SUGGESTED READINGS

Notes

1. Terrence Mech, "Public Library Directors: A Career and Managerial Profile," *Public Libraries* 28 (July/August. 1989): 228.

2. Elfreda Chatman, "The Role of Mentorship in Shaping Public Library Leaders," *Library Trends* 40 (Winter 1992): 499.

3. Mech., 228.

4. Ibid.

5. Chatman, 499-500.

6. Joy Greiner, "A Comparative Study of Management Styles and Career Progression Patterns of Recently Appointed Males and Female Public Library Administrators (1983-87)," in Gerard McCabe and Bernard Kreissman, eds. *Advances in Library Administration and Organization* 7 (Greenwich, CT: JAI Press. 1988): 4.

7. Ibid.

8. Mech, 228.

9. Greiner, 4.

10. Ibid., and Mech, 230-31.

11. Mech, 232

12. Ibid., 229.

13. Chatman,.499.

14. Ibid.

15. Brooke Sheldon ,"Library Leaders: Attributes Compared to Corporate Leaders," *Library Trends* 40 (Winter 1992): 400.

16. Mech, 231

17. Mech, 232.

18. Boss, Richard, *The Library Manager's Guide to Automation.* 3rd ed. (Boston: G.K. Hall, 1990), 131.

19. Chatman, 506-7.

20. Mech's typology is based on an interpretation of Mintzberg by Moskowitz. Mech, 233.

21. W. David Penniman, "On Their Terms: Preparing Librarians for a Competitive Environment," in Betty-Carol Sellen and Betty Turock, eds., *The Bottom Line Reader* (New York: Neal-Schuman, 1990), 4.

22. Joanne Euster, *The Academic Library Director: Management Activities and Effectiveness* (New York: Greenwood Press, 1987).

23. Joanne Euster, "The Qualities of Leadership," in Alice Gertzog, ed., *Leadership in the Library/Information Profession* (Jefferson, NC: McFarland, 1989), 6.

24. Sheldon, 394.

25. Jennifer Cargill and Gisela Webb, *Managing Libraries in Transition* (Phoenix, AZ: Oryx Press, 1988), 62.

26. J. Wesley Cochran, *Time Management Handbook for Librarians* (Westport CT: Greenwood, 1992), 4.

27. Ibid., 72.

28. Ibid., 31-33.

29. Cameron Alexander et al, "Public Library Boards and Chief Librarians: A Creative Balance," *Canadian Library Journal* (April, 1992): 136.

30. Richard Rubin, *Human Resource Management in Libraries* (New York: Neal-Schuman, 1991), 129-135.

31. Raymond Chadwick, "The Executive Search: Recruiting the Library Director," *Public Libraries* 28 (March/April 1989): 116.

Suggested Readings

Albritton, Rosie and Thomas Shaughnessy. *Developing Leadership Skills: A Sourcebook for Librarians.* Englewood, CO: Libraries Unlimited, 1990.

Blake, Virgil. *Joining City Hall: The Role of the Public Library Director in Obtaining Support for the Public Library.* New Brunswick, NJ: Rutgers University (unpublished doctoral dissertation), 1988.

Cargill, Jennifer and Gisela Webb. *Managing Libraries in Transition.* Phoenix, AZ: Oryx Press, 1988.

Gertzog, Alice, ed. *Leadership in the Library/Information Profession.* Jefferson, NC: McFarland, 1989.

Ihrig, Alice. *Decision Making for Public Libraries.* Hamden, CT: Shoe String Press, 1989.

Moran, Barbara. ed. "Libraries and Librarians: Meeting the Leadership Challenges of the 21st Century." *Library Trends* 40 (Winter 1992).

Sheldon, Brooke. *Leaders in Libraries: Styles and Strategies of Success.* Chicago: American Library Association, 1991.

Woodrum, Pat. *Managing Public Libraries in the 21st Century.* New York: Haworth, 1989.

Wozny, Jay. *Checklists for Public Library Managers.* Metuchen, NJ: Scarecrow Press, 1989.

CHAPTER 17

HUMAN RESOURCES

The best conceived library plan, firm financial footing, a deep reservoir of community good will and support all matter little unless a library is serviced by talented, able, willing employees who share purpose and commitment. A good staff breathes life into a library; a poor one saps its energy and strength.

Mounting an effective human resources program entails identifying, recruiting, hiring and utilizing appropriate staff, devising an unbiased position classification system, insuring adequate compensation and benefits, recognizing merit and encouraging job mobility and advancement. An inherently difficult task, for public libraries it is further complicated by an increasingly complex civil service system and the rapid growth of unions among library professionals and support staff.

A multitude of terms have been utilized to describe the combination of ingredients needed to staff a library. Human resources, the phrase employed in this chapter, is defined as the process

--by which jobs are organized into a cohesive career service to accomplish the institution's purposes;

--the manner in which personnel are chosen, trained and evaluated;

--how libraries deal with civil service, labor unions and federal and state personnel legislation.

STAFF SIZE AND COMPOSITION

The latest public library quantitative standards, those issued in 1966, set staff size at one employee for every 2,000 people in a service area. Recently, numerical standards have yielded to an approach that emphasizes the needs of individual libraries based on their own program definition as reached through the planning process, rather than by reliance on external factors. Staff size is now more often determined by the nature of a community and the roles the library has chosen to emphasize than by the aggregate numbers of people serviced. A community whose members have achieved high levels of education are heavier users of the library than one whose population exhibits a high degree of illiteracy and will generate the need for more staff. If, however, the library focuses on circulation of popular adult materials rather than on providing comprehensive reference services, than the demand for professional staff is lessened. On the other hand, a strong commitment to outreach and group programming is both labor intensive and professionally taxing. Staff size, then, is a function of the nature of the community a library hopes to serve and the way in which it attempts to deliver that service.

The typical public library consists of librarians and support staff. Other categories of workers -- technical experts who manage the library's automation effort or who are skilled in public relations or personnel; paraprofessionals who have training in library routines and processes, high school pages and volunteers -- may be present on the staff, but the basic division between librarians and support staff remains, with an average ratio of one of the former to three of the latter.

Professionals

Professional librarians hold at least a master's degree in library or information science, and often have earned an additional master's or a doctorate. They serve in leadership positions, direct departments, plan and develop new programs, assign execution and maintenance of ongoing programs to others and utilize their special skills to fulfill the information needs of the library's clientele. Librarians are expected to apply theory and expertise to solving library problems. In the past, many tasks assigned to librarians could have been performed by clerks. As a result, it was not uncommon for frustrated librarians to leave the field for more challenging and creative opportunities. Other librarians who remained with the library, settled for less and accepted work assignments that demanded little from them. Unfortunately, there are many holdovers from this earlier era in libraries today. Years of conditioning have made them reluctant to modify their behavior, even as their institutions experience cataclysmic change. Job security becomes the paramount concern with routine -- non-threatening and comforting -- the goal.

Professional librarians entering the field today are dissatisfied with the limitations their predecessors sometimes accepted. They seek autonomy, variety, innovation and flexibility in a quality work environment in which they can utilize their individual strengths. The "compleat" librarian, a relatively recent concept, accepts responsibilities in both public and technical services and is willing to participate holistically in the entire library, rather than only in some of its parts. Libraries can develop arrangements for staff to work together to accomplish certain tasks, a further departure on the "compleat" model.

Support Staff

Support staff use learned procedures to work out repetitive, day-to-day difficulties. Their jobs encompass a wide range of positions and abilities. They can be para-professionals, technical specialists, library assistants or clerks. The largest group of library employees, their responsibilities include the routine tasks of most departments. They can have educational backgrounds ranging from completion of high school to completion of graduate school. Public libraries have been fortunate in their ability to attract highly educated and talented employees -- generally women -- for nonprofessional positions. Unfortunately, tensions may arise when over-qualified personnel function in clerical, support positions. For instance, resentments are created when entry-level professional librarians who lack site-specific technical knowledge must be trained by seasoned, experienced support staff or when professionals are unfamiliar with routine procedures followed rotely by technical assistants. The strain can be overcome, at least partially, by encouraging an organizational climate that minimizes the division between professional and support staff, that includes the latter in staff development activities, task forces and on search committees. Some blurring between professional and support staff tasks seems inevitable. Distinctions between professional and support staff are effaced when experienced employees who lack formal credentials are placed in charge of periodicals, acquisitions, or circulation. Support staff, particularly those with advanced degrees, represent a fertile recruiting ground for professional librarians and deserve encouragement in that pursuit. Many libraries grant time off, education supplements and other incentives to support staff who choose to enroll in library schools.

Pages

Pages are an important group of library support staff. They are charged with shelving books and periodicals, or in a few libraries or with specific types of materials, retrieving them. Traditionally, high school students played this role. When differentials in the minimum wage based on age were permitted, libraries routinely recruited high school students as pages. After the law was changed to apply equally to all categories of workers, some libraries replaced teenagers with more mature workers. High school students can be undependable. They frequently fail to show up for work. They are mercurial, quitting precipitously or on short notice. But there are distinct benefits to hiring students. Generally bright and quick to learn, they are often more familiar than staff with computers and other new technology, and, they have easy relations with their peers.

Some libraries have found excellent page help among senior citizens who appear to take great pride in the condition of their shelves. The drawbacks of frequent illness and the "snowbird syndrome"-- leaving colder climates for warmer ones in wintertime -- are far outweighed by their loyalty and commitment.

Volunteers

Few matters elicit more ambivalent reactions from public librarians than does the use of volunteers. A complex group of reasons accounts for their indecisive attitudes.

The ominous cloud of uncertain funding that surrounds public libraries is caused, in part, by competition from public safety and welfare, a crumbling infrastructure and losses in state and federal funding, factors that combine to place libraries under increasing public scrutiny. Public figures, at all levels, seeking to cut whatever possible corners, have suggested replacing salaried public servants with volunteers. George Bush's message identifying volunteers as "one thousand points of light," while not explicitly directed toward substituting unpaid for paid workers, nonetheless makes the practice more thinkable, perhaps even acceptable. Librarians have been less successful than attorneys or medical doctors in convincing the public that the skills they command are special and not able to be delivered by untrained workers. Many library users never encounter a professional librarian. Circulation desks, where most public transactions occur, are serviced by support staff. It is little wonder that users are unable to distinguish clerical workers from professionals and bring equal expectations to both.

Some librarians fear that widespread use of volunteers jeopardizes community funding and support. The public may believe that library work is so devoid of content that even untrained volunteers can perform it. In addition, librarians consider volunteers to be lacking discipline, undependable, and to require more staff effort than is justified by their value.

Conversely, others contend that a carefully managed volunteer effort can prove worthwhile to public libraries. Studies indicate that volunteers are used extensively.[1] They augment overworked staffs and provide special expertise. If the right volunteer is matched with the right job, the outcome will be beneficial. Even with some attendant costs, volunteers can save money. In addition, they often become a corps of committed community library supporters.

Abundant anecdotal evidence exists both for and against the use of volunteers in public libraries. What appears critical is how volunteers are organized and how their activities are managed and monitored. Parks suggests six essential components of a successful volunteer program:

1. A program of volunteers needs to be *well organized.*
2. The *staff* needs to be included in the organization of the effort.
3. Volunteers need to be assigned *meaningful tasks.*
4. Volunteer *orientation* programs are essential.
5. The library must express *appreciation* of and to its volunteers for their efforts.
6. Someone -- a staff member, a board member, or a volunteer -- must be *designated* as the person *in charge* of the program.[2]

Volunteers need to have explicit work schedules and vacation times. Volunteer contract arrangements have been used successfully by some libraries. In these situations, volunteers commit themselves to a job description and a schedule for a period of time, after which the contract may or may not be renewed. In lieu of pay, volunteers may receive a letter of recommendation. This method is particularly valuable for people reentering the work force after a hiatus, generally women who have taken time out for child bearing and rearing.

A volunteer program of any size will require heavy staff

involvement in training and supervision. The larger the volunteer effort, the greater the need for instruction and coordination. Each individual library will have to assess the relative advantages of substantial involvement in a volunteer program. Many will find a program useful. Some will not.

LIBRARY POLICIES

Personnel practices can help to reinforce or negate a librarian's sense of worth. Carefully framed and readily available, the library's rules for and about employees in the form of a personnel policy help to create a nurturing environment, particularly if the policies have been reached through the collective efforts of staff members who have struggled to make them fair and equitable. The library's personnel policy contains information about terms and conditions of employment, promotion, termination and change of position, benefits, career ladders, grievance procedures, evaluation, access to leaves, travel funds and continuing education as well as statements about non-discrimination and sexual harassment.

The tests that employees may be asked to undergo and when they may be required should be specified. These may include: medical tests for drug abuse; lie detector tests when thefts are involved; personality tests; AIDs testing; medical histories; credit checks; and arrest record checks. Decisions about the ethics of administering these tests must be reached carefully because of their serious implications about privacy and the rights of the public weighed against those of individual citizens.

Personnel Law

The policy manual must also describe federal, state and local statutes that guide public library employment. Among these are:

Minimum Wage. The *Fair Labor Standards Act of 1938* as amended, and the wages and hours laws of various states regulate the minimum wages that can be paid to employees and also assure that hours worked in excess of 40 during any single work week are compensated at time and a half. State wage laws pre-empt the federal act when the minimum wage is set at a higher rate. The *Fair Labor Standards Act* also requires that employment records be maintained for a minimum of five years.

Discrimination in Employment. Employers may not discriminate in employment practices. Title VII of the *Civil Rights Act of 1964* declares illegal discrimination against any individual in hiring, firing, compensation and conditions and privileges of employment because of race, color, sex, religion or national origin to be a violation of federal law. The *Equal Employment Opportunity Act of 1972* extends the provisions of the Act to agencies of local or state government. The Equal Employment Opportunity Commission (EEOC) is charged with enforcement of the act.

Affirmative Action. A result of Executive Order 11246 issued in 1966, this requires government contractors to remedy the effects of past discrimination to ensure an equitable distribution of women and minorities within an institution. Affirmative action does not fix quotas, require preferential hiring or the employment of unqualified people. It merely demands that an organization determine whether there are fewer minorities and women working in particular jobs than would be expected by their availability in the workforce and to set a timetable for remedying the situation if it is found to require remediation.[3]

Sexual Harassment. One increasingly important provision of the *Civil Rights Act of 1964* deals with sexual harassment. The courts have determined that sexual harassment in the workplace falls within the jurisdiction of Title VII and holds the employer responsible for maintaining a climate that discourages this behavior. Harassment means unwelcome sexual advances, requests for sexual favors and other verbal or physical conduct of a sexual nature. Violations of the act occur when:

1. submission to such conduct is made a term or condition of an

individual's employment;

2. submission to or rejection of such conduct is used as a basis for employment decisions affecting an individual;

3. such conduct has a purpose or effect of unreasonably interfering with an individual's work performance, or creating an intimidating, hostile or offensive work atmosphere.[4]

A library could be held in violation of the law if an employee were found to be guilty of sexually harassing another employee and if the employer implicitly condoned such action by failing to exercise proper control. Ignorance of a specific occurrence may not constitute an adequate defense for an employer in cases of sexual harassment; proper diligence is required.

The Age Discrimination in Employment Act. This bans discrimination against applicants over 40 and prohibits mandatory retirement.

The Vocational Rehabilitation Act of 1973. The act protects the rights of handicapped workers. More recently, *The Americans with Disabilities Act* prohibits discrimination in public entities against physically handicapped workers. The Act requires employers to make *reasonable* accommodation to known physical or mental limitations, including perhaps job structuring, modified work schedules, acquisition of special equipment, and altering accommodations to make them accessible. Routine, pre-employment inquiries regarding physical or mental disabilities are prohibited by the Act, but medical examinations, routinely and uniformly administered are permitted.

Some additional laws affecting library practice include the *Immigration Reform and Control Act of 1986* that requires employers to verify employment eligibility and the *Occupational Safety and Health Act of 1980* (OSHA) that compels employers to or serious physical harm to employees.

Laws and regulations governing personnel are complex, continually changing, and potentially damaging to libraries which violate them. Continually tracking new legislation becomes imperative.

CONDITIONS OF EMPLOYMENT

Working conditions, remuneration and benefits are the factors that enable a library to recruit and retain staff. They influence employee satisfaction, performance and attitudes toward work. Physical facilities, hours of work, vacations, health and retirement benefits, opportunities for accomplishment and advancement, and the quality of supervision, all contribute to employees' well-being and performance.

Salaries

Salaries represent the major source of income for most librarians. A public library's ability to compete for qualified staff is greatly influenced by its salary schedule, its package of fringe benefits and how it compares with similar institutions. Salary compensation schedules stem directly from job evaluation. Properly constructed, they consider the demands of the position and the environment in which it is performed, and are equitable throughout a system. A comprehensive plan groups like positions in pay grades based on the levels of training and experience required for positions and the levels of responsibility assigned to them.

Compensation is also related to salaries paid in the geographic region as well as to those that prevail in the profession. Salaries are seen as fair when there is

1. internal equity, or what employees are being paid for the job in comparison to what other employees in the same organization are being paid to do their jobs;

2. external equity, or what employees are being paid in

comparison to what employees in other organizations are being paid for performing similar jobs.[5]

A systematic approach to salary administration produces a scale that is competitive with similar libraries in a region, provides annual increases at least equal on a percentage basis with other municipal employees and merit increases based on continuing evaluation of each employee's work. Remuneration for professional librarians are fixed by reference to salaries paid locally, regionally and nationally.

Support staff wages are based on local market areas, those in the immediate vicinity of the library. Clerical help is hard to find, harder indeed than library assistants who generally lack typing or accounting skills that would make them valuable to industry. It is particularly difficult to retain the services of clerical workers when they learn that other municipal support staff are paid at higher levels. Library assistants, often overqualified and occupying positions that require less education, may have chosen the library because it offers a good work environment, proximity to a home or flexible hours. They have willingly accepted lower pay and lower status. However, the morale and enthusiasm of both clerical and library assistants must be maintained. As far as possible, a personnel program for support staff offers commensurate salaries, appropriate classification levels, suitable working conditions, flexible schedules, job enrichment, access to internal promotion and career opportunities for promising employees.

Salary increases are generally awarded annually and are based on length of service, merit or, most commonly, some combination of the two. Length of service is rewarded because of the assumption that more experienced workers are more valuable. Merit compensates quality performance, acknowledging those who work the hardest and are the most valuable. Basing pay increments on either methods has drawbacks. Length of service does not automatically equate with increased value and merit may only be in the eyes of the beholder and may encourage favoritism.

Library salary information is readily available annually from

Library salary information is readily available annually from the American Library Association's Office of Research and Office for Library Personnel Resources. Some state associations offer salary guidelines and *Library Journal* lists starting salaries each year. Library directors at comparable institutions are generally willing to share basic information about salary ranges and classification systems.

Librarianship is not a well paid profession. Salary considerations did not govern the choice most librarians made to join its ranks. They became librarians because of the nature of the work, its importance, its inherent interest and accepted the trade-offs necessitated by their decision. Passivity, however, in the face of declining individual purchasing power when salaries do not even keep pace with inflation is inappropriate behavior.

Pay Equity and Comparable Worth

The disparity between salaries paid men and women has recently concerned the library profession. It is currently illegal to pay different wages to men and women who work in substantially equal jobs. Studies, however, have revealed that while librarianship is overwhelmingly female, males occupy the vast majority of head librarian positions, and therefore receive larger pay checks.[6] Family obligations, limited mobility, and other reasons for accepting certain types of positions may partially account for the disparity. But "evidence suggest that salary discrimination for women exists even when one allows for the personal, career, and professional variations that contribute to salary differences."[7]

Pay equity has also been examined in a broader arena. Many occupations are segregated by sex, with men occupying certain fields and women others. Women who work are paid about 28 cents less on the dollar than are men.[8] Recently comparable worth, the doctrine that calls for equal pay being accorded to positions that demand matching levels of education, has won abundant support in librarianship particularly from those who contend that the doctrine of "pay equity" will not redress the needs of women in a

Association's Committee on Pay Equity issued a program to eliminate abuses by urging every political jurisdiction to take direct action to establish equity in compensation by

--eliminating differences in compensation between men and women doing comparable jobs;
--analyzing and grouping jobs by comparable value;
--basing salary levels on the value of the position;
--taking steps to end past discrimination.[10]

Not all librarians support comparable worth. Some note the difficulties involved in establishing a mechanism to measure the worth of a job. Others point to the increased labor costs employers would experience if they had to raise salaries precipitantly and the danger to women who might be faced with the loss of a job as a result. Opponents of comparable worth fear that its imposition is likely to create more problems than it will solve.

Once political judgments become a means of setting pay, the system becomes inherently divisive. There is no objective, scientific standard of fair pay. Everyone's wages cannot go up, and those who lose out will not sit idly by.[11]

The long-range prospects of the public library movement depend on the availability of a pool of candidates at least as strong as they are today. Librarians once were recruited from the ranks of educated young women whose opportunities in other fields were limited by their gender. The women's movement has successfully opened the doors to many previously closed professions. Applauding this development does not mean that its potentially negative implications for librarianship may be overlooked. Unless the profession is able to change its market value to society, the nature and number of future applicants is likely to diminish. If it cannot compete successfully with other professions, it is unlikely that able, committed personnel will be wooable. The public library as an institution holds high esteem.[12] Translating that support into higher salaries is one of the great challenges faced by the profession.

Among the steps that managers can take is to offer decent salaries, even at the risk of being understaffed, and to demand quality in performance, never settling for inferior credentials as a trade-off against higher pay. Setting salaries above the average may be a cost-effective move for a library hoping to recruit the best possible personnel and to retain them. Training replacements for positions that have been vacated is not only expensive, but means a loss, at least for some period of time, in effective service.

FRINGE BENEFITS

Compensation includes more than salaries. Fringe benefits can represent as much as 35% of a salary package. Commonly included under this rubric are retirement, health insurance, vacations, personal days, sick leave, life insurance and disability, and other specialized benefits such as tuition remission and leaves of absence.

Libraries have been more successful in gaining good benefit packages than they have in winning high salary levels, occasionally greater benefits than those allowed other public employees. Vacations, are one such area; travel allotments another. Municipalities are willing to deviate from their normal practices if a strong case can be made that the library requires these larger fringes in order to remain competitive and that the required outlay is relatively small.

Vacations and Leaves

Most public librarians receive four weeks of vacation annually, in addition to paid legal holidays. Support staff generally receive two weeks after a year of work and may increase after five or ten years to four weeks. Sick leave is provided at a rate ranging from three-quarters of a day to one and a half days per month. The amount of sick or vacation leave employees are permitted to accrue varies, although many libraries demand that the latter be utilized within a calendar year, while allowing the former to cumulate unused sick days and cash them in at retirement. Extended employee illnesses are often covered under workers' compensation funds or other disability policies. Most libraries offer staff a small number of personal leave days. Short term paid leaves cover jury duty, service, a death in the family and other emergency purposes. Public libraries as a rule do not offer sabbatic leaves, paid time off to pursue an area of study or research, but some are willing to grant leaves without pay for the purpose. Financial pressures have slowed recognition of the importance of encouraging professional employees to distance themselves from an institution and their jobs in order to gain perspective and diminish burnout.

Health Services

Medical benefits are provided by most libraries, usually in tandem with other municipal government agencies. Increasingly, dental work and vision are covered in addition to standard medical insurance for hospitalization and doctor's fees. New technology has caused some libraries to implement periodic eye examinations for workers who routinely use computer terminals.

Retirement Benefits

Retirement benefits are a standard part of most employee packages. Generally they supplement the U.S. Social Security Insurance Program, although some states have chosen not to join the federal system. Library workers participate in municipal retirement programs, where available. Some have elected to enter the Teachers Insurance and Annuity Association/College Retirement Equities Fund (TIAA/CREF). For libraries with no coverage, the American Library Association offers similar benefits in its insurance program for individuals.

WORKING CONDITIONS

Hours

Librarians are expected to work between thirty-five and forty hours a week as are support staff. For those engaged in public service work, this will mean evening and weekend hours. A number of libraries have recently experimented with flexible work schedules -- "flextime" or "flex/time" -- in the form of varied periods of time worked, number of days, intervals between days or changed starting and finishing times. Libraries that have adopted flextime plans have experienced decreased absenteeism, increased productivity and job satisfaction, improved employee morale and motivation. The same consequences have been noted when job-sharing systems have been instituted. Both, however, are difficult to implement uniformly. It is likely that experiments in alternative staff arrangements will continue in light of the numbers of two-career families with young children, single parents and older adults in the work force.

Physical Facilities
    The lack of certain physical amenities will cause employees to become dissatisfied and, perhaps, to depart the library. Severe overcrowding, noisy, dusty, dirty buildings without adequate heating and ventilating systems may result in high turnover. Sufficient lighting, proper equipment, adequate work space, bright and attractive quarters all contribute to good morale. The link between employee satisfaction and productivity, on the one hand, and good working conditions on the other is sufficient justification to develop a schedule of systematic maintenance and improvement of library staff work areas. A comfortable physical environment is a necessary, although not sufficient, condition to motivate staff to accomplish quality work.

CIVIL SERVICE

    A product of the reform movement of the late nineteenth century, civil service was instituted in public employment to substitute merit in hiring, performance, and promotion for the "spoils system" which rewarded political supporters of those in power by placing them on public payrolls. Many public libraries now operate under either state-wide or local civil services systems that feature methods of ranking prospective employees through examination or evaluation of experience and training, or both, and of regulating promotion and transfer. Most civil service systems incorporate a well defined personnel classification and job evaluation system, a well articulated performance evaluation system and open competition for promotions.

Proponents of civil service claim that the system has been relatively successful in limiting political excesses, has introduced objective methods of evaluating potential employees and promoting present ones, and has provided a fair grievance mechanism that protects the rights of both public employees and the public.

Opponents disagree. No proof exists, they contend, about the relationship between test-taking and performing well in a position. Yet civil service demands that selections and promotions be based on scores from competitive examinations. Less qualified candidates remain on appointment lists for years, eventually securing appointment after higher ranked ones have been chosen for other positions. Civil service, critics argue, almost guarantees the appointment and retention of less qualified employees since ranking is over time experience-based and therefore rewards those least likely to be mobile and adventurous. Further, the system makes firing unproductive employees virtually impossible given the burden of proof and length of time necessary before termination is permitted.

Both sides of the civil service debate offer compelling arguments. The role of politics has been curtailed. But the system often does reward mediocrity. Some flexibility is built into civil service since choice between the top three or five candidates is generally permitted. While red tape hampers management's ability to maneuver, it also safeguards employees against unfair and arbitrary actions.

UNIONS

Union organizing activities have been singularly successful in libraries in recent years. Although the first library union was formed in 1914, significant gains have only been experienced during the past two decades. A recent estimate finds about 25% of librarians working in unionized situations, primarily in public libraries, although occasionally in academic ones. A union in a library is

> an organization of employees organized with the expressed intent of engaging in collective bargaining with the library administration on matters of wages, hours, and conditions of employment.[13]

The formation and operation of labor unions is governed by federal and state laws. The *National Labor Relations Act* limits management activities during union organizing and prohibits employers from promising employees benefits or special considerations if they do not unionize, bars them from questioning employees or spying on them in regarding their union activities, and forbids them from threatening employees engaged in union activities with reprisals.

Librarians, like white collar workers in other professions, have been ambivalent about joining unions. Many consider membership in professional organizations to be the best way to further their own interests and those of the profession and that they abandon status when they join unions. Herb White presents a compelling explanation of the recent movement of librarians into unions:

> Library employees and other professionals quickly found that their salaries were not growing as rapidly as those of skilled or even unskilled workers. In many municipalities, sanitation workers were paid more highly than teachers or librarians and the fact that this first group was unionized could not be ignored. Professional librarians and teachers found, for perhaps the first time, that they were not immune from layoffs and terminations, and that they no longer had the lifelong job security they had taken for granted. Cuts in government budgets, a decline in school age population and a shift to other programs were all taking their toll.[14]

Whatever the reasons, unions in public libraries have altered employee-management relations from established unilateral determinations of working conditions to patterns of bilateral decision making.[15] Collective bargaining has been seen either as paralleling recent movements towards participation in management, or alternately as sacrificing collegiality. Those who view collective bargaining and unions favorably point to formalized personnel policies and procedures, improved communications, increased fringe benefits and better working conditions as evidence of their positive results. Advocates assert that collective bargaining need not be destructive nor depersonalized, emotionally charged and vituperative. Rather, it can lead to a spirit of cooperation and a better library environment. Detractors maintain that labor negotiations cause more paperwork, contribute to inflexibility and rigid rules and create an adversary relationship between labor and management.

Contract negotiations are held annually or bi-annually. The substance of collective bargaining deliberations, negotiations between employee and employer representatives, can be described in three categories: *Mandatory issues,* concerns that, if raised by either party, must be bargained. These generally deal with wages, hours or conditions of employment. *Permissive issues* are non-mandatory negotiation items and might include the participation of professional librarians in the affairs of state and national asssociations. *Prohibited issues* are those specifically excluded from bargaining by law. Such matters as negotiations aimed at achieving some level of power sharing in management by unions may be prohibited by the wording of governmental statutes.

Participating in the deliberations are representatives of the administration and/or the library board and union. It has become increasingly common for management to hire a labor negotiator to lead the administrative team. Skilled labor negotiators are not only familiar with the tactics and strategies of collective bargaining, but are also knowledgeable about laws and regulations relating to employment and the contents of agreements arrived at in similar markets. The other important benefit of hiring an outside negotiator is that he or she will leave the library and perhaps the community when the negotiation ends. With the best will in the world, negotiations invariably create acrimony. If the director has led the negotiation, it becomes much more difficult for relations to return to normal. The parent union generally supplies an experienced agent who has skills similar to those possessed by the management negotiator to assist shop stewards to bargain.

The contract that emerges from negotiations spells out the formal relations between employer and employees for a specified period of time. Its contents require communication and explanation to all members of the library staff, those who will put it into practice and those it will influence. In a unionized library, the contract governs day-to-day employment relations. Shop stewards and supervisors become its principal interpreters and enforcers. Misunderstandings about clauses can lead to unnecessary grievances. In larger libraries, participants in the negotiations can lead seminars or meetings whose express purpose is to describe and discuss major alterations to the existing contract.

Differences in interpretation of the contract are resolved through the grievance process. Most grievances in a union shop arise because of differing interpretations of the contract, violations of its provisions, violations of the law and violations in work procedure. If employed properly, the grievance procedure can prevent small problems from festering and becoming larger ones. Insoluble problems that have followed the formalized, prescribed union grievance procedure, are finally resolved in arbitration. Libraries report that 75% of problems are solved at the first step, with only 5% finding their way to arbitration.

Grievances that arise when employees perceive they have been unfairly treated by management are described in a subsequent section of this chapter.

STAFF RECRUITMENT

In the hierarchy of tasks that administrators perform, none is more important that staffing the library. Every library must hire at some time or another. Turnover is normal, although some administrators feel that a

> stable, long-term staff with little or no turnover is a sign of a sound, well-functioning organization and that an organization that has frequent turnover, especially after a managerial change, is an organization that is unstable and in the throes of upheaval.[16]

These same managers tend to become incensed when an employee leaves a position in order to accept another one that offers more status or higher pay, considering the action disloyal and a personal rejection.

Other librarians find vacancies, particularly professional ones, an opportunity to bring in new blood and offer a degree of field-wide cross-fertilization. They feel flattered when their employees successfully climb career ladders, despite their departure for other work sites. Excessive turnover is to be guarded against; lack of turnover is equally undesirable.

Filling a vacancy in a library is the end product of a complex process that begins with position analysis and job description, continues through recruitment -- advertising, interviewing and checking references -- and concludes only after an employee has been oriented and trained.

Job Analysis and Position Description

When a position becomes vacant, an essential first step before attempting to fill it is to analyze the library's organization structure to determine whether the reasons why the job was originally created still prevail. In this way, administrators are forced to reexamine work flow and staffing levels. Vacancies provide opportune moments to reorganize and implement change.

Once a job analysis has been completed the position to be filled must be clearly defined, described and assigned a proper job title. Its description will include an outline of the kinds of duties to be performed, an indication of the level of the job -- whether it calls for degreed or support staff, how much supervision the employee gives and receives, the main areas of responsibility, the extent of necessary experience and training, and the salary offered. In this way a recruiter can know exactly the capabilities for which to search and the candidate knows precisely what will be expected if the job is offered and accepted.

Recruitment from Within

The objectives of any candidate search are clear:

1) the library needs staff members of the very best quality of mind and personality, in each type and level of service;

2) the only basis of consideration should be the merit of the candidates, and no discrimination or preference should be allowed on grounds unrelated to qualities needed for successful performance;

3) the selection process should operate as swiftly and inexpensively as is consistent with getting the needed results.[17]

In public institutions, as a rule, salary differentials based on merit are small. Staff motivation therefore often stems from promotional possibilities. All things being equal, appointments should be given to candidates available within the library. However, in the absence of commensurate ability, appointment of non-employees is obligatory.

The decision about whether to recruit for a position from within a library staff or to search outside may have already been made by civil service law or union contracts, both of which place limits on the way in which vacancies are filled. Civil service law typically requires that current members of the staff be considered for promotion before vacancies are advertised to non-employees. Separate civil service hiring lists are issued for promotional candidates and non-employees who have passed examinations that qualify them for positions. Even when desireable candidates appear who are not on the list, the civil service process can be so lengthy that attempting to hire non-employees becomes impractical.

Union contracts also act to favor present staff over non-employees. Contracts contain clauses requiring promotion of qualified current staff before outside recruiting can proceed. Unions, however, can only invoke clauses that have been agreed to during collective bargaining negotiations, unlike civil service requirements that are imposed by law, regardless of prevailing attitudes within local jurisdictions.

In both cases, however, some flexibility remains for management. Civil service systems and union contracts strictures all pertain to "qualified" personnel. Rigid enforcement of high appointment standards, consistently imposed and based on clear comparisons of candidates, their performance and experience, makes it more possible to fill positions with the best possible employees which is, after all, the objective of any candidate search.

Recruitment from Without

The search and selection process requires casting as wide a net as possible in order to enlarge the potential pool of candidates. Recruitment procedures vary with the level at which the job is to be filled.

High school page vacancies are filled by maintaining open files of high school students who have applied for positions, or by contacting guidance or employment counselors at local high schools. Senior citizen pages can be located through senior citizen centers and aging agencies.

Clerical and other support staff can be recruited through state and local media -- newspaper and radio advertisements -- and high school guidance counselors.

The search for professionals is conducted locally, regionally and nationally by placing advertisements in professional library publications, at library school placement offices, with state "hot lines," and by using the library grapevine, making personal phone calls to librarians.

Affirmative action, in its best sense, can assist the recruitment of new employees. Advertisements which contain such phrases as "the library is an equal opportunity employer and welcomes applicants from minorities and women" help to encourage entry into the profession of qualified applicants, regardless of racial or cultural background and should be applauded. The current composition of most library staffs in no way reflects the complexion of the community at large.[18]

Interviews
Searches are carried out by committees or by the library director depending on the size of the institution and the management style it has adopted. No matter the kind of search, however, candidates should be interviewed by more than one person given the importance of these interviews and the functions they must play in the recruitment process.

Position announcements rarely convey any real picture of either the vacancy to be filled, the character of the library that has placed the advertisement or of the culture of the community in which it is located. Candidates need to learn about the "style" of the library, the expectations which the institution may have for its employees and the expectations that a candidate may have from the institution. Institutional purposes and environments differ from library to library. Some candidates may respond best to highly structured situations. Others will flourish in fluid surroundings where creativity and flexibility predominate.

Responses to advertisements from candidates also lack character and definition. For this reason, it is important if at all possible to interview the top four or five candidates. If possible, these visits are financed by the library. If the costs are prohibitive for the library, the candidate may be offered an interview at his or her own expense. When a personal interview proves impossible, a telephone interview or an interview at a professional meeting, though clearly less satisfactory, may be substituted. It is appropriate to request candidates for professional positions to give a lecture, submit a statement or respond to a series of scenarios. Applicants for children's positions may be asked to tell a story, catalogers may be requested to catalog and classify a book and reference librarians may be given questions to address.

Recommendations

It is always appropriate to request written recommendations as part of a candidate's credentials package, along with a current vita and perhaps transcripts. On occasion, verbal references are also solicited, particularly when written ones contain ambiguities.

Appointment

The final hiring decision is the result of both objective factors and personal evaluation. Civil service and union contracts may modify the process, but nonetheless substantial discretion remains vested in management. Information gathered in interviews, recommendations and staff judgments about the suitability of the candidate for the position is weighed against the needs of the institution and a decision is made. In the absence of an outstanding candidate it is usually better to reopen the search than to settle for a less qualified person. In the face of equally, but differently qualified candidates, attention to affirmative action and each applicant's potential contribution to the library informs the decision about which one to hire.

ORIENTATION AND TRAINING

The process of staff development begins on the day a staff member accepts a position. New employees have the right to expect two kinds of training, formal and informal or on-the-job. Most libraries readily provide the latter type which focuses on the successful completion of specific tasks. Few, however, design a total orientation program that assures not only that employees are well-versed in particular job assignments, but have a sense of the institution as a whole. It is important that staff internalize the values of the organization.

While the organization's values are clarified during the development of a mission and plan of service, it is through training and orientation that values are transmitted to the staff.

The purpose, then, of formal training as an adjunct to on-the-job instruction is to create and maintain a shared staff vision of the role of the library in the community.

An orientation program for new employees includes an introduction to the overall library organization, a tour of the physical structure and its departments, an explanation of library policies and expectations and completion of forms for health benefits, parking spots, badges, E-Mail addresses and other important formalities. Knowing how the parts of a library operate and how they interact with each other helps new employees understand their place in the institution. At the end of the formal orientation and training, employees are delivered to their hiring departments. There, a training plan should be prepared for new staff members that describes all tasks that must be learned. Providing a self-completed checklist assists employees to monitor and assess their progress. Training or probationary periods normally last for a maximum of six months.

PERFORMANCE APPRAISAL

Performance appraisal is designed to provide constructive assistance to all staff members by helping them to understand the strengths and weaknesses of their job performance, to assist with decisions about promotions and salaries, and to create a paper trail in the case of less-than-satisfactory employees. Evaluation is a difficult process "that is almost unanimously disliked and mistrusted by management and employees alike."[19] The process is complicated, time-consuming, nerve-wracking and at times confrontational. Properly conducted, however, it can improve performance, and save the time, energy and expense required to replace an employee whose work could have been improved if given proper encouragement and instruction.

All staff members should be analyzed at frequent, pre-established intervals with known evaluation instruments which are seen and initialed by both supervisor and subordinate. The periodic evaluation will hold no surprises if it follows continual informal evaluations. Employees being appraised should have a channel

through which to voice disagreement with an assessment.
Performance appraisal systems vary in style and content. Most
public libraries utilize *supervisor-generated* ratings with objective
scales based on employee traits, behaviors or combinations of both.
Self-Appraisal places the primary responsibility for assessing
performance on employees and is normally followed by a
discussion with the supervisor. This role reversal helps open a
dialogue and is particularly valuable with employees who are
inclined to be defensive. *Peer Appraisal* bases the assessment on
collegial review of individual performance with the average of
appraisal scores providing the rating. *Subordinate Appraisals* tap
subordinates opinions about their supervisors. Organizations that
encourage employee participation in management are more likely
to adopt this technique. Regardless of who completes the
performance appraisal, major problems exist. People must say
things that others will not like.

Institutional emphasis on performance appraisal as a vehicle
for improvement and change, rather than as an instrument of
punishment, helps to lessen the pressure and anxiety. Despite the
difficulties of implementing formal performance appraisal systems,
the advantages of formal feedback far outweigh their drawbacks.

Among the most popular forms of performance appraisal is a
modification of the Management-By-Objectives (MBO) method
pioneered by Peter Drucker. Utilizing a planning framework that
identifies aims and goals, supervisors and employees negotiate and
agree on a set of objectives for a period to come. MBO may have
to be combined with additional assessment methods that describe
or measure other types of achievements. Assessments of support
staff tend to be rating systems that appraise performance levels and
abilities. For professionals, the evaluations are more typically
narrative in form.

Unfortunately, to quote Byron J. Langenfield,

rare is the person who can weigh the faults of others without
putting his thumb on the scale.[20]

GRIEVANCE PROCEDURES

A substantial body of law -- civil service regulations and state and federal labor statutes -- as well as union contracts between libraries and their employees, is now directed toward assuring equity and fair play in the workplace. Grievance procedures guarantee employees a path to appeal the decisions of their superiors.

> Grievance channels are ways of removing the employee from direct and complete control of the immediate supervisor. Grievance channels may discipline supervisors and act as guarantees to employees. They exist to assure employees that justice is available when they have legitimate complaints against the organization.[21]

Procedures may be mandated by civil service law, stipulated by a library's union contract, or suggested by the need to assure a process that can stand the test of fairness relating to state and federal labor laws. Typically there is an appeal process that permits employees to take their case beyond their supervisor to an administrative superior and finally to the library board, a civil service review board, an arbitrator and possibly the courts. Employees are often granted the right to bring in representatives -- attorneys, union representatives, coworkers, friends -- to help argue their case.

Supervisors or organizations are sometimes proven wrong and the appeal is won by an employee. It is foolish for a supervisor or administrator to continue to harbor resentment once the determination has been made. Accepting the decision graciously is crucial to healing the wounds.

TERMINATION OF EMPLOYMENT

Every administrator is faced, at some time, with having to terminate the employment of an employee. Sometimes the suspension stems from budgetary reductions or termination of a grant. More frequently, it is the result of inadequate job performance. No single responsibility is more detested by managers than having to fire an employee. Terminating an unsatisfactory worker is never a cause for celebration. It represents institutional failure, either in the selection or supervisory process. Every attempt at performance improvement should be documented in the periodic performance appraisals administered to the staff. Discussion with unsatisfactory employees should be summarized in writing, with copies distributed to them and placed in their personnel files. Documenting problems shows "good faith" on the part of employers. Termination is the final step. Under civil service, intermediate steps may be taken. These include less severe penalties such as loss of pay increment or demotion to a lower rank.

How an organization deals with separation from service is never lost on those who remain. Every employee is worthy of respect and civility in the way the termination is handled. Caring, responsible treatment, even in the face of hostility and anger, sets a standard of behavior for the entire staff.

BURNOUT

Burnout can be considered the end point of a continuum that begins with stress.

> This continuum runs from 1) a condition wherein, on the whole, challenges are sources of happiness and productive responses, to 2) a condition wherein perceived imbalances between demands and resources are painful, but where coping strategies restore the balance and reduce the pain, to 3) a condition where inappropriate coping strategies are out of control (i.e. are contributing to the problem) and the person's physical and mental resources are depleted.[22]

Simple stress can be managed by coping mechanisms. Distress can be contained. Burnout overwhelms individuals to the point where they no longer function effectively. Because individuals perceive emotions differently, stress to one person may be strain to another and burnout to a third.

Stress can be traced to a number of causes including work overload, feelings of inadequacy, work "underload" -- lack of sufficient challenge -- unsatisfactory inter-personal relations with staff and/or the public, lack of effective positive feedback from supervisors, lack of effective supervision, and career concerns, particularly at the entry, mid-career and approaching retirement levels. Middle managers, caught between demands from above and below, are particularly vulnerable. Studies have identified the susceptibility of certain personality types to stress, including workaholics, impatient, competitive types, unassertive people who accept too many assignments, perfectionists, young singles, and those living alternative life-styles.[23]

A number of strategies to help lessen stress and burnout problems in libraries have been identified. Some are described below:

Job Redesign. Restructuring positions to eliminate work overload or modify work levels may result in decreased anxiety, lessened boredom or other changes that have an impact on the ability to work. It may be desireable, for instance, to alternate levels of intense activity and concentration with more relaxed assignments. Periodically involving entire staffs in collaborative ventures, in contrast with individual duties, may eliminate destructive competition.

Employees who have reached a plateau or the top of the career ladder can remain interested and contributing if they are offered the opportunity to grow within their individual jobs. The profession is changing so rapidly that there are continually new techniques or theories to be learned.

Inter-Personal Relations. Job strain is often a product of interpersonal tension. By reviewing communication mechanisms, administrators can ascertain that information flow through the system is timely and to the point. Supervisory feedback to staff, particularly of a supportive nature, assuring employees maximum feasible control and autonomy over their job performance and providing training for supervisors about stress and stress management all contribute to a healthy work environment.

Support and Counseling. Libraries lend staff support when they inform employees about conditions leading to stress and burnout, when they promote greater self awareness, and when they make available as part of the health insurance package funds to pay for psychological counseling. Librarians are not therapists, nor should they attempt to be. Employees experiencing severe stress or burnout will require professional assistance, often in the form of psychological counseling.

Burnout and stress management have been the subjects of attention recently and the objects of countless remedies. Yet there has to date been little empirical research into how widespread the problem may be. Only one study has documented the existence of stress as a factor in public library life.[24] More research is needed.

ENCOURAGING STAFF

Adult education specialists distinguish between continuing education and staff development. The former they view as a choice made by employees and the latter as an employer's appraisal of the needs of the organization. In the first instance, employees may seek career mobility or individual satisfaction. In the second, the library determines skills their staff members must acquire in order to keep up with the field and successfully accomplish their work. The reference staff, for instance, must know the latest on-line data-bases or new protocols for manipulating information. Administrators require exposure to the latest management techniques. The two endeavors, continuing education and staff development, are not mutually exclusive. A librarian who enrolls in a computer course for personal reasons will undoubtedly have the opportunity to utilize the newly acquired skills on the job.

Professional literature suggests that libraries allocate up to 10% of their total personnel budgets on staff development, although the actual expenditures hover around 1%. The absence of tangible spending, however, does not mean a library has abandoned staff development.

Supervision and Mentoring

There is a real need in libraries for the kind of supervision that encourages accomplishment and stimulates cooperation toward the common good. Mentoring, an activity whose importance has received increased recognition over the past decade, is one such form of supervision. Librarians learn not only from texts and their own experience, but from the example of other librarians who act as role models. More experienced librarians willingly accept the responsibility to share with more recent entrants to the field their understanding of both the theory and practice of the profession. They assist and guide, pointing out opportunities and pitfalls; and encourage newer librarians to grow beyond the limits of their current positions into new career challenges with additional responsibility either in-house or elsewhere.

Some public libraries have institutionalized mentoring by assigning new staff to more seasoned ones who work in other parts of the organization in order to avoid authoritarian or threatening situations. The mentor serves as a guide, an advisor and a shoulder.

Meetings and Retreats

Frequent staff meetings help to build staff morale. They encourage participation and further good communication. Staff retreats lasting from a few hours to perhaps two days held in a location away from the library can stimulate fresh thinking about old problems or enthusiasm for new ventures. Brainstorming, nominal group processes and other problem-solving techniques facilitate the development of consensus and build group cohesiveness. Library brown-bag lunches with featured speakers or to discuss a new professional article is intellectually stimulating and provides yet another avenue to insure that employees are keeping up with the field.

Ethical Conduct in Personnel Matters

Employees have a right to expect that they will be judged fairly and that professional rivalries or personal bias will not intrude on decisions. The needs of the library should not impede an employee's progress. Promotions should be granted even when they may mean the temporary loss of sufficient personnel for a particular department. Requests for professional references should be met honestly and be reliable, objective and free from bias. Opening of personnel files has resulted in more positive letters of reference, but ones that are less trustworthy. It is tempting, but unethical, to commend out of proportion the few virtues of an inadequate staff member whose presence in the library is a constant irritant in the hopes that he or she will be hired elsewhere. Employees also have a right to be protected from physical harm and verbal abuse, all too common events in public libraries today.

Librarians, similarly have responsibilities to the library. Except when circumstances are intolerable, librarians have an obligation to remain in a position long enough to have achieved definite results before moving on. The training required by any job is expensive. It is some time before employers begin to reap the benefits of their investments in new employees. Common courtesy calls for librarians seriously considering another position to discuss their plans with their supervisors or with the library director. If they accept a job, professionals owe their libraries at least two or three months notice before departure. For support staff two weeks to a month will suffice.

SUMMARY

How a library recruits, pays, and considers its staff, how well it uses its human resources all help to predict the success with which the institution will operate in the community. The goal of human resources management is to assure that all employees are treated equitably and justly, and that they remain motivated to perform good work.

Civil service and union contracts, despite their drawbacks and inflexibility, have been responsible for formalizing public library personnel procedures and for introducing fairness and objective standards into the process.

Libraries are among the civilizing institutions of contemporary society. Staff treatment should reflect the same humane orientation.

NOTES AND SUGGESTED READINGS

Notes

1. Roy found, for example, that two-thirds of Illinois libraries serving communities of 25,000 - 50,000 persons use volunteers. Loriene Roy, "The Use of Volunteers in Public Libraries: A Pilot Study," *Public Library Quarterly* 8 (1987-88): 127-145.

2. Catherine Park, "Public Library Volunteers," *Texas Library Journal* 65 (Winter, 1989): 126-128.

3. Robert Stueart and Barbara Moran, *Library Management.*4th ed. (Littleton, CO: Libraries Unlimited, 1993), 179.

4. Paul John Cirino, *The Business of Running a Library* (Jefferson, NC: McFarland, 1991), 103.

5. Stueart and Moran, 162.

6. Kathleen Heim and Leigh Estabrook, *Career Profiles and Sex Discrimination in the Library Profession* (Chicago: American Library Association, 1983).

7. Ibid., 38-9.

8. Stuart and Moran, 171.

9. Sue Galloway, "Comparable-Worth Adjustments: Yes," *American Libraries* 19 (Feb. 1985): 92.

10. ALA Committee on Pay Equity, "Recommended Pay Equity Policy Language for Libraries," *Library Personnel News* 4 (Winter 1990): 13.

11. June O'Neill, "Comparable-Worth Adjustments: No," *American Libraries* 19 (Feb. 1985): 92.

12. An analysis of ratings accorded local services by sixty or more local jurisdictions revealed that library services placed second in public perceptions to local fire services and were ahead of police, schools, parks/recreation and water/sewer services. Reported in Thomas Miller and Michele Miller, "Standards of Excellence: U.S. Residents' Evaluation of Local Governmental Services," *Public Administration Review* 51 (Nov/Dec. 1991).

13. Byron Cooper, "Personnel Procedures and Practices," in Ellen Altman ed. *Local Public Library Administration* (Chicago: American Library Association, 1980), 126.

14. Herbert White, *Library Personnel Management* (White Plains, NY: Knowledge Industry Publications, 1985), 163.

15. Carlton Rochell, *Wheeler and Goldhor's Practical Administration of Public Libraries* (New York: Harper, 1981), 55.

16. Jennifer Cargill and Gisela Webb, *Managing Libraries in Transition* (Phoenix, AZ: Oryx, 1988), 113.

17. Rochell, 77.

18. Office for Library Personnel Resources, American Library Association. *Academic and Public Librarians Data by Race, Ethnicity and Sex, 1986* (Chicago: American Library Association, 1986). Also summarized in *Library Personnel News* 5 (January-February 1991), 5.

19. Cirino, 89.

20. Quoted in Cirino, 89.

21. Stueart and Moran, 175.

22. Charles Bunge, "Stress in the Library Workplace," *Library Trends* 38 (Summer 1989): 94.

23. Nathan Smith et al., "Burnout and the Library Administrator: Carrier or Cure," *Journal of Library Administration* 9 (1988): 13-21.

24. David Fisher, "Are Librarians Burning Out?" *Journal of Librarianship* 22 (October 1990): 216-235.

Suggested Readings

American Library Association. Office for Library Personnel Resources. "Managing Employee Performance." *Topics in Personnel* 11 (1988).

American Library Association. Office for Library Personnel Resources. "Writing Library Job Descriptions." *Topics in Personnel* 7 (1988).

Berryman-Fink, Cynthia. *The Manager's Desk Reference.* New York: American Management Association, 1989.

Caputo, Janette. *Stress and Burnout in Library Service.* Phoenix, AZ: Oryx, 1991.

Cargill, Jennifer and Gisela Webb. *Managing Libraries in Transition.* Phoenix, AZ: Oryx Press, 1988.

Cooper, Byron. "Personnel Procedures and Practices," in Altman, Ellen, ed. *Local Public Library Administration.* Chicago: American Library Assocation, 1980.

Creth, Sheila and Frederick Duda, eds. *Personnel Administration in Libraries.* New York: Neal-Schuman, 1981.

Library Personnel News, 1987-date.   Office for Library Personnel

Resources, American Library Association.

Lindsey, Jonathan, ed. *Performance Evaluation.* Phoenix, AZ: Oryx, 1986.

Pay Equity: An Action Manual for Library Workers. Chicago: American Library Asssociation, 1989.

Rochell, Carlton. *Wheeler and Goldhor's Practical Administration of Public Libraries.* New York: Harper, 1981.

Rooks, Dana. *Motivating Today's Library Staff.* Phoenix, AZ: Oryx, 1988.

Rubin, Richard. *Human Resource Management in Libraries.* New York: Neal-Schuman, 1991.

Stueart, Robert and Barbara Moran. *Library Management.* 4th ed. Littleton, CO: Libraries Unlimited, 1993.

Weiss, Donald. *Fair, Square and Legal.* NY: American Management Association, 1991.

White, Herbert S. *Library Personnel Management.* White Plains, NY: Knowledge Industry Publications, 1985.

CHAPTER 18

FINANCIAL MANAGEMENT

No self-supporting human being ever escapes having to deal with personal finances. Similarly, public librarians never avoid funding considerations, no matter the administrative level at which they operate. Financial concerns influence all library activities. Libraries cannot function without resources, that is staff and materials; few resources are obtainable without money; and finding money, particularly in the 1990s, can daunt the most sanguine administrator. Library board members, or trustees, bear *de jure* responsibility for operating and funding the library. *De facto*, however, it is professional library directors who deal with day-to-day monetary concerns and long-range funding problems. It is no wonder that librarians find financial matters anxiety-producing and that, for directors, they are a major contributor to "burn-out." Yet, according to W. David Penniman,

> librarians often come to [the financial] arena with an orientation and mindset that leaves them ill prepared for the contest. They have been self-selected and educationally reinforced to emphasize service. And this service emphasis has too often been equated with the inappropriateness of measuring the monetary value of a service.[1]

Survival for not-for-profit organizations, among them libraries, is precarious in an America of diminished domestic resources, enlarged global competition and a weighty deficit. Non-profit or not-for-profit organizations "were formed to deal with the health welfare, religious, educational and other matters no longer handleable on a neighbor-to-neighbor basis."[2] Their purpose is to benefit the public and to improve society through provision of a service, not a product. Unlike businesses, not-for-profit organizations survive on fixed incomes; customarily, they know at the end of one fiscal year how much they will have available to them for the ensuing one. Managing public libraries means having the knowledge to deal with, among other aspects of finance, planning, income/revenue, costs, budget construction and presentation, and implementing capital campaigns.

FINANCIAL PLANNING

A plan for library service is incomplete without a financial module, that is, without dollar amounts affixed to all current and future operations. This is accomplished annually through the budget. There is a danger, however, that budgeting anually without reference to a long-term financial plan may lead to short-term thinking and short-term remedies. Three year financial plans lead to better fiscal control by enabling financial managers to quantify goals, assess progress in meeting them, and evaluate how successful the plan has been. A financial plan projects revenues and expenses against a backdrop of societal and community conditions and library goals and aspirations. A description of the steps to be taken when creating a financial plan follows:

--Analyze the library's financial status;

--Analyze the situation. This includes the economic, legal, political, social, technological and organization factors that impact on the library;

--Do a market analysis. Look at the nature of the library's current and potential customer base, determine how responsive are its current and potential programs, services and products to that base, and identify the library's competition;

--Make assumptions about the future regarding financial goals and objectives;

--Project the outlook for a three-year period. Three-year budgetary forecasts help control annual operating budgets and bring into focus particular financial challenges.

--Design funding strategies. Distinguish sources of funding to pay for proposed growth and development.

--Evaluate and assess the success of the financial plan.[3]

The format of a financial plan is usually the one utilized for the annual budget. (Types of budgets are described below.) Fund raising from the private sector or from public or private granting bodies also profits from the existence of a financial plan that documents how the library intends to meet its future needs.

REVENUES

Public libraries realize the bulk of their funds from public sources, local, state and national. Some public administrators and students of public finance assert that a federal system of public agency support permits public goods to be financed at optimal levels of government. Goods that benefit local constituencies can be produced locally; those that benefit larger constituencies can be produced at higher levels. The interstate highway system, for instance, is offered as an example of a product that benefits the entire country and therefore is appropriately funded by the national government. Libraries, seen as fundamentally local institutions, are financed by local municipalities. In addition, these economists argue, the closer the service is to the people it serves, the more likely it is that community support will be forthcoming. Of course, municipalities vary significantly in the amounts of tax they are able to generate, and therefore in the amounts of funds they have available to spend on essential services. Some urban and rural library districts simply lack sufficient taxing resources to fund an adequate library. For this reason, other experts consider larger jurisdictions as more appropriate levels from which to support such services as education and libraries. A state with responsibility toward all of the governmental jurisdictions within its boundaries is in a better position to develop a plan for service to all districts than are individual municipalities acting on their own. Furthermore, services are becoming less local as "national information roadways," electronic data networks, are being assembled. Darlene Weingand comments:

> the extensive and growing interlibrary loan mechanisms suggest that local funding may be yesterday's solution patched into a world that is quite different and that a larger funding base, such as at the state--or even national--level would be more appropriate as we head into the next century.[4]

Many library planners regard a mix of 50% local, 30% state and 20% federal as an ideal support distribution for public libraries. Normative figures reveal that the spread is closer to 85-95% local, 5-10% state and 5% (indirect) federal.[5]

Whatever the ratio, however, of far more consequence is the recent debate over whether providing library service at public expense is appropriate or justifiable. The question shocks many librarians who count libraries as among the basic rights of citizenship, as ways of assuring freedom of access to information and as avenues to affording equality of opportunity.

The fundamental justification for government involvement in funding libraries is that its resources fit an economist's definition of a *public good*. According to this definition, a *public good* is "one that allows a consumer to consume this good without reducing the consumption by any other consumer."[6] In contrast, a private good -- gasoline, shoes, soft drinks -- is consumed by one person and cannot subsequently be used by others. Economists apply yet another test of services in the public good. They ask whether services provide "positive externalities," that is beneficial effects for the whole society. Ann Prentice says:

A public good is not exclusive, but is available to and consumable by all citizens in equal amounts. No one can be excluded from using it because of failure to pay for it voluntarily. While the motivation of the private sector is to meet goals, the motivation of the public sector is to consider the welfare of its citizens. Taxes are the price paid for public goods.[7]

Which services can be properly labelled *public good* is somewhat ambiguous and economists differ on precisely which ones are embraced. Although virtually all would include national defense, and fire and police, substantial differences about services deserving that designation appear as the list lengthens. What constitutes "positive externalities" also produces subjective judgments.

Those who take the position that libraries are not a public good and do not merit public support argue that public libraries, in contrast with other public services, are built on "voluntary use." Unlike the street cleaning department, for instance, whose service is "automatic and more or less ubiquitous," the library depends on its public to choose it, else its resources stand idle.[8] They also contend that the library does not meet other tests of a public good. Its primary beneficiaries are selected or single consumers, rather that the entire community. Most people, they say, do not use the library for information. And as they dip into the pool of books, they lessen the amount of available material. Lawrence White who holds this opinion advocates charging fees to all library users except children and students. To answer the poor person's access problems, he proposes a chit system, not unlike food stamps. In this way, not only are the library's funding problems solved, but a supply and demand mentality is allowed to prevail. Those services no longer cost effective will wither.[9]

Widespread opposition to those who favor pay library service appears likely. However, the movement to impose more users fees for what may be considered "special services" seems likely to expand. Services and items that may carry fees include on-line database searching, and rental of videos and audiovisual equipment.

PUBLIC FUNDING

Local governments derive their legal authority to provide library services from state laws, although the decision about whether or not to furnish them is usually discretionary. A few states mandate library service. The library laws of some states give local public libraries autonomy and the power to determine a tax rate within certain limits set by law. Typically, the statute will establish a ceiling on the amount that can be assessed by the library board without voter approval. A higher level requires voter referendum.[10]

Property taxes, generally taxes on the estimated value of real estate, are the foundation of most local funding which take the form either of a municipal allocation from the general fund or a library levy. Property taxes are regressive, putting undue burdens on citizens least able to pay -- homeowners and those on low or fixes incomes such as the elderly or the poor -- and commanding intense resentment. As a result, local services supported by property taxes -- police, education, courts and libraries -- are the most likely targets of taxpayer revolts, first because of their visibility and second, because they are considered within the grasp of local residents unlike federal income, sales and other taxes.

Occasionally, other taxes are used to support libraries. Among these are local income or sales, "intangible property," penal fines or dog taxes. Those "earmarked" for libraries, intangibles taxes, for instance, carry the virtue of certainty, but the drawback of framing the budget around available capital, rather than on identified need. Allocations for libraries rarely represent more than one to two percent of the tax on the total jurisdiction and are directly related to the per capita expenditures for other municipal services.

State and Federal Support

The majority of states have grant-in-aid programs utilizing

state funds to help support local public libraries. Modern state aid programs began during the 1930s when it became clear that: 1) impoverished local governments needed help in meeting library resource needs; 2) unserved and rural areas required libraries; 3) larger units of service, where tax burden could be more economically distributed, would improve the quality of libraries; and 4) equalizing library service, particularly in states with a wide disparity between the rich and the poor, would have a similar impact.

Four patterns of state contributions have been identified

--*Substantial support*, as found in Hawaii and West Virginia;

--*Support of larger systems whose boundaries are established at state level.* Illinois and New York are examples of this model;

--*Financial assistance with minimum regulation* as in California, Florida and South Carolina;

--*Aid to any legally established library.* Massachusetts follows this pattern.[11]

Most state aid programs involve formulas for distribution, based on per-capita/geographical area figures. A few states design formulas to "equalize" support. Several states confer discretionary grants, aid area administrations or reimburse libraries for certain services. Most states also impose eligibility requirements that local communities must meet in order to receive state aid. Among them are minimum local budgets; availability of trained personnel; sufficient hours of public access; membership in networks, cooperatives, or systems; willingness to share materials with other libraries; and series of supporting documents, including annual state reports. Some local jurisdictions resent having to meet these minimum standards, fearing further encroachments by state agencies.

In addition to apportioning state aid to local libraries, state libraries are responsible for distributing Library Services and

Construction Act Funds. They first decide priorities for awarding grants. They then receive proposals describing how the moneys will be used and finally, they bestow money on the worthiest grant requests. Four Titles, or sections, are of interest to public librarians:

> **Title I-Services.** Emphasis is placed on reducing the number of people unserved or underserved in rural and urban areas, on extending service to the aged, handicapped and minorities, and on sharing resources and increasing interlibrary cooperation.
>
> **Title II-Construction.** Building and/or renovating modern library facilities and removing barriers to access for the handicapped.
>
> **Title III-Cooperation.** Multitype library cooperation, special emphasis on statewide union catalogs.
>
> **Title VI-Literacy.** Aids libraries in establishing and conducting literacy programs.

Most other federal funds are available to local libraries only through grant programs. Both the National Endowment for the Humanities (NEH) and National Endowment for the Arts (NEA) support library programs, usually on a matching funds basis. The former offers money for both construction and programs, while the latter only lends support to arts-oriented endeavors.

PRIVATE FUNDING

A number of important sources of funds are available to public libraries. Care must be taken to insure that moneys received from them are not considered substitutes for municipally allocated funds, what might be called "hard money," but rather are seen as additions to be used for special purposes, and represent "soft money." Among these funds are endowments, gifts, grants, fines and other fees.

Endowments

An Endowment Fund, comprised of awards, donations, bequests, gifts, inheritances and legacies, is established for the purpose of producing interest income which the library may use to support its ongoing program. Endowment funds provide for the future and can act as cushions and hedges against bad times. The Fund's principal is rarely expended, except in unusual circumstances or for particular one-time purposes and only when the terms of the endowment allow its use. Endowment funds can mean the difference between success and failure for many non-profit organizations. Not-for-profit organizations find Endowment Funds attractive sources of support. Once acquired, they are permanent and do not require annual solicitations. Unfortunately, thick strings in the form of donor restrictions become attached to them. Favorable terms may be negotiated with the donor at the time a gift is proffered. If this proves impossible, decisions about how burdensome the stipulations are or may be in the future will have to be made. If they are excessively onerous, the Endowment Funds must be refused, or in extreme cases when the donor has died, legal attempts made to break the trust. Endowment Funds are established as separate accounting entities for purposes of accountability, that is so that expenditures drawn against them are readily identifiable and easily traceable. Depending on the size and nature of the fund, a library may chose to entrust it to a professional investment manager, establish an investment advisory committee to handle it or leave it in the hands of knowledgeable board members. Some state laws restrict how libraries may invest their funds, permitting purchase only of those secured by government, Treasury Bills or Certificates of Deposit. Where investment funds are permitted to be diversified, conservative management suggests a varied portfolio of stocks, bonds, and money markets.

Gifts

Annual solicitations for money, tribute or memorial funds and book sales are three fund-raising devices used by most libraries. The annual campaign for support is a function of the library board or the Friends, never of the staff. It is inappropriate, and in some places illegal, for public employees to engage in activities designed to provide their own remuneration. Repeated every year the drive solicits, often by direct mail, small gifts from many individuals and uses the funds for current operations. Some fundraisers see the annual appeal as paving the way for a major capital drive by establishing a list and a tradition of giving to the library.

Tribute or memorial funds are almost always book funds. Donors either donate the cost of a particular book or contribute to the general book fund in honor or memory of a person. Notification is sent to the honoree or to the family of the deceased. When a particular title is chosen, a plate specifying the honoree or the deceased and the donor is placed in the book.

Book sales are always successful, raising large amounts of money for libraries and carrying the additional advantage of acting as a means to recycle books and other materials. Other fundraising projects that may be undertaken by Friends groups are discussed in Chapter 15.

Just as refusing certain endowments may become necessary because of the restrictions placed on them, other gifts, too, primarily books and periodicals may be declined. Saying "no" to unwanted material is discussed in Chapter 8.

Grants

We live in a grants society. Kenneth Boulding has estimated that somewhere between 20 % and 50 % of the United States economy is centered around grants.[12] Only a handful of human services agencies today can avoid the realities of grant financing -- the very smallest, and the least and most successful. Grants to libraries are for the most part program/project oriented, rather than in support of a library's operation. Often they are designed to push recipients into activities they might not otherwise have preferred. Title III of LSCA, for instance, supports cooperation and networking. Only libraries willing to participate in collective activities should apply. But if the carrot is large enough -- that is, the grant funds substantial -- libraries with little enthusiasm about cooperation may be willing to participate.

Successful grant applications depend on a carefully conceived program to meet a clearly defined goal presented to the right funding source at the ideal time.[13] Grants should be made for programs that are consistent with the overall purpose of the library as defined in its plan. They also require carefully crafted proposals that follow guidelines, the required format, and are written simply and without jargon. Grants beget grants. There is a multiplier effect. Establishing a track record of earned grants insures credibility. The chances of winning an award are enhanced by a respectable list of past awards.

Activities of major foundations can be located in *The Foundation Directory, The Foundation Grants Index* and *Marquis' Annual Register of Grants Support.* Corporate sources sometimes demand less information from applicants than do governments or foundations. Requesting funds from federal and state agencies can be complicated and entail substantial amounts of paperwork. Before embarking on any application process, it is well to insure that the central program being promoted in the grant is one that supports the mission of the institution and that there is a fit between the agenda of the library and that of the funding body.

Caution should also be taken to assure that the *cost* of the grant does not outweigh its potential benefits. All grants involve expenditures of local operating funds. Some grants (LSCA, for instance) do not permit the inclusion of indirect costs. If these costs are not allowable, the requester must judge whether the administrative costs in time, energy and accounting make the grant worth pursuing.

It is almost axiomatic that grant funds should not be sought for general operations, first because foundations and other granting agencies do not find these requests exciting and second, because of their temporary life spans. Similarly decisions must be made at the outset as to whether or not the program can be continued after the grant period.

Among the most important tasks associated with grants submission is that of keeping municipal funding bodies apprised of applications and outcomes. Without information to the contrary, officials could easily assume that grant funds may be substituted for those already allocated to the library. A breakdown in communication at this juncture courts disaster.

Fines and Fees

Most libraries levy fees for some of their services, but not for basic loan or information. Money is collected for making microform prints and photocopies. Many libraries ask that patrons compensate the library for online searching after offering some portion of it free. The question of fees for service is discussed in Chapter 11. Non-residents, those who live outside the normal service area of a library, are also asked to pay for borrowing privileges, although not for in-house access to materials. Overdue fines are levied by most libraries, although their efficacy has been questioned. Charges for borrowers' cards and the imposition of fines are discussed in Chapter 10.

EXPENDITURES

Public libraries expend two kinds of funds, operating and capital. Operating funds are those utilized in every day activities. Capital funds are used for large, one-time purchases. Expenses under operating funds include salaries, fringe benefits, materials and supplies, contracted services, travel, maintenance, utilities, and insurance. Those under capital funds might be a new building, remodeling, new furniture, or a computer system.

As of 1990, public libraries spent about $16.28 per capita. These moneys were apportioned as follows:

Personnel. Expenditures for personnel, including fringe benefits, represent about 60% of the library's total, give or take 10%. Of this percentage, fringes represent somewhere between 15 and 35%, depending on what the library offers in benefits.

Materials. Approximately 20-30% of the library's expenditures are accounted for by materials, depending on whether cataloging and processing are included.

Other. The remaining 10-20% is allocated for all other library expenses, among which are building and maintenance costs, equipment and so on.

Many libraries have recently adopted a program approach to library finances. All activities of the library, reference, children's services, and so on, are seen as programs that can be costed and assessed in terms of cost-benefit. Aggregate financial figures are incomprehensible to most people unless they have worked with them over a period of time. Presenting them in a program format enables officials and others to see what services are being purchased for the amount of money allocated the library. Each library decides what constitutes a program. For one, it may be all branch libraries; for another, each branch is its own program.

The expense of a program is a product of direct costs, those easily assigned to a specific activity -- personnel, materials and supplies -- and indirect costs, those not specifically associated with the program, but which together form "overhead" -- administration, finance, utilities, security and custodial services. Calculating overhead is particularly important when determining the additive costs of a new service.

Turock and Pedolsky suggest a method for arriving at a program's indirect labor costs:

1. Take annual salaries of the staff and prorate them in proportion to the total time given to the task. Add to that benefits, also prorated.
2. Summarize other direct costs -- materials, supplies, telephone, postage and equipment.
3. Estimate indirect -- administration, finance/accounting,

maintenance, utilities and security -- by multiplying all direct labor costs by the library's total labor costs.
4. Determine actual program costs.[14]

The cost benefit of each program can be computed by weighing its costs against demand and projected benefits. Programs that are in high demand and are low cost are obviously most desirable and those that are in least demand and most expensive are less attractive. The ones in the middle, those with low cost and low demand and those with high cost and high demand, require priority determinations. Projected benefits, the third element in the matrix, are less amenable to quantity judgments than are cost and demand, yet can be made in terms of how well a program meets the goals of the library. Cost comparison data can be useful in helping libraries assess their performances over time. However, since each library operates in a unique community and there may be hidden factors that influence costs even in communities that are apparently similar, they must be used with care.

Purchasing
Efforts to assure that all legitimate vendors or contractors have the opportunity to participate in public enterprises, that libraries spend the least amount on products or services, and that conflicts-of-interest do not intercede in decisions have led to the imposition by many states and localities of regulations about purchasing in the public sector. Some of these entail formal procedures with public notices and sealed bids. Others merely require a number of competitive proposals from which a supplier emerges. Most involve the delineation of specifications in order to make comparisons relatively easy. Whenever possible, the library retains the right to reject all bids and requires bid and performance bonds, particularly for those projects involving capital expenditures.

THE BUDGET PROCESS

The library's budget translates the organization's plan into financial terms and assigns dollar amounts to goals and objectives to enable administrators to estimate the money they will need to furnish the program during the coming year. The budget's legitimacy and authority derives from its dependence on long and short term plans.

In more practical terms, the budget is an estimate, an itemized summary of probable expenditures and incomes for a given time period that usually includes a systematic plan for meeting expenses. It is a planning document used by an organization, typically prepared and presented in standard accounting formats emphasizing dollar revenues, expenditures and costs.[15]

All budgets depend on a clearly defined and articulated library, one whose program has been devised from a profound understanding of its unique community, whose services have been weighed and accorded priorities and whose procedures have been examined for cost effectiveness.

Budgets appear in two sections, operating and capital. The operating budget describes for one year the costs of service, either by department or by program, and anticipated revenue. The capital budget often covers a number of years and includes moneys for equipment, construction and other large purchases.

Types of Budgets

Library budgets take various forms. If the library is a part of a city or county government, a specific method of budget preparation or format presentation may be prescribed. If the library constructs its budget differently than required by the municipality, it must later be translated to cohere with those produced by other departments.

Line-Item Budget is the most common type of budget. It uses broad institution-wide categories to describe expenses. All personnel costs are grouped, all materials, all utilities and so on. Most line-item budgets are created by extrapolating last year's spending level into next year, adding increments for anticipated increases in costs, and further expanding the budget to include new projects and programs.

The assumption of a line-item budget is that the activities engaged in last year are essential to this year's program and therefore must be continued for the coming year at the same or somewhat increased levels. An underlying premise is that all the services are now performed in the most cost-effective manner.

Line-item budgets are simpler to construct and easier to compute than other types of budgets. The individual items are clearly defined; no difficulties arise in categorizing activities or assigning costs. Among the drawbacks are that they do not stress services to the public, but rather describe the services and commodities that are purchased. No cost-benefit analysis is possible with a line-item budget.

Zero-based Budget, popular during the Carter Administration, expects all programs both new and ongoing to justify their value on an annual basis. They assume that an institution starts with a blank slate each year and builds from point zero. Decision packages are developed in which each activity or program is described. These packages are then ranked for decision-making. Those with the highest order of importance through cost/benefit analyses are retained; those at the lower end discarded. Few libraries today use zero-based budgeting.

Program Budget utilizes the program approach described above under costs associated with them and expenditures, that is programs are isolated and costs, both direct and indirect, attached. In a full program budget, all costs are allocated between the various programs so that alternatives can be logically considered and adopted. The library's standard programs are those of acquiring materials, organizing them for use, and disseminating and interpreting them through activities of circulation, administration, reference and outreach. The needs of the institution will determine the extent to which these activities or programs will be further subdivided. A library may have isolated the improvement of interlibrary loan services as an objective for its current year. Assigning costs to the program and examining alternative methods of providing the service will help to determine whether it is over or under funded to achieve the goals set for it. Program budgets can feed into line-item budgets.

The figures on the pages following show examples of line-item and program budgets.

The Process

Library directors maintain primary responsibility for the budget although as many staff members should be encouraged to participate in its construction as can be accommodated by the process. Not only is the quality of decision-making improved, but participation promotes collaboration among staff and management, allows staff to acquire knowledge of and skills in planning, budgeting and evaluation and grants the organization cohesiveness in its view of the library's mission, goals and priorities for the time period.[16] In other words, everyone will be more willing to buy into the final product if they have had to opportunity to provide information and advice.

Previous year's budgets and expenditure statements form part of the database necessary to compile a new budget. In certain categories, the previous year's expenditures will predict the minimum amounts necessary for the following year. If, for instance, the utility budget was overspent because the cost of fuel rose unexpectedly during the fiscal year, an increased amount must be built into the following year's budget unless a decision is made to curtail hours. Data collected as output measures can also inform the budget distribution process. Some libraries allocate one-half of their budget to the central library and one-half to branches. Of the amount for branches, 40% is distributed equally, the other 60% based on variables of patron count. Another library uses collection size, items added per year, circulation, number of reference and information questions and number of programs per location as the basis for apportioning its funds.[17]

Figure 13
THE LINE-ITEM BUDGET

Account Code	Object	Actual Expenditure 1987	Request 1988
100300	Personnel		
100301	Full Time	$748,322	$800,705
100302	Part Time	110,218	117,933
100303	Overtime	8,240	8,817
200300	Benefits		
200301	Social Security	51,959	55,596
200302	Pension	75,345	80,619
200303	Health Insurance	32,000	34,240
	TOTAL PERSONNEL	$1,026,084	$1,097,910
300300	Materials		
300301	Books	26,250	28,046
300302	Periodicals	18,611	19,913
300303	Databases	21,816	23,343
300304	Documents	5,300	5,671
	TOTAL MATERIALS	$71,977	$77,015
400300	Supplies		
400301	Office	5,250	5,618
400302	Computer	3,190	3,413
500300	Communication		
500301	Postage	12,600	13,482
500302	Telephone	4,500	4,815
500303	Datalines	13,500	14,445
600300	Conferences & dues	8,500	9,095
700300	Staff Development	4,000	4,280
	TOTAL OPERATING	$123,517	$132,163
	GRAND TOTAL	$1,149,601	$1,230,073

from Barry Devlin, "Basic Budget Primer," in Sellen and Turock. 32.

Figure 14
THE PROGRAM BUDGET

Account Code	Object	Actual Expenditure 1987	Request 1988
100300	Personnel		
100301	Full Time	$140,971	$150,839
100302	Part Time	29,680	46,758
100303	Overtime	--	--
200300	Benefits		
200301	Social Security	18,320	19,236
200302	Pension	13,380	14,532
200303	Health Insurance	10,503	11,028
	TOTAL PERSONNEL	213,314	$242,393
300300	Materials	24,600	24,950
300301	Books	14,760	15,245
300302	Periodicals	16,810	15,731
300303	Databases	4,500	4,500
300304	Documents	$60,670	$60,426
	TOTAL MATERIALS		
400300	Supplies		
400301	Office	5,250	1,500
400302	Computer	2,109	1,100
500300	Communications		
500301	Postage	10,010	11.011
500302	Telephone	10,308	10,300
500303	Datalines	18,402	13,462
600300	Conferences & dues	4,210	4,210
700300	Staff Development	4,200	4,280
800,300	Programming	8,250	8,250
900,300	Van Maintenance	--	500
	TOTAL OPERATING	$59,989	$54,533
	GRAND TOTAL	$353,973	$357,352

from Barry Devlin, "Basic Budget Primer," in Sellen and Turock. 33.

Flexibility is one aspect of a good budget. The opportunity to purchase some new equipment or sets of books, to act cooperatively with regional libraries to establish a new network should not be overlooked because they are not specifically described in the budget, as long as they fulfill the spirit of a budget allocation. Caution, however, is required when shifting large sums of money from one category to another--from staff to materials, for instance -- and permission from the library board or even the municipality should probably be obtained before the transfer is executed.

Several months in advance of the fiscal year, guidelines for preparation of the budget are formulated and distributed to participants. They will be given a timetable for stages of submission and informed of any constraints such as a ceiling in percentage increase or retrenchment requirements. Departmental units and other administrators gather information about current operations, future programs, personnel and equipment needs, and other unusual expenses. Larger libraries may operate on a system of departmental budget requests submitted to an administrative body for evaluation and modification.

When the budgets for all library programs have been merged, they are presented in preliminary form to the Finance Committee of the Board for consideration. New programs and anticipated revenue requests are explained. The Board approves the final budget, which is then transmitted to the funding body(ies) and explained at public hearings. The municipality(ities) collates all budget requests of community organizations and agencies and makes an allocation based on its assessment of need and merit, what is, in reality, a negotiated distribution of resources.

Retrenchment Budgets

Creating retrenchment budgets is painful for librarians. Too often, of late, they have had to confront this unpleasant task with the only three strategies available: cut services, increase organizational productivity, or identify new sources of financial resources to supplement existing ones. There are advantages to having to analyze costs and benefits, establish priorities and make choices between and among them. Cost-benefit studies can reveal the value of an investment in a particular service. Efforts to stave off budget cuts may sometimes be successful if the impact is described in terms meaningful to the community.

The first step in retrenchment is often to *freeze* employment. If personnel cutbacks become necessary, labor contracts and civil service may dictate how this will be achieved. If not, the next step is to reduce or eliminate part-time workers, and then use seniority as the criterion for further cuts.[18] The most common retrenchment practice is to reduce the materials budget temporarily. This may be a short-sighted strategy that causes permanent harm to the quality of the collection.

Implementing budget cuts is best affected by dividing the proposed cut into segments. If a 50% cut is required, first reduce service by 25% and then by an additional 33%. Some budget managers begin their proposed budgets at 90% and identify what programs this would eliminate. So successful is this exercise in revealing possible change and substitution that managers often find the proposed cuts remaining and new programs instituted when the budget is rebuilt to 100% or beyond.

Capital Budgets

Capital budgets are multi-year plans for acquiring what the federal government labels "big-ticket" items. They are based on a capital improvement list, derived from the library's plan, arranged in priority of execution, assigned probable costs, possible methods of financing and other pertinent information. They use the same principles of budgeting as applied to annual budgets. Capital expenditures draw on different sources of revenue, referenda, specific fund-raising campaigns, or borrowing.

Maintaining an up-to-date capital plan not only rationalizes the library's future, but also positions it to apply for new grant funds as they become available. When LSCA Title II funds for construction suddenly were released after the Title had remained unfunded for a decade, libraries with capital plans and budgets were ready to make application for them.

BUDGET PRESENTATION

The People endow the government with the responsibility of allocating society's resources. They do this through the political process in which government apportions the funds it has raised from taxes among competing persons and purposes. Invariably there are more demands on the funds than there are moneys available. Decisions made about a governmental budget are signals, messages sent about the preferences of the society. Municipal allocations are based on precedent. The fact that something was done before means that it will probably be done again. Usually a governmental unit will proceed from an existing foundation, using an incremental approach, and basing its decisions on some notion of "fair share." Fair share relates to the base an agency has established, but also to

> the expectation that it will receive some proportion of funds, if any, which are to be increased over or decreased below the base of the various governmental agencies. Fair share, then, reflects a convergence of expectations on roughly how much an agency is to receive in comparison to others.[19]

The community's notion of fair share is made manifest during the budget process. Agencies perceived as receiving more than their share of material wealth may be squeezed back into shape in the next fiscal cycle. Traditions can be changed; shares of the community pie sliced differently. But this requires time, patience and establishing meaningful relations with those responsible for awarding the funds. Credibility and community confidence are achieved in two ways. First, by being what decision makers think *they* themselves are. Funding bodies consider themselves efficient, effective, devoted to their work and careful with taxpayers' money. They think of themselves as aboveboard, fair, square-shooters, and frank persons. Second, by being forthright and honest in dealing with municipal officials, not by trading in lies, misstatements and deceptions. Playing it straight with funding bodies should, over time, produce a relationship of mutual trust between requester and grantor, one that enhances the bargaining position of the agency and simplifies the negotiating process.[20]

Defense of the budget in a public forum requires careful preparation. Presentations are the responsibility of the board and senior administrators. Often the board president will make an initial statement and the director will conclude. Simple visual aids, charts and slides help to provide clear pictures of the library's program. The aim is to convince the governing body that its funds have been used effectively and that those being requested are necessary to meet a need and will be well spent. Statistics, presented as raw data or as per capita figures, that show achievement or that highlight local deficiencies can be persuasive. Comparing per capita support of libraries in a region to illustrate the relative poverty of the local one is better than using aggregate numbers. On the other hand, demonstrating growth by presenting growth in circulation statistics or numbers attending programs can be impressive. Fund requests are best translated into service terms. For instance, explaining that a $20,000 increase in the materials budget would purchase 1,000 more books and result in 4,000 additional circulations based on per volume circulations is more effective than simply requesting the money.

Knowing the municipal officials helps to avoid possible landmines. "One set of commissioners may be proud of the library's standing as best-funded in the state; another set will find this an indication that the library's budget can be cut."[21]

FINANCIAL REPORTING

Librarians prepare, or have their financial managers prepare, monthly statements of revenues and expenditures for presentation at board meetings. These generally compare current status with anticipated amounts based on the budget forecasts. Often, percentages of category allocations already spent and still remaining are provided, in addition to the dollar amounts.

Monthly reports feed into annual financial reports, quantitative statements of how well the library has achieved its financial goals, that is, met its budget. Typically, the financial report is embedded in a qualitative and statistical report describing the libraries service accomplishments for the year. It answers the need to be accountable and often includes comparative and benchmark figures. Annual reports, both numerical and qualitative, provide information for internal management, patrons, governing boards, municipalities and others. A professional looking document serves as an excellent public relations vehicle and can be used in conjunction with presentations to various business and civic groups.

Libraries are responsible for arranging for an annual audit conducted by an independent CPA whose services have been secured through a process of competitive bidding. Audits assure that public funds have been spent appropriately, that there has been no misappropriation of funds nor any improper practices. There are dangers in using the same accountant over too long a time period. Practices become institutionalized, readily recognizable and therefore amenable to theft. State libraries, particularly those who dispense aid, require reports that document expenditures, revenues and usage, sometimes in exquisite detail and frequently in categories not consistent with a library's accounting practices.

FINANCIAL PRACTICES

Libraries must gear their financial practices to state statutes and regulations that apply to them. These are found both in state laws relating to libraries and in general state laws dealing with financial practices of local government.

Handling Money

Libraries generate substantial amounts of cash during the course of a day as they collect fines and fees for photocopying and other services. These require speedy, daily handling, orderly accounting and swift deposit.

Petty cash funds are established to pay for small, everyday library expenditures. These funds, too, must be carefully recorded and monitored. The amounts of money kept in the petty cash fund are modest and replenished as they are expended in order to discourage their being used for more expensive purchases. Postage stamps and supplies are likely targets of petty theft. Caution suggests that only enough for current needs remain accessible.

Library Bookkeeping

The fundamental purpose of library bookkeeping is to keep expenditures and encumbrances within the budget. Categories harmonizing with the budget and reporting requirements are established and transactions recorded within them. In some municipalities, major accounting is handled by the central administration, but most libraries keep their own records, as well. Endowment funds are separated from municipal appropriations for purposes of accountability.

Automating Financial Records

Library finances are amenable to automation. Computer programs have facilitated budget preparation, monthly reporting, and producing annual and other financial reports. Computers have also eliminated numerous errors. Unfortunately, computational problems continue to recur because people manipulate data and people make mistakes. They are unavoidable.

Insurance

For insurance purposes, up-to-date inventories and evaluations of library materials, catalog records and equipment is obligatory. Fire and extended coverage insurance is maintained on buildings and contents by most libraries. Three elements are used to estimate the amount of insurance required to safeguard the library's contents. The first, covering the bulk of the collection, is based on an average per volume cost plus acquisition and accession fees. The second specifically applies to rare books, original paintings and the like, which may have to be listed and evaluated individually. The third includes the contents of the catalog, the cabinets or computers and the terminals themselves. The rate of obsolescence within disciplines varies and must be accounted for in the insurance estimate. A document listing the size of collections according to classification, using the shelf list to estimate the items within a category, accompanied by an average cost of replacement for each discipline, should be maintained and can be used as the library's evaluation of the cost of its materials. The policies should be reviewed every three or four years to assure that the coverage remains adequate.[22]

SUMMARY

The financial responsibility of the library can be described as a stewardship carrying the obligation to use the public's money in a manner that protects its investment and produces results that meet its needs. Libraries, as "public goods" have been seen as appropriate recipients of public funds. Taxes collected by local municipalities are major providers of library funds. However, there is increasing interest in seeking resources from higher levels of government and from private sources.

Many libraries have fallen on hard times and predictions abound about continuing difficulties. There are steps that can be taken to diminish the extent of budget reversals. Careful financial planning and role setting, both long-range and short-term, increased productivity, and priority determinations all help to stay the course. Clear and consistent budgets and reports attest to responsible fiscal administration. Libraries that have earned respect and fulfill their proper functions are most likely to receive their "fair share" of community resources.

NOTES AND SUGGESTED READINGS

Notes

1. W. David Penniman, "On Their Terms," in Betty-Carol Sellen and Betty Turock eds., *The Bottom-Line Reader* (New York: Neal-Schuman, 1990), 4.

2. Tracy Connors and Christopher Callaghan, *Financial Management for Non Profit Organizations* (New York: American Management Association, 1982), 2.

3. Betty Turock and Andrea Pedolsky, *Creating a Financial Plan* (New York: Neal-Schuman, 1992), 4.

4. Darlene Weingand, *Administration of the Small Public Library* (Chicago: American Library Association, 1992), 82.

5. Alphonse Trezza, "Sources of Funding for Public Libraries," in Pat Woodrum and Sul Lee eds. *Managing Public Libraries in the 21st Century* (New York: Haworth Press, 1989), 67.

6. Randall Holcombe, "Introduction: Library Funding and the Concept of Federalism," in Alphonse Trezza ed., *The Funding of Public and Academic Libraries: The Critical Issue for the '90's* (Boston: G.K. Hall, 1992), 1.

7. Ann E. Prentice, *Financial Planning for Libraries* (Metuchen, NJ: Scarecrow Press, 1983).

8. Lawrence White, *The Public Library in the 1980s* (Lexington, MA: D.C. Heath and Company, 1983), 6.

9. Ibid., 144-47.

10. Ibid.

11. Barratt Wilkins, "State Aid to Libraries: A National Perspective," in Alphonse Trezza, *Funding of Public and Academic Libraries* (New York: Macmillan, 1992) 53.

12. Kenneth Boulding, *A Preface to Grants Economics* (New York: Praeger, 1981), 2.

13. Irene Moran, "Writing a Winning Grant Proposal," in Sellen and Turock, 169.

14. Turock and Pedolsky, 109-10.

15. Barry Devlin, "Basic Budget Primer," in Sellen and Turock, 1990, 31.

16. Jan Keene, "Distribution of Library Funds in the 21st Century," in Woodrum and Lee, 1989.

17. Ibid., 106-7.

18. Donald Sager, *Managing the Public Library* (Boston: G.K. Hall, 1989), 78.

19. Aaron Wildavsky, *The New Politics of the Budgetary Process* (Glenview, IL: Scott, Foresman), 1987.

20. Ibid., 74-77.

21. Robert Burgin, "Creative Budget Presentation: Using Statistics to Prove Your Point," in Sellen and Turock, 39.

22. Gerald Myers, *Insurance Manual for Libraries* (Chicago, American Library Association, 1977) and Marvina Brand, ed., *Security for Libraries* (Chicago: American Library Association, 1984).

Suggested Readings

Lynch, Mary J. *Non-Tax Sources of Revenue for Public Libraries.*

Chicago: American Library Association, 1988.

Morris, John. *The Library Disaster Preparedness Handbook.* Chicago: American Library Association, 1986.

Prentice, Ann E. *Financial Planning for Libraries.* Metuchen, NJ: Scarecrow Press, 1983.

Ramsey, Inex and Jackson Ramsey. *Library Planning and Budgeting.* New York: Franklin Watts, 1986.

Roberts, Stephen A. *Cost Management for Library and Information Services.* London: Butterworths, 1985.

Rosenberg, Philip. *Cost Finding for Public Libraries.* Chicago: American Library Association, 1985.

Sellen, Betty-Carol and Betty Turock. *The Bottom-Line Reader.* New York: Neal-Schuman, 1990.

Smith, G. Stevenson. *Managerial Accounting for Libraries and Other Non-Profit Organizations.* Chicago: American Library Association, 1991.

Turock, Betty and Andrea Pedolsky. *Creating a Financial Plan.* New York: Neal-Schuman, 1992.

Trezza, Alphonse. *Funding of Public and Academic Libraries.* New York: Macmillan, 1992.

Trumpeter, Margo and Richard Rounds. *Basic Budgeting Practices for Librarians.* Chicago: American Library Association, 1985

Wildavsky, Aaron. *The New Politics of the Budgetary Process.* Glenview, IL: Scott, Foresman, 1987.

Woodrum, Pat and Sul Lee. *Managing Public Libraries in the 21st Century.* New York: Haworth Press, 1989.

CHAPTER 19

THE LIBRARY BUILDING AND EQUIPMENT

For reasons still not fully understood, a building's structure, its materials, the organization of its space, and

> the cubic area of the separate spaces which comprise it, constitute a language through which men believe they can express values, norms and beliefs.[1]

Library buildings do, indeed, make symbolic statements, sometimes unintentional ones, about themselves and about their communities. From monumental to pedestrian, library architecture mirrors the temporal and spatial ethos of the environment which produced it.

EARLY BUILDINGS

Many American cities and towns still have massive neo-Classic, Victorian, French Provincial, or even English medieval style libraries dating from an earlier age. No matter their architectural mode, they share a major element. They are designed as monuments. Like kindred American public buildings, they celebrated the arrival of a distinctly American culture, one that promised to remain for years to come. Change came slowly, almost imperceptibly, to early American society and its institutions. The solid, inflexible construction of libraries and other public buildings reinforced the prevailing belief that culture was permanent and unlikely to experience radical transformation. Of the twenty-two large public library buildings constructed before 1900, only six have been demolished.[2]

A typical library, circa 1880-1930, contained long stairways, thick walls, and many load-bearing partitions on the main floor to support its massive structure. Its description would have included words like impressive or majestic, rather than cozy. Carnegie libraries typified these structures. Solid in design, they often incorporated into their plans neo-classical columns, weighty pediments and high front stairs. Their exterior and internal walls were always heavy. Standard features of interiors of libraries built during this period were a large central control point from which radiated separate rooms for reference, periodicals, and other spaces designated as study areas. The circulating collection could be found at the rear of the structure in multi-tiered stacks. Furniture was built for endurance not comfort. Buildings of this style, with their load-bearing interior walls and heavy exterior ones, proved inflexible and difficult to adapt and expand to altered conditions.

By necessity, as well as perhaps by preference, early libraries contained large numbers of small spaces, the antithesis of library architectural styles that followed. Ironically, despite their monumental appearance, the buildings were actually small, and quickly became inadequate in the face of rapid population growth, universal automobile travel, widespread literacy, increased educational achievement, and new activist roles for librarians. Later, steel beams and wide use of concrete would make practical other building forms. Changed constituencies and changed services produced a need for innovative structures.

During the period 1929-1945, including the Depression and World War II years, building new library structures held very low priority and few were erected. Some buildings were constructed by the Works Progress Administration (WPA), a federal jobs program designed to put people back to work during the Depression. For most libraries, the question of a new building never arose. Rehabilitating an old one was the only option and those who could aspire to that goal considered themselves fortunate. How to accommodate the massive structures of the past to present and future purposes became a preeminent problem. The difficulties and frustrations of adapting these fortress-like buildings led many to feel nothing but contempt for them.

OPEN OR MODULAR CONSTRUCTION

Reaction against the traditional "monumental" library set in as early as the mid-1930s when Angus Snead MacDonald, a manufacturer of library shelving, first began to speak of new kinds of library buildings. They would, he predicted, be constructed with light, hollow steel weight-bearing columns in which heating ducts could be placed, utilize flush mounted lighting, and have non-load-bearing partitions that could be easily relocated to divide areas. Above all, these buildings would be "modular" in construction, that is, composed of modules of standard size that could be changed at will and permit great flexibility.[3]

Joseph Wheeler, the Dean of American library building consultants, described the objective of this new kind of library design:

The whole trend in library planning is toward keeping the main floor as open as possible, reducing the structural cost, eliminating the waste of space caused by obstructions, and permitting easy shifts later on.[4]

Not only did Wheeler apply this doctrine of "open" space to new libraries, but he utilized these principles in the rehabilitation of existing buildings, as well. He explains why:

The open view of the busy, interesting interiors of libraries in operation is an effective publicity device which expresses the library's desire to welcome and serve everyone. Complete face lifting of old buildings should be sought, even if enlargement does not go with it...The problem is to have the new space if possible at the front, to open up or cover up or demolish the old front (usually including a heavy portico and space consuming stairs and entrance) by a strip of strategic new structure across the old front, as wide as possible.[5]

The result was a mixed blessing. Many rehabilitated libraries became more functional.   However, outstanding examples of American architecture were defaced or even destroyed in the process. Only in recent years has architectural heritage become of sufficient importance to prompt communities to undertake serious efforts to save what still remains.

During the post-World War II period, increased availability of funds resulted in the erection of many libraries. The new structures tended to be modular, creating open spaces with few load-bearing or other kind of partitions. Many were built on concrete slabs. Few had basements. Often, form did follow function, producing, once again, mixed results. While most of the new buildings proved far more functional than their predecessors, aesthetic considerations were sacrificed, resulting in unattractive, dull structures.

Nolan Lushington describes their appearance.

> Concrete and glass boxes were created in the International style with identical large open spaces and masses of fluorescent lights in the ceilings. Large glass sides brought the outside into the building, whether it was a busy, noisy street, or a crowded parking lot...These libraries at their worst gave little clue to users as to whether they were gyms, airplane hangers, or parking garages.[6]

Functional modular libraries, designed to combine utility with economy, are still being constructed, but some attention, at least, is paid to matters of aesthetics.

Contemporary library design and construction is based on the conviction that architecture should flow from an understanding of, first, the nature of the service to be provided, second, the community in which it is housed, and third, an explicit set of library goals and objectives defining the role of the library in the community. From this mix is derived the specific information needed to create a program and construct a building.

Design changes in recently constructed public libraries stem from the currently prevailing view that there are many "publics," rather than a monolithic "public," each using the library differently. The challenge has now become to provide multiple environments for different kinds of groups and uses. There is little doubt that technology, too, will create changed relationships between activities and their patterns of use and drastically alter how libraries look and how they are functionally arranged. Twenty-first century buildings will have to accommodate to a variety of formats -- print, microforms, audio, video and ones yet to be developed.

THE PLANNING PROCESS AND THE BUILDING EFFORT

The Public Library Association asserted, in 1966, that:

Fundamentally a library is not a building but a service organization. The pattern of service to be rendered in a specific community will determine the nature of its physical facilities; there is no standard building plan for public library operation.[7]

If a library is a service organization rather than a building, then service concerns must be addressed before they become building questions. Buildings are tools shaped by purpose. Until the purpose is clear, shaping an efficient tool is impossible.

During the process of planning, the library's aims and goals are explored, community needs assessed and current services, service opportunities, and service constraints examined. A natural outgrowth of the process is a determination of building needs. Effective planning is an ongoing, cyclical process. So, too, is the continuing review of facilities integral to the library's current plan of service.

Frequent evaluation, including facilities requirements, can help libraries avoid the recurring library nightmare of insufficient time to plan when an opportunity to embark on a building project suddenly arises. Creating a plan of service for a community library requires at least nine months and sometimes a year, an amount of time not always available when an unexpected bequest or new governmental funding appears. Pressed for time, library service considerations may remain insufficiently explored and take a back seat to applying for and obtaining the money. In this case, building problems that could easily have been avoided often develop and fester.

DETERMINING NEED

Decisions to take action are triggered by the needs of those to be served and informed by prevailing conditions. Three questions about buildings must be answered before any action is taken:

1. What is the library's current inventory of facilities?
2. Given the role of the library in the community, as defined in its plan of service, what kind of facilities are required?
3. Which new facilities are necessary to bring the inventory of facilities up to the required level?

Answering the first question entails drawing up a list of the strengths and weaknesses of the current library physical plant and of its furniture and equipment, as well as the maintenance schedule. Responding to the second involves compiling a list of facilities a particular community would find necessary in order to support optimal library services. To reply to the final question a comparison must be made between the answers to questions one and two and a list generated of currently unmet needs, including furniture, equipment and proper maintenance.

All of the knotty issues that surface in the development of a plan of improvement connect with question two above because the process of assessing the needs of a community for library facilities is so imprecise. Translating pertinent data about the community, both current and future projections, into concrete building recommendations is filled with uncertainties. Tradition suggests that needs for building facilities should be projected twenty years into the future.[8] On the other hand, the rapid rate of change has led to doubts about whether twenty-year projections are reliable.

Given the cost of construction or even renovation, in most cases a more modest ten-year population projection serves as a better basis for action. The larger question of how best to assign space values to service needs presents more intricate considerations. The problem does not lie in decisions about particular items. We know that one reader's chair occupies approximately 30 square feet of housing in libraries. Similarly, it is relatively easy to set space specifications for shelving and work space. Shelving is produced in three foot wide modules ranging in height from a low of forty-two inches to a high of ninety inches. The standard depth of most book shelving is eight inches, although some materials demand deeper shelves. Generally, circulating collections can be calculated at seven volumes per linear foot or shelving, or twenty-one volumes per three foot shelf. This leaves one-quarter to one-third of each shelf empty for expansion, book shifting, and easy removal and insertion of volumes. Staff work space is normally calculated at between fifty and one hundred and fifty square feet per employee depending on the specific purpose. The real difficulty lies in estimating the *number* of seats that will be needed by a library in that community ten years from now, the *number* of staff who will be working or the number of books a library requires.

Unfortunately, formulas developed to assist librarians in gauging future building needs are anything but scientific. Rather, they are educated guesses calculated from observation and normative behavior. Formulas used today are almost all derived from ones developed by Joseph Wheeler in his landmark 1941 book. What he, and architect Alfred Githens, had suggested as a point of departure is that the total space needs of any community library be calculated on the basis of the number of seats required (the ratio of seats to population served), the number of volumes to be shelved (the ratio of books to projected population) and a value drawn from the number of books the library circulates each year. They assumed that the larger the population, the smaller the per capita space required. Utilizing the VSC formula (volumes, seats, circulation), a sliding scale ranging from .5 to .7 square feet per capita, depending on community size projected 20 years into the future, was calculated. [9] Wheeler's formula was widely accepted, [10] although he himself observed that he may have erred in overestimating space needs, perhaps creating a formula that was too generous.

Ironically, by 1980, Lushington and Mills were suggesting anywhere from .6 of a square foot per capita for populations of 100,000 or more to more than 1 square foot for the smallest of communities. [11] Most recently, Raymond Holt proposed that space requirements be developed incrementally without recourse to formula, considering, instead, existing facilities and collections, population projections for 15 to 20 years, work space needs, and unassigned space. [12] Stairways, mechanical equipment rooms and other space unusable for staff or the public generally occupy 20 to 30% of the total building space.

Reduced to its basic premises, the Wheeler formula suggested that each community of a given size should have available a specific number of seats or volumes. While it was always anticipated that local libraries would adjust the formula to meet local conditions, the question of how the criteria might be refined was never explained.

Formulas offer a point of departure, but are never definitive. Professional judgment and observation, based on thorough knowledge of the community, are in the last analysis the true determinants of how many volumes or seats will meet the service needs of a particular library. Library use studies lend additional insight into the extent to which a population will utilize services.

BUILD, REHABILITATE OR ADAPT

Once the assessment has been completed, and deficiencies of the present structure identified, decisions about how best to remedy the situation become paramount. Four courses of action are possible. First, the structure can be renovated. Second, it can be added to and remodelled. Third, the library can occupy and convert a building originally designed for another purpose. Finally, a completely new building can be erected. Most librarians prefer the final option. Following that path, however, may prove too costly or politically unwise because it will displease important community members who are attached to the present structure.

Each library arrives at its own solution, reached through deliberations made within a broad context and after careful review of all alternatives. Proposals have sometimes been rejected when they undergo scrutiny from the wider community and when questions arise that have gone unconsidered.

Among the important questions that figure into deliberations are: How much additional space must the system provide? Can the existing space be renovated to gain sufficient room? Many buildings, particularly those dating from Pre-World War II, are virtually impossible to alter because of construction difficulties or cost. Adding on, too, can be more expensive and less satisfactory than starting anew. The supposition that money can be saved by an addition is often illusory. Not only must the addition be funded, but renovation of the existing structure is usually essential, as well, generating further expense. Post World War II library buildings, cheap rectangles erected between 1950 and 1980, pose expansion problems. Not only are they poorly constructed, but the faceless character of the original design does not lend itself to enlargement.

In many cases, the space deficiency is insufficiently dramatic to necessitate either a new building or an addition, but is amenable to remedy by more efficient usage of current space. Shortages of shelving room, for instance, can sometimes be alleviated by intensive weeding. Converting large unused closets to offices may solve staff space needs, at least for the short term. Rearranging furniture and shelving can occasionally gain space, as can converting parts of the collection to microform.

Making a decision about whether to construct anew, or to move into a facility erected for other uses, compels gathering as much data about anticipated expenditures as possible and comparing the figures with the price tag on a new building. Costs can be calculated by learning the "going rates" for similar kinds of construction in the area. Any financial outlay for site acquisition and improvement is built into the price. Library standards play an important role in assessing the wisdom of converting existing space to library use. Library floors, for instance, must support extremely heavy loads, particularly in book stack areas where at least 150 pounds per square foot is required. The cost of shoring up commercial construction which rarely has need for those levels of support may be costly. Further, older buildings may contain so many load-bearing partitions on the first level that conversion to library purposes would be prohibitively expensive. In the long run, the expense of adapting an existing structure may be comparable to the price of an entirely new building.

The final judgment on the relative merits of various options normally proceeds along two lines, one financial, the other functional. Which path is cheapest and which will provide the most efficient building? Library directors have generally reported a higher level of satisfaction with the utility and functionality of new buildings than with additions and/or additions and conversions.[13] Moreover, less functional buildings are more expensive to operate. Lower initial prices may lead to misapprehension about real costs. Future operating costs must also be tallied and factored in. It is not unusual for a less costly original investment to prove more expensive in the long term when increased operating costs more than offset the initial price tag. Librarians should be vigilant against illusory, short-term savings.

SITE SELECTION

A review of building alternatives is incomplete without consideration of site location and adequacy. Wheeler, as far back as 1941, noted that:

> The ideal site for a library building is where a large department store, a popular bank, or the busiest office building or drug store could be successfully located.[14]

The definition of an advantageous site would be altered today to include busy places in suburban and rural areas that lack a traditional "downtown," but the emphasis on a well-trafficked site remains sound. A good location incorporates sufficient acreage to permit adequate public and staff parking, as well as space for expansion. As a rule, the number of parking spaces should equal half the total seats contained in the building. Approximately 100 parking spaces, each occupying about 350 square feet, or at least three-quarters of an acre for the parking area would satisfy a library with 200 seats. Alternately municipal zoning laws often use a gauge of 3.5-5 parking slots for each 1,000 square feet of building.

Sites should be tested to discover the existence of unusual subsoil conditions. Both bed-rock or marshy terrain can be expensive to overcome, as can excessive slope. Traffic conditions surrounding any potential site may have an impact on library use. Excessive traffic that creates problems of gaining access to the building or parking lot will discourage patronage.

The potential placement, or orientation, of a building on the site is yet another consideration. For instance, a location that enables the longer part of the building to face north and south is favored over one that faces east and west because the latter orientation may necessitate louvers or other window treatments and additional air conditioning.

THE BUILDING TEAM

Most public library facilities projects, whether new buildings, rehabilitations or expansions, are guided by "building teams," groups that supervise the project from beginning to completion. Serving on the team are the architect, representatives of the governing body -- library trustees or local government officials -- the library director, and, where there is one, the library building consultant. Other staff, and perhaps lay community members, may also be represented. Participation by those who use the building both as staff and public serves to broaden the perspective of the team as it addresses questions. Few library matters command as much staff interest, attention and excitement as does planning a new library facility. Used to living with past mistakes, library staff will do anything possible to help planners avoid future errors. Sadly, the problem sometimes is to convince the building team to listen in advance to their advice.

Many libraries have "in-house" building committees, created by boards of trustees and consisting of board members, even when no expansion is in view. Generally, their work is limited to immediate concerns such as how the library will cope with a leaking roof, rather than considering facilities that may be necessary during the next ten years. Trustee building committees should, however, also serve as long-term planners focusing on the needs of the library, advising the administration and the governing body about all facility requirements, including maintenance, rehabilitation and construction.

Frequent field trips to library systems with new or recently renovated facilities will enlighten board building committees about inadequacies in their own building, as well as introduce them to recent developments in library architecture. On-site visits make real what pictures and descriptions can only suggest. Raising the consciousness of board members, expanding their horizons and imaginations, always redounds to the library's benefit. In recent years, public libraries have entered into a variety of interesting relationships with other agencies. Some share quarters with bookstores. Others have been built with cafés in their basements. Senior citizen centers, elementary schools, and other community agencies have embarked with libraries on cooperative ventures sharing quarters, resources and personnel. Innovations in concepts have produced branches that reflect the ethnic character of their neighborhoods, or the type of clientele. When the building plan is transformed from wishful speculation to actuality, conversations with librarians who have recently experienced construction projects can help avoid many serious mistakes.

Forming the Group

Once the decision to "go" is finally made, the existing building committee may be expanded to include "experts" -- staff, community persons, architects, consultants, interior designers, clerks of the works, whoever is necessary -- or a totally new committee can be formed with board representatives, staff, municipal delegates and community members. The library director is responsible for all aspects of library service and will be deeply involved in the committee's deliberations.

A long and bumpy road faces those who agree to participate. Usually committee members pursue a coordinated, unified process in guiding the project and it proceeds smoothly as a team effort. On occasion, individuals follow their own agendas, making the already complex project tortuous. It is acceptable for team members to disagree on aspects of the work, but controversies should be aired in the presence of the entire building team, prior to the time when reports are submitted to other bodies rather than after.

Many staff members will covet a place on the building team. The choice may rest on a staffer's ability to meet certain demands of serving on it. For instance, will he or she have a sufficient amount of available time to fully participate? Simply mastering the mass of information is time-consuming. Countless meetings add to the burden. A second consideration is the qualities staff members can contribute to the team. Do they work well with others? Are they alert? Can they represent a wide range of staff and public interests?

Non-staff local members must also agree to commit sufficient time to participate fully in the project. Frequently, trustees and local officials lacking the time and/or inclination nonetheless accept membership on the building team, only to miss meetings and otherwise fail to live up to their commitments. Without their participation, the perspective of the building team is altered, which may, in turn, produce severe problems. By agreeing to join the team, trustees or governmental officials tacitly imply active participation. The committee should understand that non-functioning members will be removed and replaced. Local team members fill seats on the basis of their ability to cooperate and for their insight. They should not be selected for partisan reasons and care must be exercised to insure they are without hidden motives, or vested interests. A building team is not the place to reflect the greater community's political differences.

Of critical importance to the entire project is the quality of outside, paid professionals -- the architect, building consultant, interior designer and construction superintendent or clerk of the works -- engaged by the library to develop and complete the project.

THE ARCHITECT

The architect, the library's building design and construction expert, creates the structure and later certifies that accepted plans are being followed and that construction is proceeding according to specifications. It follows, therefore, that there must be supreme confidence in the capacity of the architect to discharge his or her responsibilities. While architects usually understand well that they must communicate and work with library trustees and local government officials, they sometimes give short shrift to other participants, particularly library staff. Some architects have been known to resent building consultants and/or interior designers. Ignoring anyone during the design and construction phases of a project is both foolish and potentially costly.

Most problems that emerge between librarians and architects are generated by conflicting goals for the facility in question. Architects want to look at completed projects as products of good design. Librarians seek structures that accommodate quality library service, security and control. The best approach to avoiding adversarial relations is for architects and librarians to be aware of the end product each seeks.

Determining which architect will best serve the library can be difficult. Architects commonly possess a minimum level of competence and experience, and will present themselves as both eager and agreeable. But how does a library select from among a group of applicants? The first step is to evaluate critically all of the information presented with the application. Letters of reference are helpful. More useful, however, are telephone calls to former clients, those agreeing to serve as referees, as well as others. Probing questions regarding the architect's quality of design, ability to administer a building project -- particularly within set financial constraints -- and willingness to work with a group of people should be posed.

The nature and quality of past work is another consideration. Has the architect ever built a library, or designed and constructed a public building? Is she or he aware of pertinent legal statutes and regulations? How does the architect establish projected costs for a building? Have there been cost over-runs on previous projects, particularly public ones? This information, too, is probably best acquired through informal channels, that is, conversations with past employers.

Testimony of any one previous client, however, should be received with caution. It may be unreliable. It is preferable to focus on patterns of performance, rather than on single assessments that may be skewed by personal bias. In fairness, architects being considered should be aware that the library intends to solicit a wide range of comment about their abilities. Visits to some of an architect's completed projects are helpful in judging performance, particularly if they include conversations with those who may have been involved in the undertaking. Building team members often have visceral reactions to the structures and this, too, provides useful, if highly subjective, information.

Personal interviews with architects, and, if they choose, their firm's key consultants including engineers of various kinds, represent another worthwhile evaluative tool. Delegated members of the building team, particularly representatives of the governing body, as well as the library director usually conduct the interviews. Others may be invited to attend in an advisory capacity. The same kind of information as was developed from the background check is usually elicited during the interview, but the architect has an opportunity to place on the record insights that she or he might have about the particular project. In addition, it may be possible to learn how the architect's personality will mesh with those of committee members and, particularly, with the library director whose subjective judgment is crucial, and, in the final analysis, of greatest moment.

An architect's lack of previous library design experience is not necessarily fatal. While prior experience is certainly preferable, some architectural firms untested in library construction display such talent, imagination, and energy that they warrant serious consideration, even when compared with firms that have built libraries. This is particularly true for projects utilizing a building team approach, with an experienced library building consultant. Working within that framework, the novice library architect can draw on the collective experience of other team members. The amount of the fee for service levied by the architect will also have an impact on the choice. Architectural fees normally range from 6 to 9 % of the building's cost. In some communities, a premium is put on hiring the lowest bidder. Every librarian wants to complete a building for as little cost as possible, but choosing the least expensive architect is probably short-sighted because he or she may well be the least competent of the applicants.

The community may have an ongoing relationship with an architectural firm and expect the library to use it, as well. Too often, this firm will have little or no understanding about or experience with libraries, making the team's job more difficult. Also, architects are marked by certain styles that characterize their work. To hire a local architect may be tantamount to purchasing a certain building look, one already existing in a number of community structures. On the other hand, using a local firm has some advantages. Easier, more frequent and more economical consultation is possible. A local architect who feels pride in the community and in the region may work that much harder.

CONSULTANTS AND OTHER TEAM MEMBERS

The question of whether or not to engage a library building consultant should usually be answered in the affirmative, particularly with large projects -- those expected to cost more than

$50,000.[15] Most library directors and most architects have been involved with few, if any, library building projects. Library consultants offer experience. It is possible, but not likely, that a library director will produce an effective building program and provide excellent leadership within the building team. Weighed against the costs of serious mistakes in the building process, this seems a needless risk. Consultants can be considered as necessary and relatively inexpensive insurance policies.

Consultants serve another important function on the building team. They bring with them what might be called a "tyranny of expertise" which can work to the benefit of the library. The words of librarians often carry less weight with architects or municipal officials than they should. An outside consultant, on the other hand, is a library advocate whose authority and advice command respect. Some building consultants are hired by the architectural firm designing the library as part of the service they provide. This arrangement can work well, but it may limit the consultant's advocacy role since the employer is the architect, not the library. The process of selecting a library building consultant is similar to that followed in engaging an architect. Both demand careful review of past assignments and a personal interview. Further, the team must ascertain that the building consultant has the same understanding about his or her role as it does.

Building consultant fees are calculated in a variety of ways. They can be based on a percentage of the building project cost, a per diem rate or an hourly one. Hourly rates for experienced consultants range from $50 to $150. Part-time consultants with full-time jobs tend to charge less than do full-time ones because they have no overhead, but they are sometimes less experienced.

Every library engaged in translating a building plan into an actual structure faces supervision problems. Architects normally provide general supervision to a project, but continual on-site direction can only be assured if a project supervisor or clerk of the works is employed, either through the architect as part of his or her team, or directly by the library. On-site supervision is advisable to make certain that the library receives what it has contracted for.

Despite frequent architect on-site visits, deficiencies arise when shoddy work is covered up and hidden from sight. For smaller projects, supervision should be included in the architect's contract, so that work can be easily coordinated. On larger ones, the library may hire a firm whose business it is to provide project supervision. Charges for full-time supervision are a percentage of building project cost. Fees for small projects are provided on a cost plus basis, or cost plus profit margin, approximately 10% of the cost.

Furniture and equipment selection is an integral part of the building project, and specifications for their purchase should be developed early in the process. Interior design should never be an afterthought. The task of creating a furniture and equipment package rests most easily in the hands of an experienced designer, operating either as an independent contractor or as part of the architect's design team. In either case, the interior designer must have sound aesthetic judgment and a clear awareness of how a library functions. If possible, the interior designer should attend preliminary design conferences, particularly those that deal with areas on which the architect and other members of the building team must cooperate.

THE BUILDING PROGRAM

The building program, the first in what will be a series of basic documents, has a two-fold purpose. First, it must convey to any reader a sense of the spirit of the building in prospect. Second, it must itemize the specific space needs of every element in the building and describe their relationships to each other and to the building as a whole. This document informs staff, trustees, the public and government officials about criteria and guidelines for the new facility and presents a functional context for the development of the architect's building design. A library building consultant may prepare the actual written program, but if active planning has preceded the report, the other members of the building team will already have significantly influenced the document. The building program is not a permanent, unchangeable instrument. To the contrary, it usually signals the beginning of a dialogue about the nature of the building to be erected. Just as the architect may be asked to scrap preliminary designs and redevelop ideas, the building consultant must also be prepared to reconsider approaches and compromise as the building program is refined.

RECURRING BUILDING CONCERNS

All of the recurring concerns with major impact on building projects involve who will use the building, for what purpose, and in what way. Use, here, refers to both the public and the staff and extends to all elements from shelving to sound.

Shelving

Every public library user or worker can attest to the lack of utility of the 90 inch high, seven shelf book section, for so long a fixture in American public libraries. Patrons and staff alike have difficulty reaching both its upper and lower ranges. Dropping down to six shelves may utilize more floor space for shelving, but it will improve real use of the collection. Similarly, the traditional three foot aisle between book stacks is inadequate, and should be widened at least to 42 inches, if not to four feet. The book stack, itself, with shelves set at a ninety degree angle to the ground makes it difficult to read book spines. Bookstores have long used tilted up shelves so that titles can be read with relative ease. Some libraries have started to shelve portions of their popular book collections with covers facing out in order to stimulate public interest. This, too, results in increased floor space needs. The impact of many of these steps on shelving space requirements points up, once again, the inadequacy of space formulas still widely accepted.

Seating and Sound

How public seating is arranged may predict the manner in

which it will be utilized. Most people, though not all, prefer space that gives them a sense of privacy. For some, however, isolation is unwelcome. Finding a proper balance is necessary, albeit difficult.

Sound control has grown increasingly problematic in recent years, partially as a consequence of the open style of library architecture utilized during the post World War II era. With little or no noise containment, the public library that functions as a quiet place to study is almost a relic. The rising decibel level, exacerbated by improved access of younger children to adult collections and services, can be irritating to senior citizens. Librarians forget that different patrons place different demands on the library, sometimes conflicting ones. A group of teen-agers discussing a joint project is bound to annoy an older patron who seeks a quiet study area, especially if they are in close proximity to one another. Young people growing up with rock music, television, and "boom boxes," probably experience sound, itself, differently than do those of previous generations. Loud to an older person may be normal to a younger one. Saddled with "open space," the library is able to satisfy neither user. Compounding this generational problem is the fact that a single user may use differing kinds of space at different times. This single dimensional approach is usually justified by the need to maintain control of space with a minimum of staff. However, multiple environments can be shaped to meet different uses and still provide central control and service points. Smaller rooms enclosed by glass partitions can be created or spaces formed on more than one level, reasonably isolated, yet amenable to supervision.

Lighting

The question of what constitutes sufficient library lighting has absorbed the attention of librarians and architects for much of this century, yet the appropriate amount remains debateable. Over the last fifty years, the argument has come full circle. In 1941, Wheeler noted that even distribution of light was probably the key to a successful illumination scheme, and deemed 20 foot candles at the reading level adequate.[16] The next 30 years witnessed a movement toward increasing the intensity of light to 100 or more foot candles, often creating excessive glare and shadow. As energy grew more expensive, a reaction set in.

By 1981, Rochell was recommending 30 foot candles in reading areas.[17] Experts now agree on lower levels of intensity than were used in the 1950-1975 period, and continue to stress even diffusion of light as a key to more effective illumination, a return to the spirit of the 1941 recommendations. There is a growing awareness that lighting depends on the tasks to be performed. For instance, terminals, whether for staff or public, are particularly susceptible to glare.

New Technology

"Wire," as in cable, is a word that contemporary library planners must always keep in mind. Wiring requirements today bear little resemblance to those of only ten years ago. The same statement will probably be accurate again in another ten years. Providing adequate, flexible power and communication capabilities is critical. The building must be "forgiving," that is, amenable to widespread change in the amount and location of wire in the foreseeable future.

The library as a vital element in the "wired community" demands that transmission lines be available to offices and residences as well as from and to great distances. The location of computer terminals, particularly those for the public, presents considerations that never arose when determining the placement of the card catalogs. Situating terminals in stack areas provides far better access to collections and solves many problems of multi-level buildings. A separate computer station adapted for public use takes up about a forty square foot area. Installing one utilizes a minimum amount of space. But allowing for four or five in one place, or many throughout a library, could cause problems if not factored into the building during the design stage.

Children's Rooms

Providing children's rooms or areas never provokes hostile questions or opposition. In fact, children's rooms in public libraries have been subject to more experimentation than any other section of the library, sometimes to their profit and occasionally to their detriment. Designs for children's rooms have ranged from down-sized replicas of adult facilities to cloying versions of childhood envisioned by Hollywood in 1930s films. The object should be to design and furnish a space especially for children that will delight and welcome them. The maximum height for children's book stacks should be five feet, with picture book shelving a maximum of forty two inches high. Table heights, seats and counter spaces should be scaled to children's sizes, and at least several inches lower than in adult areas. The exact dimensions of children's furnishings will depend on how many young persons there are in the community and their age distribution, and the age at which a child moves into the library's adult section. A children's room that keeps children longer will supply a higher percentage of full-sized furniture than will a library that passes children on at a younger age. Where possible, the story hour area -- perhaps story steps, a viewing area for audio-visual products and a place to hold programs including live performances -- should be located in or in close proximity to the children's room.

Meeting Rooms

Almost all contemporary public libraries have meeting rooms, although they remain "frills" in the minds of some trustees and some members of the public. This question gains legitimacy only when libraries have not clearly articulated their goals and objectives and spelled out how the meeting rooms help to serve institutional purposes. Meeting rooms are almost always "multi-purpose," sufficiently flexible to house widely varying activities. They accommodate art exhibits, concerts, dance recitals, receptions, films and formal meetings. Adaptability is enhanced by including kitchen facilities; providing wall strips, demountable art panels and exhibit cases for art work; designing an oblong room for screening films; and using room dividers to create more and smaller separate meeting spaces. Unfortunately, most meeting facilities permit the library to do many things, but nothing very well given the number of compromises that have been made so that a wide range of activities can be offered.

Storage Space

One building problem that seldom receives proper attention is the provision and placement of adequate storage and maintenance support space, perhaps because maintenance foremen rarely serve on building teams and because no building storage standards have been promulgated. Realization that inadequate quarters for this purpose in new and renovated buildings, as well as in old ones, have generally been allowed should serve as sufficient warning that an especially long look at the problem by building teams is warranted.

Staff Quarters

The proportion of space occupied by staff is small in contrast with that utilized by collections and readers. Nonetheless, adequately housing personnel is important and too frequently given short-shrift by building planners. Library staff quarters become congested and inadequate long before others parts of the library do. Contrary to current library practice, we believe that all professional personnel in public libraries should have their own offices, or at least share a room with one or two others. An average of 150 to 175 square per staff member is probably sufficient. While some contend that technology will reduce the number of staff members, the space required for an automated work station will be somewhat larger than for its manual predecessor. Some suggest that an additional 10 square feet should be added to a secretary's work state where use of a microcomputer or word-processing terminal is involved.

Handicapped Access

The aim of those involved in constructing library buildings, whether new or renovated, is to serve the entire community population, including those for whom access to traditional buildings poses special problems. Concerns for those with disabilities that limit access to public facilities and to equal employment opportunities has caused the federal government to enact legislation designed to remove the barriers that prevent them from participating in mainstream American life. This body of law, together with applicable state and local laws and regulations, constitute the framework for action of those subject to the legislation.

Federal law regarding handicapped persons can be seen as a series of increasingly broader and more inclusive steps.

The *Civil Rights Act of 1964* dealt generally with problems of discrimination in the Society;

Section 504 of the Rehabilitation Act of 1973 made it illegal for either federal agencies, or other organizations outside the federal government that received any form of federal funding to discriminate against any one based on their disabilities;

The Americans with Disabilities Act (ADA), Public Law 101-336, extends the provisions of Section 504 to public entities regardless of whether or not they receive federal funds for any purpose. ADA regulations affecting public employment became effective on July 26, 1992.

The federal government has been signaling its intention to end discrimination against those with disabilities since 1973. Section 504 lists the steps that must be taken to eliminate barriers that limit access and frame the basis of the regulations included in the

Americans with Disabilities Act. The ADA provisions are not unreasonable. They do not mandate actions that would result in fundamental changes in a library's public service program or that would present undue financial or administrative burdens. The law intends that a doctrine of reasonableness govern compliance. However, when new facilities are constructed all of the provisions of ADA must be met. The same holds true for *substantial* alterations, rehabilitations and building expansions. Only when renovation work is minor is it possible to claim exemption from ADA provisions. Universal access to library resources and services has been a tenet of American Public Library faith. Actions taken by any library to circumvent the regulations would be difficult to defend.

Library practitioners must become familiar with the law itself, and with regulations and relevant cases that touch on its meaning and intent. At present, libraries are responsible for complying with one of two building guidelines, either Americans with Disabilities Act Accessibility Guidelines for Buildings and Facilities (ADAAG) or Uniform Federal Accessibility Standards (UFAS). These guides to barrier free access to public accommodations deal with such problems as

> *Freedom of Access* - entrances with free access to those with disabilities, including entrances located on ground level, or with ramp access, doors wide enough for wheelchair access and light enough to be used by those with disabilities.

> *Freedom of Movement within the Building* - adequate aisle space, and elevators connecting all building levels.

> *Proper Design of Furniture and Equipment* - tables which can accommodate wheelchairs, controls within reach of those in wheelchairs.

> *Devices that expedite use for patrons with other special*

needs - Telecommunication instruments for the Deaf, TDD's, signs in Braille.

Special Designs to make restrooms accessible.

The design specifications for patrons with special needs are extensive, but meeting the requirements is not necessarily costly, particularly in new buildings. Even with older structures, the design constraints imposed by ADA are, in most cases, simply corrections that should have been made had the Act never existed.

Security

The degree to which security systems are necessary depends, to a great extent, on the particular institution. All public libraries provide emergency exits, fire controls and fire and police call systems. Most librarians now prefer to have a public address system which can be used for emergencies as well as to notify patrons of closing times. The decision about whether to acquire book theft detection systems and equipment alarms are more discretionary and dependent on the environment. A library in a community where vandalism is high will add security measures that might be unnecessary in a library located elsewhere. For instance, many libraries have installed burglar alarms that alert police to illegal or forced entry when the library is closed. Where the security of readers in the stacks is a matter of concern, buildings must be designed with as many areas of stacks as possible in sight of and capable of being supervised by library personnel.

FUNDING THE LIBRARY BUILDING

The major source of funding for new or renovated public libraries is local government, a dismaying fact given the intense competition with other public agencies for limited dollars. Remaining accountable helps to assure that in the eventuality that money becomes available the library will be considered. Part of accountability is keeping municipalities informed of all plans, projected and actual. Developing a building plan whose foundation is emerging service requirements both demonstrates documented need and responsible behavior.

A second major source of library capital funding may be found in other levels of government -- county, state and federal. County coffers have from time-to-time been tapped for limited assistance in capital projects. Occasionally, funding for public library projects has been available from state treasuries. The perspective of both county and state government is different than that of local government. Both are interested in library service that transcends local jurisdictions. Funding from municipalities at this level may be tied to developing service for wider areas.

The federal government has offered money through the Library Services and Construction Act (LSCA) on and off for many years, generally in programs administered by state library agencies. In addition, special federal programs, including Works Project Administration (WPA) in the 1930s, and, more recently, Appalachian Regional Funds, Economic Development Act funds and National Endowment for the Humanities Challenge Grants have included libraries among their recipients for construction aid.

Governmental funding is part of the political process. Making building money available is a political judgment and is made on the basis of the political viability of such a move. If librarians want governmental aid in the future, it will be necessary for them to promote this cause in the political arena.

The private sector may also be a source for building funds. Foundations, endowments, wealthy individuals and a capitol campaign are all possibilities. The public library is one of the few local services for which non-public funds can be raised. The act of attempting to raise funds from these sources not only provides concrete evidence of the library's eagerness to place as little stress as possible on the local budget, but also allows the library to focus public attention on library problems. Since librarians, trustees and local officials are not likely to be skilled fund raisers, hiring an experienced consultant to explore fundraising potential and or to oversee a campaign should be considered.[18]

THE BUILDING CYCLE

What occurs in that period between the development of preliminary designs and cutting the ribbon at the opening is the building construction, itself. Fraught with a wealth of peculiar problems, this sometimes long period is made even more difficult when questions that have not been resolved before the cycle begins must now, at last, be addressed.

The first step in the cycle, sometimes referred to as the "schematic design" phase, results in the production of functional sketches. Next is a preliminary plan that includes walls, doors, windows, and other general features of the design, perhaps delineating preliminary furniture layouts, as well. The interior designer becomes involved at this stage. Until now, the project is still fluid. Changes in approach are to be expected, even encouraged, in the interest of achieving the best possible design solutions. It is illegitimate for the architect to levy additional charges for alterations made before preliminary designs are accepted. However, once full approval has been given by the library's governing body, the architect will begin to produce working drawings after which any changes will incur additional cost, as well as delay. In order to avoid causing both extra outlays of time and money, the building team must review all plans in an orderly, systematic and timely fashion.

Successful navigation through the hazards of document development, bidding, and construction demands careful attention to detail and the recognition that all elements of the design documents and of the construction flow from the building program and approved preliminary designs. Efforts to assure that the construction documents follow those original reports will result in greater efficiency.

Most public projects are subject to public bidding at which time competing contractors quote their "best" prices for construction of the building. Public law mandates that the lowest *responsible* bid be accepted. To meet that stricture, library authorities require proof of a contractor's sound financial condition, and a solid record of previous construction, often before a contractor is permitted to bid. Typically, bids are accompanied by *bid bonds,* insured guarantees that the bidder will execute the contract, if awarded, and *performance bonds,* insured guarantees that the building will be completed at the bid price. With this evidence in hand, a contract between the library and the contractor will be drawn and signed after the contractor has provided evidence of satisfactory liability insurance.

The architect plays a dominant role during the design period. However, the building consultant also has an important part to play, assuring that from a library perspective that what has been developed is functionally sound. During the construction phase, the project clerk or the works or project superintendent assumes a commanding place, affirming that actual work reflects the intention of design documents.

SUMMARY

Developing and executing a building program is one of the most exacting, yet exciting, challenges that a public librarian will face. Elements of the process are uncontrollable. Political issues surface; constituent groups alter the context of public consideration by raising new, often peripheral, issues; contractors chosen prove incompetent.

Librarians, however, have the power to act in the library's interest to contain the problems. Certainly, they can influence those matters over which they have dominion. They can advise about which road to follow, about which professionals are competent to design the project. They can create a structure within which careful planning and execution will proceed. An orderly process is the best defense against unexpected challenges that arise to derail a project.

A building program articulates the library's vision of the project. The architect's preliminary sketches translate and interpret the concept into visual form. Later drawings reassemble and rearrange the pieces into an integrated and harmonious, yet affordable structure. Ascertaining that the program is actualized as written is the responsibility of the library director whose failure to monitor the ongoing process will almost invariably lead to a faulty structure. It is probably well to remember, as the distinguished architect Ralph Adams Cram is reported to have insisted about cathedrals, "nothing is unimportant."

NOTES AND SUGGESTED READINGS

Notes

1. Robert Gutman, "Library Architecture and People," in Ernest DeProspo ed., *The Library Building Consultant* (New Brunswick, NJ: Rutgers University Press, 1969), 28-29.

2. Donald Oehlerts, *Books and Blueprints* (New York: Greenwood Press, 1991), 130.

3. Angus Snead McDonald, "Modular Library Planning," in American Institute of Architects *The Library Building* (Chicago: American Library Association, 1947), 16-18.

4. Joseph Wheeler and Herbert Goldhor, *Practical Administration of Public Libraries* (New York: Harper, 1962), 555.

5. Ibid., 552-53.

6. Nolan Lushington and Willis Mills, *Libraries Designed for Users* (Hamden, CT: Library Professional Pub., 1980), 28-29.

7. Public Library Association, *Minimum Standards for Public Library Systems, 1966* (Chicago: American Library Association, 1967), 60.

8. Wheeler, Joseph and Alfred Githens, *The American Public Library Building* (Chicago: American Library Association, 1941), 43.

9. Ibid.

10. Wheeler himself restated it in his revised text Wheeler and Goldhor, 1962; Carleton Rochell repeated it in his revision, Carlton Rochell, *Wheeler and Goldhor's Practical Administration of Public Libraries* rev. ed. (New York: Harper, 1981); American Library Association standards adopted part of the formula, and it was used again by Keith Doms in "Public Library Buildings," in Roberta Bowler's *Local Public Library Administration* (Chicago: International City Manager's Association, 1964).

11. Lushington, 48.

12. Raymond Holt, *Planning Library Buildings and Facilities* (Metuchen, NJ: Scarecrow, 1989), 13-27.

13. Gerald Cecil Sandy, *Evaluation Comparison* (Ann Arbor, MI: University Microfilms, 1981), 100.

14. Wheeler and Githens, 45.

15. Richard Boss, *Information Technologies and Space Planning for Libraries and Information Centers* (Boston: G.K. Hall, 1987), 102.

16. Wheeler and Githens, 396-405.

17. Rochell, 397-99.

18. A list of fund-raising consultants can be obtained by writing to the American Association of Fund-Raising Counsel, Inc., 500 Fifth Avenue, New York, NY 10036.

Suggested Readings

Brown, Carol. *Selected Library Furniture.* Phoenix, AZ: Oryx, 1989.

DeProspo, Ernest, ed. *The Library Building Consultant.* New Brunswick, NJ: Rutgers University Press, 1969.

Dewe, Michael, ed. *Library Buildings: Preparation for Planning.* Munich, Germany: Saur, 1989.

Holt, Raymond. *Planning Library Buildings and Facilities.* Metuchen, NJ: Scarecrow Press, 1989.

Holt, Raymond, ed. *Talking Buildings: A Practical Dialogue on Programming and Planning.* Delmar, CA: Holt Assoc., 1986.

Lushington, Nolan and James Kusack. *The Design and Evaluation of Public Library Buildings.* Hamden, CT: Library Professional Pub., 1991.

National Service for the Blind and Physically Handicapped. *Planning Barrier Free Libraries.* Washington, DC: Library of Congress, 1981.

Oehlerts, Donald. *Books and Blueprints.* Westport, CN: Greenwood Press, 1991.

Smith, Lester. *Planning Library Buildings: From Decision to Design.* Papers from a Library Administration and Management Association Buildings and Equipment Section Preconference at the 1984 ALA Conference, Dallas, TX. Chicago: American Library Association, 1986.

Thompson, Godfrey. *Planning and Design of Library Buildings.* 3rd ed. London: Butterworth Architecture, 1989.

Veatch, Julian, Jr. *Library Architecture and Environmental Design.* Jacksonville, FL: Florida State Univ. Doctoral Dissertation, 1989.

CHAPTER 20

EVALUATION

Library evaluation, difficult at best, is made even more complex by the ambiguity and elusiveness of such words as "good," and "adequate," both of which we use in a number of ways. We distinguish, for instance, between an object's intrinsic "goodness" and that which it is good for. One of these "goods" refers to quality, and the other to value. We might ask, on the one hand, "How good is a library?" (quality) and/or "What good does a library do?"(value)[1] A comprehensive collection of medical books on arterial sclerosis would undoubtedly contain information needed by a patron to help understand his arthritis symptoms. All things being equal, the system is capable of meeting the user's needs. On the other hand, if the patron has a reading level of sixth grade, the holdings would be of little or no value to him.

A recently completed investigation into the concept of "goodness" -- defined as effectiveness -- in public libraries found that "the definition and measurement of effectiveness in libraries...is ambiguous because of intangible outputs, shifting goals, indeterminant technology, multiple constituencies, and vulnerability to the political process."[2] In the search for indicators or dimensions of public library effectiveness, they found public libraries to be judged good (effective) by staff, the public, trustees and municipal officials in the following areas:

Intellectual Freedom
Staff-User contact
Use (circulation and equipment usage)
Relations with other libraries

Freeness of Library
  Materials
Public Opinion
Variety of users

Libraries were found most lacking or least effective in the areas of:

Community relations (awareness of service, public involvement/community analysis	Staff size and staff expenditure
Parking	Board Activeness
Library Products	Energy Efficiency

The study also revealed that the four most popular roles for libraries were as a
1) Reference library; 2) Popular materials center; 3) Preschoolers' door to learning; 4) Community Information center.

Difficult as the assessment of "goodness" may be, evaluation is nonetheless a necessary undertaking for any library. It enables librarians to make rational, informed decisions about allocating resources, to determine whether to continue old programs and/or institute new ones, to monitor progress, to report accurately to administrators and funding bodies, to demonstrate responsibility and accountability for activities, to diagnose problems, to compare programs and services with like institutions, and to establish benchmarks for the historic record and for longitudinal analysis. Evaluating the effectiveness of a service means assessing how well the service has met the demands or needs of the community it serves in comparison with some standard that has been established either by the library itself, or by an agency or individual external to it.

Evaluation is an on-going process. At any given time, some library service should be subjected to scrutiny, to posing and answering questions such as "what is being done, why is it being done and how and how much is being done."[3] But systematic evaluation should never be taken lightly. It is difficult, time-consuming and easily misinterpreted and, therefore, potentially harmful to a library.

What should be evaluated? Everything may be evaluated, and, further, a method can be found to evaluate anything. However, simply data-snooping without focus or clarity of intent spawns muddy results. Any evaluation commences with the questions:

What information is required? by whom? and for what purpose? This allows assessments to be made at the appropriate level and with the best methods to secure the desired information. While most evaluations do not *require* the use of computers, the ability of high speed calculators to process large amounts of information and generate reports rapidly makes using them attractive when large quantities of data are available for manipulation.

Librarians seeking to evaluate their operations and programs would do well to consult Lancaster *If You Want to Evaluate Your Library*; Van House et al. *Output Measures for Public Libraries;* coupled with McClure *Planning and Role Setting for Public Libraries;* and Zweizig and Robbins *Are We There Yet?*[4] Manuals for evaluating specific activities such as reference service or the collection are included when applicable.

TYPES OF EVALUATION

The most useful library evaluation assesses the degree to which the library staff has met the goals and objectives that it has set for the library, based on the needs of its community; that is, how well a library has performed within its own staff's expectations and aspirations as measured by pre-chosen performance indicators.

In recent years, performance evaluation in librarianship has moved toward judging effectiveness by appraising how well a service satisfies demands placed on it by users. Performance evaluations are always a cyclical process involving:

1. An indication of what constitutes effectiveness or success for the services, the person or the institution to be evaluated;
2. formulated criteria or objectives;
3. criteria translated into measures;
4. data collected using the measures that have been established;
5. results compared with the definition of effectiveness.[5]

Because generous commitments of time and staff are needed to undertake detailed evaluation, many librarians, who also may fear the unknown, choose less demanding forms. The most frequent types of assessments utilized by public librarians are counting and comparing inputs. Inputs are quantitative measures of resources and activities. They tend to be institution, rather than user, oriented, and do not assess the quality or effectiveness of a service. Among the inputs frequently measured are: the level of support for a library, the number of questions asked of reference staff, the number of users served, the numbers of materials circulated, the size of the staff, acquisition rates, hours of service, size of building and periodical holdings. These inputs are amenable to cross-institutional comparison or against standards promulgated by national or state associations. Unfortunately, inputs do not always correlate reliably with the effectiveness of a program.

Outputs, on the other hand, measure use. The variables become circulation per capita or circulation per volume owned or reference questions per capita, rather than aggregate circulation figures or aggregate numbers of reference questions asked. In other words, they report services delivered and uses made of the library. Output measures not only reflect library performance, but user success, as well.[6] Unfortunately, conditions can be manipulated to improve performance on a measure without improving service. In addition, comparison is limited to institutional or service goals, and there are no "good" or "bad" scores.

Even with output measures, librarians are still likely to base judgments about quality and effectiveness only on quantitative results, some of which are immutable, no matter how diligent are their attempts to influence and better them may be. In the absence of qualitative assessment, there is no information, for instance, about whether patrons are using library books as doorstops and little insight into whether a reference question has really been addressed or whether the response reflects a librarian's misperception of what the question might have been.

There is a close relationship between different input and output criteria. For example, the fact that Library A has available for immediate use 75% of the titles sought by its public on a given day while Library B can only supply 60% might lead to the assumption that Library A is doing a better job in satisfying need. However, if Library A has registered only 20% of its public, while Library B has registered 55%, then the assumption may prove imprecise or erroneous. Output measures are most useful when tracking performance in the same institution over time.

Evaluation can be internal or external, administered by members of the library or carried out by others. Some happen automatically. At budget time, for instance, municipalities review programs. An allocation reflects many factors, but probably indicates, at least to some extent, the satisfaction or attitudes of decision-makers about the library.

Self-study should always precede or be the firm foundation for planning efforts so that the plan finally adopted is based upon a clear sense of a library's strengths and weaknesses. Self-study is often undertaken as a response to a specific, perceived problem, perhaps an articulated dissatisfaction with the library's collection, space shortages, or high staff turnover.

The appraisal of the library by an outside expert independent of any accrediting or professional group is usually associated with a particular project -- automating services or constructing a new building -- or is the result of unhappiness on the part of the community or the board. Whatever the motivation for calling in an outside consultant, the appraisal should be viewed as an opportunity rather than a threat, and should use the consultant's presence to generate recommendations and suggestions that will enhance the library's position.

Recently, focus groups, user surveys and other opinion tapping processes have been utilized by public libraries to help them collect more subjective -- qualitative -- data. Information gathered through these methods reflects thoughts, attitudes and feelings. They can be utilized to help interpret quantitative data developed from other sources but should not be considered a scientific sample of public opinion.

Among the elements to be factored into any evaluation are appropriate scheduling of the projected study, choosing, for instance, a typical week to sample; enough time to complete the task; clear instructions and expectations from participants; familiarity with methods of collecting and analyzing the data; and careful interpretation of the results, bearing in mind that most data is expressed in quantities and does not answer questions about "why," or "how" or "what next." The inferences and speculations reside in the minds of interpreters.
The following caveats also apply:

1. Biggest is not always best.

2. The item being evaluated remains more important than the measure itself. There is a danger that counting things can lead to judging the process more important than the thing being counted.

3. Not everything consequential that happens in a library can be accounted for in quantitative terms.[7]

There may be value in conducting a study as a consciousness-raising device, but acting on the results is what produces the broadest change. Participants, as well as others, need to learn the findings. After analysis, correctives for problems should be framed and implemented. The objective of evaluation is not only to learn what a library is are doing, but to improve service.

STANDARDS

When applied to libraries, *standards* usually refer to a set of guidelines or recommended practices developed by a group of experts based either on their expertise or on statistical or research data documenting current library practice that can serve as a guide to good, adequate or excellent library service.[8] Traditional public library planning tended to treat all communities of a given size alike, making widespread use of input targets -- so many books per capita, so many staff per capita and so on. The general standards applied to public libraries were always clearly designated as "minimum," but no formulas were offered to guide libraries to "good" or "optimal" levels. In other words, they described adequacy rather than excellence. Standards did function to establish a floor of services -- building, staff, materials or services -- beneath which libraries might not fall, lest they be judged inadequate in comparison with other institutions or by a state library agency responsible for dispensing financial aid. In some cases, standards provided and continue to provide the incentive for "substandard" libraries to develop, grow and reach minimum levels. On the other hand, for many libraries, the quantitative standards proved more a trap than a target particularly in the hands of fiscally conservative local officials or citizens.

Even in 1956, when the last quantitative American Library Association standards for local public libraries were issued, users were warned that they represented guiding principles, rather than standards:

> These guiding principles are not standards, but are basic to the establishment of standards. They are neither objective, concrete, nor statistical. As principles, they require interpretation when applied to individual libraries. They cannot be used like a yardstick which determines the length of an object, without subjective interpretation, no matter what the scientific nature of the measures.[9]

After decades of struggling to devise standards and measures that could be used to evaluate public libraries, most librarians now acknowledge that absolute criteria, universally applicable, are not only nonexistent, but are probably undesirable. Public libraries differ in their missions. The nature of library service depends on an individual community's traditions, wealth, social structure, education, geography, particular needs, library leadership and the other contextual and environmental elements that have been stressed throughout this book. These provide the data for making decisions about community needs and for choosing the roles on which they wish to concentrate, and then for setting the goals and objectives that are projected to be accomplishable. Goals and objectives are translated into measurable data, collected annually and assessed in quantitative and qualitative terms. In this way, libraries set their own standards and compare their actual performances with their own projections. Comparisons made on this basis must be done with care. Some self-comparisons represent "moving targets." That is, in the interim between the time objectives have been set and evaluation takes place, the stakes have changed.[10]

The process loosely described above replaced standards and was articulated for public librarians in *A Planning Process For Public Libraries*, published in 1980. This was followed in 1982 by a manual to help determine *Output Measures for Public Libraries*. A revised version of *A Planning Process*, published in 1987, and called *Planning and Role Setting for Public Libraries*, added a methodology for determining and placing in priority order desirable roles for local public libraries. A second edition of *Output Measures*, issued in 1987, incorporated the roles established in *Planning and Role Setting*. The final component, *The Public Library Data Service*, collects data from selected output measures, role choices that libraries have made, input data including holdings, staff and operating expenditures and community data such as population, age distribution and income for participating libraries.[11]

The primary effect of the new method was to offer libraries a variety of ways of conceiving their mission and consequently their effectiveness. It provides no measures, only options.

The definition of public library effectiveness depends on an individual library's mission, goals and objectives -- how the library chooses to operate within local constituencies. The concept of the public library, then, and its effectiveness is situational.

While quantitative input standards were, in reality, nothing more than educated guesses and statements of normative behavior, they carried with them the weight of authority, of outside expertise. Many librarians feel uncomfortable without access to numerical standards despite their limitations. Forty state libraries still retain *prescriptive* standards and many still issue reports of public library activity based on them. The new measures provide flexibility and sensitivity to local conditions. However, they do not answer the basic questions: "What constitutes a good public library? How do we know how well a specific library is doing?" The U.S. Department of Education issued the first of its projected annual collections of public library statistics in June 1992. Composed primarily of input data, the report included information from all 50 states about numbers of public libraries, the populations they served, the numbers and types of full-time equivalent (FTE) staffs, income, expenditures, size of collections, hours of service, library use by annual attendance and reference transactions and circulation, both inhouse and interlibrary loan.

The procedures that have been developed for evaluating various aspects of public libraries are treated here under seven headings: 1) administration, 2) staff, 3) finance, 4) physical plant, 5) technical processes, 6) materials collections, and 7) public services, which is subdivided into reference, programming, and use.

ADMINISTRATION

Evaluating library administration means considering how well the library is organized and administered to meet its purposes. It involves examining formal and informal governance and organizational characteristics and assessing the degree to which these enable the institution to fulfill its mission. For instance, does the reporting mechanism insure that the channels of communication between the library and the municipality and between the library and the board are open and clear, without intervening "noise" caused by mixed signals? If the library is a municipal department, does the librarian report to an official at an appropriate level and is this person a community leader? Does board membership carry with it prestige? Is it a sought after position? Have clear lines of responsibility been drawn between the board and the administration? Does the board accept its responsibilities for funding the library and setting its policies?

Has the library created long and short range plans of service based on careful community analysis and assessment of needs? Has it set measurable objectives, evaluated the extent to which they have been met and devised alternate strategies for their achievement when they have not been accomplished? In assessing the library's internal administration, a determination is made about whether the work has been organized in a way that insures maximum productivity. Is the staff involved in decision-making? Are positions clearly defined? Is the library staffed with well-trained personnel. Are there appropriate levels of responsibility and authority. Is the structure amenable to change? Does the organization provide mechanisms for problem-solving? Is there frequent formal communication with staff?

Any evaluation of administration should also look at the informal mechanisms that play a role in how the library functions. Relationships, rituals and other societal patterns have a significant impact on the course of events in a public library. The "grapevine," for instance, is a pivotal communication mechanism for transmitting attitudes and values. Examining its path, participants and messages is one aspect of understanding organizational behavior.

Among the most exciting uses of automation has been the development of management information systems which permit administrators to work on the "what if" questions, those which utilize varying input data to test outcomes. What impact, for instance, will building a new branch have on established neighborhood use patterns. Modeling of this sort requires large volumes of operational data. With the development of comprehensive models of the library, it is possible to manipulate variables, produce paper outputs of various scenarios and never have to disturb current operations.

STAFF

State standards may dictate, for example, that there be one staff member (full-time or equivalent) for each 2,000 people in the service area,[12] and normative data indicate that approximately 20%

of full-time equivalent (FTE) staff is professional, that is, has an earned master's degree in librarianship.[13] Neither quantitative gauge, however, measures staff quality, a far more important predictor of library effectiveness.

Ways to evaluate employees have been described in Chapters 16 and 17. Performance appraisals, based on preestablished and mutually agreed-upon objectives, rather than ones which consider traits, would seem to produce the most valuable results. The director's performance, too, should be regularly evaluated, both from above and below, as well as by the board. Comprehensive reviews which relate the director's performance to library outcomes provide information that can enhance library effectiveness. One practical method of evaluating administrators is simply to record how they spend their days. Time studies sometimes reveal that they are working on tasks that are inappropriate and expensive.

The lack of staff turnover, or an excess of it, the number and qualifications of applicants for positions, staff attainment of higher positions -- either internally or in other workplaces -- are all key indicators of the attractiveness of the library as a workplace and reflect the extent to which it is competitive with other institutions. If beginning salaries have not kept pace with comparable public libraries, then recruitment will be more difficult. If the library is unable to offer a quality package of fringes and some incentive for and assistance with skill improvement, then new newcomers may be reluctant to join the staff.

Lack of consensus on the library's current roles among library staff may be a factor in poor morale. "People with different expectations of the same library can be expected to differ in their evaluation of that library."[14]

FINANCE

American libraries spend over 4 billion dollars annually, about $16.28 for every citizen. Among the states, Arkansas' per capita operating expenditures at $6.44 is the lowest and New York's $30.42 the highest.[15] However, there are no absolute standards to apply in measuring the adequacy of a library's financial support because the amount of money required depends on the goals of the library and the extent and quality needed to support those goals. While placing a dollar value on the manner in which a reference librarian shows a patron how to use a certain major bibliographical tool is difficult, there have been recent attempts to determine the cost effectiveness of various library services. A measure of internal operating efficiency, cost-effectiveness of a service can be improved by holding costs constant while either raising the level of effectiveness or maintaining a particular level of effectiveness and reducing cost.[16] For instance, a reference department may consider that it performs adequately by answering 80% of the questions addressed to it. However, it may also judge that its expenditures for that reference service are too high. In order to lower the cost, a decision is made to discontinue subscriptions to some lesser used reference materials. If the department's ability to respond to questions remains unchanged, the library has improved its cost-effective ratio. Cost effectiveness determinations about the best allocation of resources are far easier to make about a single service than they are about the library as a whole.[17] The danger, however, is that reallocation may cause improvement in some services and deterioration in others.

Several formulas have been developed for allocating available resources within a public library. Like other formulas, they represent normative, generalized prescriptions with no mention of roles or priorities. Formulas all have their weaknesses. In the last analysis, the library budget will be determined by the traditions governing its relationship with the municipality, its "fair share" of available resources, and the extent to which the library has been successful in convincing its community that

1) it needs the money it has requested to supply library service;
2) it has, in the past, made judicious use of its allocations.

Most commonly, in evaluating and justifying the library budget, public librarians keep careful records of expenditures from year to year, compare the growth over a period of years, and compare the library's progress against the financial progress of other libraries of comparable size, program and community.

PHYSICAL PLANT

In judging the building and equipment, considerations should be given to the adequacy of book and seating capacity, how the arrangement of books and readers encourages the use of library materials, how well the climate controls and building maintenance program protect the collection, the space and convenience of staff working quarters, the comfort and variety of furnishings, the flexibility of the building plan to allow for rearrangement and expansion, and such important physical conditions as good lighting, ventilation, and noise control. In addition, the state of the building, how well it is maintained and the relative shabbiness of its interior decoration should be examined. If not already in effect, a plan for regularly scheduled improvements and replacements should be adopted.

Appendix B presents a form for evaluating the physical appearance of a library, including condition and signage.

TECHNICAL PROCESSES

The procedures for ordering, cataloging and classifying both printed materials and nonprint media should be considered in evaluating the library. The evaluator must confirm that sound management principles are being applied, that there is a reasonable division between clerical and professional duties and that the various steps in the technical processes are being carried out in an economical and efficient manner. Technical processes are more amenable to quantitative measurement than are many other parts of the library. It is possible to evaluate, for instance, the efficiency of technical services using time and cost factors. The cost of purchasing an item, cataloging it and preparing for the shelf can be determined. In addition, how long it takes to do any one of those processes is calculable. Data can be gathered by observation or by logs, and costs computed from invoices, overhead estimates and staff salaries. Comparisons can be made from employee to employee, or with like institutions, or by type of material and performance goals established.

Based on these data, it is easy to establish objectives and performance measures. These might call for the acquisition of a given number of titles or volumes per year, cataloging new acquisitions within a specified time period or checking in new serial titles within a number of days of their receipt.

Staff tenure is an important factor in the efficiency and economy of processing services. If staffing has remained relatively constant in size for a number of years, an increase in the number of titles cataloged may indicate improved conditions of work assignment and procedures or a reduced labor turnover in the staff. On the other hand, a decline in titles cataloged and classified may reveal the library's difficulty in retaining qualified staff at its present salary levels, or in motivating those who remain to work at a satisfactory pace.

Routine inspection of books on the shelves reveals whether the staff is alert to those requiring mending, binding, or other preservation techniques. Journals in the current periodical area too are checked to determine if they are regularly collected and bound promptly. In binding, the question of quality is a primary concern, but speed in getting material back to the shelves after the volumes are returned from the bindery is also important.

REFERENCE SERVICE

Reference service evaluation examines how well the library responds to user requests and how efficiently the service is performed.[18] There are no national standards stating minimum number of reference questions or reference transactions that should be received or handled. The national statistics reveal that, on average, citizens ask .92 questions per capita.[19]

Evaluation of reference services has experienced a checkered career. Librarians have traditionally collected input data about the reference department. They have reported the number of personnel, examined their duties, described their organization and staffing patterns, and their educational and experiential backgrounds. They have also counted and described the reference collection and assessed the quality of the materials.

Analysis of reference questions has focused on enumeration and classification, including the number of questions posed, and to a lesser extent, the number which have been answered correctly. Various categories have been devised to sort these questions. The most common ones describe the ease or difficulty of answering them. Time spent in finding an answer has usually played a role in how the categories are established. Some variation of the following tripartite classification is commonly employed:

Directional - questions requiring the location of an item or service

Ready Reference - questions requiring a single, usually readily accessible factual answer or source.

Search - questions requiring information on a specific subject from one or more books.

While of use, the categorization is only as precise as those who share an understanding of its meaning. Dan, for instance may classify a question about the former name of Namibia as a Search question, while Carol may consider it Ready Reference because she knows it to be South West Africa without ever having to consult a Historical Atlas.

Robbins and Zweizig suggest that, in view of the difficulties in defining and categorizing reference questions, "any inquiry in person or by mail or phone, from either a child or an adult, that requires the use of library materials or the professional judgment of the librarian to answer the question" be counted. In this way "location" and "hours" questions would not be considered reference. They also advise that sampling be substituted for routine tallying of reference transactions given the tediousness of the process and the wide margins of error.[20]

Librarians have used four approaches to determine the quality of a reference transaction. They themselves have judged the process to be successful (self-reported); the patron has reported satisfaction (user feedback); proper reference procedures have been followed (peers or supervisors have judged it to be so); the information supplied is true (usually based on manufactured questions and objective testing). Each of these approaches has corresponding problems: the librarian may be wrong; the patron may have low expectations and accept bad answers or reject good ones; a shortcut may lead to the best results; and test questions may not represent a true load.[21] Determining accuracy is complicated. How is accuracy defined? If the source reports inaccurate information and neither the librarian nor the patron knows it, can the transaction be counted as successful?

In the last two decades, so-called unobtrusive methods have been employed to evaluate reference service. An unobtrusive study is one in which the object being studied is not aware of the researcher. True unobtrusive measures would be those in which there was no interaction between the researcher and those being studied. For instance, measuring the wear on tiles in a bathroom to determine the pattern of use would be genuinely unobtrusive. Unobtrusive studies of reference service have used manufactured questions, submitted in a way that permits researchers to be treated as "real" users with "real" questions. While not genuinely unobtrusive, these simulations have produced results that suggest that patrons' questions are answered accurately 50-60% of the time, a much lower rate than that recounted by users or self reported by librarians. Murfin and Guechuk have explained some of this discrepancy by the inadequacy of forms used to survey patrons about their satisfaction with the reference product.[22]

Baker and Lancaster recommend that reference evaluation is better accomplished by an informed evaluator with less vested interest in the outcome than by librarians reporting outcomes such as perceived reference fill rate as suggested by the *Output Measures*.

In the most recent development, appraisal of librarian behavior has been added to the evaluation matrix. Questions are asked about the manner in which the reference interview developed the patron's underlying need; which strategies were used in the search; whether the source of the answer was provided; and whether, in the absence of a suitable answer, the question or the patron were referred elsewhere. Four aspects of the reference interview have been found to influence accuracy:

1. the degree to which the librarian negotiated the question;
2. how well the librarian understood the question and how much attention was given to it;
3. how comfortable the librarian was with the question
4. whether the librarian checked to see if the patron was satisfied with the final response.[23]

In an encouraging development, it has been demonstrated that reference librarians subject to intensive training that emphasizes proper conduct of a reference interview, heightened awareness of current practices, and thorough training in correct behaviors accompanied by opportunities for practice with feedback from coaches will substantially improve their accuracy rate.[24]

THE COLLECTION

The measure of a public library's "goodness" to library patrons is often derived from their perception of the depth and breadth of its collections, or, alternately the collection's ability to satisfy their needs and desires. Here, too, "goodness," is subjective and difficult to judge. While the older evaluations used to look at quantities and types of materials owned, new ones are more likely to examine use, reasserting the "good" and "good for" arguments described in the beginning of this chapter.

There are a number of approaches that can be used in collection evaluation. The first is to have an outside evaluator -- an expert in the field -- appraise the collection. Sometimes called the "impressionistic" approach, this permits a library to look at the collection or its major parts as a totality, rather than on an item-by-item basis. A major drawback to this method, as well as to several others that will be mentioned, is its lack of attention to the community. The collection may be good in its completeness or in its ownership of recommended titles, but it may not serve its community well. In addition it is often costly and is also non-replicable.

A second approach involves checking a library's holdings against lists of standard or core bibliographies. Public libraries might use, for instance, the *Fiction Catalog* or the *Public Library Catalog*. These tools purport to present the "best" books, and are useful in identifying major collection gaps. They are easy to administer and cost little. But they also carry the danger that what is best for some is useless to others.

In yet another evaluation technique, the absolute size of a collection and its growth rate are compared with quantitative standards issued by the profession. The last local library standards called for libraries of at least 100,000 volumes of currently useful books, 300-400 periodicals, adding annually at least 1/5 of a book per capita.[25] Current national statistics report an average of 2.5 volumes per capita in legal service areas.[26] Not only can size be compared with standards, but it can also be matched with collections serving similar communities.

Baker and Lancaster contend that the

> concept of absolute size is important because a library is unlikely to function effectively if a collection falls below a certain level. Presumably, the larger the collection, the greater the probability that it will satisfy the information needs of its users.[27]

But comparing holdings in numerical terms reveals nothing about the quality of the collection, nor how useful it is to its public.

The relative age and condition of the collection are two important dimensions to public library use. The premium placed on "currently useful" suggests that most of the collection should be up-to-date. Sampling the shelf list, or its computer equivalent, will reveal average copyright dates of material.

Computer-based systems have the potential to provide libraries with excellent descriptions of the collection and its use that were virtually unattainable manually. Information can be generated and tabulated about language, country of origin, subject (using classification), format, and type of materials being used in the library. Systems can be programmed to monitor, analyze, and project growth and to help plan for future collection development. Decisions about preservation, storage and weeding can be reached less subjectively and intuitively.

USE STUDIES

The degree of collection use, and how well it is meeting the needs of its users are among the crucial questions that can be asked of a library and the answers surely provide important indications of a library's quality.

Public libraries have traditionally kept statistics of items loaned, both in aggregate and per capita, usually categorized by age group, and sometimes by type of material, subject classification, interlibrary loan, and less often, by in-house use. Consistently maintained, reported and interpreted these statistics -- incomplete as they are -- have some value. They represent the volume of circulation activity during a given year, volume that can be compared with circulation of previous years, as well as with libraries in like communities. The national statistics report current annual circulation of materials from public libraries at 1.4 billion loans, with a per capita circulation of 5.75.[28]

For the first time, libraries with computer-based systems can develop an accurate, detailed portrait of library users and non-users and of the use made of discrete parts of the collection. The categories of patrons who are borrowing what types of material is readily accessible through automated management information systems.

Collection turnover rate has been used as an output measure. It indicates the numbers of times each item of library material would have circulated if the circulation had been spread evenly throughout the collection. Calculated by dividing the annual circulation by the number of items in the collection, it can then be associated with specific types of library materials as well as with the collection as a whole. A public library geared to heavy circulation of its current materials would expect to find a fairly high turnover rate in contrast to a university library whose retrospective holdings are a more important indicator of "goodness." Improving turnover rate can be accomplished in a number of ways, the easiest of which is weeding. Obviously, less books means higher turnover. On the other hand, too high a turnover rate may indicate an insufficient number of materials, demonstrating once again that measures do not have intrinsic meaning, but must be interpreted in light of other information.

Another approach to evaluating the utility of the collection is to maintain statistics on numbers of books and titles requested that remain unfilled from a library's own collections. This permits establishing targets for decreasing their numbers, as well as the opportunity to examine the titles of those materials the library is unable to supply to learn whether patterns of non-purchase and request appear.

Resource-sharing activities, particularly interlibrary loan, can be evaluated both from an effectiveness of cooperation stance and as an indicator of an individual library's holdings. Other interlibrary loan data available at most libraries can be used to evaluate fill rate and delivery speed, as well as transactions, labor hours, and total cost per request.

Circulation and stock sampling can be used to learn about the absence or presence in the collection at any given time of a title as an indicator of material availability. Four major reasons account for materials being unavailable in libraries:

1. the library may not own the needed item (Acquisition);
2. another patron may be using the item (Circulation);
3. a library error, misshelving, for instance, may prevent the material from being located (Library);
4. a patron error, for example misreading the call number, may

prevent the item's being found (Patron).[29]

Buckland has identified two possible actions that could raise the availability level significantly. First, the library could systematically duplicate copies to achieve higher satisfaction levels. The cost could be substantial. Second, the library could establish a variable-length loan policy, giving the most popular books shorter loan.[30]

USER SURVEYS

User studies, based on surveys which tap behavior in and attitudes towards the library, can be of great help in understanding patron library experience. Chit systems, questionnaires, interviews and focus groups are frequently employed methods. Their usefulness, and the validity of their results, depends on the attitudes and cooperation of the people who choose to participate -- to complete the questionnaire, or agree to be interviewed and those charged with interpreting the findings. Another limitation is that most library users want to praise the library, rather than condemn it. There is a "well-established 'halo'" effect that surrounds public libraries -- an essentially non-critical, positive view of the institution is held by the general populace.[31]

As a result, librarians who take at face value the results of surveys, without objective corroborations of the information, develop a false security that may be at odds with how the community really views the library.

Despite methodological limitations in questionnaires and interviews, the data they produce can prove helpful in revealing how the public library is used. Philip Clark has discovered, for instance, that patrons are unlikely to both borrow books and use the reference facilities of the library on the same day. They come with a purpose, fulfill it, and leave.

Properly worded, user surveys also afford clues to the satisfaction and dissatisfaction that patrons have with discrete parts of the library, and what suggestions they may have for improving library service. A word of caution: Questionnaires and interview schedules are delicate instruments. Those planning to administer them should consult a specialist in survey design and data gathering techniques prior to creating them. Mail questionnaires can provide information from large numbers of people who are geographically dispersed. They are particularly useful when simple or factual information is required and little probing is necessary. However, because returns are usually low and from a self-selected group, questionnaires cannot be considered valid samples of public opinion.

LIBRARY AND PROGRAM ATTENDANCE

Much library use is unmeasurable by circulation statistics. Vast numbers of people come daily to read newspapers and other material, to consult reference books or for a variety of other reasons. Library attendance then becomes another measure by which to gauge activity. The national statistics report 3.13 visits per capital to the library annually.

Studies of when -- that is at what time, on which day, and in what month -- libraries and/or their departments are used should help to determine the hours to open or close the library, how many staff and at what level should be available, whether weekend hours are advisable and, if so, at which times. Limitation imposed by current practice must be considered when study findings are presented. For instance, a library that closes on Friday evenings cannot track use during those hours.

Programs, their nature and attendance, should be evaluated routinely inasmuch as they are often expensive and always labor intensive. Program attendance per capita is one of the key output measures. It is possible also to determine average attendance per program, to separate children's and adult's programs, and to analyze attendance by type of program. Based on the findings, the library may decide to have more programs, to publicize them more effectively, to broaden the types of programs offered, or to repeat successful ones at different branches.[32]

CHILDREN'S SERVICES

Evaluation of services for children and young adults focuses on output measures similar to those applied to the library as whole. They include:

Library use: children's library visits per child, building use by children, and furniture and equipment use;

Materials use: circulation of children's materials per child, in-library use of children's materials per child, turnover rate of children's materials;

Materials availability: children's fill rate, homework fill rate, picture book fill rate;

Information services: children's information transactions per child, children's information transaction completion rate;

Programming: children's program attendance per child;

Community Relations: class visit rate, child care center contact rate, annual number of community contacts.

Additional evaluations look at the nature of the children's program, its success in reaching disparate audiences and the participation of caregivers. Focus groups with children can produce useable data. However, children tend to be literal and questions must be framed precisely in order to generate the information being sought.

SUMMARY

In recent years, public librarians have come to appreciate the importance of evaluation. As Mary K. Chelton wrote:

Evaluation is neither magic or a panacea for stupidity. The main reasons to do it are: first, to make the invisible visible so that our decisions can be informed rather than intuitive; secondly, because it has become blatantly apparent that nobody at least in the public library field is going to do it for us.[33]

Research into procedures, policies, personnel and other aspects of public library service has produced countless methods to evaluate and judge how institutions are doing and whether they are doing what they are supposed to be doing. No single approach answers all assessment questions.

Evaluation is an ongoing process, one that requires constant checking to see how much progress has been made towards a stated goal. The importance of systematic evaluation cannot be underestimated. Nor, however, should instinct and educated guesswork be undervalued. Experienced librarians develop a sixth sense about their institutions. Eyeballing a shelf of books often produces instantaneous knowledge about the condition of the collection and the degree to which particular parts of it are being utilized. While instinct can never replace formal evaluation, it can easily be accommodated into the picture and can sometimes serve as a warning signal that more rigorous examination is required.

It may be, as Russell Shank contended, that human nature makes one inquisitive so that counting things and arraying the tally in various displays comes with the genes.[34] But data are not information. They must still be analyzed, interpreted and put to use.

NOTES AND SUGGESTED READINGS

Notes

1. R.M. Orr , "Measuring the Goodness of Library Services," *Journal of Documentation* 19 (September, 1973): 315-32; Michael Buckland, *Library Services in Theory and Context* (New York: Pergamon Press, 1983), 194-5.

2. Thomas Childers and Nancy Van House, *The Public Library Effectiveness Study* (ERIC document ED1.302:L61/4), 6.

3. Sharon Baker and F. Wilfred Lancaster, *The Measurement and Evaluation of Library Services*, 2nd ed. (Arlington, VA: Information Resources Press, 1991), 1.

4. F.W. Lancaster, *If You Want to Evaluate Your Library* (Champaign, IL: University of Illinois Press, 1988); Nancy Van House et al., *Output Measures for Public Libraries*, 2nd ed. (Chicago: American Library Association, 1987); Douglas Zweizig and Jane Robbins, *Are We There Yet?* (Madison, WI: School of Library and Information Studies, University of Wisconsin-Madison, 1988).

5. Van House, 29.

6. Ibid.

7. Virginia Walter, *Output Measures for Public Library Service to Children* (Chicago: American Library Association, 1992), 20.

8. Baker and Lancaster, 326.

9. *Public Library Service: A Guide to Evaluation with Minimum Standards* (Chicago: American Library Association, 1966).

10. Zweizig and Robbins, 1.

11. Vernon Palmour, et al. *A Planning Process for Public Libraries* (Chicago: American Library Association, 1980); Douglas Zweizig and Eleanor Jo Rodger, *Output Measures for Public Libraries* (Chicago: American Library Association, 1982); Charles McClure et al. *Planning and Role Setting for Public Libraries* (Chicago: American Library Association, 1987); Van House.

12. *Minimum Standards for Public Library Systems, 1966* (Chicago: American Library Association, 1966).

13. *Public Libraries in the United States, 1990* (Washington, DC: National Center for Education Statistics, U.S. Department of Education, 1992), 24.

14. Childers and Van House, 5.

15. *Public Libraries in the United States,* 42.

16. Baker and Lancaster, 7.

17. Lancaster, 15.

18. Zweizig and Robbins, 76.

19. *Public Libraries in the United States,* 83.

20. Zweizig and Robbins, 76.

21. Paul Kantor, "Quantitative Evaluation of the Reference Process," *RQ* 21 (Fall 1981): 43-52.

22. Baker and Lancaster, 241.

23. Ibid., 249.

24. Sandy Stephan et al., "Reference Breakthrough in Maryland," *Public Libraries* 27 (Winter 1988): 202-03.

25. *Public Library Service:,* 36.

26. *Public Libraries in the United States,* 66

27. Baker and Lancaster, 55.

28. *Public Libraries in the United States,* 84

29. T. Saracevic et al., "Causes and Dynamics of User Frustration in an Academic Library," *College and Research Libraries* 38 (January 1977): 7-18.

30. Described in Baker and Lancaster, 164.

31. Childers and Van House, 5.

32. Van House, 72.

33. Mary K. Chelton, "Developmentally Based Performances Measures for Young Adults Services," in Robbins and Zweizig, 101.

34. Russell Shank, *Library Automation as a Source of Management Information*, ed. by Wilfred Lancaster (Champaign, IL: Graduate School of Library and Information Science, University of Illinois, 1982), 2.

Suggested Readingsg

Baker, Sharon L. and F. Wilfred Lancaster. *The Measurement and Evaluation of Library Services*. 2nd ed. Arlington, VA: Information Resources Press, 1991.

Curran, Charles and F. William Summers, eds. *Library Performance, Accountability and Responsiveness: Essays in Honor of Ernest R. DeProspo*. Norwood, NJ: Ablex, 1990.

Hernon, Peter. "Research and the Use of Statistics for Library Decision Making," *Library Administration and Management* 3 (Fall, 1989): 176-79.

King Research Limited. *Keys to Success: Performance Indicators for Public Libraries*. London: HMSO, 1990.

Lancaster, F.W. *If You Want to Evaluate Your Library...* Champaign, IL: University of Illinois, 1988.

McClure, Charles et al. *Planning and Role Setting for Public Libraries*. Chicago: American Library Association, 1987

Public Libraries in the United States: 1990. Washington DC: National Center for Education Statistics, U.S. Department of Education, 1992.

Robbins, Jane and Douglas Zweizig. *Are We There Yet? Evaluating Library Collections, Reference Services, Programs and Personnel.* Madison, WI: School of Library and Information Studies, University of Wisconsin, 1988.

Van House, Nancy and Thomas Childers. *The Public Library Effectiveness Study: The Complete Report.* Chicago: American Library Association, 1993.

Van House, Nancy et al. *Output Measures for Public Libraries.* Chicago: American Library Association, 1987.

Walter, Virginia. *Output Measures for Public Library Service to Children* Chicago: American Library Association, 1992.

Appendix A

Library Bill of Rights

The American Library Association affirms that all libraries are forums for information and ideas, and that the following basic policies should guide their services.

1. Books and other library resources should be provided for the interest, information, and enlightenment of all people of the community the library serves. Materials should not be excluded because of the origin, background, or views of those contributing to their creation.

2. Libraries should provide materials and information presenting all points of view on current and historical issues. Materials should not be proscribed or removed because of partisan or doctrinal disapproval.

3. Libraries should challenge censorship in the fulfillment of their responsibility to provide information and enlightenment.

4. Libraries should cooperate with all persons and groups concerned with resisting abridgement of free expression and free access to ideas.

5. A person's right to use a library should not be denied or abridged because of origin, age, background, or views.

6. Libraries which make exhibit spaces and meeting rooms available to the public they serve should make such facilities available on an equitable basis, regardless of the beliefs or affiliations of individual or groups requesting their use.

The Freedom to Read

1. It is in the public interest for publishers and librarians to make available the widest diversity of views and expression, including those which are unorthodox or unpopular with the majority.

2. Publishers, librarians and book sellers do not need to endorse every idea or presentation contained in the books they make available. It would conflict with the public interest for them to establish their own political, moral; or aesthetic views as a standard for determining what books should be published or circulated.

3. It is contrary to the public interest for publishers or librarians to determine the acceptability of a book on the basis of the personal history or political affiliations of the author.

4. There is no place in our society for efforts to coerce the taste of others, to confine adults to the reading matter deemed suitable for adolescents or to inhibit the efforts of writers to achieve artistic expression.

5. It is not in the public interest to force a reader to accept with any book the prejudgment of a label characterizing the book or author as subversive or dangerous.

6. It is the responsibility of publishers and librarians, as guardians of the people's freedom to read, to contest encroachments upon that freedom by individuals or groups seeking to read, to contest encroachments upon that freedom by individuals or groups seeking to impose their own standards or tastes upon the community at large.

7. It is the responsibility of publishers and librarians to give full meaning to the freedom to read by providing books that enrich the quality and diversity of thought and expression. By the exercise of this affirmative responsibility, bookmen can demonstrate that the answer to a bad book is a good one, the answer to a bad idea is a good one.

Request for Reconsideration of a Book

Author_____

Title_____

Publisher and publication date_____

Request initiated by_____

Telephone_____Address_____

Is Complaint from a group or individual?_____If group, name_____

1. To what in the book do you object? Be specific, cite pages or passages._____

2. What do you feel will result from reading this book?_____

_____

3. For what age group would you recommend this book?_____

4. Did you read the entire book?_____What parts?_____

5. Is there any thing good about this book?_____

6. Do you know what literary critics have said about the book?_____

7. What would you like the library to do about this book?_____

8. Is there a book you would suggest that could replace this book?_____

_____
Signature of Complainant

Appendix B

Library Walkabout

External

Is there a clear indication that this is a Library?
Can the library sign be easily spotted even by a passing motorist?
Is there a bookdrop?   Bicycle racks?
How is the landscaping?
What overall impression does the exterior leave?

The Lobby

What first meets the eye?
Is the area welcoming?   Does it lead you inside?
Do the doors open easily?
Are the days and hours clearly posted?
Is there a map of the functional areas posted in the library?
Are signs phrased in positive or negative language?
What changes might be recommended?

An Overview

When you enter from the lobby, what is your overall impression?
Is it physically attractive?   Clean?
Does it require painting?
What word(s) best describe the initial reaction?

welcoming	distant	attractive	crowded
active	exciting	friendly	inviting
standoffish	peaceful	open	dull
comprehensible	light	confusing	empty
cluttered	busy	spacious	quiet
dark	noisy	cluttered	alive

Designed for children?   Designed for Adults?
Are there elements that should be visible as you enter that are not
present?
Are functional areas clearly delineated so that they can be identified
from the entrance?
Is there clear and large-sized signage over Children's, YA, Reference,
Circulation, etc.
Is supervision possible from all parts of the library?
Where does patron gain first access to information?
     An information section of the circulation desk?
     A separate information desk?
Is it clearly delineated and obvious (are you led to it through signs or
placement?)
Is staff available?   Are they welcoming?
Is the "information place" user friendly (height, location, appearance)?
What kinds of orientation and explanatory materials about the library
are available as handouts?
Are there materials about the community available?
Is the area for registering new patrons clearly marked?
Are circulation functions -- checkout, return -- indicated?
     Are there lines waiting to do one or the other?
Is there adequate staff work space at the circulation desk?
     Patron work space?
Is the terminal designed for patron use centrally located?
     Clearly indicated?   Are there lines waiting to use it?
Is there adequate, comfortable seating and work space?
     Is it arranged for ease of use with library materials?
     Comfortable chairs near periodicals?
     Work tables in close proximity to reference materials?
Is there task-oriented lighting?
Does the temperature/humidity feel right?
Is there acoustical control?
Are there bulletin boards highlighting community events?
Comments?

Collections - A Bird's Eye View

Are collection areas clearly delineated and marked by signs (not only

Dewey numbers, but subjects as well)?
Are there notations on book stacks of Dewey numbers and general
subjects?
What is the condition of the shelves (crowded, empty, misshelved, etc.)
Are bookstack heights considered?
Are the aisles between bookstacks sufficiently wide?
Is there adequate light?
What is the general condition of the books (tattered, unused)?
Are book exhibits well planned and inviting?
Are periodicals well displayed?
 Back periodicals accessible?
 Newspapers readily available?
 Are the periodicals orderly and in fairly good condition?
Is information about AV materials easily accessible to public?
Are children's services clearly delineated? also YA?
Is there age appropriate furniture?
Is there a children's services desk? Is it staffed?
Are the services available to children clearly indicated?
Are there children's exhibits and displays?
What impression does the collection leave (full or empty shelves,
signage, tattered or unused)?

Amenities, etc.

Is the restroom easily discovered?
 Is it clean and equipped (towels, soap, etc.)
 Graffiti free?
Is there a water fountain? Is it findable?
Is there a public phone? Is it conveniently placed?
Are there adequate staff amenities (lounge, microwave, refrigerator)?
Is the meeting room clearly marked?
Are the exit signs visible from all over the library?
Are there handicap impediments that might be removed?

Summary

What positive aspects of the library stand out?
What, if any, are the negative aspects that can be changed?

INDEX

581

ABOUT THE AUTHORS

Alice Gertzog (AB Antioch College, MLS Catholic University of America, Ph.D. Rutgers University) has served as a librarian in public, academic and special libraries. She has been Director of the Meadville (PA) Public Library and of the Crawford County (PA) Federated Library System, as well as a staff member of the New Haven (CT) Free Library and the Brooklyn (NY) Public Library. Dr. Gertzog has also been a library educator, a library consultant, is the author of *Lyle's Administration of the College Library,* with Caroline Coughlin (Scarecrow Press, 1992), *Casebook in College Library Administration* (Scarecrow Press, 1992) and editor of *Leadership in the Library/Information Profession* (McFarland, 1990). She is a frequent contributor to library periodical literature.

Edwin Beckerman (AB University of Missouri, MLS Columbia University) has been a public librarian, library consultant, educator and contributor to books and periodicals in the library field. He has worked in the New York Public Library, served as Director of the Woodbridge (NJ) Public Library, as Assistant Director of the Yonkers (NY) Public Library and as a Branch Librarian in the Leicester (England) City Public Library in conjunction with the Department of State Exchange of Persons Program. He is the author of over one hundred consulting reports on library organization management and library building issues and has taught courses in library management and planning at Rutgers University School of Communication, Information and Library Studies.